Lecture Notes in Artificial Intel

Subseries of Lecture Notes in Computer Sc
Edited by J. G. Carbonell and J. Siekmann

Lecture Notes in Computer Science

Edited by G. Goos, J. Hartmanis and J. van Leeuwen

Springer

Berlin
Heidelberg
New York
Barcelona
Hong Kong
London
Milan
Paris
Singapore
Tokyo

Tom Wagner   Omer Rana (Eds.)

Infrastructure for Agents, Multi-Agent Systems, and Scalable Multi-Agent Systems

International Workshop on Infrastructure
for Scalable Multi-Agent Systems
Barcelona, Spain, June 3-7, 2000
Revised Papers

Springer

Series Editors

Jaime G. Carbonell, Carnegie Mellon University, Pittsburgh, PA, USA
Jörg Siekmann, University of Saarland, Saabrücken, Germany

Volume Editors

Tom Wagner
University of Maine, Department of Computer Science
228 Neville Hall, Orono, ME 04469-5752, USA
E-mail: wagner@umcs.maine.edu

Omer F. Rana
Cardiff University, Department of Computer Science
Queen's Building, Newport Road, Cardiff CF24 3XF, Wales, UK
E-mail: O.F.Rana@cs.cf.ac.uk

Cataloging-in-Publication Data applied for

Die Deutsche Bibliothek - CIP-Einheitsaufnahme

Infrastructure for agents, multi-agent systems, and scalable multi-agent
systems : revised papers / International Workshop on Infrastructure for
Scalable Multi-Agent Systems, Barcelona, Spain, June 3 - 7, 2000. Tom Wagner ;
Omer Rana (ed.). - Berlin ; Heidelberg ; New York ; Barcelona ; Hong Kong ;
London ; Milan ; Paris ; Singapore ; Tokyo : Springer, 2001
  (Lecture notes in computer science ; Vol. 1887 : Lecture notes in
artificial intelligence)
  ISBN 3-540-42315-X

CR Subject Classification (1998): I.2.11, I.2, C.2.4, D.2

ISBN 3-540-42315-X Springer-Verlag Berlin Heidelberg New York

Springer-Verlag Berlin Heidelberg New York
a member of BertelsmannSpringer Science+Business Media GmbH

http://www.springer.de

© Springer-Verlag Berlin Heidelberg 2001
Printed in Germany

Typesetting: Camera-ready by author
Printed on acid-free paper   SPIN: 10722484   06/3142   5 4 3 2 1 0

Topic A: Infrastructure and Requirements for Building Research-Grade Multi-Agent Systems

Topic A review committee & organizers:

Tom Wagner	University of Maine
K. Suzanne Barber	University of Texas at Austin
Keith Decker	University of Delaware
Tim Finin	University of Maryland Baltimore County
Les Gasser	University of Illinois
Marcus Huber	Intelligent Reasoning Systems and Oregon Graduate Institute
Victor Lesser	University of Massachusetts
Richard Metzger	Air Force Research Lab

Topic B: Infrastructure Scalability

Topic B review committee:

Omer F. Rana	University of Wales, Cardiff, UK
Lyndon Lee and Steve Corley	BT Labs, UK
David Walker	Oak Ridge National Lab, USA
Murray Woodside	Carleton University, Canada
Roy Williams	CACR, Caltech, USA
Kate Stout	Sun Microsystems, USA
Peter Harrison	Imperial College, London, UK
Craig Thompson	OBJS, USA
Jan Treur	Vrije University, Amsterdam, The Netherlands
Denis Caromel	INRIA, France
Michael Luck	University of Warwick, UK
Mark d'Inverno	University of Westminster, UK
Michael Shroeder	City University, UK

The Panel Session

Panelists:

K. Suzanne Barber	University of Texas at Austin
Keith Decker	University of Delaware
Tim Finin	University of Maryland Baltimore County
Katia Sycara	Carnegie Mellon
David Wolpert	NASA Ames

Preface

Building research grade multi-agent systems requires a large amount of software infrastructure. Many systems require planning, scheduling, coordination, communication, transport, simulation, and module integration technologies and often the research interest pertains to only a portion of the technology or to aggregate system performance. To advance scientific progress, we, as a community, need to share this infrastructure wherever possible – reuse in this context may enable more researchers to build functioning experimental systems and to test their theoretical ideas in actual software environments.

When these research ideas are translated to commercial systems, scalability issues become significant. Commercial success for multi-agent systems will require scalable solutions – in infrastructure and software design approaches, to enable re-use and effective deployment of both mobile and intelligent agents.

This volume contains papers of two topics that are joined under the common umbrella of addressing questions that will make deployed and large scale multi-agent systems a reality. The first topic focuses on available infrastructure and requirements for constructing research-grade agents and multi-agent systems. The second topic aims to consider support in infrastructure and software design methods for multi-agent systems that can directly support coordination and management of large multi-agent communities. Study of performance and scalability techniques are necessary to make some of the multi-agent systems being developed at research institutions usable in commercial environments.

The papers presented here are derived from the Workshop on Infrastructure for Scalable Multi-Agent Systems that was held at the 4th International Conference on Autonomous Agents, June 3–7, 2000, in Barcelona, Spain. There were over 80 registered participants at the workshop and lively discussions and panel sessions contributed to the refinement of these ideas. The organizers and panelists are credited below.

We would like to thank the contributors to this volume, the workshop organizers, the workshop participants, and the panelists.

We hope that this volume proves to be a valuable resource in furthering research in agents and multi-agent systems and to helping this paradigm realize its potential.

March 2001   Tom Wagner and Omer Rana

Table of Contents

**Infrastructure and Requirements
for Building Research-Grade Multi-Agent Systems**

MAS Infrastructure Definitions, Needs, and Prospects 1
  Les Gasser

Tools for Developing and Monitoring Agents
in Distributed Multi-agent Systems.................................... 12
  *John R. Graham, Daniel McHugh, Michael Mersic, Foster McGeary,
  M. Victoria Windley, David Cleaver, Keith S. Decker*

Agora: An Infrastructure for Cooperative Work Support
in Multi-agent Systems 28
  *Mihhail Matskin, Ole Jørgen Kirkeluten, Svenn Bjarte Krossnes,
  Øystein Sæle*

Sensible Agent Testbed Infrastructure for Experimentation 41
  K.S. Barber, D.N. Lam, C.E. Martin, R.M. McKay

The MADKIT Agent Platform Architecture........................... 48
  Olivier Gutknecht, Jacques Ferber

An Architecture for Modeling Internet-Based
Collaborative Agent Systems 56
  Roberto A. Flores, Rob C. Kremer, Douglas H. Norrie

Frameworks for Reasoning about Agent Based Systems 64
  Leon J. Osterweil, Lori A. Clarke

Integrating High-Level and Detailed Agent Coordination
into a Layered Architecture 72
  *XiaoQin Zhang, Anita Raja, Barbara Lerner, Victor Lesser,
  Leon Osterweil, Thomas Wagner*

Adaptive Infrastructures for Agent Integration 80
  David V. Pynadath, Milind Tambe, Gal A. Kaminka

The RoboCup Soccer Server and CMUnited:
Implemented Infrastructure for MAS Research 94
  Itsuki Noda, Peter Stone

An Agent Infrastructure to Build and Evaluate Multi-Agent Systems:
The Java Agent Framework and Multi-Agent System Simulator 102
  Regis Vincent, Bryan Horling, Victor Lesser

Design-to-Criteria Scheduling: Real-Time Agent Control 128
  Thomas Wagner, Victor Lesser

Integrating Conversational Interaction and Constraint Based Reasoning
in an Agent Building Shell 144
  Mihai Barbuceanu, Wai-Kau Lo

An Enabling Environment for Engineering Cooperative Agents 157
  Soe-Tsyr Yuan

Agent Mobility and Reification of Computational State:
An Experiment in Migration 166
  Werner Van Belle, Theo D'Hondt

As Strong as Possible Agent Mobility 174
  Tim Walsh, Paddy Nixon, Simon Dobson

An Architecture for Adaptive Web Stores 177
  Giovanna Petrone

Performance Issues and Infrastructure Scalability in Building Multi-Agent Systems

A Performance Analysis Framework for Mobile Agent Systems 180
  Marios D. Dikaiakos, George Samaras

A Layered Agent Template for Enterprise Computing 188
  Carmen M. Pancerella, Nina M. Berry

A Community of Agents for User Support
in a Problem-Solving Environment 192
  Line Pouchard, David W. Walker

Scalable Mobile Agents
Supporting Dynamic Composition of Functionality 199
  In-Gyu Kim, Jang-Eui Hong, Doo-Hwan Bae, Ik-Joo Han, Cheong Youn

A Formal Development and Validation Methodology
Applied to Agent-Based Systems 214
  Giovanna Di Marzo Serugendo

A Proposal for Meta-Learning through a Multi-Agent System 226
  Juan A. Botía, Antonio F. Gómez-Skarmeta, Juan R. Velasco,
  Mercedes Garijo

Scalability Metrics and Analysis of Mobile Agent Systems 234
  Murray Woodside

Improving the Scalability of Multi-Agent Systems 246
    Phillip J. Turner, Nicholas R. Jennings

Mobile Agents for Distributed Processing 263
    Penny Noy, Michael Schroeder

Scalability of a Transactional Infrastructure for Multi-agent Systems 266
    Khaled Nagi

Towards a Scalable Architecture for Knowledge Fusion 279
    Alex Gray, Philippe Marti, Alun Preece

Towards Validation of Specifications by Simulation 293
    Ioan Alfred Letia, Florin Craciun, Zoltan Köpe

Open Source, Standards and Scaleable Agencies 296
    Stefan Poslad, Phil Buckle, Rob Hadingham

Infrastructure Issues and Themes for Scalable Multi-Agent Systems 304
    Omer F. Rana, Tom Wagner, Michael S. Greenberg, Martin K. Purvis

Author Index 309

MAS Infrastructure
Definitions, Needs, and Prospects

Les Gasser

Graduate School of Library and Information Science
University of Illinois at Urbana-Champaign
501 East Daniel St., Champaign, IL 61820
gasser@uiuc.edu
WWW: http://www.uiuc.edu/~gasser

Abstract. This paper attempts to articulate the general role of infrastructure for multi-agent systems (MAS), and why infrastructure is a particularly critical issue if we are to increase the visibility and impact of multi-agent systems as a universal technology and solution. Second, it presents my current thinking on the socio-technical content of the needed infrastructure in four different corners of the multi-agent systems world: science, education, application, and use.

1 Why MAS Infrastructure is an Issue

MAS have the potential to meet two critical near-term needs accompanying the widespread adoption of high-speed, mission-critical content-rich, distributed information systems. First, they can become a fundamental enabling technology, especially in situations where mutual interdependencies, dynamic environments, uncertainty, and sophisticated control play a role. Second, they can provide robust representational theories and very direct modeling technologies to help us understand large, multi-participant, multi-perspective aggregates such as social systems, ecologies, and large information processing systems. Many people inside and outside the MAS community can now legitimately envision a future in which we clearly understand how information and activity of all kinds can be managed by (automated) teams and groups (not individuals), and in which we naturally and ubiquitously manage it that way: a vision of "MAS everywhere."

Progress toward systematic scientific principles and robust coordination/interaction technologies for MAS has been underway for the past thirty years. Though more fully articulated knowledge is needed, we are on the way toward developing the knowledge that will eventually give MAS a comprehensible. predictable operational character. MAS researchers have developed some fairly sophisticated theories and technologies for multi-agent interaction; coordination; coalition formation; conflict resolution; dynamic organization and reorganization; network and organization design; fault-tolerance, survivability, and robustness; multi-agent learning; and real-time multi-agent behavior. In a theoretical sense, there is much interesting work and many good

T. Wagner and O.F. Rana (Eds.): Infrastructure for Agents, LNAI 1887, pp. 1–11, 2001.

results, many of which point the way to more intriguing questions. It is fair to say that in several of these areas---coordination, teamwork, coalition-formation, dynamic reorganization, for example---the approaches developed in the multidisciplinary MAS community are among the most detailed, sophisticated and general that are available.

But from a practical point of view, our understanding is really just beginning. A number of deep scientific issues (such as managing dynamic heterogeneity [10] and understanding system-wide pathologies [9]) are very under-explored and have implications that will only arise clearly when we begin to have widespread, interacting, fielded MAS. Currently there is a very small number of fielded MAS systems, and in general there are very few---if any---systems in routine operational use that actively exploit the most sophisticated MAS theoretical developments such as robust inter-agent coordination techniques, multi-issue negotiations, dynamic organizational efficiencies, or multi-agent learning.

Moreover, even if the next generation of MAS technical milestones are met and new capabilities are created by researchers, widespread use of MAS won't occur until a critical mass of fielded systems, services, and components exists and network effects take hold to blossom the user population and public interest. The public incentives for widespread attention to and use of analogous technologies such as Web browsers and cell phones appeared only with the development of a) a stable, reliable, accessible infrastructures, and b) a critical mass of "content" (e.g., broadly interesting websites) that compelled potential users. Similarly, until we have a stable, operational, widely accessible, and low-apparent-cost MAS infrastructure populated with a critical mass of MAS services and systems that provide value to prospective users, MAS is likely to languish as a technology with potential, not kinetic, energy.

Another critical impact of the failure to have a variety of fielded MAS is that we lack practice and experience in building and operating MAS in situ. In virtually every case of implemented experimental or commercial MAS, the theoretical and technological frameworks used rely on standard, homogeneous agents and limited, inflexible standards of interactivity. Each project or application is generally self-contained and its components can accommodate only a very limited, predictable range of interaction. In the research community, each group's projects are quite often similarly isolated. Though there are some widely distributed MAS tools (see e.g., [1]) it is rare that one group's tools and technologies work with those of others in an integrated way, and cross-group testing generally doesn't happen. (However, see [17],[14].)

An important exception to this is recent experiments in constructing and using joint simulation environments and shared physical environment, such as the RoboCup simulations. Still, under these conditions there is generally still careful centralized control over interaction possibilities, determined for example by simulator APIs or controlled physical environments. Also worth mentioning are the newly emerging infrastructure tools, such as the Nortel FIPA-OS implementation, many attempts at KQML tools, and many XML frameworks e.g., for e-commerce [19]. It's not yet clear to what extent these will actually serve to integrate agent behaviors (see e.g., [18].) The bottom line is that despite the compelling vision of ubiquitous multi-agent technology, we simply have hardly any real experience building truly heterogeneous, realistically coordinated multi-agent systems that work together, and this almost no basis for systematic reflection and analysis of that experience.

Finally, the current prospects for advanced pedagogy in MAS are very weak, especially in terms of demonstration of MAS and experimentation in MAS behavior and implementation. How will the MAS communities create pedagogical environments and tools that will help develop, transfer, and extend the MAS knowledge and skills to impact widening groups of people? Simply put, there are few if any sharable tools with a serious pedagogical aims.

2   MAS Infrastructure Elements and Attributes

An infrastructure is a technical and social substrate that stabilizes and rapidly enables instrumental (domain-centric, intentional) activity in a given domain. Said another way, (technical) infrastructure solves typical, costly, commonly-accepted community (technical) problems in systematic and appropriate ways. In this way, infrastructure allows much greater community attention to unique, domain-specific activities. As Star and Ruhleder have pointed out [15] infrastructures have the general character of being: embedded "inside" other structures; transparent (not needing reinvention or re-assembly each time); of wide reach or scope; learned as part of community membership; linked to conventions and norms of community practice; embodying standards, shaped by pre-existing installed bases of practice and technology; and invisible in use yet highly visible upon breakdown. Infrastructure is also an effective leveling device: it unifies local practices with global ones, both providing coordination and creating shared knowledge. For the purposes of this paper, I've divided spheres of MAS activity into four categories, each of which has different infrastructure needs---that is to say, the communities in each sphere have different views of their own "typical, costly, commonly-accepted community technical problems" and different notions of what are the most "systematic and appropriate" solutions to them. These four categories are MAS science, MAS education, MAS application, and MAS use. The most critical infrastructure needs are not the same across these focus areas, and not all of these area are developing with equal force or speed. (E.g., MAS science is way ahead of MAS use, and MAS application is somewhat ahead of MAS education). Table 1 presents a schematic view of MAS infrastructure elements and characteristics, and their relationship to each of the four MAS spheres. I'll treat each of these in more detail below.

3   Needed Elements of MAS Infrastructure

Rows of Table 1 show the main elements of MAS infrastructure, categorized into System Elements, Services, Capabilities, and Attributes. Table 1 shows the relationships of these infrastructure elements to needs in the four different categories of MAS activity.

MAS Infrastructure Needs	MAS Science	MAS Education	MAS Application	MAS Use
System Elements				
Communication Languages	E	E	E	N
Components (content and processes)	E	E	E	E
Comprehensive, Implemented MAS	E	E	E	E
Design Methodologies	D	D	E	N
IDEs	E	D	E	N
Implementation Frameworks	E	E	E	N
Active Services				
Certification Services	D	E	E	E
Economic Services	P	E	E	E
RDD Services	E	E	E	E
Security Services	D	E	E	E
Specialized Domain Services	D	D	E	E
Capabilities				
Analysis	E	D	P	N
Data Collection	E	E	P	P
Experiment Construction	E	E	D	N
Information Exchange	E	E	P	P
Intentional Failure	E	D	P	N
Measurement	E	E	E	N
Representation of MAS Concepts/Data	E	D	E	D
Simulaton	E	E	D	N
Transfer	E	D	E	D
Attributes (of Elements/Services/Capabilities				
Administrative/Economic Practicality	E	E	E	E
Illustrativeness	D	E	P	N
Openness	E	D	E	P
Packaging	D	E	E	E
Progressive Complexity	D	E	E	P
Robustness	D	E	E	E
Scalability(many dimensions of scalability)	E	P	E	E
Sharablility	E	E	D	P
Standardization	D	D	D	D
Support	P	D	E	E
Usability	E	E	E	E
Visibility	E	E	P	P
Widespread Availability	D	E	E	E
Other				
Community	E	E	D	P
Open Source Projects	E	E	E	E
User Groups and Interest Groups	D	P	E	E

E = Essential
D = Desirable
P = Possibly useful
N = Not Critical

Table 1

The two primary categories of infrastructure elements are System Elements and MAS Services. System Elements are tool-level MAS needs important for actually constructing MAS. Services, both generic and specialized, refer to active online services needed for effective integration of MAS in one or more of the four "spheres." Capabilities refere to operational capabilities provided by MAS elements or services. Attributes describe ideal, valuable MAS-relevant characteristics of one or more of the elements and services. Finally, there are several infrastructure issues that fall outside this framework. Below, "MAS Infrastructure" is usually abbreviated to "MASI."

3.1 System Elements

Communication Languages: Support for Agent Communication Languages (ACLs) and their underlying support bases (e.g. belief knowledgebases for MAS based on KQML, FIPA, FLBC, etc.).

Components (content and processes): There should be extensible, easily used libraries of components that provide multi-agent oriented capabilities and tools.

Comprehensive, Implemented MAS: Complete, operational MAS in particular, useful, significant domain areas that are available for experimentation and extension.

Design Methodologies: Systematic engineering methods for the design and construction of MAS, that increase productivity and integrity of the resulting products.

IDEs: Integrated Development Environments specialized for construction, operation and use of MAS.

Implementation Frameworks: Implementation Frameworks (IFs) are implemented, sharable architectural templates that can be filled in with specific MAS codes and data for applications. Examples include some existing agent-building toolkits with multi-agent capabilities [1]. IFs must capture multi-level models; models of the MAS operational environment and infrastructure (e.g. hardware models; failure), message communications; agents and their activities; tasks and problem-level interactions and dependencies (E.g. GPGP and TAEMS [2],[3]); agent ensembles and their interactions; possibly environmental models, such as physical landscapes or structures (these are notoriously hard).

The lowest-level implementation frameworks should enforce no fixed agent architecture beyond message passing, execution, tracing, and some database capability. Above this, there should be infrastructural support for a set of multi-level, complex, sophisticated architectural templates to rapidly instantiate agents with specific architectures, knowledge, and policies, such as BDI agents and blackboard agents. Actually a variety of such templates is desired, ranging across the following:

-- Simple agents with simple message passing facilities (send-message) and simple, "flat" (non-hierarchical) reactive or programmatic decision models.

-- Agents with flat structure, some significant communication support such as structured Agent Communication Languages (ACLs) and simple procedural or reactive reasoning.

-- Agents with flat structure but some significant communication (e.g. structured ACLs) and knowledge-based reasoning such as JESS, Prolog, etc.

-- Agents with some significant communication support such as structured ACLs, XML, or GPGP [3], and with sophisticated, multi-level, multi-component reasoning/control architectures such as BDI, sophisticated blackboard control architectures; reasoning with a variety time horizons such as organization-level and problem-level (e.g. planning) horizons, etc.

3.2 Active Services

Online, continuously running or demand- callable infrastructures or servers with a growing set of standard agents with general expertise in various tasks. These would provide the basis for an ongoing, growing, sharable agent service infrastructure.

Certification Services: Third-party security services that certify the origin or the security of an MAS and its components.

Economics Services: Services for charging and managing economic interactions in MAS.

Resource Description/Discovery (RDD) Services: Services for real-time and non-real-time description, offering, and discovery of MAS resources such as active teams; contracting partners; new markets; etc. (Also called Matchmaking services [4],[16].)

Security Services: Services that create and enforce trust, truth-telling, and system integrity, including protecting property and other rights.

Specialized Domain Services: Specialized MAS services for particular operational domains that are available on an interactive basis, possibly subject to RDD, certification, economic, and security processes.

3.3 Capabilities

Analysis: Ability to effectively make sense of MAS data and information to synthesize new principles and to verify known ones.

Data Collection: User-defined probes for gathering data on states and events at level of:

-- operational infrastructure (e.g. message delivery; agent execution; size of agent queues)

-- agents (e.g., agent behavior; size/quality of agent database)

-- problem or task (e.g. goal creation, task assignment, goal mix, other "metadata"

Experiment Construction: Large-scale experiments involving large, heterogeneous MAS in differing local circumstances are very hard to set up, initiate, deploy and run under varying operational parameters. Tools and support are needed for this, including batch modes for multiple runs (e.g., overnight Monte-Carlo simulations). Support (i.e., tools and languages) for easily specifying and constructing large MAS models is also needed. "Large MAS models" means large (100 to 100,000) ensembles of possibly sophisticated, possibly simple heterogeneous agents with heterogeneous relationships and connections, to significant collections of information and knowledge content, possibly via external content-bases. This is necessary to start and run experiments of realistic and interesting scale and scope.

Information Exchange: Open exchange of MAS information through written articles and reports; direct contact, and open availability of core materials such as source code

Intentional Failure: Intentional failure of agents must be supported for experimental purposes, Other failures that should be modeled and simulated include failure of infrastructure (e.g., communications) and communication delays.

Measurement: The ability to operationalize, capture, and measure aspects of MAS performance at a number of levels.

Representation of MAS Concepts/Data: Easy capture and representation of MAS concepts and data, e.g., teams and groups; distributed knowledge; distributed interpretation.

Simulation: The ability to run controlled (repeatable) simulations and to gather a wide variety of data from them is critical. To avoid behavioral artifacts of synchronous simulation, controlled randomization of individual agent actions and agent interactions, and explicit agent execution ordering are also necessary. These should incorporate MVC (model-view-controller) paradigms for realtime control/influence and observation of simulations. Serious multi-agent simulations trade off capability and complexity: large-grained agent architectures with sophisticated control reasoning use large amounts of simulation resources, and cry out for distributed approaches. However, distributed simulation techniques are very complicated, the moreso in conditions where inter-agent dependencies are emergent and not definable until runtime [8].

Transfer: Ability to transfer MAS and MAS components/elements to entirely new operating and community substrates with no loss of functionality. Ability to "unplug" agents and attach them to other systems or environments with simple runtime support or wrappers. This includes technology transfer of MAS infrastructure ideas.

3.4 Attributes of Elements/Services/Capabilities

Administrative/Economic Practicality: Good fit between resource needs and administrative requirements of the MAS and availability of same in the community of partici-pants [11].

Illustrativeness: The ability to use the MAS to illustrate a principle or phenomenon by controlling its operating parameters and/or its execution process, and by offering support for visualizing or otherwise communicating results meaningfully. The ability to capture pictures and data streams for analysis and for papers and articles is also useful.

Openness: The ability to incorporate agents that are heterogeneous on many dimensions (architecture, resource used; interactivity; scale), possibly except for minimal 'wrapper', protocol, or API technology.

Packaging: Available as a complete self-contained package with supporting documentation and needed resources [11].

Progressive Complexity: The ability to progressively increase or decrease some aspect of the complexity of the MAS or its tasks or environments. This is useful for experimentation (variance), pedagogy (showing effects of increasing/decreasing complexity), and application development (prototyping, robustness testing). A collection of progressively more complex pedagogical agents and agent ensembles that illustrate important principles in MAS would be very useful. Ideally there would be some agents in such a collection that would be component-based, and for which components would be incrementally aggregatable. Thus students and teachers could explore alternative architectures and differentially complex agents, and could easily experiment with how added capabilities give added sophistication in multi-agent behavior.

Robustness: Continued operation of the MAS over a wide range of operating conditions and environments; Failure-tolerance and soft (progressive rather than precipitous) failure.

Scalablility (many dimensions of scalability): In terms of support for numbers of agents, MASI elements should support a range of from one or two agents to at least a hundred thousand. In the MASI Science realm, this is in part because the study of emergent large scale phenomena may require orders of magnitude different scale to exhibit the changes in phenomena.

Sharability: For community use, the MASI needs to be easily usable, easily comprehensible, and easily implementable/runnable in a variety of settings. It also must be sharable administratively.

Standardization: Conforming to community-wide standards for some dimension(s) of operation or interaction; Common, widely-used programming and agent-building languages such as Java. In many (but certainly not all) cases, MAS infrastructure will benefit from standardization of components, architectures, languages, interfaces, etc. [5]. Managing heterogeneity is an active area of MAS research [10], and we should be sensitive to alternatives to standardization that can provide both robustness and adaptability in addition to integration and sharability.

Support: Existence of some party responsible for extensions, modifications, upgrades; responsive to changes in its own infrastructure [11].

Usability: A high degree of correspondence between the skills, knowledge, resources, and organizational context of users and those required for effective use of the MAS.

Visibility: The ability for builders and/or users to access and to visualize internal dimensions, processes, interactions, and architectures of MAS in meaningful ways.

Widespread Availability: The degree of accessibility to and usability by a wide range of MAS participants and communities, including shared ownership, open source access, free modification/extension, Ease of location, retrieval, setup, and operation.

3.5 Other

Community: Thriving, communicative, responsive community ("community of practice") surrounding MAS.

Open Source Projects: MAS projects with protected free availability; open rights to modify, and complete representations (e.g., source code and documentation).

User Groups and Interest Groups: Communities of users and participants who actively share resources and knowledge to refine mutual understanding of MAS issues and to solve problems are actually infrastructure.

4 Conclusions

A vision of "MAS everywhere" means being strategic about infrastructure. Infrastructure needs for MAS are not uniform, and there are several constituent MAS communities that are important for progress in research, development, and application. Infrastructure is much more than specific abilities for standardized communication and resource discovery, and principles from other successful technologies should be investigated and used for inspiration in the MAS case.

5 Acknowledgements

My recent thinking on the issues discussed in this paper has benefited greatly from conversations with (alphabetically) Jean-Pierre Briot, Zahia Guessoum, Larry Jackson, Besiki Stvilia, Jun Wang, and others in the UIUC WEDAM and Agents and Multi-Agent Systems (AMAG) research groups. This work has been supported in part under NSF Grant 9981797.

References

[1] AgentBuilder, Inc, "Agent Construction Tools"
http://www.agentbuilder.com/AgentTools/, 2/2001

[2] Keith S. Decker. TAEMS: A framework for analysis and design of coordination mechanisms. In G. O'Hare and N. Jennings, editors, Foundations of Distributed Artificial Intelligence. Wiley Inter-Science, 1995.

[3] Keith S. Decker and Victor R. Lesser. "Generalizing the Partial Global Planning Algorithm." International Journal of Intelligent and Cooperative Information Systems, 1(2):319--346, June 1992.

[4] Keith Decker, Katia Sycara, and Mike Williamson, "Middle-Agents for the Internet." In Proceedings of the 15th International Joint Conference on Artificial Intelligence, Nagoya, Japan, August 1997.

[5] K. Decker, T. Finin, C. Manning, M. Singh, and J. Treur. "Implementing multi-agent systems: languages, frameworks, and standards (a report from the 1997 IW-MAS workshop)." AAAI-98 Workshop on Software Tools for Developing Agents, Technical Report, Computer Science Department, University of Delaware, AAAI-TR WS-98-10, August 1998.

[6] Les Gasser, Carl Braganza, and Nava Herman, "MACE: A Flexible Testbed for Multi-Agent Systems Research", in M.N. Huhns, Ed. Distributed Artificial Intelligence, Pitman, 1987.

[7] Les Gasser and Jean-Pierre Briot, "Agents and Concurrent Objects", IEEE Concurrency, October-December, 1998.

[8] Les Gasser, "Design Considerations for the MACE3J Simulation Environment", Working Paper LG-2001-02, Graduate School of Library and Information Science, University of Illinois at Urbana-Champaign, February, 2001

[9] Mark Klein, "Exception Handling in Agent Systems." Proceedings of the Third International Conference on Autonomous Agents, Seattle, Washington, 1999.

[10] A. Ouksel, A. Sheth (Eds.), Semantic Interoperability in Global Information Systems, Special Issue of ACM SIGMOD Record, Vol. 28, No. 1, March 1999, pp. 47-53.

[11] H. Van Dyke Parunak, "Industrial and Practical Applications of DAI", Chapter 9 in G, Weiss, (Ed.), Multi-Agent Systems: A Modern Approach to Distributed Artificial Intelligence. MIT Press, Cambridge, MA., 1999.

[12] Onn Shehory, "A Scalable Agent Location Mechanism," in Lecture Notes in Artificial Intelligence, Intelligent Agents VI, Springer, 1999.

[13] Onn Shehory, "Architectural Properties of Multi-Agent Systems," Technical Report CMU-RI-TR-98-28, Robotics Institute, Carnegie Mellon University, December, 1998. (http://www.ri.cmu.edu/pubs/pub_479.html)

[14] Onn Shehory and Katia Sycara "The Retsina Communicator." In Proceedings of Autonomous Agents 2000, Poster Session (to appear).

[15] S.L. Star and K. Ruhleder, "Steps to an Ecology of Infrastructure." Information Systems Research, 7(1), March, 1996.

[16] Sycara, K., Klusch, M., Widoff, S. and Lu, J. "Dynamic Service Matchmaking Among Agents in Open Information Environments". In [Ouksel and Sheth, 1999].

[17] Tambe, M., Pynadath, D. and Chauvat, N., "Building Dynamic Agent Organizations in Cyberspace," IEEE Internet Computing, Vol 4, number 2, March, 2000.

[18] Wooldridge, Michael, "Semantic Issues in the Verification of Agent Communication Languages." Autonomous Agents and Multi-Agent Systems, 3(1), March, 2000.

[19] The XML Catalog, XML.Org, http://xml.org/xmlorg_registry/index.shtml

Tools for Developing and Monitoring Agents in Distributed Multi-agent Systems

John R. Graham, Daniel McHugh, Michael Mersic, Foster McGeary,
M. Victoria Windley, David Cleaver, Keith S. Decker

University of Delaware
Newark, DE, 19716, USA
{graham,mchugh,mcgeary,windley,cleaver,decker}@cis.udel.edu
http://www.eecis.udel.edu/ decaf

Abstract. Before the powerful agent programming paradigm can be
adopted in commercial or industrial settings, a complete environment,
similar to that for other programming languages, must be developed.
This includes editors, libraries, and an environment for the completion
of agent tasks. The DECAF[8] Agent architecture is a general purpose
agent development platform that was designed specifically to support
concurrency, distributed operations, support for high level programming
paradigms, and high throughput. The architecture has been designed
with built-in scalability which adapts itself to multiple processor architecture and highly distributed multi-agent systems. DECAF supports
research efforts in planning and scheduling with modular design. The architecture also supports application development and has current developments in social modeling, middle agents, information extraction, and
proxy operations. DECAF also supports the next step in the progression
of the programming paradigm by allowing "flexible" and "structured
persistent" actions [7]. This paper is a case study of the development of
the DECAF architecture, tools that have been developed concurrently
to support programming and testing, and some of the more significant
applications designed using DECAF.

1 Introduction

Providing an environment for the execution of a software agent is very similar to
providing an operating system for the execution of general purpose applications.
In the same fashion that an operating system provides a set of services for
the execution of a user request, an agent framework provides a similar set of
services for the execution of agent actions. Such services include the ability to
communicate with other agents, maintaining the current state of an executing
agent, and selecting an execution path from a set of possible execution paths.

Agent systems are composed of a collection of autonomous units that have
local information and local capabilities. In multi agent systems, local information and goals are normally insufficient to achieve larger goals independently.
To support the achievement of larger, non-local goals, agents must communicate

T. Wagner and O.F. Rana (Eds.): Infrastructure for Agents, LNAI 1887, pp. 12–27, 2001.

and exchange information with other agents. This scenario of solving problems imposes design constraints which an agent architecture must support in order to be effective. **Communication.** Agents are distributed across networks and need to communicate. **Concurrency.** Concurrent activities are essential for an architecture in order to improve the availability of its services. Working on task solutions at the same time as processing incoming messages, for example. **Language Support.** Agent programming includes all of the usual programming paradigms as well the extensions that make agent programming unique, such as flexible actions. **Testability.** Repeatability is essential for designing solutions to complex tasks.

There are two major design features of DECAF that support these design constraints. First, DECAF consists of a set of well defined control modules (initialization, dispatching, planning, scheduling, execution, and coordination) that work in concert to control an agent's life cycle. Each of the modules is implemented as a separate thread in Java. Secondly, there is one core task structure representation that is shared between all of the control modules. The task structure can be annotated and expanded as needed with details that may be understood by only one or two modules, but there is still one core representation.

In addition, a separate goal of the architecture is to develop a modular platform suitable for our research activities. DECAF distinguishes itself from many other agent toolkits by shifting the focus away from the underlying components of agent building (such as socket creation, message formatting, and the details of agent communication) to allow agent developers to focus on the logic of the task or in the case of research, allowing focus on one particular aspect of the architecture.

In support of these goals a set of tools has evolved to assist programmers and researchers: Component libraries, GUI programming, Agent Management Agent (AMA) and middleware (ANS (agent name server), Matchmaker and Broker). The remainder of this paper discuses each of the control modules and the support tools. Lastly, an overview of the research projects and applications that have been developed using DECAF.

2   The DECAF Architecture

DECAF (Distributed, Environment-Centered Agent Framework) is a toolkit which allows a well-defined software engineering approach to building multi agent systems. The toolkit provides a stable platform to design, rapidly develop, and execute intelligent agents to achieve solutions in complex software systems. DECAF provides the necessary architectural services of a large-grained intelligent agent [5,14]: communication, planning, scheduling, execution monitoring, coordination, and eventually learning and self-diagnosis [9]. This is the internal "operating system" of a software agent, to which application programmers have strictly limited access. The overall internal architecture of DECAF is shown in Figure 1.

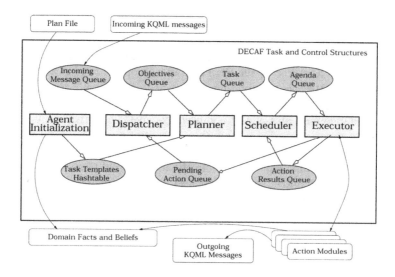

Fig. 1. DECAF Architecture Overview

2.1   Agent Initialization

The execution modules control the flow of a task through its life time. After initialization, each module runs continuously and concurrently in its own Java thread. When an agent is started, the *Agent Initialization* module runs. The agent initialization module will read the plan file as described above. Each task reduction specified in the plan file will be added to the *Task Templates Hash table* (plan library) along with the tree structure that is used to specify actions that accomplish that objective.

2.2   Dispatcher

Agent initialization is done once per agent, and then control is passed to the Dispatcher which waits for an incoming KQML (or FIPA) message. These messages will then be placed on the *Incoming Message Queue*. An incoming message contains a KQML *performative* and its associated information. An incoming message can result in one of two actions by the dispatcher. First the message is attempting to communicate as part of an ongoing conversation. The Dispatcher makes this distinction mostly by recognizing the KQML :in-reply-to field designator, which indicates the message is part of an existing conversation. In this case the dispatcher will find the corresponding action in the *Pending Action Queue* and set up the tasks to continue the agent action.

Second, a message may indicate that it is part of a new conversation. This is the case whenever the message does not use the :in-reply-to field. If so a new *objective* is created (equivalent to the BDI "desires" concept[12]) and placed on the *Objectives Queue* for the Planner. An agent typically has many active objectives, not all of which may be achievable.

2.3 Planner

The Planner monitors the Objectives Queue and matches new goals to an existing task template as stored in the Plan Library. A copy of the instantiated plan, in the form of an HTN corresponding to that goal, is placed in the *Task Queue* area, along with a unique identifier and any provisions that were passed to the agent via the incoming message. If a subsequent message arrives requesting the same goal be accomplished, then another instantiation of the same plan template will be placed in the task networks with a new unique identifier. The Task Queue at any given moment will contain the instantiated plans/task structures (including all actions and subgoals) that need to be completed in response to an (as yet) unsatisfied message.

2.4 Scheduler

The *Scheduler* waits until the Task Queue is non-empty. The purpose of the Scheduler is to determine which actions *can* be executed now, which *should* be executed now, and in what order they should be executed. This determination is currently based on whether all of the provisions for a particular module are available. Some provisions come from the incoming message and some provisions come as a result of other actions being completed. This means the Task Queue Structures are checked every time a provision becomes available to see which actions can be executed now.

A major research effort is underway to add reasoning ability to the scheduling module. This effort involves annotating the task structure with performance and scheduling information to allow the scheduler to select an "optimal" path for task completion. Optimal in this case may mean some definition of quality or deadline and real-time goals.

2.5 Executor

The *Executor* is set into operation when the Agenda Queue is non-empty. Once an action is placed on the queue the Executor immediately places the task into execution. One of two things can occur at this point: The action can complete normally (Note that "normal" completion may be returning an error or any other outcome) and the result is placed on the *Action Result Queue*. The framework waits for results and then distributes the result to downstream actions that may be waiting in the Task Queue. Once this is accomplished the Executor examines the Agenda queue to see if there is further work to be done. The Executor module will start each task in its own separate thread, improving throughput and assisting the achievement of the real-time deadlines. Alternatively, an action may fail and not return, in which case the framework will indicate failure of the task to the requester.

3   Architecture Development

Currently, DECAF is being used as a research platform for some classical AI problems in scheduling and planning. The following sections briefly describe these research efforts.

3.1   Scheduling

DECAF supports the idea of "soft" real time execution of tasks. To achieve this, the concept of execution profiles and a characterization of agent execution that will lead to optimal or near optimal scheduling of agent execution has been developed. This work is leveraged from the Design to Criteria (DTC) work at the University of Massachusetts [15]. Using the agent execution profile and characterization, currently, DECAF can be run with a simple non-reasoning scheduler or with the DTC scheduler. Under development is DRU (Dynamic Realtime Update), a scheduler that is faster than DTC and improves reliability by taking advantage of the Java Virtual Machine (JVM) to run redundant efforts to achieve deadlines in the event of failure of the primary solution.

3.2   GPGP

Generalized Partial Global Planning (GPGP) is a task structure centered approach to coordination [3]. The basic idea is that each agent constructs its local view of the structure and relationships of its intended tasks. This view is then augmented by information from other tasks, and the local view changes dynamically over time. In particular, commitments are exchanged that result in new scheduling constraints. The result is a more coordinated behavior for all agents in the community.

3.3   Planning

The focus of planning in our system is on explicating the basic information flow relationships between tasks and other relationships that affect control flow decisions. Most control relationships are derivative of these more basic relationships. Final action selection, sequencing and timing are left up to the agent's local scheduler. Thus the planning process takes as input the agent's current set of goals and set of task structures and produces as output a new set of current task structures. The important constraint on the planning module is to guarantee at least one task for each goal until the goal is accomplished or until the goal is believed to be unachievable.

The planner includes the ability to plan for preconditions and plan to achieve abstract predicate goals (instead of decomposition by task names). The planner also designs plans to allow runtime choices between branches to be made by an intelligent scheduler, based on user preferences that can change between plan time and runtime. This feature provides real time flexibility, since the scheduler can react to a dynamic environment by exploiting choice within a plan, rather than forcing the planner to do costly replanning.

4   Agent Development tools

4.1   Plan Editor

The control or programming of DECAF agents is provided via an ASCII *Plan File* written in the DECAF programming language. The plan file is created using a GUI interface called the *Plan-Editor*. In the Plan-Editor, executable actions are treated as basic building blocks which can be chained together to achieve a larger more complex goal in the style of an HTN (hierarchical task network). This provides a software component-style programming interface with desirable properties such as component reuse (eventually, automated via the planner) and some design-time error-checking. The chaining of activities can involve traditional looping and if-then-else constructs. This part of DECAF is an extension of the RETSINA and TÆMS task structure frameworks [16, 2].

   The DECAF Plan-Editor attaches to each action a performance profile which is then used and updated internally by DECAF to provide real-time local scheduling services. The reuse of common agent behaviors is thus increased because the execution of these behaviors does not depend only on the specific construction of the task network but also on the dynamic environment in which the agent is operating.

   For example, a particular agent may be "persistent", or "flexible" [17] meaning the agent will attempt to achieve an objective, possibly via several approaches, until a result is achieved. This construction also allows for a certain level of non-determinism in the use of the agent action building blocks. Figure 2 shows a PE session.

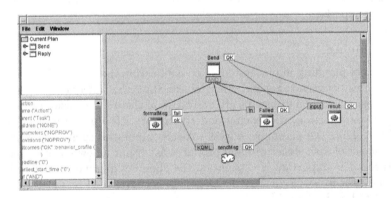

Fig. 2. Sample PE Session

   The PE facilitates code generation in multiple languages through the use of a common data structure, the *PEComponentData*. A PEComponentData is created to represent each object in a Plan File (tasks, actions and non-local actions). This representation is independent of any particular language and is easily used to generate any output language. Currently the PE can generate compilable Java code, the DECAF Language, and TÆMS. This process replicated for generation of any language by creating a new Java method to translate the PEComponentData into that language.

4.2   Agent Construction

One of the major goals of building the DECAF framework is to enable very rapid development of agent actions and task structures. This is accomplished by removing the agent interaction details from the programmers hands. The developer does not need to write any communications code, does not have to worry about multiple invocations of the same agent, does not have to parse and schedule any incoming messages, and does not have to learn any Application Programmer Interface (API) in order to write and program an agent under the DECAF architecture. Note that, since the Plan File incorporates all of the data flow of an agent, the programmer does not have to write code for data flow between actions.

The plan file represents the agent programming and each leaf node of the program represents a procedure that the user must write. The DECAF language supports all of the usual programming constructs such as selection and looping, but it also supports the idea of "structured persistent actions". One feature of an agent oriented approach to problem solving is the ability to describe in broad terms the method for achieving a goal. The programmer does not have to build from scratch an explicit solution, rather they can build an encapsulation that continuously tries for success without accounting for all possible conditions. For example, to look up a quote for a stock may require may queries to many price databases. The programmer does not have be concerned with details of which database is used or what remote format the data is in, only that eventually the price will be returned or that the price is not available.

The PE session in Figure 2 demonstrates some important programming concepts built into DECAF. In this case the task is named "Send". Generically this task will format a KQML message, send it to the designated recipient and await the response. There are three actions the programmer must write and all the rest is handled by DECAF. If the "formatMsg" task fails, the failure is reported to the "Failed" action which does the error processing and reports that the task is complete. Otherwise, the message is sent to the cloud construct. In DECAF the cloud represents a non-local action or task. Internally, the cloud takes cares of all communication, timeouts, and retries for message delivery and ultimately delivery of the response to the downstream action. This is true whether there is one message or a stream of messages to be sent or received. All that remains for the programmer is to process the replies.

4.3   Test Generation Tool

To properly test the DECAF architecture, it is necessary to generate random plan structures. However, simply generating random structures is not enough.

The test generation program for DECAF allows random plan files to be created with certain features, that allow testing of different aspects of DECAF. These features include the average depth of the tree, the average breadth, and the amount of enablements within a tree level. With only a few minor parameter changes, many different types of plan files can be quickly generated and used.

5   Middleware

Middle agents support the flow of information in a MAS(Multi-Agent System) community. They do not contribute directly to the solution of the goal. For example, a middle agent that lists all of the airlines traveling from New York to Chicago does not find you a ticket for the trip. However, in order to get such a ticket, you need the list of airlines. You could of course program such functionality into your ticket finding program but it is easier to have such a list available as a middle agent.

5.1   Agent Name Server

The current DECAF Agent Name Server is based on a version in use at Carnegie-Mellon University. This is a stand alone program with a fixed API which does the registration of agents. The new DECAF ANS under development will be written as a DECAF agent. This will allow interaction with the ANS through KQML messages. It also allows new functionality to be easily added via new task structures to a DECAF plan. To avoid excessive message traffic and to maintain directories, the ANS agent will have a known port and listen to simple socket connections from other agents. Simple activities with the ANS, such as registering, unregistering and looking up other agents can be handled by these simple socket connections. These simple protocols and other more complex ones can be handled through the normal message port of the ANS. This design will lead to more complex behaviors by the ANS. Agent Name Server Agents could register with each other, and a protocol could be developed similar to DNS for finding an agent's location given it's name as well as for increased security.

5.2   Matchmaker and Broker Agents

Two middle agents that have been developed using DECAF are *Matchmaker* and *Broker*. The Matchmaker agent serves as a yellow pages tool to assist agents in finding other agents in the community that may provide a service useful for their tasks. An agent will *advertise* its capabilities with the Matchmaker and if those capabilities change or are no longer available, the agent will *unadvertise*. The Matchmaker stores the capabilities in a local database. A requester wishing to ask a query will formulate the query to the Matchmaker and *ask* for a set of matching advertisements. The requester can then make request directly to the provider. A requester can also *subscribe* to the Matchmaker and be informed when new services of interest are added or removed.

A *Broker* agent advertises summary capabilities built from the providers that have registered with one Broker. The Broker in turn advertises with the Matchmaker. For example, one Broker may have all the capabilities to build a house (plumber, electrician, framer, roofer, ...). This broker can now provide a larger service than any single provider can, and more effectively manage a large group of agents.

5.3 Information Extraction Agent

The main functions of an information extraction agent (IEA) are [4]: Fulfilling requests from external sources in response to a *one shot query* (e.g. "What is the price of IBM?"). Monitoring external sources for *periodic* information (e.g. "Give me the price of IBM every 30 minutes."). Monitoring sources for patterns, called *information monitoring* requests (e.g. "Notify me if the price of IBM goes below $50.")." These functions can be written in a general way so that the code can be shared for agents in any domain.

Since our agent operates on the Web, the information gathered is from external information sources.The agent uses a set of *wrappers* and the wrapper induction algorithm STALKER [10], to extract relevant information from the web pages. When the information is gathered it is stored in the local IEA "infobase" using Java wrappers on a PARKA [13] database/knowledge-base.

5.4 Proxy Agent

DECAF agent can communicate with any object that uses the KQML or FIPA message construct. However, web browser applets cannot (due to security concerns) communicate directly with any machine except the applet's server. The solution is a *Proxy* agent. The Proxy agent is constructed as a DECAF agent and uses fixed addresses and socket communication to talk to Java applets or any application. Through the Proxy agent, applications outside the DECAF or KQML community have access to MAS Services.

5.5 Agent Management Agent

The Agent Management Agent (AMA) creates a graphical representation of agents currently registered with the ANS, as well as the communication between those agents. This allows the user to have a concept of the community in which an agent is operating as well as the capabilities of the agents and the interaction between agents. The AMA frequently queries the ANS to determine which agents are currently registered. These agents are then represented in a GUI. The AMA also queries the Matchmaker to retrieve a profile provided by each agent. This profile contains information about the services provided by an agent. This profile is accessible to the AMA user by double-clicking on the agent's icon. In the future, the AMA will also have the capability of monitoring and displaying communications between these agents. Each agent will send a message to the AMA whenever it communicates with another agent, so that the user may then monitor all activity between agents.

6   Scalability

DECAF operates by reading a *plan file* which contains a list of tasks that this instantiation of the architecture is capable of performing. A plan file is an ASCII representation of a Hierarchical Task Network (HTN) that details the actions and sequences to complete a task. The actual syntax of the plan file is an extension of the RETSINA and TÆMS structure detailed in [16, 2]. In broad terms, a plan file is tree[1]. The plan defines execution paths along the various branches of the tree and the critical measurement of complexity of the plan is the number of actions (represented as tree leaves) to be executed.

Testing Scalability is a matter of observing results when the underlying architecture (such as number of CPU's) is varied or the software architecture (threaded vs. non-threaded) is changed. In order to scale a complex task it is essential to make sure the Java Virtual Machine (JVM) makes use of threads and multiple processors in the expected fashion. There should be a relation between the number of agent actions and the execution time.

Three tests were run to verify the activities of threads in the JVM. First, a plan file with sets of computationally complex agent actions (computation of π) were run in a non-threaded version of the architecture on 1,4 and 14 processor machines. The results were as expected and the execution time was a direct relation to the number of tasks and independent of the number of processors. (Figure 3)

Next, the same experiment (same plan file and same agent actions) was run where the execution module of DECAF was parallelized (threaded). In this case the number of processors greatly improved results. Figure 4 is the result of threading and shows that the JVM works in the expected manner.

The benefits of threading vary greatly depending on the type action being performed. I/O bound activities show much greater benefit (even on single processor machines) than compute bound actions. Our development of a more reliable scheduling algorithm depends on the ability to parallelize actions even on a single CPU machine. The ability to do this depends on the execution profile of the agent actions required to complete a task. The third test in this series used plan files that had programmed varying ratios of compute bound tasks and I/O bound tasks. If the threading works as anticipated, the execution time will be related to the number of compute bound tasks while the I/O tasks run in parallel on the single processor. Figure 5 shows the expected result. These results show the low level threaded activities of the JVM act as would be expected from any robust threading architecture.

So far, two significant agents have been developed that take advantage of threading. First, a Resource Management Agent (RMA) has been developed. The goal of RMA is to allow the use and scheduling of resources that may be local to one agent, available to the entire agent community. To do this required used of a distributed deadlock detection agent and development of a resource

---

[1] "Tree" is not quite a totally accurate term for an HTN plan, but for purposes here it will serve well.

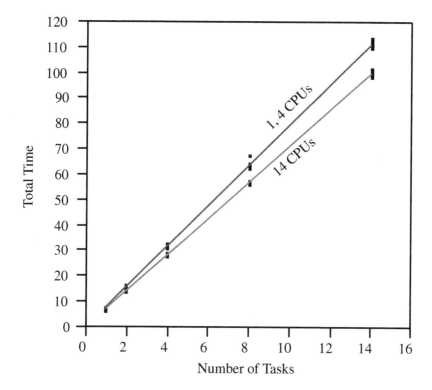

Fig. 3. Non-Threaded Execution Results

management protocol. During the testing of this agent, up to 160 agents were run on machines from 1 to 14 processors and also distributed over a local network of up to 4 hosts.

The Virtual Food Court (VFC, see Section 7.1) also tests the ability of the architecture to scale to a large agent community. VFC is unique from RMA in that each agent in RMA was essentially the same. In VFC each agent has a different task and a much higher volume of message traffic. Also, the life cycle of each agent is unique. A VFC agent may be persistent (in the case of a restaurant) or may be come and go (in the case of a diner or an employee). The VFC has been scaled to include 25 agents serving thousands of meals to 10 or more diners. Tests are underway to measure the network overhead as a function of message traffic.

7   Current Development

7.1   Modeling with the Virtual Food Court

Virtual Food Court (VFC) is a small artificial economy. VFC models diners, workers, and entrepreneurs. These economic entities are participants in transac-

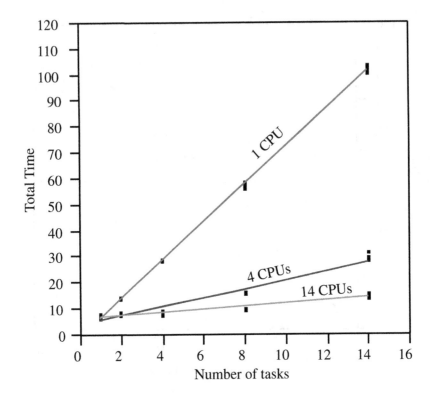

Fig. 4. Threaded Execution Results

tions that take place within a simplified shopping mall food court. Although caricatures, the entities exhibit behaviors, chosen from a repertoire of self-interested behaviors, sufficient to allow VFC to contain a labor market, markets for food service equipment, and markets for food products. For example, accepting a contract to perform labor and forming an organization (i.e., offering the labor contract) are reciprocal events. Because both of these are voluntary actions, we believe it necessary to model and explain both sides of the transaction simultaneously. This is what we do in VFC, planning to extend our results to model organizational structures more complicated than a simple employment contract (while still, of course, basing the analysis on the need for there to be reciprocally voluntary contracts). We expect that such models will also have to be expanded to include aspects of governance and perhaps non-economic social forces as we explore the long term control and stability of such structures.

The initial configuration of VFC is shown in Figure 6 Lines represent the KQML communications and the boxes are DECAF agents. Arrowheads reveal the direction of the initial message. Agents need to know of the Matchmaker in order to register their existence with it. Workers and Restaurants know of the existence of the Government because they report data to it.

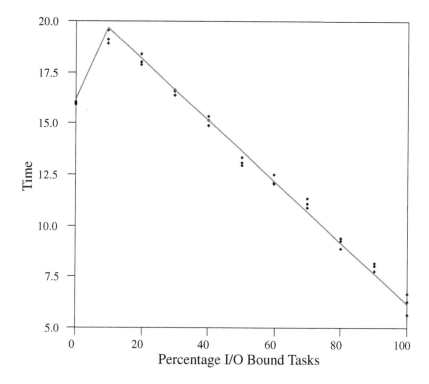

Fig. 5. Task Type Results

7.2   GeneAgent

GeneAgent is a bioinformatics-gathering system based on the RETSINA agent organizational concept of Interface Agents that work with humans, Information Extraction Agents that wrap various web resources, and Task Agents that include both middle-agents and domain task analysis agents. GeneAgent interfaces with a biologist via a browser and applets that use the DECAF Proxy Agent to communicate with the rest of the information gathering system. The Information Extraction Agent class has been used to build wrappers for several necessary Internet resources such as the NCBI BLAST servers that allow searching for protein sequences in GenBank; Protein Motif (sequence pattern) databases such as SwissProt, and local databases of organism-specific genetic sequences. Initial analysis agents provide services such as notification of new BLAST results and automated customized annotation of local genetic sequence information. Figure 7 shows the basic architecture of GeneAgent.

8   Conclusions and future work

Currently the most widely used agent development approaches use the "toolkit" concept, meaning there is an API that the programmer must use to completely

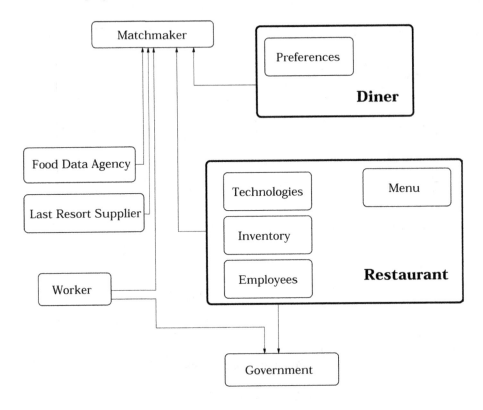

Fig. 6. Virtual Food Court Architecture

build the agent task. Also, there is no convenient representation in a language or GUI that can be written to program the agent. *JATlite* from Stanford University and *Bond* from Purdue University are good examples of this approach. *DESIRE* [1] and *ConCurrent METAtem* [6] are language formalizations but they must be developed by hand and do not allow the coordination mechanisms specified by DECAF and TÆMS. ZEUS [11] is an example of such an extended framework similar to DECAF. ZEUS is a collection of tools (primarily visual) that assist the agent developer in building agent code. As a complete collection of tools it is somewhat more advanced than DECAF. However, ZEUS allows only very simple coordination specification between agents components and does little or no reasoning about agent action scheduling or planning.

DECAF is currently the basis for several AI projects and projects involving organizational development and bioinformatics information gathering. It has also been used as a programming tools for graduate level classes on agent development.

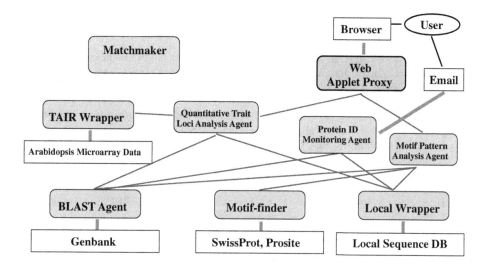

Fig. 7. GeneAgent Architecture

9   Acknowledgments

Primary development of DECAF was done by John Graham with extensive improvement by Mike Mersic. Development of the VFC was by Foster McGeary. The Test Generation Tool was developed by David Cleaver. The PE GUI and code generation was developed by Daniel McHugh and Victoria Windley. This material is based upon work supported by the National Science Foundation under Grant No. IIS-9812764.

References

1. F. M. Brazier, B. M. Dunin-Keplicz, N. R. Jennings, and J. Treur. Desire: Modeling multi-agent systems in a compositional formal framework. *International Journal of Cooperative Information Systems*, 6(1), 1997.
2. K. S. Decker and V. R. Lesser. Quantitative modeling of complex computational task environments. In *Proceedings of the Eleventh National Conference on Artificial Intelligence*, pages 217–224, Washington, July 1993.
3. K. S. Decker and V. R. Lesser. Designing a family of coordination algorithms. In *Proceedings of the First International Conference on Multi-Agent Systems*, pages 73–80, San Francisco, June 1995. AAAI Press. Longer version available as UMass CS-TR 94–14.
4. K. S. Decker, A. Pannu, K. Sycara, and M. Williamson. Designing behaviors for information agents. In *Proceedings of the 1st Intl. Conf. on Autonomous Agents*, pages 404–413, Marina del Rey, Feb. 1997.
5. K. S. Decker and K. Sycara. Intelligent adaptive information agents. *Journal of Intelligent Information Systems*, 9(3):239–260, 1997.

6. M. Fisher. Introduction to concurrent metatem. 1996.
7. L. Gasser. Agent and concurrent objects. *An interview by Jean-Pierre Briot in IEEE Concurrency*, 1998.
8. J. R. Graham and K. S. Decker. Towards a distributed, environment-centered agent framework. In N. Jennings and Y. Lespérance, editors, *Intelligent Agents VI — Proceedings of ATAL-99*, Lecture Notes in Artificial Intelligence. Springer-Verlag, Berlin, 2000.
9. B. Horling, V. Lesser, R. Vincent, A. Bazzan, and P. Xuan. Diagnosis as an integral part of multi-agent adaptability. Tech Report CS-TR-99-03, UMass, 1999.
10. I. Muslea, S. Minton, and C. Knobloch. Stalker: Learning expectation rules for simistructured web-based information sources. Papers from the 1998 workshop on ai and information gathering. technical report ws-98-14, University of Southern California, 1998.
11. H. S. Nwana, D. T. Ndumu, L. C. Lee, and J. C. Collis. ZEUS: A toolkit for building distributed multi-agent systems. (6), 1998.
12. A. Rao and M. Georgeff. BDI agents: From theory to practice. In *Proceedings of the First International Conference on Multi-Agent Systems*, pages 312–319, San Francisco, June 1995. AAAI Press.
13. L. Spector, J. Hendler, and M. P. Evett. Knowledge representation in parka. Technical Report CS-TR-2410, University of Maryland, 1990.
14. K. Sycara, K. S. Decker, A. Pannu, M. Williamson, and D. Zeng. Distributed intelligent agents. *IEEE Expert*, 11(6):36–46, Dec. 1996.
15. T. Wagner, A. Garvey, and V. Lesser. Criteria-Directed Task Scheduling. *International Journal of Approximate Reasoning, Special Issue on Scheduling*, 19(1-2):91–118, 1998. A version also available as UMASS CS TR-97-59.
16. M. Williamson, K. S. Decker, and K. Sycara. Unified information and control flow in hierarchical task networks. In *Proceedings of the AAAI-96 workshop on Theories of Planning, Action, and Control*, 1996.
17. M. Wooldridge and N. Jennings. Intelligent agents: Theory and practice. *Knowledge Engineering Review*, October, 1994.

Agora: An Infrastructure for Cooperative Work Support in Multi-Agent Systems

Mihhail Matskin, Ole Jørgen Kirkeluten, Svenn Bjarte Krossnes and Øystein Sæle

Department of Computer and Information Science,
Norwegian University of Science and Technology
N-7491 Trondheim, Norway
{Mihhail.Matskin,Ole.Jorgen.Kirkeluten,Svenn.Bjarte.Krossnes,
Oystein.Sale}@idi.ntnu.no

Abstract. In this paper, we describe an infrastructure for cooperative work support in Multi-Agent Systems (MAS). The infrastructure is based on a concept of Agora which can be considered as a facilitator of cooperative work. Basic features of the Agora based system as well as some implementation details (including communication adapter, message wrapper, proxy and default agent) are presented. An example of Virtual Shopping Mall as a general framework for modeling agent-based intelligent software services in mobile communications is used for illustration of the approach.

1 Introduction

Recent interest to agents and expectations from the agent technology are quite high. Almost everywhere customers and application developers accept agents as an interesting and promising paradigm. However the next question they usually ask is – how it is possible to take a practical advantage of agents or which tools, platforms, infrastructures can be used for implementing agent-based systems? An answer to this question is not very obvious because of agent-based tools are not enough developed yet. In addition there is a great variety of requirements from agent system developers who may need tools of various levels. From this perspective an infrastructure for MAS may consist of many different levels and components. Some of these components are as follows:

- language and communication,
- architectural platforms,
- middleware
- generic modules, components
- testbeds
- application-specialized systems

T. Wagner and O.F. Rana (Eds.): Infrastructure for Agents, LNAI 1887, pp. 28–40, 2001.

It is not necessary that all this levels are presented in the infrastructure but it is important to decide about which level(s) should be supported in particular platform. We focus our work only on support of cooperative work in MAS which is positioned at the middleware level and we try to define interfaces with other levels and components of MAS infrastructure.

The rest of the paper is organized as follows. First we describe what do we understand by infrastructure for cooperative work support. This part is related to the Agora concept which is presented in the next Section. After that we briefly consider an example of Virtual Shopping Mall as an illustration of Agora-based infrastructure and its application to modeling intelligent software services for mobile communications. Then we describe some details of our implementation. Finally we summarize our results and indicate some future works.

2 The Agora Concept

Our approach to agents cooperative work support is based on a concept of Agora [3,4]. Agora is a node (meeting point) where agents can register their interests (for example, skills, tasks they can perform and tasks they are interested in, working context, common knowledge etc.) and get support for common work. We introduce the Agora concept after analysis of a representative set of generic scenarios [3] of cooperative work. The analysis has been done from the following perspectives:

- functionality,
- data sources,
- cooperative work points

The functionality and data sources mostly reflect the user's view to a system and we support them but don't select as a basis for architecture and we consider their influence to architecture to be rather implicit than explicit. At the same time the cooperative work points relate to a system organization view and provide us with ideas about the architecture explicitly.

According to the above-mentioned analysis we consider cooperative work in MAS as a set of communication, coordination and negotiation acts between participants (agents). We call such communication, coordination and negotiation acts as cooperative points. Using such terminology anytime we have a cooperative work we can identify participants and cooperative points in such work. In this case support of cooperative work assumes identification of cooperative points between participants in the cooperative work and providing infrastructure for these cooperative points. Such infrastructure is provided by Agoras. In other words Agora can be considered as a facilitator of cooperative work which

- manages proper protocol for negotiation and coordination
- restricts context for negotiation, coordination and communication
- presents template of situation for cooperative work

Each Agora contains registered and default agents. The registered agents represent participants of cooperative activity and default agents correspond to management, service and matchmaking agents which are created by default when a new Agora is generated. The default agents can be redefined/overridden by the customer when needed. An example of Agora network is presented in Fig. 1. We would like to notice that agents can be registered at several Agoras and that there could be interrelations between Agoras.

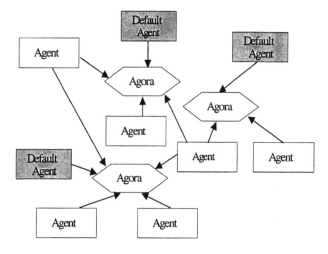

Fig. 1. Agoras network

The most closely related architectures to Agora are Blackboards [2] and KQML facilitators [1]. The main difference with Blackboard architecture is that Agora doesn't presents a model for introducing control into MAS but rather emphasizes infrastructure support. Other differences with Blackboards are as follows:

— Agora does not allow global access
— Agora uses registration of participants/agents
— Agora allows flexible its creation and it has adjustable/customizable control unit,
— Agora is oriented to cooperative work support and it always has negotiation and/or coordination agents
— Agora has richer content than a blackboard including various types of knowledge
— We consider Agora to be higher level architecture than traditional blackboards or hierarchies of blackboards

Facilitators in KQML have very nice properties which allow to use them in typical communication situations. They have support for predefined communication protocols. The main differences of KQML facilitators compare to Agora we see as follows:

- customized Agoras can be created and destroyed dynamically
- protocols supported by Agora can be adjusted/overridden by registration of manager, negotiation and/or coordination agents
- protocols supported by Agora are functionally oriented to facilitation of different elements of cooperative work rather than only communication
- Agoras can be connected and interrelated

In order to demonstrate the Agora concept more practically we consider an example of multi-agent system for modeling virtual shopping mall.

3 An Example: Virtual Shopping Mall

We are interested in applying agent-based intelligent software services in mobile communications [5]. In such applications agents may, for example, represent customers and service providers or network providers. Each of the agents personalizes some interests and has goals to be achieved. For example, customer is interested in comparison of available services and choosing one according to price-quality relation and service provider could be interested in involving a greater number of customers into its service network and in having a reasonable profit. In spite of the fact that these interests may be non-cooperative customers and providers may reach mutually acceptable solution via exchange of information and negotiation. In this case the process of service selection may be treated as a trading process. We consider how such trading process between agents can be supported. As a more general modeling framework we use a virtual shopping mall case where agents represent buyers and sellers (who may play roles of customers and service providers in our application).

The problem is described as follows. We assume that there is a virtual shopping mall on the Internet containing different shops and there are customer agents who represent customers in such shopping mall. We do not assume some predefined scenario for buying-selling but we are rather interested in creating an infrastructure for such mall which should be flexible enough to support various shopping scenarios.

One of possible situations in the virtual shopping example could be described as follows (just to be more concrete rather than to consider only one situation). A customer enters a shopping site on the Internet. The site is a portal to Virtual Shopping Mall where several shops and enterprises are presented. The customer registers at the mall and gets access to a personal agent who helps him to get required information and to make purchases. The personal agent may retrieve some basic information about the customer such as personal data, intentions, some goals, tastes and, maybe, typical negotiation strategies. On the other end shops are also represented by agents and they may communicate to customer agents and to each other. The process of purchasing may be done by communication of customer agents to shop agents and to each other in order to collect information about products which might be of interest for the customer. Agents may also negotiate about price or other terms of delivery and inform the customer about the results (or ask confirmation for achieved agreements). We may also assume that the customer doesn't always have precise plans what to buy and, therefore, phases corresponding to needs identification or product advertising may be also involved.

In order to implement the Virtual Shopping Mall we first identify participants of the cooperative work. They can be identified by roles they play in the mall (see [9]). Finally we may come up with the following agents:

— Customer Agent – represents a customer. If the customer would like to have more than one Customer Agent, there have to be an Agora where these agents can be coordinated
— Shop Agent – represents a seller in a shop. When a shop manager needs to have more than one Shop Agent, there have to be an Agora where the agents can be coordinated
— Price Negotiation Agent is a service agent and it represents a negotiation manager (for example, auctioneer). It controls the negotiation process in a neutral way and initiates the payment process if a purchase is agreed
— Marketing Agent – represents a marketing manager. It can connect to Customer Agoras for active performance of marketing towards the Customer Agents
— Mall Agent – represents a mall manager. It is a coordinator that mainly keeps an overview of customers and shops participating in the virtual mall. For simplicity we assume only one Mall Agora, but in a general case it would be not reasonable to restrict the customer/shop overview to one Agora only
— Bulk Purchase Agent – represents a coordinator of agents coalition. Agents can organize coalitions both for a product information exchange and for uniting buying resources in order to get a better price for a particular product. Such coalitions can be represented by Bulk Purchase Agora. At this Agora the Bulk Purchase Agent meets and coordinates the Customer Agents that try to enter into bulk purchases
— Multi-product Agent – represents a coordinator of another kind of agent coalition for coordinated buying of multi-products. This is similar to the Bulk Purchase Agent and Bulk Purchase Agora with some differences in details of coordination and marketing

Cooperative points for agents work in our problem can be identified, for example, as follows:

— Coordination of the Mall activity
— Coordination of different Customer Agents
— Coordination (information gathering) and negotiation between Shop and Customer Agents
— Coordination of multi-product and bulk purchasing

These cooperative points can be mapped into the following set of Agoras:

- Customer Agora – coordinates work of different Customer Agents representing different interests of the same customer
- Shop Agora – supports work coordination of Customer Agents and Shop Agents in the virtual shop. Each shop is represented by own Shop Agora with a corresponding set of Shop Agents. The Shop Agents meet Customer Agents, give these agents information about products and try to sell their shop's products through negotiation with the Customer Agents. In addition the Shop Agents can connect, for example, to the Multi-product Agora to enter into a multi-product agreement with other Shop Agents belonging to other shops
- Mall Agora – coordinates work of the shopping mall
- Bulk Purchase and Multi-product Agoras – coordinate Customer Agents coalitions

Interrelations and connections among agents and Agoras are presented in Fig. 2. Lines between Agoras mean that agents from connected Agoras can be registered on both of them. Shadow Agoras mean that there can be more than one Agora of this type. We would like to say that the presented Fig. 2 is not complete and it serves only for illustration of the ideas rather than description of particular implementation. Coordination and negotiation agents manage corresponding protocols (auctions, Contract Net Protocol [6], notifications etc.).

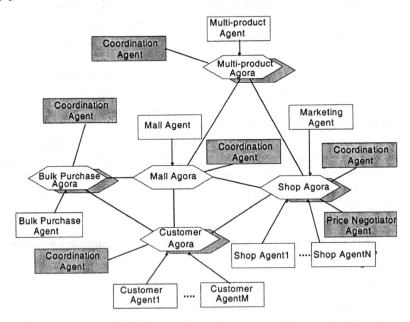

Fig. 2. Virtual Shopping Mall

We can summarize usage of Agora platform in problems like the above described as follows:

– Having a problem first identify participants of cooperative work
– Identify cooperative points in the problem by finding coordination and/or negotiation activities
– Map participants to agents
– Map cooperative points to Agoras
– Choose coordination and negotiation agents according to identified activities

Agora platform provides an infrastructure where the above-mentioned steps can be supported by corresponding tools.

4 Implementation Details

4.1 Agora Functionality

As it is mentioned in the Section 2 Agora contains default and registered agents. The registered agents are divided into:

– coordination agents,
– negotiation agents,
– participant agents

The first two types of agents supervise/manage coordination and negotiation activities to be performed at the corresponding Agora. The participant agents represent participants of cooperative activity.

Default agents are Agora manager, service and matchmaking agents. We consider first matchmaking function of default agent in more details as the basic one, while other functions will be mentioned briefly later.

Each participant agent presents offered and wanted activities at Agora. Offered Activity (OA) may be any task the agent can perform by itself. In the case of the Virtual Shopping Mall example an offered activity could be a product offered by a seller for sale. Wanted Activity (WA) could be any requested task from other agents. For example, in the case of shopping mall it could be a product the customer would like to buy. General operation loop is shown in Fig. 3. It includes:

– registration of Offered and Wanted activities by participants
– starting matchmaking by some event (for example, clock event)
– matching Offered and Wanted activities registered by participant agents and producing the following outputs:
    -- failure – no matched activities
    -- info – inform involved participant agents about matched activities
    -- perform negotiation – communicate to negotiation agent to perform a negotiation process with involved participants about matched activities

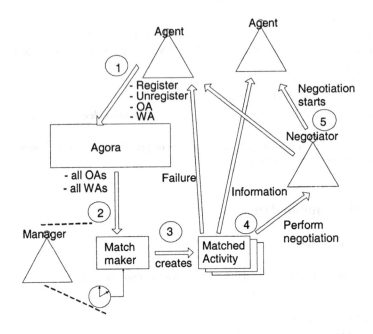

Fig. 3. Matchmaking in Agora

Complexity of matchmaker can be customized for different applications. In particular direct matching of OA and WA is provided by default. However the default matchmaker can be overridden to support semantical matchmaking using ontology, synonymous etc.

Other default agent functionality may include:

- advance event handler – a complex decision making procedure for starting matchmaking process, including filtering events, reasoning about necessity of matchmaking, selective matchmaking etc.
- decision making about registration of particular negotiation and/or coordination agent
- processing queries about registered activities, ontology used and other general information
- handling registration/unregistration protocols
- pro-active reasoning with available knowledge
- reflection support by perceiving environment
- history maintenance and analysis

All functional features of default agents can be overridden by customer via registration of his own default agents.

4.2 Agents

The Agora platform provides a mechanism for agents deployment. Agents created by the Agora system have the following modules:

– *GoalAnalyzer* module perceives the environment, synthesizes a goal description, evaluates incoming messages, selects a plan from a collection of alternative plans
– *Knowledge Base* module maintains storage, retrieval and querying knowledge (performative base, ontology etc.)
– *Planner* module creates a collection of plans based on the goal and knowledge base
– *Scheduler* module creates a task (a plan that is ready for execution) which contains run-time information and if there are found enough resources then the task is delivered to the agent for execution
– *ActionCreator* module performs an action which corresponds to a particular step in the plan. *ActionCreator* decides which module or procedure should be executed (internally or externally by message passing), finds correct performative and ontology
– *Communication Threads* are communication ports of the agent and they are created for each communication channel/activity

The proposed generic agent architecture doesn't contain agents mental states and can be considered as a low-level machinery for support of basic agent functions. Intelligence of a particular agent depends on complexity of the *GoalAnalyzer* and *Planner* modules and it can be added by customer via overriding standard modules. The goal of the above-mentioned architecture is to provide an extensible and generic machinery platform rather than to cover complete functionality of agents.

At the current version of the platform default *Planner* and *GoalAnalyzer* are quite simple and we consider development of a set of various planners as a possible extension of the platform.

Plans in the current implementation are presented in the Extensible Markup Language (XML) format.

4.3 Negotiation and Coordination Agents

Both Negotiation and Coordination agents are ordinary registered agents with some predefined functionality in the Agora platform. Their specificity lays in maintenance of corresponding negotiation and coordination protocols. The protocols are presented as plans to be performed by the agents. Plans are described as XML files and they may include description of communications between involved parties. At the moment a set of implemented negotiation protocols include Contract Net Protocol and basic auction protocols. In the current version of the system we implemented only awareness via deadlines managing as coordination activities.

4.4 Communication Adapters and Message Wrappers

As it is mentioned in the Introduction we are focused on support of cooperative work. As a solution for communication/language component we adopt a concept of speech act-based Agent Communication Language (ACL). In particular a concept of Message Wrapper is implemented. The Message Wrapper format is used for communication inside Agoras and agents. While outside of them an external communication format (like FIPA [7] or KQML [1]) is used. The Message Wrapper format is quite general and it uses ideas both from FIPA and KQML. A general idea/intention of introducing message wrapper is to make independent (to some degree) internal communication between agents and Agoras from the external format. At the moment we use JATLite package [8] (KQML-based) for implementation of communication, however, moving to a FIPA-based solution should not be a problem for customers who run tasks in Agora environment.

Message Wrapper performatives are almost identical to the FIPA performatives as more standardized solution while parameters both from FIPA and KQML are supported (usage of both type parameters in the same communication act is not recommended but technically possible).

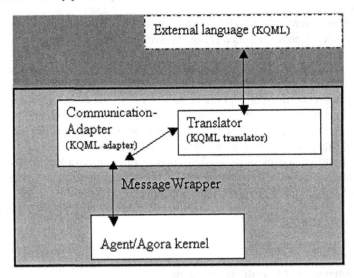

Fig. 4. A Communication Adapter

For translation between Message Wrapper and external formats Communication Adapter is implemented (see Fig. 4). Agents and Agoras communicate by exchanging communication objects in the Message Wrapper format. These objects are passed to the Communication Adapter who converts the objects to external communication language or external constructions into communication objects. The Communication Adapter should exist for each external ACL and it can be extended or overridden by user if needed. In the current version only translation from Message Wrapper format to KQML (so called, KQML-adapter) is implemented.

We consider a Communication Adapter solution as a practical solution in case of uncertainty about the ACL to be used. However even in case of standardization of language and, what is more important, supporting communication environment (naming, routing etc) usage of communication adapter can bring a flexibility into infrastructure.

4.5 Agora and agents

A general view to functioning of the Agora system is presented in Fig. 5.

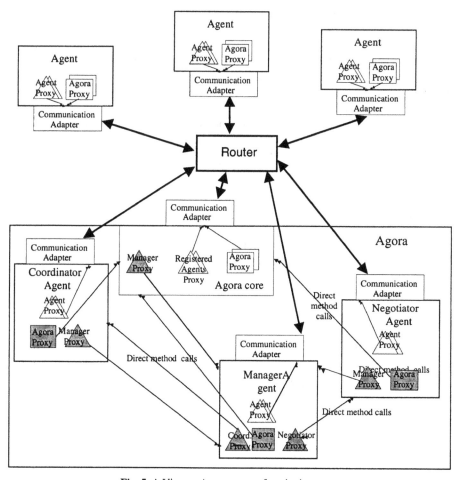

Fig. 5. A View to Agora system functioning

Agents and Agoras contain proxy objects – local representatives of objects in a different address space. Both Agora and agents have proxies of each other. This allows performing method calls locally on the proxy-object as if the remote Agent/Agora were really available locally. Particular implementation of message passing by proxy may vary and it may or may not involve communication adapter. This means that all components of Agora and agents can be distributed among the network, however, when such high distribution is not efficient (or not necessary) the communication can be easily implemented by local method calls.

5. Conclusions and Future works

A multi-agent system infrastructure may include different levels and components. We are focused only on cooperative work support component in the infrastructure which we consider to be at MAS middleware level. The platform we developed is based on the Agora concept as a facilitator of cooperative work. Advantages of such approach are that in addition to methodological and instrumental basis it also allows accumulate and re-use knowledge about cooperative work by developing templates and libraries of typical solutions for cooperative work. For example, such typical solutions might be generic shop or customer Agoras in the example we considered in the Section 3.

The Agora platform is implemented in Java and it provides two basic possibilities for its usage:

– Application Program Interfaces (API) and
– A simple Graphical User Interface (GUI)

In the second case Agoras and agents can be created from standard windows and plans for agents can be presented as XML files. Our future work is oriented to development of more advance and flexible GUI as well as extension of functionality of default components and maintenance of library of templates for typical agents and Agoras.

Acknowledgements

This work is partially supported by the Norwegian Research Foundation in the framework of the Distributed Information Technology Systems (DITS) program and the ElComAg project.

References

1. Finin, T., Labrou, Y., Mayfield, J.: KQML as an Agent Communication Language. In: Bradshaw, J. M. (ed.): Software Agents. AAAI Press/The MIT Press: Menlo Park, CA. (1997) 291-316
2. Hayes-Roth, B.: A Blackboard Architecture for Control. Artificial Intelligence, 26(3) (1985) 251-321
3. Matskin, M., Divitini, M., Petersen, S. A.: An Architecture for Multi-Agent Support in a Distributed Information Technology Application. International Workshop on Intelligent Agents in Information and Process Management on the 22nd German Annual Conference on Artificial Intelligence in Bremen (KI-98), TZI-Bericht Nr. 9, Germany, September 15-17, (1998) 47-58
4. Matskin, M.: Multi-Agent Support for Modeling Co-operative Work. In: T. Yongchareon, F. A. Aagesen, V. Wuwongse (eds.) Intelligence in Networks. The Fifth International Conference SMARTNET'99, 22-26 November 1999, Thailand, Kluwer Academic Publishers, (1999) 419-432
5. Matskin, M.: Agents in Telecommunication-Based Services. Invited talk, Proceedings of Networking'2000 conference, Mini-Conference "IATE - Intelligent Agents for Telecommunication Environments", Paris, May 16, (2000) 77-90
6. Smith, R. G.: The Contract Net Protocol: High-Level Communication and Control in a Distributed Problem Solver. IEEE Transactions of Computer Science, 29(12). (1980) 1104-1113
7. URL: http: //www.fipa.org
8. URL: http://java.stanford.edu
9. Wooldridge, M., Jennings, N., Kinny, D.: A Methodology for Agent-Oriented Analysis and Design. Dept. of El. Eng. – Queen Mary & Westfield College – London. (1999)

Sensible Agent Testbed Infrastructure for Experimentation

K. S. Barber, D. N. Lam, C. E. Martin, and R. M. McKay

The Laboratory for Intelligent Processes and Systems, ENS 240
Electrical and Computer Engineering Department, The University of Texas at Austin
Austin, TX 78712
http://www.lips.utexas.edu
phone: (512) 471-6152
fax: (512) 471-3652
{barber, dnlam, cemartin, ryanmckay}@mail.utexas.edu

Abstract. The design and analysis of multi-agent systems is difficult due to complex agent capabilities and rich interactions among agents. Experimentation is a crucial step in gaining insight into the behavior of agents. Experiments must be flexible, easily configurable, extensible, and repeatable. This paper presents the Sensible Agent Testbed, which supports these requirements. The CORBA infrastructure of the Testbed platform and the formally-defined interfaces among Testbed components are described. The Testbed promotes many levels of modularity, facilitating parallel development of agents and agent capabilities. This approach provides many opportunities for different types of experiments. Experimental setup through a configuration file is simplified using the Init File Maker, which has the capability to automate the production of multiple configurations. Overall, the Sensible Agent Testbed provides a solid infrastructure supporting multi-agent experiments.

1   Introduction

The ability to experimentally analyze multi-agent systems greatly enhances the understanding of multi-agent technology as well as its application to specific problem domains. Such experiments provide insight into the behaviors of distributed software-based problem-solvers and allow researchers to support or refute theoretical claims. However, providing this experimental capability presents many challenges. First, an experimental infrastructure must be provided that supports a variety of experimental tasks and problem domains. This experimental infrastructure must be flexible, easily configured, and extensible. It must also support experimental repeatability. Second, the experimental infrastructure must allow agents, agent sub-components, the environment, and/or individual algorithms to be easily interchanged to support experimental comparisons. Third, due to the size and complexity of many multi-agent research projects,

This research was supported in part by the Texas Higher Education Coordinating Board (#003658452), a National Science Foundation Graduate Research Fellowship, and the Naval Surface Warfare Center – Dahlgren. The content of the information does not necessarily reflect the position or the policy of the Government and no official endorsement should be inferred.

T. Wagner and O.F. Rana (Eds.): Infrastructure for Agents, LNAI 1887, pp. 41–47, 2001.
© Springer-Verlag Berlin Heidelberg 2001

the experimental infrastructure must support the integration of software that is produced in parallel by multiple developers. Several multi-agent testbeds have recently addressed these challenges to varying degrees [3;5;6;8]. (For a survey of previously developed multi-agent testbeds, see [4].) These testbeds differ in many respects, including degree of domain independence, degree of agent-architecture independence, types of constraints placed on agent interaction with the world and other agents, level of on-the-fly configuration for experimental runs, and type of data logging and experimental feedback.

This paper describes the Sensible Agent Testbed [2], which provides an experimental infrastructure addressing the challenges described above. It should be noted that Sensible Agent functionality (e.g. conflict resolution, planning, truth maintenance, team formation) and Testbed infrastructure functionality (e.g. such as environmental simulation) has been delineated into logical components. The existence of well-defined interfaces among the components of the system helps provide the necessary capabilities and features. Because development activity is distributed across multiple developers working in parallel, it can be very difficult to test an individual's work for correct, much less optimal, behavior. Therefore, it is crucial that users have the ability to see what implementations are available for testing, and to configure desired components into a testable system. In addition, many experiments require repeatability and a level of control over environmental conditions that is not feasible in the real world. Repeatability in a simulated-world experiment requires repeatability in setting up experiments and repeatability in running experiments. Finally, the ability to record data from experiments is required. Since a wide variety of data may be appropriate for various experiments, a great deal of flexibility in specifying what types of data to record during the experiment is necessary. The purpose of this paper is to describe how the Sensible Agent Testbed meets the requirements described above, focusing on its facilities for experimentation. The remainder of the paper discusses the structure of the Sensible Agent Testbed including the underlying CORBA-based infrastructure and the realization of deterministic interactions between the agents and the simulation environment. It also discusses facilities provided by the Testbed to setup experiments and gather data.

2   SENSIBLE AGENT TESTBED DESIGN

The Sensible Agent Testbed is composed of three main parts: the agents, the environment, and the user interface for visualization. Each agent in the system is represented by a Sensible Agent System Interface (SASI). The SASI encapsulates the four Sensible Agent internal modules (PM-Perspective Modeler, AR-Autonomy Reasoner, AP-Action Planner and CRA-Conflict Resolution Advisor) and provides each agent with a single point of contact to the rest of the system. The abstraction of the SASI allows agents with different internal architectures to be introduced to the system with no impact on the infrastructure. Each SASI instance controls the creation and synchronization of its own internal modules, if such internal modules exist for that instance. The creation and execution of the SASIs and simulation environment are controlled by a single component called the Testbed System Process (TSP). The Testbed is truly distributed because every Testbed component (SASIs, simulation, internal agent modules, user interface, etc.) can be spawned on different processors. All agent interactions, including communication, are carried out through the simulated environment via sensors and actuators registered with the simulation (these may or may not be noisy). The TSP also allows user-interface components to register with the agents or simulation-environment components. Depending on which events these user interfaces subscribe to, the agents or simulation environment will publish information to be displayed on these interfaces.

2.1   DESIGN SPECIFICATION AND IMPLEMENTATION FLEXIBILITY

In order to facilitate rapid and parallel agent development, both in-house and by third parties, the objective was to place very few restrictions on implementation language (Lisp, Java, and C++) and platform (Linux, Unix, WindowsNT). The Sensible Agent Testbed uses CORBA to provide the required flexibility in these two areas. Figure 1 logically depicts how the Sensible Agent Testbed system components interact with the ORB. Different ORBs can use the Internet Inter-ORB Protocol (IIOP) to communicate with each

other. OMG's Interface Definition Language (IDL) formally specifies the services that each component will provide in a language-independent, object-oriented manner.

Although the Sensible Agent Testbed supports interchanging entire agents, experiments up to this point have found the interchangeability of internal agent modules to be more useful. If agents operating in the Testbed conform to the Sensible Agent architecture [1], multiple implementations of various internal modules may already be available for comparison testing. The agent

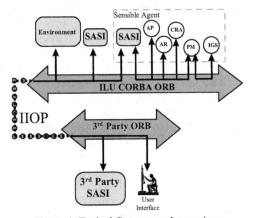

Figure 1: Testbed Component Interactions

designer specifies which implementation to use with a name. The name is a pointer to a factory that "makes" that type of component. A factory is a design pattern for instantiating distributed objects. In this case, factories provide objects satisfying some IDL specification. A name is used to retrieve a factory from a naming service. With this approach, experimenters can access any kind of implementation they want, as long as a factory has been published to the nameserver. The TSP is responsible for factory lookup and retrieval to create the simulation and all the SASIs for an experiment. Each of the SASIs is, in turn, responsible for using factories to obtain its internal module instances.

2.2   AGENT-ENVIRONMENT INTERACTION

In the Sensible Agent Testbed, agents must interact with a simulated environment. Requirements for this environment include the ability to: (1) accept actuator input from and provide sensor information to multiple agents, (2) model the passage of time, (3) determine the state of each agent and the environment, (4) maintain and apply models of environmental characteristics and mechanisms (e.g. radar signal propagation, e-commerce market status, movement and position of physical entities), and (5) halt and reset to produce multiple experimental runs in batched mode, (6) record data about states and events for experimental analysis. These experimental results should not be affected by the relative speed of or transient load on the hardware during a given experimental run. This is especially important in a distributed system, where components are running on multiple computers.   Therefore, to achieve repeatability for experiments, the simulation environment must (7) handle agent-agent and agent-environment interactions deterministically.

The simulation environment in the Sensible Agent Testbed is based on a time-tick paradigm for repeatable simulation operation. Each time tick is composed of a simulation active phase and an agent active phase. The simulation enters its active phase after all agents have reported that they are finished processing for the previous time tick. During the simulation active phase the simulation takes the following steps:

1.   sends a halt signal to each agent (SASI) and to each sensor and actuator,
2.   increments the time tick counter,
3.   applies simulation mechanisms (e.g. calculating new positions from velocity information),
4.   polls all actuators for new events,
5.   deterministically applies all actuator actions to the environment,
6.   calculates the world state (e.g. current position of all entities) including what information goes to each sensor (e.g. sent messages may not arrive at a given communication sensor due to environmental loss, if so modeled)
7.   sends new information (if any) to each sensor
8.   records performance data for this time tick, and
9.   checks for conditions signaling the end of the run.
      o   If these conditions are met, it resets all actuators, sensors, and agents
      o   Otherwise, it advances each agent, sensor, and actuator to the next time tick (starting the agent active phase)

To ensure repeatable simulation runs, the agents must remain inactive while the simulation updates the world state. The agents must also behave deterministically during their active phase. At the beginning of every agent active phase, a consistent world state is presented to each agent. During the agent active phase, Sensible Agents employ a state machine to coordinate the interactions of their internal modules [7]. In this manner, race conditions among internal agent components due to variables such as machine load, processor speed, and distribution of agent processes are eliminated.

3   SETUP FOR EXPERIMENTS

The primary purpose of the Sensible Agent Testbed is to test and analyze technology resident in SA modules as well as overall agent behavior and performance. In this section, we will discuss how the Testbed facilitates: (1) ease and repeatability in configuring the system components and setting initial conditions, and (2) ease in specifying what types of data to record. Each internal module in a Sensible Agent uses its own language to set its experimental specification (initial conditions and data to be logged), instead of developing a common experimental specification language that all the components understand. This gives individual SA module developers the freedom to develop their own setup language, which no other components in the system need to understand. Although this approach makes development and testing easier with respect to a single module, this approach makes it more difficult for users to set the experimental specification for modules that they did not develop. A tool has been created to help users easily setup the SA modules and will be described after an explanation of the specification file.

The implementation of our approach consists of a textual experimentation setup file. This file uses a XML-like tagged meta-language to abstract away from each SA module's experimental specification language. There is a <RunSpec> tag in the setup file for each run in an experiment, which specifies the settings for a respective run. A <BaseSpec> tag specifies default settings that remain constant across experimental runs in batched mode. This feature helps reduce the size and complexity of the initialization file.

Each agent has a setup specification set off by the <AgentBaseSpec> tags. Within this tag, the various <Factory> tags specify what CORBA factories to use for each of the agent's SA modules. As can be surmised, each agent can have different module configurations, so factories must be specified for each agent. Following the factory specifications are the four SA modules tags. Within those tags, SA module developers can code their information using any format they prefer because only their module will see it. In this way, the module specifications can be independently developed without integration problems.

Another tag of interest is the <PerfDataLog> tag. This tag is used to specify the types of data that the user desires to be logged during the experiment. In contrast with the methodology used for the BaseSpec and RunSpec, the contents of this tag are global – they are sent to the simulation and to each SASI during initialization. Each SASI passes the information on to its modules. The rationale for this methodology is that the types of data to be logged are often not specific to any particular module. However, we do allow for module-specific values in this tag – other modules simply ignore values that they do not understand.

To aid in the creation and modification of experimental setup files, the Init File Maker (IFM) tool was produced. This tool presents several different graphical views of the setup file: (1) Tree view, (2) QuickView, (3) TableView, (4) BaseAgents view, and (5) RunSpec view. Each view has a different focus and allows manipulation of data in different ways. These views will now be described in more detail.

Since the experimental setup file is in a hierarchical, tagged format, a parse tree is a natural graphical view of it (left-hand side of Figure 2). The right-hand side of the figure displays the information of the selected tag, which is in the form of a table for the <EnvironmentSpec> tag. The user can also directly traverse down a specific branch of the tree to edit the attribute values directly. Due to the large amount of information that can be contained in the setup file, the tree can become very deep, making it difficult to locate specific tags. In which case, the user can access the other tab panels, such as QuickView and BaseAgents, which provide convenient access to a subset of the information in the tree structure. These tab panels offer the capability of representing the tagged information in a concise and user-friendly interface, allowing various settings to be selected by radio buttons or from a list of options.

The QuickView tab panel presents the user with general attributes (e.g. the locations of factories) and a list of possible logging options that records performance data. The TableView tab panel displays the tables of all the tags that hold table-like information, such as the information in the <EnvironmentSpec> tag shown on the right-hand side of Figure 2.

The BaseAgents tab panel displays all the information needed to configure each agent. Figure 3 shows the interface for setting up the <ARSpec> tag for agent "1." This interface allows an experimenter to configure the Autonomy Reasoner (AR) in different ways (e.g. disabling AR functions, setting random seeds and default values). To support large sets of experiments in batch mode, the IFM has the ability to produce all combinations of configuration settings given a list of possible values for any number of attributes. For example, given nine possible values for agents' positions, as well as three possible emitter strengths for communication, the IFM will produce configuration information for 27 runs.

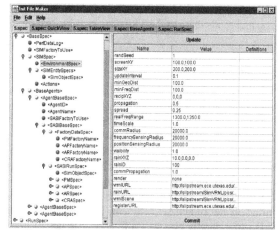

Figure 2: Construction of tree from input file 5.spec

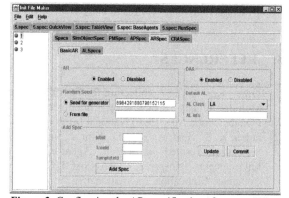

Figure 3: Configuring the AR specifications for agent "1"

Each variation of configuration settings is appended as a single "RunSpec" tag in the tree. Once all modifications have been made, the IFM encodes the information and sends the output to a setup file that can be used to run a complete experimental session in batch mode.

Once the setup file has been created, the user may start the experiment. The process is as follows: The user starts the Testbed System Process (TSP) and loads a setup file of his or her choice. The TSP parses the file to obtain the simulation factory name and the SASI factory name for each agent. The TSP then obtains a simulation and agent wrappers from the appropriate factories. The TSP then sends to each component its corresponding BaseSpec and its first RunSpec. The BaseSpec allows the initialization of the simulation environment, allows agents to instantiate their submodules, and allows agents to register with the simulation sensors and actuators. Once each SASI has obtained its modules, it sends to each module its respective portion of the BaseSpec and RunSpec. The dispersion of experimental specs and the aggregation of data at the end of the experiment are mirrors of each other – the same pattern of abstraction is used. Just as the SASI passes an experimental spec to each of its SA modules, oblivious to its content, the SASI also requests experimental reports from each of its SA modules, wraps the textual reports in tags, and sends them to the TSP as part of its own report.

4   SUMMARY

This paper presents a platform for multi-agent experimentation called the Sensible Agent Testbed.   The Sensible Agent Testbed uses CORBA as language- and platform-independent middleware.   This allows software developers the freedom to write their components in the language of their choice, and run their components on their own machines.   This paper describes the interactions between Sensible Agents and the Testbed's simulation environment, focusing on repeatable experimental behavior. Specifically, the description focuses on the functionality provided by the Testbed for setting up and running experiments as well as collecting desired data. The Init File Maker (IMF) tool greatly aids in configuring batches of experiments through a set of graphical user interfaces.   In conclusion, the Sensible Agent Testbed is a full-featured, highly flexible and configurable tool for running multi-agent experiments.

5   REFERENCES

[1] Barber, K. S.: The Architecture for Sensible Agents. In Proceedings of International Multidisciplinary Conference, Intelligent Systems: A Semiotic Perspective (Gaithersburg, MD, 1996) National Institute of Standards and Technology, 49-54.

[2] Barber, K. S., Goel, A., Han, D., Kim, J., Liu, T. H., Martin, C. E., and McKay, R. M.: Simulation Testbed for Sensible Agent-based Systems in Dynamic and Uncertain Environments. *accepted to* TRANSACTIONS: Quarterly Journal of the Society for Computer Simulation International, Special Issue on Modeling and Simulation of Manufacturing Systems, (2000).

[3] Barber, K. S., McKay, R., Goel, A., Han, D., Kim, J., Liu, T. H., and Martin, C. E.: Sensible Agents Capable of Dynamic Adaptive Autonomy: The Distributed Architecture and Testbed. *accepted to* IEICE Transactions on Communications, Special Issue on Autonomous Decentralized Systems, (2000).

[4] Decker, K. S.   Distributed Artificial Intelligence Testbeds. In Foundations of Distributed Artificial Intelligence. Sixth-Generation Computer Technology Series, O'Hare, G. M. P. and Jennings, N. R., (eds.). John Wiley & Sons, Inc., New York, (1996) 119-138.

[5] Decker, K. S. Task Envrionment Centered Simulation. In Simulating Organizations, Prietula, M. J., Carley, K., M., and Gasser, L., (eds.). AAAI Press / The MIT Press, Menlo Park, CA, (1998) 105-130.

[6] Horling, B., Lesser, V., and Vincent, R.:   Multi-Agent System Simulation. In Proceedings of Sixteenth IMACS World Congress 2000 on Scientific Computation, Applied Mathematics and Simulation (Lausanne, Switzerland, 2000)

[7] McKay, R. M. Communication Services for Sensible Agents. Master's Thesis, Electrical and Computer Engineering, University of Texas at Austin, 1999.

[8] Noda, I., Matsubara, H., Hiraki, K., and Frank, I.: Soccer Server: A Tool for Research on Multiagent Systems. Applied Artificial Intelligence, 12 (1998) 233-250.

The MADKIT Agent Platform Architecture

Olivier Gutknecht and Jacques Ferber

Laboratoire d'Informatique, Robotique et Micro-Electronique de Montpellier
C.N.R.S. - Université Montpellier II
161, rue Ada - 34392 Montpellier Cedex 5 - France
gutkneco@lirmm.fr - ferber@lirmm.fr

Abstract. In this paper, we present MadKit (multi-agent development kit), a generic multi-agent platform. This toolkit is based on a organizational model. It uses concepts of groups and roles for agents to manage different agent models and multi-agent systems at the same time, while keeping a global structure.

We discuss the architecture of MadKit, based on a minimalist agent kernel decoupled from specific agency models. Basic services like distributed message passing, migration or monitoring are provided by platform agents for maximal flexibility. The componential interface model allows variations in platform appearance and classes of usage.

1 Introduction

1.1 The heterogeneity issue

A major characteristic in agent research and applications is the high heterogeneity of the field. By heterogeneity, we mean both *agent model heterogeneity*, characterizing agents built and described with different models and formalisms; *language heterogeneity*, with agents using different communication and interaction schemes, and finally *applicative heterogeneity*, as multi-agent systems are used with various goals and in many applicative domains.

Many successful theories and applications has been proposed in different fields of multi-agent research: interface agents [6], mobile agents [5], information retrieval agents [8], etc. We believe that being able to take advantage of this diversity of approaches simultaneously is important to build complex systems while keeping heterogeneity manageable. An "one size fits all" seems rather adventurous; thus, the interesting question is how to establish conceptual models *and* software toolkits to facilitate integration.

We also advocates that interoperability in agent system should be envisaged at agent level. Existing interoperability mechanisms in software engineering (CORBA, XML, ...) are interesting for the foundations they procure, but are not the universal answer to our preoccupation. At least, the relationship between the underlying interoperability platform and the agent layer be clearly defined and identified.

T. Wagner and O.F. Rana (Eds.): Infrastructure for Agents, LNAI 1887, pp. 48–55, 2001.

1.2   MadKit as a multi multi-agent system

We have designed a model, called AALAADIN, that structures multi-agent systems, and implemented a platform based on this model. The platform itself has been realized to take full advantage of the model. In this paper, we will particularly focus on the MADKIT platform. We will see that a structural model at multi-agent systems level can ease agent diversity integration within a platform, hence this qualification of "multi multi-agent systems". The MADKIT toolkit was motivated by the need to provide a generic, highly customizable and scalable agent platform. The goal of building a foundation layer for various agent models was essential, as well as making the basic services provided completely extensible and replaceable.

We briefly introduce the AALAADIN conceptual model in section 2. Section 3 describes the platform architecture. It presents the concept of "agent microkernel", how system services are provided by agents and gives an overview of the agent interface model. Section 4 presents some experiments and systems built with MADKIT. Section 5 briefly talks about future work and concludes.

2   The agent/group/role model

The MADKIT platform architecture is rooted in the AGR (agent-group-role) model developed in the context of the AALAADIN project. MADKIT both implements and uses for its own management this model. We will just summarize it here, and refer to [2] for a more general overview of the project and [3] for a detailed description of its formal operational semantics. In summary, we advocate that considering organizational concepts, such as groups, roles, structures, dependencies, etc. as first class citizens might be a key issue for building large scale, heterogeneous systems.

In our definition, an organization is viewed as a framework for activity and interaction through the definition of groups, roles and their relationships. But, by avoiding an agent-oriented viewpoint, an organization is regarded as a structural relationship between a collection of agents. Thus, an organization can be described solely on the basis of its structure, i.e. by the way groups and roles are arranged to form a whole, without being concerned with the way agents actually behave, and multi-agent systems will be analyzed from the "outside", as a set of interaction modes. The specific architecture of agents is purposely not addressed.

2.1   Agent

The model places no constraints on the internal architecture of agents. An *agent* is only specified as an active communicating entity which plays *roles* within *groups*. This agent definition is intentionally general to allow agent designers to adopt the most accurate definition of agent-hood relative to their application. The agent designer is responsible for choosing the most appropriate agent model as internal architecture.

2.2 Group

Groups are defined as atomic sets of agent aggregation. Each agent is part of one or more groups. In its most basic form, the group is only a way to tag a set of agents. In a more developed form,in conjunction with the role definition, it may represent any usual multi-agent system. An agent can be a member of n groups at the same time. A major point of AALAADIN groups is that they can freely overlap. A group can be founded by any agent.

2.3 Role

The role is an abstract representation of an agent function, service or identification within a group. Each agent can handle multiple roles, and each role handled by an agent is local to a group. Handling a role in a group must be requested by the candidate agent, and is not necessarily awarded. Abstract communication schemes are thus defined from roles.

The model is not a static description of an agent organization. It also allows to define rules to specify the part of the dynamics of the agent organization. Note that the particular mechanism for role access within a group is not defined (systematic acceptance or refusal, admission conditioned by skills or by an admission dialog, relation to a group metrics,...).

3 Architecture

The MADKIT platform is built around this model. In addition to the three core concepts, the platform adds three design principles:

- Micro-kernel architecture
- Agentification of services
- Graphic component model

MadKit itself is a set of packages of Java classes that implements the agent kernel, the various libraries of messages, probes and agents. It also includes a graphical development environment and standard agent models

The basic philosophy of the MADKIT architecture is to use wherever possible the platform for its own management: any service beside those assured by the micro-kernel are handled by agents. Thus the platform is not an agent platform is the classical sense. The reduced size of the micro-kernel, combined with the principle of modular services managed by agents enable a range of multiple, scalable platforms and construction of libraries of specialized agent models.

Agent groups have been proposed in other architectures, such as [1], although the mechanism is specific to mobile agents and lacks our ability to handle multiple groups and multiple roles in a generic model.

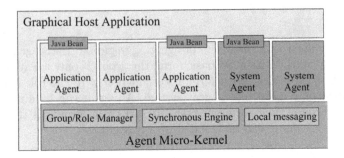

Fig. 1. MadKit Architecture Diagram

3.1   Agent micro-kernel

The MADKIT micro-kernel is a small (less than 40 Kb) and optimized agent kernel.

The term "micro-kernel" is intentionnaly used as a reference to the role of micro-kernels in the domain of OS engineering. We could directly translate their motto into: *'incorporating a number of key facilities that allow the efficient deployment of agent toolkits."*

The MADKIT kernel only handles the following tasks:

Control of local groups and roles As most of the interoperability and extensibility possibilities in MADKIT relies on the organizational layer, it is mandatory that group and role are handled at the lowest level in the platform, to provide this functionality to any agent The micro-kernel is responsible for maintaining correct information about group members and roles handled. It also checks if requests made on groups and roles structures are correct (ie: evaluating - or delegating evaluation - of role functions).

Agent life-cycle management The kernel also launches (and eventually kills) agents, and maintain tables and references of agent instances, it is the only module in MADKIT that owns direct references to the actual agents. It also handles the agent personal information and assigns it a globally unique identifier (kernel address plus agent identification on the local kernel) , the `AgentAddress` upon creation. This identifier can be redefined to accept standardized agent naming schemes.

Local message passing The kernel manages routing and distribution of messages between **local** agents. The basic mechanism relies on a copy-on-write implementation to avoid unnecessary operations.

The kernel itself is wrapped in an special agent, the `KernelAgent`, which is created at bootstrap. It permits control and monitoring of the kernel within the agent model.

Kernel hooks The kernel itself is fully extensible through "kernel hooks". Any entitled agent (i.e. an agent that has been allowed to be member of the *system* group) can request to the `KernelAgent` to subscribe or intercept a kernel hook. These hooks are the generic subscribe-and-publish scheme allowing extension of the core behavior of the platform. Every kernel function (adding an agent to a group, launching an agent, sending a message) implements this mechanism. For instance, this is how are written the agents that monitor the population or organization in the platform.

For instance, a system *communicator* agent can inject in the local kernel a message received through a socket connection with a distant madkit platform.

3.2   Agents

The generic agent is MADKIT is a class defining basic life-cycle (what to do upon activation, execution, and termination).

- Control and life-cycle. The main agent class in MADKIT defines primitives related to message passing, plus group and role management, but does not implement a specific execution policy. A subclass adds support for concurrent, thread-based execution, which is the natural model for coarse-grained collaborative or cognitive agent. Additional subclasses implements synchronous execution through an external scheduler, focused on reactive or hybrid architectures: many fine-grained agents.
- Communication is achieved through asynchronous message passing, with primitives to directly send a message to another agent represented by its `AgentAddress`, or the higher-level version that send or broadcast to one or all agents having a given role in a specific group.
- Group and roles actions and requests are defined at action level. The agent developer is completely free to define the agent behavior, but the organizational view will be always present.

Message passing Messages in the MADKIT platform are defined by inheritance from a generic `Message` class. Thus specific messages can be defined for intragroup communication, and allows a group to have its specific communication attributes. Messages receivers and senders are identified with their `AgentAddress`. MadKit do not define interaction mechanism, which can be defined on an ad-hoc basis, or built in a specific agent model library.

Agent models Several specific agent libraries have been built above this infrastructure, notably:

- Bindings to the Scheme language
- An agent model that wraps the JESS rule engine [4].
- Various models for artificial life / reactive systems, such as a "turtle kit" that mimics some functions of the StarLogo environemente [7].
- An actor model implementation
- Agent construction tools running themselves as agents in the platform.

3.3   Agentification of services

In contrast to other architectures, MADKIT uses agents to achieve things like distributed message passing, migration control, dynamic security, and other aspect of system management. These different services are represented in the platform as roles in some specific groups, defined in an abstract organizational structure. This allows a very high level of customization, as these service agents can be replaced without hurdle.

For instance, external developers have built a new *group synchronizer* agent that use a shared JNDI directory to maintain group information across distributed kernel instead of relying on our provided (but MadKit-specific) system. Their agent uses some hooks in the kernel to achieve its goal and replaced the provided *group synchronizer* agent by requesting the same role in the *system* group. Other agents did not notice the change.

The role delegation principle has the other interesting effect to allow easy scaling. An agent can hold several roles at the beginning of a group, and as the group grows, launches other agents and delegates them some of these roles.

Communication and distribution As messaging, as well as groups and roles management use the `AgentAddress` identifier, and as this identifier is unique across distant kernels, MADKIT agents can be transparently distributed without changing anything in the agent code. Groups can spawn across different kernels, and agents usually do not notice it.

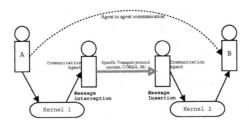

Fig. 2. Communication agents

Since the communication mechanisms are built as regular agents in the platform, communication and migration could be tailored to specific platform requirements only by changing the communication agents, for instance in disconnected mode for laptop. An MADKIT platform can run in full local mode just by not launching the communication agents.

These services are not necessarily handled by only one agent. For instance the *communicator* agent can be the *representative* for a group gathering agents specialized in sockets or CORBA communications and delegate the message to the appropriate agent

3.4 Componential graphical architecture

MADKIT graphic model is based on independent graphic components, using the Java Beans specification in the standard version.

Each agent is solely responsible for its own graphical interface, in every aspects (rendering, event processing, actions...) An agent interface can be a simple label, a complex construction based on multiple widgets, or a legacy bean software module. A "graphic shell" launches the kernel and setup the interfaces for the various agents and manage them in a global GUI (for instance: each agent has its own window, or is mapped in a global worksheet, or is combined with another agent interface,...).

As the graphic shell is a classic software module, it can be wrapped in an agent for maximum flexibility, allowing control of other agent interfaces by a regular MADKIT agent that can be part of any interaction scenario.

3.5 Consequences and discussion

The conjunction of the agent micro-kernel and the decoupled agent GUIs as well as a modular set of agent services allows important customizations of the MADKIT platform.For instance, the following "varieties" of the platform have been developed:

- A complete graphical environment to develop, and test multi-agent systems, called the "G-Box". It allows graphical control of agent life-cycle (launch, termination, pause), dynamic loading of agents, and uses introspection on agent code to discover at runtime groups and roles, references to other agents, and offer direct manipulation of these structures.
- A text-only mode, only running the micro-kernel without instantiating graphical interfaces of running agents. This platform is useful to keep a small "agent daemon" running on a machine and agents providing services of brokering, naming or routing for other machines.
- An applet wrapper, which carries the agent micro-kernel with some application agents, and executes in a distant browser.
- A "classic" application that would embed a MadKit kernel and hosts agents that handles the collaborative / dynamic aspects.
- A version of MADKIT tailored for the Palm Pilot. The kernel is slightly tweaked to only use the set of classes allowed on the Java Platform Micro Edition. A specific *communicator* handles infrared messaging.

4 Applications

MadKit has been used in various research teams for nearly two year in projects covering a wide range of applications, from simulation of hybrid architectures for control of submarine robots to evaluation of social networks or study of multi-agent control in a production line.

For instance, Wex, developed by Euriware S.A., is a complex MADKIT framework for knowledge-management applications. It federates information from different data sources (databases, support tools, web search engines, current page browsed by the user and parsed...) and present unified views of these highly heterogeneous knowledge sources. Agents have been implemented to encapsulate the various mechanisms to retrieve and transform information. The abstract organizational structure has been defined, and the various agents can plugged in to adapt the platform to the client specific needs.

5   Conclusion and future work

In this paper, we presented an agent toolkit based on an organizational model, and we argued that that large and complex agent systems should be able to cope with heterogeneity of models, communications and individual agent architectures.

We plan to extend this work in three directions. We plan to continue work on the underlying model, especially in the context of formal expression and design methodologies. Secondly, we will extend the platform itself by refining existing system agents, proposing more predefined agents and groups libraries. Finally, we are planning to built additional layers and models for multi-agent based simulation.

References

[1] Joachim Baumann and Nikolaos Radouniklis. Agent groups in mobile agent systems. In *IFIP WG 6.1, International Conference on Distributed Applications and Interoperable Systems (DAIS 97)*, 1997.

[2] Jacques Ferber and Olivier Gutknecht. A meta-model for the analysis and design of organizations in multi-agent systems. In *Third International Conference on Multi-Agent Systems (ICMAS '98) Proceedings*, pages 128–135. IEEE Computer Society, 1998.

[3] Jacques Ferber and Olivier Gutknecht. Operational semantics of a role-based agent architecture. In *Proceedings of the 6th Int. Workshop on Agent Theories, Architectures and Languages*. Springer-Verlag, 1999.

[4] Ernest J. Friedman-Hill. *Jess, The Java Expert System Shell*. Distributed Computing Systems, Sandia National Laboratories, Livermore, CA, 2000.

[5] Frederick C. Knabe. An overview of mobile agent programming. In *Proceedings of the 5th LOMAPS Workshop on Analysis and Verification of Multiple-Agent Languages*, Stockholm, Sweden, June 1996.

[6] Brenda Laurel. Interface agents: Metaphors with character. In Brenda Laurel, editor, *The Art of Human Computer Interface Design*, pages 355–365. Addison-Wesley, 1990.

[7] Mitchel Resnick. *Turtles, Termites, and Traffic Jams: Explorations in Massively Parallel Microworlds*. MIT Press, 1994.

[8] E. M. Voorhees. Software agents for information retrieval. In O. Etzioni, editor, *Software Agents — Papers from the 1994 Spring Symposium (Technical Report SS-94-03)*, pages 126–129, March 1994.

An Architecture for Modeling Internet-based Collaborative Agent Systems

Roberto A. Flores[1], Rob C. Kremer[1], Douglas H. Norrie[2]

[1] Department of Computer Science, University of Calgary, 2500 University Dr. NW,
Calgary, Canada, T2N 1N4
`{robertof, kremer}@cpsc.ucalgary.ca`
[2] Department of Mechanical & Manufacturing Engineering, University of Calgary, 2500
University Dr. NW, Calgary, Canada, T2N 1N4
`norrie@enme.ucalgary.ca`

Abstract. This paper describes an architecture for modeling cooperating systems of communicating agents. The authors' goal is not that of providing a framework to implement multi-agents systems (there are tools—such as CORBA, Java and DCOM—that do an excellent job on that), but rather to provide an architectural metaphor upon which collaborative multi-agent systems could be modeled. The approach is based on requirements defined with a practical view of the communicational and resource-oriented nature of distributed collaborative multi-agent systems.

1 Introduction

Increasingly, the Internet will be used for commerce, industry, and educational interactions between multiple parties. These interactions are intermittent but sustained over days, months, and years. They will involve multiple sources of information and often record, transform, and store considerable quantities of information for subsequent access and re-use. The Collaborative Agent System Architecture (CASA) presented in this paper provides a structural framework to support the modeling of such distributed, collaborative multi-agent systems.

In this architecture, agents are seen as software entities that pursue their objectives while taking into account the resources and skills available to them, and based on their representations of their environment and on the communications they receive [1]. In the case of agents in collaborative systems, agents are also capable of delegating task realization to agents capable of performing the required task. Internet-based systems pose an additional challenge to this scenario in that agents collaborate in a dynamic, distributed environment where agents from heterogeneous sources could interact.

It is common to find collaborative mechanisms in currently available implementation frameworks; however, modeling systems based on these facilities result in systems with less flexibility and adaptation to changes given previous design commitments to the underlying framework. The collaborative architecture presented here aims to separate the modeling of multi-agent systems from the specifications that

T. Wagner and O.F. Rana (Eds.): Infrastructure for Agents, LNAI 1887, pp. 56–63, 2001.

designers need to commit given the low-level mechanisms of proprietary frameworks used in the implementation of multi-agent systems.

There are three elementary components that we have identified as fundamental in the design of collaborative multi-agent systems: computer resources, agents, and owners. These are interrelated, since both agents and computer resources are bound by the regulations set by the human institutions owning and controlling those agents and resources. The latter are further described below.

- Computer resources: Computer resources are hardware and software resources that are available to agents for the execution of their tasks
- Agents: Agents are communicational and collaborative entities that perform their duties using the computational resources available to them. Agents can take the role of requesters or suppliers without these being one of their intrinsic characteristics. Agent requesters and providers rely on the definition of roles and on mechanisms of advertisement to locate other agents that can perform tasks for them.

2 Architecture Requirements

In this architecture, we model communities of agents in two ways: based on the computer resources agents use, and on the communicational contexts upon which they interact.

On the one hand, agents are seen as communicational entities that interact with other agents to achieve their goals. In this view, agent communities are formed as a result of interactions and the preferred locations in which interactions take place.

On the other hand, agents are seen as entities with affiliation, performing their tasks on behalf of human institutions that endorse and exert authority over them. In this view, affiliation enables resource-oriented communities by binding agents and resources. It is common that affiliation is addressed in terms of the low-level mechanisms implemented by different frameworks. We believe that these decisions should be reflected at the modeling stage, independently from the proprietary mechanisms offered by implementation frameworks.

Based on the concepts introduced above, we present several minimal requirements upon which we base our architecture.

1. The architecture should provide means (for humans) to organize computer resources in identifiable clusters.
2. The architecture should provide means to control agents' usage of computer resources according to human policies.
3. The architecture should provide means for agents to locate other agents for the purpose of collaboration and delegation of tasks.
4. The architecture should provide means for agents to create and maintain settings where agents interact (settings may include the state and history of agent interactions, and any artifacts pertinent to the context of interaction).

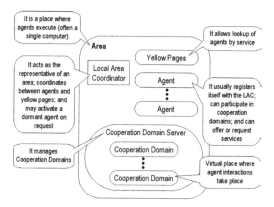

Fig. 1. Basic concepts in the CASA architecture

3   The Collaborative Agent Systems Architecture

In this section we describe a structural framework for the modeling of collaborative agents in distributed environments based in the requirements from the section 2.

Basic to this architecture are the concepts of areas (bounded resource-oriented regions), each of which contain a local area coordinator (an agent that is—in principle—responsible to negotiate with other agents the use of resources in an area), yellow pages (agents to which services offered by agents are advertised and queried), and cooperation domains (virtual contexts of interaction that may last over time, and which are supported by cooperation domain servers). These concepts (illustrated in Figure 1) are further described in the subsections below.

3.1   Areas

To satisfy the requirement that "The architecture should provide means (for humans) to organize computer resources in identifiable clusters" (requirement 1) we include the concept of areas.

Areas are bounded regions comprising computer resources owned by human institutions. Areas could be formed of partial resources from one computer, an entire computer, or a group of computers. Agents in areas form communities whose common denominator is being accepted under the usage policies and regulations set by the owners of the area's resources. Just as in a human club or sports association, membership is granted based on regulations that members are expected to abide by. In this view, membership does not necessarily imply awareness of other members of the area, since areas are facilities-oriented associations rather than associations for communication and interaction among the members. This is not to say that the latter is not important: cooperation domains are explained a later sub-section.

3.2   Local Area Coordinators

To satisfy the requirement that "The architecture should provide means to control agents' usage of computer resources according to human policies" (requirement 2) we include the concept of local area coordinators.

Local area coordinators (LAC) are agents who put into effect the usage policies given by the human institutions owning the computer resources allocated in an area. Agents requesting the use of resources in an area need to go through a registration process with the LAC in that area. Agents succeeding in their registration are expected to surrender some of their autonomy in exchange for the use of resources. Depending on the usage policies assigned to the area, agents' executable code could be required to reside in one or more of the area's resources, and its use of resources could be influenced by the usage regulations assigned to these resources.

In addition to provide an abstraction for a group of computer resources, areas and LAC can also help to encapsulate the execution state of registered agents. For example, if a communication is requested for a non-running agent or an agent whose execution is suspended, the LAC could allocate resources to enable that agent to resume execution and react to the communication, or it could refuse the communication on the basis of the agent unavailability.

3.3   Yellow Pages

To satisfy the requirement that "The architecture should provide means for agents to locate other agents for the purpose of collaboration and delegation of tasks" (requirement 3) we include the concept of yellow pages.

An agent attempting a task that requires more resources or abilities than it is capable of supplying could break down the task into several sub-tasks, and then distributed these among several agents. To succeed, this division of labor should take into account the functionality provided by agents and the actions required by the tasks that are delegated. This understanding of an agent's functionality (i.e., what the agent can do) can be based on roles (skills that are known to be performed by individuals supporting that role), or on the identities of specific instances (skills that specific agents are known to perform). From these, roles have the advantage that they allow agents to plan a division of labor without committing to any specific agent instance. This is of importance given that agents can unpredictably appear and disappear from the environment.

In any event, agents that offer or request services need to rely on mechanisms for the advertising and requesting of services. Agents can make available a set of skills (represented as a role) for others to request, or they could post the need for an agent with a specified set of skills. These two functions are akin to that of yellow pages and job posting boards, respectively. In the case of the CASA architecture, we define an agent called Yellow Pages to support these functions. Yellow Pages are just a special case of ordinary agents. An agent may access yellow pages through a database of known yellow pages kept by LAC.

3.4   Cooperation Domains

To satisfy the requirement that "The architecture should provide means for agents to create and maintain settings where agents interact" (requirement 4) we include the concept of cooperation domains.

Cooperation domains can be conceptualized as virtual places in which purely communicational resources (i.e., resources that are manipulated through communications) are made available to agents in the place. The functionality of cooperation domains can be paralleled to that of Internet multi-user dungeons, where participants enter rooms in which objects are located and shared, and where agents' actions can be perceived by all other participants.

Our rationale in pursuing this functionality is based on the fact that meaningful interactions in dynamic environments cannot be accomplished on the sole basis of message exchange [3]. In this view, we devise cooperation domains as entities where messages are linked to the settings in which they are produced. In the architecture, cooperation domains are supported and maintained by cooperation domain servers.

Possible applications for cooperation domains include that of acting as centralized state and message repositories. One example is the one implemented in jKSImapper [2], where agents join cooperation domains to access and modify (using messages) the state of a diagrammatic structure shared among the participants of the cooperation domain.

4   Architecture Implementation

This section addresses the implementation of conversation policies for the agents we have built for the architecture. The current implementation was done using the Java programming language; and messages are communicated in KQML format.

In the CASA architecture, agents are expected to recognize and exchange messages by following agreed-upon conversation policies [3] in the domain of interaction.

Conversation policies are patterns of communication to be adhered to by interacting agents. These policies define causal-relation sequences of messages communicated among types of agents; and they describe how agents should react to these messages during interactions.

We have defined several basic policies that enable agents to interact in the architecture. These are:

- Registration: To register (to a LAC) as part of an area.
- YP Locations: To query a LAC about known yellow pages.
- Advertisement: To advertise services in Yellow Pages.
- Search: To query advertised services in Yellow Pages.
- Cooperation Domain Subscription: To join a Cooperation Domain.
- Cooperation Domain Invitation: To invite another agent to join a CD.

In addition to these primitive conversations, it is expected that particular domain-specific applications will develop and include new conversation policies appropriate to the agent interactions in their domain.

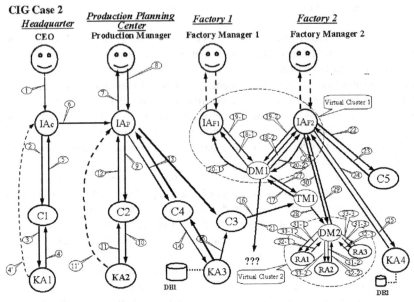

Fig. 2. A production planning scenario

5   Modeling a Production Planning Multi-Agent System

Figure 2 shows a multi-agent system scenario in the domain of production planning. This scenario was modeled using the Infrastructure for Collaborative Agent Systems [4], which is a high-level infrastructure composed of both vertical and horizontal functional layers.

5.1   Test Case: Brief Overview

The production planning test case scenario (illustrated in Figure 3) is composed of a number of agents, including humans. These agents are, at the top level, humans that interact with interface agents (IA), which then interact with collaboration (C) and mediator (DM and PM) agents, some of which interact with knowledge management (KM) agents, found at the bottom level in the figure.

The dynamics of this scenario are as follows (a more detailed description is found in [5]): Initially, the CEO receives a production order for a product B, and based on this request it looks for a production manager to carry on with the order. This process is realized as follows: the CEO asks her interface agent (IAc) for a suitable production manager. IAc asks a collaboration agent (C1) where to find an agent knowledgeable in production managers, leading (in this case) to KA1, which then provides the requested information back to IAc, etc.

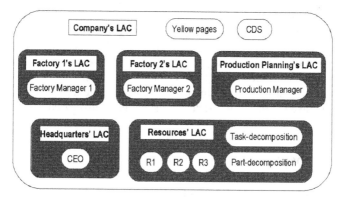

Fig. 3.. A CASA structural model for the Production Planning scenario

5.2   Modeling the Test Case using CASA

There are several ways on which this scenario could be modeled using the CASA architecture. For simplicity, we assumed that all agents in the scenario belong to the same company. Figure 5 shows one possible model. In this case, one company-wide area is encompassing all agents. Under this approach, it is expected that general organizational regulations could be applied by the LAC at this level. Next, we defined a yellow pages and cooperation domain server to assist in the interaction of agents within the company.

The interaction dynamics of the test case scenario under this model are as follows (for simplicity, we assume that all agents have registered with their respectively areas and that all service provider agents have advertised to the yellow pages—the dynamics of these interactions should be observable from the descriptions below).

Initially, the CEO receives an order for product B, and sets off to find about available production managers for this order. In this example, the (human) CEO and the IAc are considered under the single agent CEO. The agent CEO contacts the headquarters LAC and asks about known yellow pages. The headquarters' LAC then forwards the request to the company's LAC, and a reply with the location of the YP is sent back to CEO. The CEO then queries the YP for known production managers, to which the yellow pages replies with the location of the production manager in the production planning area. The CEO sends a request to the production manager for the production of the order (this, through a application specific conversation policy), etc.

6   Summary

The Cooperative Agent Systems Architecture is a software model that aims to simplify the implementation of multi-agent systems in a flexible and minimally intrusive way. The various architectural components are derived from four fundamental specifications, and further implied implementation details, such as conversation policies, and a possible agent model are also described. Finally, the architecture is applied to an example problem taken form the production planning domain.

One of the principal advantages of this model is that it supports agent discovery with a minimum of meta-information to be provided to agents. Specifically, the only information that agents need to be given is that of the location of the LAC where they initially subscribe as part of a system. Once agents are able to register to the specified area, they will have the means to locate agents that have advertised services.

Acknowledgments

The authors thank all other members of the Intelligent Systems Group at the University of Calgary for their contribution to the development of the Collaborative Agent System Architecture, and detailed discussions on the case study. Financial support for this work is provided by the Natural Sciences and Engineering Research Council of Canada (NSERC) and SMART Technologies Inc. of Calgary.

References

1. Ferber, J. (1999) Multi-Agent Systems: An Introduction to Distributed Artificial Intelligence. Addison Wesley Longman.
2. Flores, R.A. (1997) Programming Distributed Collaboration Interaction Through the WWW. M.Sc. Thesis, Department of Computer Science, University of Calgary, Canada, June, 1997
3. Greaves, M., Holmback, H., and Bradshaw, J. (1999) What is a conversation policy? Proceedings of the Third International Conference on Autonomous Agents (Agents 99), Workshop on Specifying and Implementing Conversation Policies, M. Greaves and J. Bradshaw (eds.), pp.1-9, Seattle, WA.
4. Shen, W., Norrie, D.H. and Kremer, R.C. (1999) Towards an Infrastructure for Internet Enabled Collaborative Agent Systems. Proceedings of the 12th Workshop on Knowledge Acquisition, Modeling and Management (KAW'99), B.R. Gaines, R.C. Kremer and M. Musen (eds.), Vol. 1, pp. 3-3-1: 3-3-15, Banff, Canada.
5. Shen, W., Norrie, D.H., and Kremer, R., (1999) Developing Intelligent Manufacturing Systems Using Collaborative Agents. Proceedings of the Second International Workshop on Intelligent Manufacturing Systems (IMS 99), pp. 157-166, Leuven, Belgium.

Frameworks for Reasoning about Agent Based Systems

Leon J. Osterweil and Lori A. Clarke

Department of Computer Science, University of Massachusetts,
Amherst, MA 01003 USA

Abstract. This paper suggests formal frameworks that can be used as the basis
for defining, reasoning about, and verifying properties of agent systems. The language, Little-JIL is graphical, yet has precise mathematically defined semantics.
It incorporates a wide range of semantics needed to define the subtleties of agent
system behaviors. We demonstrate that the semantics of Little-JIL are sufficiently
well defined to support the application of static dataflow analysis, enabling the
verification of critical properties of the agent systems. This approach is inherently a top-down approach that complements bottom-up approaches to reasoning
about system behavior.

1 Introduction and Overview

The use of agent based systems continues to grow, promising the prospect that important societal functions will be supported by systems of agents [1, 4, 9, 11, 12]. With this
growth, however, comes worries about the reliability, correctness, and robustness of systems of agents. We intuitively understand that agents are software components that can
"sense their environment", can "negotiate with each other", are logically "mobile", and
can "acquire and use resources." Agent based systems are then informally understood
to be "communities" of these software items that, acting as a community, can come up
with creative and opportunistic approaches to problems. But, while these characterizations provide enough intuition to suggest how such systems might be used to benefit
societal objectives, they do not help us to feel more confident that we can keep these
systems under control. Indeed, the very flexible and proactive nature of such systems
suggests that part of the reason for their creation is that they may indeed behave in ways
that may not have been completely planned a priori.

It seems imperative that we establish the basis for reasoning about the behaviors of
such systems sufficiently well that we can determine unequivocally that they will never
behave in ways that are harmful, while still leaving the systems free to be proactive
and innovative. To be able to make such unequivocal determinations, there must be
rigorous frameworks not only for describing what agents do as individuals, but also
for defining the structure of their collaborations in the context of the larger job to be
done. In our work we have defined just such rigorous frameworks, with mathematically
precise semantics, and are demonstrating that these frameworks are sufficiently robust
that powerful analysis techniques can be applied to agent systems that have been defined
in terms of them.

Earlier work has focused on the agents themselves [15] and has attempted to synthesize inferences about overall systems of such agents from a "bottom up" perspective.

T. Wagner and O.F. Rana (Eds.): Infrastructure for Agents, LNAI 1887, pp. 64–71, 2001.
© Springer-Verlag Berlin Heidelberg 2001

While interesting results have been obtained, it seems clear that this approach should be complemented with a more "top down" view. In our work we view the agents as components in a larger distributed software system. We propose to demonstrate that many of the important properties of the overall agent system can be determined more effectively by studying the structure of this overall system.

From our point of view, an agent is an entity (either software or human) that has been assigned the responsibility for the successful execution of a task, where the task has a well defined position in a rigorously defined problem specification, defined in terms of our framework. Within the context and constraints of that overall structure and framework, the agents are free to go about performing their assigned tasks. But the overall structure acts as a set of constraints that limits the activities of the agents. This structure can be engineered to assure that the behavior of the overall agent system never violates critical properties and always adheres to required behaviors.

Our view of agent systems as distributed systems of software components suggests that traditional software engineering development and analysis approaches should be useful in developing agent systems. But the translation of this notion into successful practice is complicated by the fact that agent systems are particularly complex and challenging software systems. As noted above, agents are software components that "negotiate" with each other, are often "mobile", acquire, consume, and release "resources", and exhibit a range of behaviors that traditional software systems often do not exhibit. Thus, successful engineering and analysis of agent systems requires technologies that deal with these behaviors. This, in turn, requires a mathematically sound framework for specifying what is meant by these terms and then building technological capabilities atop these semantics. A "bottom up" approach entails using the semantics of the coding languages in which agents are written as the basis for analysis of their behaviors, and then the behaviors of the overall systems of agents. In practice this is difficult, as the multitudes of details in a coding language complicate analysis and can obscure the larger scale system behaviors that we seek to study.

The "top down" approach that we advocate suggests that we use a modeling language as a framework with which to represent the overall structure of the agent system, and then apply analyzers to models defined through the use of such a language. Specifically, what seems needed is a modeling language that is effective in supporting the rigorous definition of the full range of behaviors of agents operating within agent systems. The language must support, among other things, the modeling of resources and how they are used, the specification of real time constraints, the representation of contingencies, and the specification of a range of communication and coordination mechanisms. Contemporary software modeling languages do not offer this semantic range, nor do they offer the depth of semantic rigor needed to support definitive reasoning.

We suggest the use of our Little-JIL language as a vehicle for defining models of agent systems. We believe that Little-JIL has the semantic range to cover agent behaviors, as well as the semantic rigor needed to reason about systems defined in the language. The semantic rigor derives principally from the use of a finite state machine model of Little-JIL execution semantics. We have demonstrated that this model can be used to translate Little-JIL definitions into flowgraph-like structures that are then amenable to analysis using finite state verification systems, such as our FLAVERS dataflow analyzer. The overall effect of the application of these technologies is a facility for precisely specifying agent systems as rigorously defined models that can then be definitively analyzed to assure that the systems have desired properties. In addition, as Little-JIL's semantics are executable, it is then possible to translate the Little-JIL model into the structure that actually coordinates agent activities, thereby implementing an agent system.

We now describe Little-JIL, providing indications of why we are confident that it can be used effectively to model agent systems. We then describe FLAVERS, indicating why we believe that it can be effective in the analysis of Little-JIL definitions. Our hypothesis is that this "top down" approach of modeling the overall structure of an agent system provides a valuable complement to existing approaches to gaining confidence in agent systems.

2   Modeling Agent Systems with Little-JIL

In earlier work we defined the overall structure of the coordination of agents in a problem solving activity as a process [8, 14]. From that point of view, we viewed Little-JIL as a process definition languages. Little-JIL is a visual language that supports the view that activities should be viewed as hierarchies of tasks, augmented by a scoped exception handling facility, where completion of each task is assigned to a specific agent. Little-JIL does not support definition of the agents nor how they do their work, only how the activities of the agents are coordinated. Thus, from a slightly different perspective, Little-JIL is also viewed as an agent coordination language. We now provide a very brief overview of some key Little-JIL language features and indicate how this language is a strong basis upon which to build analytic capabilities for assuring the reliability of agent systems.

A Little-JIL step is an abstract notion that integrates a range of semantic issues, all represented by an icon as shown in Figure 1. Each step has a name and a set of badges that represent key information about the step, including the step's control flow, the exceptions the step handles, the parameters needed by the step, and the resources needed to execute the step. Each step is declared once in a Little-JIL process definition,

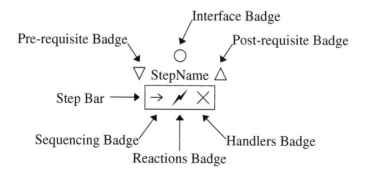

Fig. 1. A Little-JIL step and its constituent parts

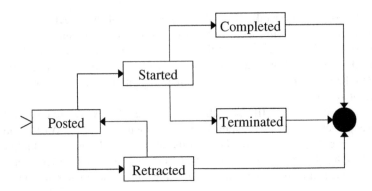

Fig. 2. Finite state machine model of step execution

but a step can be referenced many times. These references are depicted by a step with its name in italics and no badges. This enables reuse and iteration. In addition, a non-leaf step is connected to its substeps and exception handlers by edges, each of which can carry a specification of the flow of artifacts, such as parameters and resources.

The execution semantics of a Little-JIL step are defined by means of a finite state automaton (FSA), with five states: posted, retracted, started, completed, and terminated. Figure 2 shows the normal flow of control for a Little-JIL step. The step's execution can end when it is in any of the three states that have an arrow pointing to the filled circle. A step is moved into the posted state when it is eligible to be started. A step is moved into the started state when the agent assigned that step's execution indicates that the agent wants to start the work specified by the step. When the work specified by a step is successfully finished, the step is moved into the completed state. A step that has been started is moved into the terminated state if the work specified by the step cannot be successfully completed. A step is put into the retracted state if it had been posted, but not started, and is no longer eligible to be started.

A Little-JIL process is represented by a tree structure where children of a step are the substeps that need to be done to complete that step. All non-leaf steps are required to have a sequencing badge. The sequencing badge describes the order in which the substeps are to be performed. There are four types of sequencing badges. A **sequential step** performs its substeps one at a time, from left to right. A **parallel step** indicates that its substeps can be done concurrently, and that the step is completed if and only if all of its substeps have completed. A **choice step** indicates that a step's agent must make a choice among any of its substeps. All of the substeps are made available to be performed, but only one of them can be selected at a time. If a selected substep completes, then the choice step completes. A **try step** attempts to perform its substeps in order, from left to right, until one of them completes. If a substep terminates, then the next substep is tried.

A step in Little-JIL can also have pre- and post-requisites. These are attached to the appropriate requisite badges of a step. A **pre-requisite** is performed after a step starts, but before the work of the step can be initiated. A **post-requisite** has to be done before a step can complete. Requisites, when they fail, generate exceptions. A step terminates if one of its requisites terminates.

Steps in Little-JIL can throw exceptions, either directly or via requisites, to indicate that their agents were unable to complete the work of the step successfully. Exceptions thrown by a step are handled by an ancestor of that step. Exception handlers are shown underneath the handler's badge and indicate what exceptions the step is able to handle and how to proceed after handling the exception. In Little-JIL there are four different ways to proceed after handling an exception: restart, continue, complete, and rethrow. An exception handler is a Little-JIL step, which may be null. The exception management specification capability of Little-JIL is particularly powerful and flexible. Our experience suggests that this power is necessary for the specification of the kinds of (potentially nested) contingencies that actually arise in complex systems. Little-JIL's scoping and visualization make the exception management easier to understand intuitively. But the semantics of Little-JIL exception management are also precisely defined in terms our FSA model. Thus, exception flow can be modeled accurately using flowgraph models that can then be the subject of the analyzers that we propose here.

Interface badges are used to declare what parameters a step has, what exceptions it throws, and what resources it needs. The resource specification is made using a separate specification language that specifies the types of the resources that are required by the step. The agent for the step is a resource, namely that resource that is needed to assume responsibility for execution of the step. At execution time, the needed resources are requested and a separate resource management module is invoked to match the resource types requested with specific resource instances available for allocation. Should needed resources not be available, a resource exception is thrown, and the Little-JIL exception management facility is used to specify a reaction to this contingency. Little-JIL's facilities for specifying resources also provides the basis for analyses , such as "dead" resource allocations and schedulability.

The semantics of a timing annotation on a step specify that the step's agent must complete execution of the step by the time specified. If the agent fails to do this, then a exception is thrown. Here too, the incorporation of timing specifications as part of the Little-JIL step structure paves the way for potential analysis, such as real time scheduling and planning.

Space does not permit a fuller discussion of the language, but Figure 3 contains an example of a simple Little-JIL definition of an auction agent. Explanation of this example can be found in [3]. A full description of Little-JIL can be found in [13].

3   Analysis of Little-JIL Agent System Specifications

FLAVERS (FLow Analysis for VERification of Systems) is a static analysis tool that can verify user specified properties of sequential and concurrent systems [5,6]. The model FLAVERS uses is based on annotated Control Flow Graphs (CFGs). Annotations are placed on nodes of the CFGs to represent events that occur during execution of the actions associated with a node. Since a CFG corresponds to the control flow of a sequential system, this representation is not sufficient for modeling concurrent system such as agent systems. FLAVERS uses a Trace Flow Graph (TFG) to represent concur-

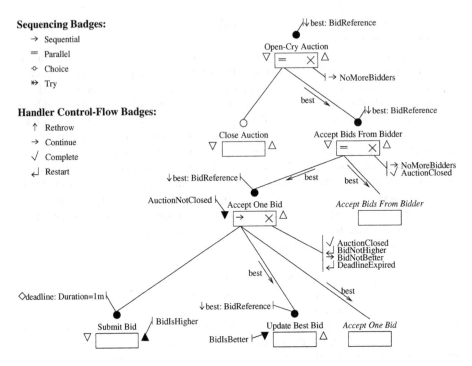

Sequencing Badges:
→ Sequential
= Parallel
⋄ Choice
↠ Try

Handler Control-Flow Badges:
↑ Rethrow
→ Continue
√ Complete
↲ Restart

Fig. 3. Little-JIL process definition of an open cry auction

rent systems. The TFG consists of a collection of CFGs with May Immediately Precede (MIP) edges between tasks to show intertask control flow.

As we have indicated above, a Little-JIL agent system definition is translatable into such CFGs and TFG. The fundamental activity here is to build a control flow graph for each of the steps in a Little-JIL definition, to connect these graphs to each other as specified by the language semantics, and then finally to compute the MIP edges. Some details of the complexities involved are described in [3]. Suffice it to say, however, that these complexities can be considerable. While the overall visual appearance of a Little-JIL definition appears straightforward (by careful design), the actual flows of control can be very intricate, involving subtle concurrency, nested exception flow, and dependencies upon resource utilization. Our early experience suggests that some of the subtlety and complexity is often overlooked or oversimplified by humans. This reinforces our belief in the importance of analysis

The annotated TFG is used as the basis for reasoning about properties that are of interest to the analyst. Examples of such properties are livelocks and race conditions. While many such properties can be specified in advance for all agent systems, many other properties are specific to a particular agent system and must be specified by an analyst. FLAVERS supports user specification of properties.

FLAVERS uses an efficient state propagation algorithm to determine whether all potential behaviors of the system being analyzed are consistent with a specified property. Given an annotated TFG and a (possibly user specified) property, FLAVERS will either return a conclusive result, meaning the property being checked holds for all possible paths through the TFG, or an inconclusive result. Inconclusive results occur either because the property indeed can be violated, or because the conservative nature of FLAVERS analyses causes the analyzer to consider some paths through the TFG that may not correspond to possible executable behavior. Unexecutable paths are an artifact of the imprecision of the model. An analyst can incrementally add constraints to determine whether a property is conclusive or not. This gives analysts control over the analysis process by letting them determine exactly what parts of a system need to be modeled to prove a property.

The FLAVERS state propagation algorithm has worst-case complexity that is $O(S * N^2)$, where N is the number of nodes in the TFG and S is the product of the number of states in the property and all constraints. In our experience, a large class of interesting and important properties can be proved by using only a small set of feasibility constraints. Thus FLAVERS seems particularly well suited to the analysis of agent systems precisely because of its computational complexity bounds. It compares very favorably with model checking approaches (e.g., SPIN [7] and SMV [2, 10]) that have exponential worst case complexity bounds. The FLAVERS low order polynomial bound holds the promise of supporting analysis on the large scale required by complex agent systems.

A major thrust of our work is the application of FLAVERS to verify properties of agent based systems. Our goal is to determine how successful FLAVERS is in definitively verifying the various kinds of properties of agent based systems that are of interest. We have had some success in verifying some user-specified properties of some agent systems and expect to also be able to prove more generic properties, such as the absence of erroneous synchronization and race conditions. We also are interested in how well FLAVERS analysis scales. As noted above, FLAVERS uses analysis algorithms that have low-order polynomial time bounds, but it seems necessary to come to a good understanding on the size of the systems it can be applied to, and characterizations of the sorts of properties to which it is best applied.

4   Conclusions

Our work suggests the possibility of applying powerful forms of analysis to models of agent systems that are particularly comprehensive, yet precisely defined. We are continuing our studies of the applicability of the Little-JIL agent coordination language to the precise specification of agent systems. In doing so, we expect to be able to add substantial power to the arsenal of tools that analysts will be able to apply in establishing the reliability of agent systems.

Acknowledgements

We are grateful to our colleagues, both past and present, in the Laboratory for Advanced Software Engineering Research, for their help with this work. Specifically, Sandy Wise, Stan Sutton, Aaron Cass, Eric McCall, and Barbara Staudt Lerner have all been very active participants in the definition, development, and evaluation of Little-JIL. In addition, Hyungwon Lee, Xueying Shen, and Yulin Dong have been helpful in writing Little-JIL process programs to help evaluate the language. Jamie Cobleigh led our efforts to apply FLAVERS to Little-JIL process programs. Finally we wish to acknowledge the financial support of the Defense Advanced Research Projects Agency, and the US Air Force Material Command Rome Laboratory through contract F30602-94-C-0137.

References

1. N. S. Barghouti and G. E. Kaiser. Multi-agent rule-based development environments. In *5th Annual Knowledge-Based Software Assistant Conference*, pages 375–387, Syracuse NY, 1990.
2. J. R. Burch, E. M. Clarke, K. L. McMillan, D. L. Dill, and L. J. Hwang. Symbolic model checking: 10^{20} states and beyond. In *Fifth Annual IEEE Symposium on Logic in Computer Science*, pages 428–439, 1990.
3. J. M. Cobleigh, L. A. Clarke, and L. J. Osterweil. Verifying properties of process definitions. In *ACM SIGSOFT 2000 International Symposium on Software Testing and Analysis*, Portland, OR, 2000. To appear.
4. K. S. Decker and V. R. Lesser. Designing a family of coordination algorithms. In *First International Conference on Multi-Agent Systems*, pages 73–80, San Francisco, CA, 1995. AAAI Press.
5. M. Dwyer and L. A. Clarke. Data flow analysis for verifying properties of concurrent programs. In *Second ACM SIGSOFT Symposium on Foundations of Software Engineering*, pages 62–75, 1994.
6. M. B. Dwyer and L. A. Clarke. Flow analysis for verifying specifications of concurrent and distributed software. Technical Report 99-52, University of Massachusetts, Computer Science Dept., 1999.
7. G. J. Holzmann. The model checker SPIN. *IEEE Transactions on Software Engineering*, 23(5):279–294, 1997.
8. B. S. Lerner, L. J. Osterweil, S. M. Sutton, Jr., and A. Wise. Programming process coordination in Little-JIL. In *6th European Workshop on Software Process Technology (EWSPT '98)*, pages 127–131, Weybridge, UK, 1998. Springer-Verlag.
9. V. R. Lesser. Multiagent systems: An emerging subdiscipline of AI. *ACM Computing Surveys*, 27(3):340–342, 1995.
10. K. L. McMillan. *Symbolic Model Checking: An Approach to the State Explosion Problem*. Kluwer Academic Publishers, Boston, 1993.
11. T. Sandholm and V. Lesser. Issues in automated negotiation and electronic commerce: Extending the contract net framework. In *First International Conference on Multi-Agent Systems (ICMAS-95)*, San Francisco, 1995.
12. T. Wagner and V. Lesser. Toward ubiquitous satisficing agent control. In *AAAI Symposium on Satisficing Models*, 1998.
13. A. Wise. Little-JIL 1.0 language report. Technical Report 98-24, Department of Computer Science, University of Massachusetts at Amherst, 1998.
14. A. Wise, B. S. Lerner, E. K. McCall, L. J. Osterweil, and S. M. Sutton, Jr. Specifying coordination in processes using Little-JIL. Technical Report 99-71, Department of Computer Science, University of Massachusetts at Amherst, 1999.
15. P. R. Wurman, M. P. Wellman, and W. E. Walsh. The Michigan internet AuctionBot: A configurable auction server for human and software agents. In *Second International Conference of Autonomous Agents*, Minneapolis, MN, 1998.

Integrating High-Level and Detailed Agent Coordination into a Layered Architecture *

XiaoQin Zhang, Anita Raja, Barbara Lerner
Victor Lesser, Leon Osterweil, Thomas Wagner
Department of Computer Science
University of Massachusetts at Amherst

June 28, 2000

1 Introduction

Coordination, which is the process that an agent reasons about its local actions and the (anticipated) actions of others to try to ensure the community acts in a coherent fashion, is an important issue in multi-agent systems. Coordination is a complicated process that typically consists of several operations: exchanging local information; detecting interactions; deciding whether or not to coordinate; proposing, analyzing, refining and forming commitments; sharing results, and so on. We argue that facets of these different operations can be separated and bundled into two different layers. The lower-layer pertains to *feasibility* and *implementation* operations, i.e., the detailed analysis of candidate tasks and actions, the formation of detailed temporal/resource-specific commitments between agents, and the balancing of non-local and local problem solving activities. In contrast, the upper-layer pertains to *domain specific* coordination tasks such as the formation of high-level goals and objectives for the agent, and decisions about whether or not to coordinate with other agents to achieve particular goals or bring about particular objectives. Detailed domain state is used at this level to make these high-level coordination decisions. In contrast, decisions at the lower-level do not need to reason about this detailed domain state. However, reasoning about detailed models of the performance characteristics of activities, such as their temporal scope, quality, affects of resource usage on performance, is necessary at this level. In this view, the layers are interdependent activities that operate asynchronously.

* Effort This material is based upon work supported by the National Science Foundation under Grant No. IIS-9812755 and the Air Force Research Laboratory/IFTD and the Defense Advanced Research Projects Agency under Contract F30602-97-2-0032. The U.S. Government is authorized to reproduce and distribute reprints for Governmental purposes notwithstanding any copyright annotation thereon. Disclaimer: The views and conclusions contained herein are those of the authors and should not be interpreted as necessarily representing the official policies or endorsements, either expressed or implied, of the Defense Advanced Research Projects Agency, Air Force Research Laboratory/IFTD, National Science Foundation, or the U.S. Government.

T. Wagner and O.F. Rana (Eds.): Infrastructure for Agents, LNAI 1887, pp. 72–79, 2001.
© Springer-Verlag Berlin Heidelberg 2001

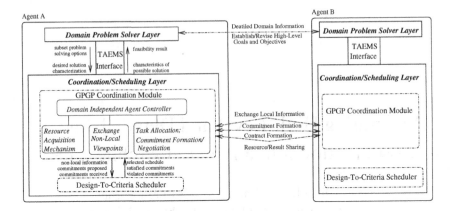

Figure 1: Integrating Coordination Agent Framework

In this paper, we describe the layered coordination model and introduce a general agent architecture based on the model (Section 2). In Section 3, we explore the layered model by integrating the Design-to-Criteria (DTC) [3] scheduler and the Generalized Partial Global Planning (GPGP) [2] coordination system as the lower layer with the Little-JIL framework as the higher layer.

2   Integrating Coordination Approaches

Figure 1 presents a general agent framework based on the layered model.The domain problem solver layer models the domain problem, manages the system state, reasons and plans on how to solve problems, and establishes the performance criteria for the agent.Different domain problem solvers may use different description languages, modeling structures, reasoning and analyzing strategies to solve problems. The coordination/scheduling layer evaluates the feasibility of performing goals/subgoals recommended by the domain problem solver layer, and, based on detailed resource constraint analysis, sets up the detailed temporal sequence and choice of local activities so that the multi-agent system meets its performance objectives. It has the following functions:

- **Reasoning about the feasibility of activities**
- **Choosing from and sequencing possible activities**
- **Assisting the task allocation**
- **Assisting the resource allocation**

The TÆMS task modeling language [1] is a domain-independent framework used to model the agent's candidate activities. It is a hierarchical task representation language that features the ability to express alternative ways of performing tasks, statistical characterization of methods via discrete probability distributions in three dimensions (quality, cost and duration), and the explicit representation of interactions between tasks.

Figure 5 contains an example of a TÆMS task structure. The TÆMS framework serves as a bridge that we use to connect the Domain Problem Solver Layer and the domain independent Coordination/Scheduling Layer.

This agent framework works as follows: the domain problem solver analyzes its current problem solving situation and establishes high level goals it want to achieve; also through the communication with other agents, it may decide some goals/tasks need to be cooperatively performed. The coordination/scheduling layer reasons about possible solutions to achieve the goal and sequences local activities. In this reasoning process, the criteria requirements such as the balance between achieving a good result quickly versus achieving a high quality result in a longer time, resource requirement and interaction with other agents are all considered. The communication and reasoning process in the coordination/scheduling layer are transparent to the domain problem solver. The GPGP coordination module communicates with other potential participant agents and builds proposed commitments for the common goal. The DTC scheduler reasons about local activities and these proposed commitments and verifies the feasibility of these commitments. If the proposed commitments are not suited for the current objective, the GPGP module refines the commitments after negotiating with other agents. The GPGP module may also receive requests from other agents to establish commitments to achieve a particular result.The DTC scheduler also reasons about these requests given the current scheduled activities and verifies if these commitments are feasible. The scheduled activities and established commitments are returned to the domain problem solver for execution. In short, the idea is that the domain problem solver decides what to do, the coordination/scheduling layer decides how to do it and when to do it.

3   Coordination in Little-JIL

3.1   Our Work With Little-JIL

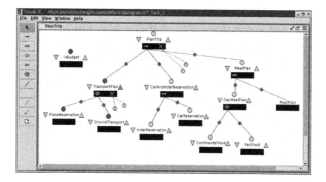

Figure 2: the personal assistant agent's task in Little-JIL

Little-JIL [4] is a process-programming language that is used to describe software development process and other processes. Little-JIL represents processes as compositions of steps, which may be divided into substeps. The specification of a step is defined in terms of a number of elements. Each element defines a specific aspect of step semantics, such as data, control, resource usage, or consistency requirements. Little-JIL language provides a description of a multiagent process. It describes control flows, data flows, resource requirements of a process. However, if there are alternative ways of accomplishing subtasks, the agent needs to reason about the effects of the choice on the overall process's characteristics. This problem is more difficult when this process is distributed among multiple agents, agents need to coordinate with each other to find a solution that meets the global criteria function. Furthermore, there are interactions among steps that agents need to coordinate over, which poses problems for multi-agent coordination.

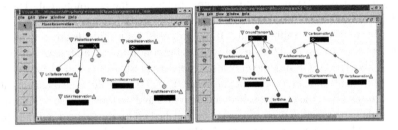

Figure 3: the secretary agent's task and the travel agent's task in Little-JIL

Our solution to these problems is to integrate our coordination module with the Little-JIL process problem solver. Figure 4 describes the infrastructure of an agent that works on a Little-JIL process program. The Little-JIL process program is generated by the Little-JIL editor(outside of the agent) or is received from another agent(task assignment). The Little-JIL problem solver receives and executes this process program.This Little-JIL process program is sent to the Little-JIL unwinder, which opens this process

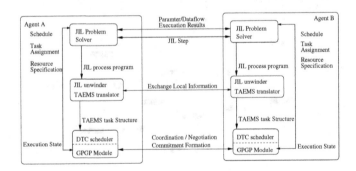

Figure 4: Little-JIL Agent Architecture

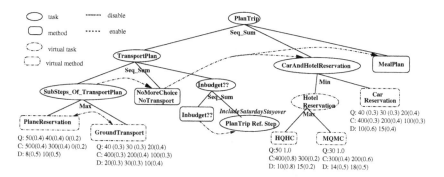

Figure 5: the personal assistant agent's task structure

program, discovers the interactions among agents, and extracts the resource requirement information. In the unwinding process, some steps are detected as non-local
tasks (for example, the *PlaneReservation* step should be executed by a TravelerAgent),
these non-local tasks are treated as virtual tasks: they will be analyzed but not executed locally. The TÆMS translator takes this process program and the information
provided by the Little-JIL unwinder and generates a TÆMS task structure. The Design-
To-Criteria scheduler uses this TÆMS structure to generate an end-to-end schedule to
meet the global criteria requirement. Based on this first round of scheduling, the agent
negotiates with other agents to find appropriate commitments for the non-local tasks
through the GPGP module. Because the other agent may not be able to perform the
task as specified by the local scheduler, re-scheduling or re-assignment may be needed
to achieve a satisfactory commitment. In this negotiation process, the agent also should
take the resource requirements into consideration, making sure resources are available
when they are needed. The "final" schedule with task assignments and resource specifications are returned to the Little-JIL problem solver and the process is executed as
scheduled.

3.2 Example

For example , there are three agents which work together to plan a trip. They are the
personal assistant agent, the travel agent and the secretary agent. To plan a trip(*PlanTrip*)
the personal assistant agent needs to do three things in sequence: first plan the transportation (*TransportPlan*), then reserve a car and a hotel (*CarAndHotelReservation*),
then plan the meal(*MealPlan*). To plan the transportation, there are two choices, either ask a travel agent to make the plane reservation (*PlaneReservation*) or ask the
secretary agent to plan the ground transport. To make the plane reservation(Figure 3,
right), the travel agent will try United Airlines(*UnitedReserveration*) first, if it fails,
then try USAir (*USAirReserveration*). To plan the ground transportation(Figure 3,
left), the secretary agent has three choices, either take a bus (*BusReservation*) or take
the train(*TrainReservation*), or drive a car (*SelfDrive*). Similarly, there are two choices

to reserve the hotel - *DaysInnReservation* or *HyattReservation*; there are three ways to reserve car - *AvisReservation*, *HertzReservation*, and *HyattCarReservation*. The personal assistant agent has the high level global view of the *PlanTrip* task(Figure 2), but it has no detailed information of each process. Both the travel agent and the secretary agent have detailed process information about their local tasks, but they don't have a global view of the *PlanTrip* task and they don't know the context of their local tasks.The context is constructed when the Little-JIL unwinder opens the process program, exchanges local information and discovers those interactions among agents.

One kind of communication is caused by the supertask/subtask relationship. For example, the personal assistant agent recognizes it is the travel agent who really performs the *PlaneReservation* task, which is a non-local task for itself. In this case, the personal assistant agent would like to use some quantitative information on the performance of non-local tasks from the travel agent and the secretary agent. This information may describe possible different approaches to do the non-local task, each approach has different performance characteristics, as the *HotelReservation* task in Figure 5, or the information is only the estimation of the quality, cost, duration. This information is used to help the personal assistant agent construct a reasonable plan that best matches its criteria requirement. The NLE(Non Local Effects) relationship is discovered though the information exchanging. For example, the Hyatt car can be reserved only if the Hyatt hotel has been reserved. This restriction is represented as an *enables* edge from the *HyattReservation* task to the *HyattCarReservation* task in TÆMS task structure.

The TÆMS translator takes the process program and those interaction relationships discovered by the unwinder and translates the Little-JIL process program to the TÆMStask structure. In the translation process more NLE relationships are discovered and recorded. They come from the context of Little-JIL steps. For example, because the *TransportPlan* step is a *choice* step, this means only one step of the *PlaneReservation* and the *GroundTransportation* steps needs to be successfully completed. This relationship is represented as a disables edge from the *PlaneReservation* task to the *GroundTransportation* task and vice versa. In the translation process, the resource requirements also are translated and recorded in the TÆMS language. For instance, the *DaysInnReservation* step requires a computer because the reservation needs to be done on the Internet.

After the unwinding and the translating process, every agent has a TÆMS task structure that includes related NLE relationships and necessary resource specifications(Figure 5, 6). It should be noted that the agent may also have other local tasks besides those tasks in this *PlanTrip* task. The environment we are studying is a multi-agent, multitask environment. The GPGP module and the DTC scheduler will work on the agent's local task group to find out a reasonable and efficient local scheduler, with negotiation and coordination with other agents. We will use the following examples to explain how this module performs the functions described in section .

Reasoning about the feasibility of activities The personal assistant schedules its local task based on its criteria function (i.e.High Quality and High cost: a trip with higher quality accommodation while is more costly is acceptable) and on the performance characteristics of each step; th following schedule is recommended by the DTC scheduler(Figure 7) From this schedule, the

78   X. Zhang et al.

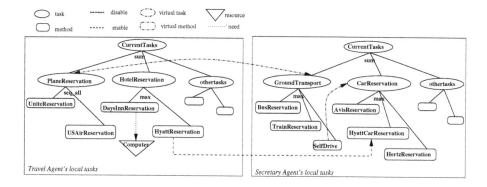

Figure 6: the travel agent and the secretary agent's task structure

travel agent and the secretary agent will obtain three kinds of information that guide their local activities. One is a time constraint on its tasks, specifying when is the earliest time they can start and when is the latest time they should be completed. For example, the travel agent will try to schedule its local activities so as to complete the *PlaneReservation* task by time 19. The second is the context information, i.e. the secretary agent can only execute the *GroundTransport* task if the *PlaneReservation* task fails. The third is the criteria related information, e.g. after *HotelReservation(HQHC)*(a high-quality, high cost approach) task is chosen by the person assistant, the secretary agent is likely to choose the *HyattReservation*(it has higher quality/cost) task instead of the *DaysInnReservation* task.

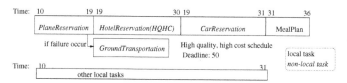

Figure 7: the high quality, high cost schedule of the *PlanTrip*

Choosing from and sequencing possible activities As discussed above, the high level schedule (HotelReservation(HQHC)) helps guide agents(the secretary agent) make local choices (*HyattReservation*) regarding how to meet the global criteria function. Also because an agent may have multiple local tasks, it is also important for the agent to sequence its local activities. This is a negotiation process. For example, the personal assistant agent wants the *PlaneReservation* to be done by time 19, the travel agent finds it is impossible to meet this deadline and instead offers time 35 as a completion time. The personal assistant thinks it is too late, then asks for an earlier time. The travel agent offers time 25 on the condition that it would do a narrower search exploring only a few airline companies. The personal assistant thinks it is OK because meeting the deadline is critical and the budget is not tight. It will reschedule the *PlanTrip* task based on the commitment that the *PlaneReservation* task is done by time 25. This negotiation process is done by the commitment formation/negotiation module in GPGP.

Assisting the task allocation After scheduling local activies, the agent may need to relocate some tasks in order to obtain higher global utility. For example, after the travel agent chooses the *HyattReseveration*, the secretary agent finds it is better to ask the travel agent to do the *HyattCarReservation* task also because there is an overlap between these two tasks. So the negotiation goes on between this two agents about this task allocation process. This is done by the task allocation module in GPGP.

Assisting the resource allocation When the agent sequences its local activities, the resource requirement should also be taken into account. For instance, the travel agent needs a computer to perform the *DaysInnReservation* task, and the computer is shared with other agents. The travel agent needs to negotiate with other agents or the manager of the computer to make sure the computer is available when it plans to do the *DaysInnReservation* task. If not, it needs to reschedule its local activities to allow the *DaysInnReservation* task to be performed when computer is available. This resource acquisition process is done by the resource acquisition module in GPGP.

4   Conclusion and Future Work

We view coordination as a multi-level process in which the higher level uses domain state to model coordination while the lower level uses quantitative information about the performance constraints to make decisions. In this paper, we have used the Little-JIL framework as an example of a high level coordination framework and GPGP/DTC as the lower level coordination framework. We have shown how these two frameworks can be integrated in order to develop a sophisticated approach to agent coordination.In the future, we are going to do some experiments to evaluate this intergration work, we would like to compare how the agents work differently with and without the coordination/scheduling module.

References

[1] Decker, K., Lesser, V. R. Quantative Modeling of Complex Environments. In International Journal of Intelligent Systems in Accounting, Finance and Management. Special Issue on Mathematical and Computational Models and Characteristics of Agent Behaviour., Volume 2, pp. 215-234, 1993.

[2] Keith S. Decker and Victor R. Lesser. Designing a family of coordination algorithms. In *Proc. of the 1st Intl. Conf. on Multi-Agent Systems*, pages 73–80, June 1995. AAAI Press.

[3] Thomas Wagner, Alan Garvey, and Victor Lesser. Criteria-Directed Heuristic Task Scheduling. *Intl. Journal of Approximate Reasoning, Special Issue on Scheduling*, 19(1-2):91–118, 1998.

[4] Alexander Wise, Barbara Staudt Lerner, Eric K. McCall, Leon J. Osterweil, and Stanley M. Sutton Jr. Specifying Coordination in Processes Using Little-JIL. November 1999. Submitted to the International Conference on Software Engineering 2000.

Adaptive Infrastructures for Agent Integration

David V. Pynadath, Milind Tambe, Gal A. Kaminka

Information Sciences Institute and Computer Science Department
University of Southern California
4676 Admiralty Way, Marina del Rey, CA 90292
{pynadath,tambe,galk}@isi.edu

Abstract. With the proliferation of software agents and smart hardware devices there is a growing realization that large-scale problems can be addressed by integration of such stand-alone systems. This has led to an increasing interest in integration infrastructures that enable a heterogeneous variety of agents and humans to work together. In our work, this infrastructure has taken the form of an integration architecture called *Teamcore*. We have deployed Teamcore to facilitate/enable collaboration between different agents and humans that differ in their capabilities, preferences, the level of autonomy they are willing to grant the integration architecture, their information requirements and performance. This paper first provides a brief overview of the Teamcore architecture and its current applications. The paper then discusses some of the research challenges we have focused on. In particular, the Teamcore architecture is based on general purpose teamwork coordination capabilities. However, it is important for this architecture to adapt to meet the needs and requirements of specific individuals. We describe the different techniques of architectural adaptation, and present initial experimental results.

1 Introduction

With the ever increasing number of information-gathering agents, user agents, agents in virtual environments, smart hardware devices and robotic agents, there is a growing need for agent integration infrastructures. Such infrastructures would allow different agents and humans to work effectively with each other[2, 1, 4]. To this end, these infrastructures must address several important issues, such as locating relevant agents (or humans) for a task, facilitating their collaboration and monitoring their performance. This paper focuses on the challenge of facilitating agent collaboration in the context of heterogeneous agents, which have different capabilities, developers, and preferences. For instance, humans may differ in their requirements for obtaining coordination information and the cost they are willing to pay to obtain such information. Humans may also differ in the types of coordination decisions they will allow (or want) automated. Software agents have still differing requirements for information and automated coordination. Such heterogeneity leads to the difficulty of encoding large numbers of special purpose coordination plans, specialized not only for each new domain, but also tailored for each individual agent requirements. Furthermore, given that these requirements may vary over time, these plans would need to be modified frequently.

T. Wagner and O.F. Rana (Eds.): Infrastructure for Agents, LNAI 1887, pp. 80–93, 2001.
© Springer-Verlag Berlin Heidelberg 2001

Our approach to addressing the above challenge is to devise an agent integration architecture, with built-in general-purpose teamwork coordination capabilities. However, we enable the architecture to adapt such capabilities (via machine learning) for the needs and performance of specific individuals. General teamwork knowledge avoids the need to write large numbers of coordination plans for each new domain and agent. Yet, further adaptation enables the integration architecture to cater to individual coordination needs and performance. Starting with the teamwork knowledge is critical for adaptation here, since learning all of the coordination knowledge from scratch for each case would be very expensive.

The agent integration architecture we are building is called Teamcore. Here, the agents or humans to be coordinated are each assigned Teamcore proxies, where the proxies work as a team. Each proxy contains Steam[9], a general teamwork model that automates the proxies' coordination with other proxies in its team. Starting with this teamwork model, Teamcore adapts to the agents in the team, sometimes those which they represent, sometimes those represented by others, where the adaptations span the different dimensions of interactions between the agents and their proxies. Here, we have identified several key interaction dimensions: (1) The *adaptive autonomy* dimension refers to a proxy's adapting its level of decision-making autonomy, so that it learns to defer some/many decisions to the human or agent it represents; (2) the *adaptive information delivery* dimension refers to a proxy's adapting to an agent's costs and reliabilities of its different communication channels, and the different values the agent associates with the coordination information. (3) The *adaptive monitoring* dimension refers to the proxies' adapting to agents' differing requirements for information about the global state of the on-going collaboration (beyond the the local coordination information discussed in dimension 2); (4) The *adaptive execution* dimension relates to proxies' adapting their execution in response to agents' varying capabilities and performance. A key novelty in our approach is that adaptation is done in the context of a team, not necessarily just an individual proxy. For instance, the proxies may cause the team to communicate more to improve monitoring.

We begin this paper by presenting the Teamcore architecture, and its application in two complex domains. These applications motivate the need for Teamcore's adaptation, which is discussed next.

2 Teamcore Framework

Figure 1 shows the overall Teamcore agent integration framework. The numbered arrows show the stages of interactions in this system. In stage 1, human developers interact with TOPI (team-oriented programming interface) to specify a team-oriented program, consisting of an organization hierarchy and hierarchical team plans. As an example, Figure 2 shows an abbreviated team-oriented program for the evacuation domain. Figure 2-a shows the organization hierarchy and Figure 2-b shows the plan hierarchy. Here, high-level team plans, such as **Evacuate**, typically decompose into other team plans and, ultimately, into leaf-level plans, that are executed by individuals. There are teams assigned to execute the plans, e.g., *Task Force* team is assigned to jointly execute **Evacuate**, while *Escort* subteam is assigned to the **Escort-operations** plan. These teams or individual roles are as yet not matched with actual agents.

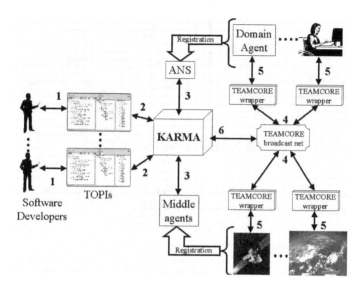

Fig. 1. The overall Karma-TEAMCORE framework.

TOPI in turn communicates the team-oriented program to Karma (stage 2). Karma is an *agent resources manager* — it queries (stage 3) different middle agents and ANS services for the "domain agents" (which may include diverse software agents or humans) with expertise relevant to the team-oriented program specified in stage 1. Located domain agents are matched to specific roles in the team plans (by Karma or developer or both). In stage 4, the Teamcore proxies jointly execute the team-oriented program. Here, each domain agent is assigned a Teamcore proxy. The proxies work as a team in executing the team plans, autonomously coordinating among themselves by broadcasting information via multiple broadcast nets (stage 4). Teamcores also communicate with the domain agents (stage 5). Karma monitors and records information about agent performance (stage 6). All communications occur in KQML.

A key feature of our framework is the proxies' in-built Steam domain-independent teamwork model. Steam provides a Teamcore with three sets of domain-independent teamwork reasoning rules: (i) *Coherence preserving* rules require team members to communicate with others for coherent initiation and termination of team plans; (ii) *Monitor and repair* rules ensure that team members substitute for other critical team members who may have failed in their roles; (iii) *Selectivity-in-communication* rules use decision theory to weigh communication costs and benefits to avoid excessive communication. Armed with these rules, the proxies automatically execute much of the required coordination, without it being explicitly included in the team oriented program. For instance, if a *domain agent* in *Task Force* executing **Evacuate** in Fig 1 were to fail, Teamcore proxies will automatically ensure that another team member (domain agent)

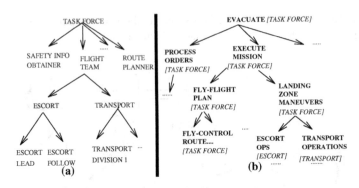

Fig. 2. A team-oriented program.

with similar capabilities will substitute in the relevant role — such coordination is not explicitly programmed in the team-oriented program.

2.1 Application 1: Evacuation Rehearsal

We have applied the Teamcore framework to the problem of rehearsing the evacuation of civilians from a threatened location. Here, an integrated system must enable a human commander (the user) to interactively provide locations of the stranded civilians, safe areas for evacuation and other key points. A set of simulated helicopters should fly a coordinated mission to evacuate the civilians. The integrated system must itself plan routes to avoid known obstacles, dynamically obtain information about enemy threats, and change routes when needed. The software developer was able to create a team-oriented program for this problem, using the following agents:

Quickset: (from P. Cohen et al., Oregon Graduate Institute) Multimodal command input agents [C++, Windows NT]

Route planner: (from Sycara et al., Carnegie-Mellon University) Path planner for aircraft [C++, Windows NT]

Ariadne: (from Minton et al., USC Information Sciences Institute) Database engine for dynamic threats [Lisp, Unix]

Helicopter pilots: (from Tambe, USC Information Sciences Institute) Pilot agents for simulated helicopters [Soar, Unix]

As seen above, these agents have different developers, they are written in different languages for different operating systems, they may be distributed geographically and have *no pre-existing teamwork capabilities*. There are actually 11 agents overall, including the Ariadne, route-planner, Quickset, and eight different helicopters (some for transport, some for escort).

We successfully used the Teamcore framework to build and execute a team-oriented program for evacuation mission rehearsal from these agents. An abbreviated portion of the program is seen in Fig 2. This program has about 40 team plans. There are 11 Teamcore proxies for the 11 agents, which execute this program by automatically communicating with each other (exchanging about 100 messages), while also correctly communicating with the domain agents.

2.2   Application 2: Assisting Human Collaboration

We are also using Teamcore to build an application to assist human teams in routine coordination activities in industrial or research organizations, using our own research team as a testbed. In this application, each human user has a Teamcore proxy that co-ordinates with other proxies on behalf of its user. These proxies communicate with the users using their workstation screens or their hand-held wireless personal digital assistants (PDAs). The distributed Teamcore architecture is well-suited in this domain, since each human maintains control on its own Teamcore and its information, rather than centralizing it.

Our current focus is facilitating coordination of meetings within our team or with visitors, at our institute or outside. For instance if currently an individual gets delayed (e.g., because she is finishing up results), other meeting attendees end up wasting time waiting or attempting to reach those missing. To help avoid such miscoordination, a Teamcore proxy keeps track of its user's scheduled meetings (by monitoring his/her calendar). These meetings are essentially the team plans to be executed jointly by the different Teamcores. Using Steam rules, the Teamcore proxies ensure coherent beliefs about the current state of the meeting. In particular, the proxies track the user's where-abouts (e.g., by using idle time on the user's workstations), and automatically inform other meeting attendees about meeting delays or about absentees. The proxies also automatically communicate with user's PDAs. Additionally, if an absent team member was playing an important role at the meeting, such as leading a discussion, Teamcore proxies attempt to get another person with similar capabilities to take over.

3   Adapting to team member heterogeneity

While the promising results of the applications discussed above indicate the benefits of founding the integration architecture on a proven model of teamwork, they also indicate ways in which the architecture must adapt to agent heterogeneity. The following sub-sections present four different methods of adaptation, each using a suitable technique. The overall theme in these adaptations is that in interacting with a heterogeneous team member (who may be human), the Teamcore proxies either adapt together as a team, or a single proxy adapts in the context of the team.

3.1   Adapting the level of autonomy

A key challenge in integrating heterogeneous agents is that they may have differing requirements with respect to the autonomy of the integration architecture to make decisions on their behalf. For instance, in the human collaboration application discussed in Section 2.2, a Teamcore proxy may commit its human user to substitute for a missing discussion leader, knowing that its user is proficient in the discussion topics. However, the human may or may not want the proxy to autonomously make this commitment. The decision may vary from person to person, and may depend on many diverse factors. Conversely, though, restricting the proxy to always confirm its decision with the user is also undesirable, since it would then often overwhelm the user with confirmation requests for trivial decisions.

Thus, it is important that a proxy have the right level of autonomy. Yet, to avoid hand-tuning such autonomy for each human (or agent), it is critical for a proxy to automatically adapt its autonomy to a suitable level. We rely on a supervised learning approach based on user feedback. Here, a key issue that contrasts our work with previous work on autonomy adaptation (e.g., [7]) is that the the level of autonomy is not only dependent on the individual but also on the the other agents being integrated. For instance, in the discussion leader example above, the number of other attendees and their state might be factors in the autonomy decision. Thus, in our approach we emphasize the use of knowledge about other team members (in addition to the preferences of the integrated agent) in using supervised learning techniques. Each proxy learns what decisions it can take autonomously, and what decision need be confirmed with the agent—*in the context of particular scenarios involving other agents.*

Specifically, the Teamcore proxies for humans can make coordination and repair decisions autonomously to aid in team activities like meetings (e.g., the human-collaboration domain). Eleven attributes are used in learning, some of which have been inspired by existing meeting scheduling systems, such as "MeetingMaker", which include meeting location, time, resources reserved etc. However, other attributes describe the state of the other agents participating in the meeting—e.g., the number of persons attending and the most important member attending (in terms of the organizational hierarchy). These attributes are extracted from the user's schedule files, organizational charts, etc. In the training phase, a proxy suggests a coordination decision and a query as to whether the user would wish it to make such a decision autonomously. C4.5[6] is used to learn a decision tree from the interactions with the user.

3.2 Adaptive execution

A proxy's decision, whether autonomous or after consultation with its domain agent, is focused on executing a team activity. Here, the proxies may dynamically adapt their team plans at execution time, based on the performance of member agents. In particular, performance of complex domain agents is likely to vary during the lifetime of the proxy organization. It is thus important that the Teamcore proxies be able to make runtime decisions about plan execution based on the performance of the domain agents. Indeed, the Teamcores can (as a team) dynamically decide whether or not to execute any plans the team programmer marks as optional. Karma gives each Teamcore an initial specification of its domain agent's capabilities, including parameters such as response time (e.g., average, min/max response times are recorded from past runs). However, if the actual runtime performance of a domain agent greatly differs from expectations (e.g., so that the cost in agent response time greatly exceeds the benefits from its results), the Teamcore proxies together modify the optional plans and avoid using this particular domain agent.

More specifically, the Teamcores begin executing an initial plan sequence that they determine to be optimal given costs and benefits of including the optional plans in the sequence. However, they can dynamically choose to omit optional plans if a particular domain agent's response time should deviate from the expected time cost. For instance, if they had initially decided to include the route planning plan, but the route planner is taking longer than expected, the Teamcores can compare their current plan sequence against alternate candidates, taking into account the increased cost of the current response time. If the time cost outweighs the value of route planning, the Teamcores can change sequences and skip the route-planning step, knowing that they are saving in the overall value of their execution.

In theory, to fully support such decision-theoretic evaluation, the developer must specify the value of executing each team plan in terms of its time cost and possible outcomes. We would then represent these as a probability distribution and utility function over possible states, with $\Pr(q_1|q_0, p)$ representing the probability of reaching state q_1 after executing plan p in state q_0, and with $U(q, p)$ representing the utility derived from executing plan p in state q. However, to ensure that the decision-theoretic evaluation remains practical, several approximations are used. First, the states here are not complete representations of the team state, but rather of only those features that are relevant to the optional plans. For instance, when evaluating route planning, the Teamcores consider only the length of the route and whether that route crosses a no-fly zone prior to route-planning. Second, the decision-theoretic evaluation is only done in terms of the more abstract plans in our team-plan hierarchy, so developers need not provide detailed execution information about all plans and Teamcores need not engage in very detailed decision-theoretic evaluations. Third, for most plans, the derived utility is simply taken as a negative time cost. However, in the evacuation scenario, the team plans corresponding to helicopter flight have a value that increases when the helicopters reach their destination and that decreases with any time spent within a no-fly zone.

The probability distribution over outcomes allows the developer to capture the value of plans that have no inherent utility, but only gather and modify the team's information. For instance, the mission begins either in state q_{safe} with an overall route that does not cross any no-fly zones or in state q_{unsafe} with a route that does. The developer also specifies an initial distribution $\Pr(q)$ for the likelihood of these states. When executing the route-planning plan in state q_{unsafe}, the route planner creates a route around no-fly zones, so we enter state q_{safe} with a very high probability. The developer then provides the relative value of executing the *flight* plan in the two states through the utility function values $U(q_{safe}, flight)$ and $U(q_{unsafe}, flight)$.

The Teamcores use this probability and utility information to select the sequence of plans $p_0, p_1, \ldots, p_n$ that maximizes their expected utility. In the evacuation scenario, there are only four such sequences, because only two team plans (out of the total of 40) are optional. They reevaluate their choice only when conditions (i.e., agent response times) have changed significantly. Thus, whenever a domain-level agent associated with either of these plans takes longer than usual to respond, its Teamcore proxy can find the optimal time (with respect to the specified utility function) for terminating the current information-gathering step and using a different plan sequence for the rest of the team program.

3.3 Adaptive monitoring

In addition to executing team activities, Teamcore proxies must also monitor these activities, to detect task execution failures and to allow humans to track the team's progress. To this end, a Teamcore proxy relies on plan recognition to infer the state of its team members from the coordination messages normally transmitted during execution. Such messages do not convey full information about agent state, but can provide hints as to the senders' state. This plan-recognition-based method is non-intrusive, avoiding the overhead of the proxies having to continually communicate their state to other proxies.

Teamcore proxies therefore monitor the communications among themselves. Applying their knowledge of their own communication protocols, the proxies identify exchanges of messages such as those establishing or terminating a team plan. When a plan is terminated/selected, the monitoring Teamcore proxies can infer that execution has reached at least the stage corresponding to the plan. However, in general, every plan may not lead to communication, and hence the plan-recognition process faces ambiguity. For instance, in the evacuation scenario, the Teamcore proxies communicate initially to jointly select the **Obtain-orders** plan. To a monitoring proxy, until a second message is observed, any of the following steps is a possibility. Unfortunately, such ambiguity interferes with monitoring.

To reduce ambiguity in recognized plans, the monitoring system utilizes two adaptation techniques. The first simple technique is to use learning to predict when messages will be exchanged. Such predictions can significantly reduce the number of hypothesized states, since the system knows that the monitored team will not get into certain states without a message being received. At first, an inexperienced system cannot make such predictions. However, as it observes messages being sent, it can construct a model of when such communications will be sent, and use this model to disambiguate the recognized plans. Here, Teamcore currently uses rote-learning successfully; but, other techniques will be investigated in the future.

The second adaptation technique is to have the Teamcore team actively adapt its own behavior to make monitoring less ambiguous. Based on the feedback of the monitoring system, the team of proxies changes its model of communication costs and benefits, so as to ensure that that the proxies communicate at specific points during execution at which ambiguity interferes with the monitoring tasks. For example, when monitoring the evacuation-rehearsal scenario, the human operators often complained that they are unable to distinguish two important states–the state in which the team was flying towards (or from) the landing zone, and the state where the team is carrying out its landing zone operations. When the monitoring system provided this feedback, the proxy team communicated when jointly-selecting the landing-zone maneuvers plan, and the ambiguity in recognized plans was greatly reduced.

3.4   Adjustable information requirements

When executing or monitoring team activities, proxies must also inform the domain agents they represent. However, agents can differ in the amount of information they need in order to successfully carry out their team responsibilities. In the evacuation scenario, the Teamcore proxies sent messages to their domain agents as mandated by the team plans' requirements for tasks and monitoring conditions, without considering communication costs incurred by these messages. More complex agents (including humans) would rather sacrifice some of these messages rather than incur high communication costs. For instance, in our human collaboration scenario, if the system delays a meeting, it can notify the attendees of this delay by sending messages to their PDAs. However, wireless message services usually charge a fee, so some users may prefer not knowing about small delays. The Teamcore proxies should weigh the value of the message (to the user, *as well as to the overall team plan*) against the cost of sending the message to the user.

In addition, heterogeneous agents may have multiple channels of communication, each with different characteristics. In the evacuation scenario, the agents communicated through a single KQML interface. However, with the human agents in our collaboration scenario, the Teamcore proxy can pop up a dialog on the user's screen, send an email message to a PDA (if the user has one), or send email to a third party who could tell the user in person. The dialog box has very little cost, but it is an unreliable means of informing the user, who may not be at the terminal when the message arrives. On the other hand, having a third party tell the user in person may be completely reliable, but there is a high cost.

We can model a communication channel's reliability with a probability distribution over the amount of time it takes for the message to reach the user through that channel. For simplicity, our initial implementation represents this time with an exponential random variable, so that the probability of the message's arriving within time t is $1 - e^{-\lambda t}$, for some reliability parameter λ. We model the cost of the channel and the values of the various messages as fixed values.

Whenever the Teamcore proxy decides to send a message to the user, it first pops up a dialog box on the screen with the message. If the user does not explicitly acknowledge the dialog, the proxy considers using alternate channels. It evaluates the expected benefit of using such an alternate channel by computing the increase in the likelihood of the message reaching the user, based on the comparative reliabilities of any channels used so far and those under consideration. If the product of this increased likelihood and the value of this message exceeds the channel's cost, the proxy sends the message through the new channel.

We have implemented a simple reinforcement learning algorithm to evaluate the communication channel parameters for individual users. For each channel used for a given message, the dialog box on the screen (which is always used during the proxy's learning phase) allows the user to provide feedback about whether the proxy's use of the channel was appropriate and whether the channel transmitted the message to the user in time. Feedback on the former (latter) increments or decrements the channel's cost (reliability) parameter as appropriate.

4 Evaluation

For evaluation, we begin with the evaluation of individual adaptation capabilities, followed by the evaluation of Teamcore's basis on a principled teamwork model. We begin with an evaluation of the adjustable autonomy component of the Teamcore proxies (Section 3.1). Here, we used actual meeting data recorded in users' meeting-scheduling programs, totaling 58 meetings. Five different data sets were constructed out of these, each by randomly picking 36 meetings for training data, and 22 for test data (random sub-sampling holdout). Figure 3 shows the accuracy of the adjustable autonomy prediction plotted against the number of examples used to train the agent (out of the 36 training examples), for the five different data sets. For each data set, we observe that the autonomy learning accuracy increases, usually up to 91%. However, even using more than 36 examples did not improve the accuracy further. Thus, while these results are promising further improvements in the attribute set may be needed to improve accuracy.

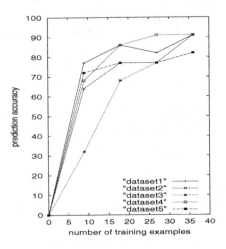

Fig. 3. Adaptation of Teamcore autonomy.

We can also evaluate the benefit of the Teamcores' runtime plan modification capabilities (see Section 3.2). Figure 4 shows the results of varying Ariadne's response times on the time of the overall mission execution. In the evacuation plan, Ariadne provides information about missile locations along a particular route. If there are missiles present, the Teamcores instruct the helicopters to fly at a higher altitude to be out of range. The team could save itself the time involved with querying Ariadne by simply having the helicopters *always* fly at the higher safe altitude. However, the helicopters fly slower at the higher altitude, so the query is sometimes worthwhile, depending on the Ariadne's response time. In Figure 4, we can see that when Ariadne's response time exceeds 15s, the cost of the query outweighs the value of the information. In such cases, the Teamcores with the decision-theoretic flexibility skip the query to save in overall execution cost (here, equivalent to time, according to the designer-specified utility function).

We have also conducted experiments in adaptive monitoring. Figures 5 presents the results from experiments run in the evacuation scenario with and without the two monitoring adaptation techniques. The X axis notes the observed joint-selections/terminations as the task is executed. Each such observation corresponds to an exchange of messages among the proxies in which they jointly select or terminate a team plan. As execution progresses, we move from left to right along the X axis. The Y axis notes the number of recognized plans based on the current observations, i.e., a higher value means greater ambiguity (worse).

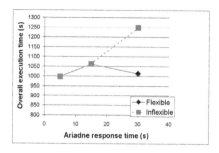

Fig. 4. Adapting to variable agent performance.

Figure 5 shows the results of learning a predictive model of the communications. We see that without learning, a relatively high level of ambiguity exist which is slowly reduced as more observations are made, and past states are ruled out. However, the system cannot make any predictions about future states of the agents, other than that they are possible. When the learning technique is applied on-line, some learned experience is immediately useful, and ambiguity is reduced somewhat. However, some exchanges are encountered late during task execution, thus they cannot be used to reduce the ambiguity while learning. The third line corresponds to the results when the model has been fully learned. As can be seen, it shows significantly reduced ambiguity in the recognized plans.

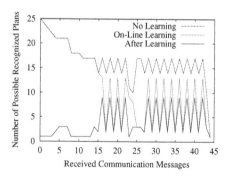

Fig. 5. Adaptive monitoring: communication model.

Figure 6 shows the proxy team's adaptation of its communication behaviors significantly reduces the ambiguity in recognized plans, to provide better monitoring. The line marked "Prior to Behavior Adaptation" shows the results of using a fully-learned model of communications to disambiguate recognized plans. The user has decided to disambiguate between the **fly-flight-plan** and the **landing-zone-maneuvers** plans, by causing the agents to explicitly communicate about the joint-selection of the **landing-zone-maneuvers** plan. This corresponds to an additional exchange of messages among the agents (observation 24). This additional observation has an effect much earlier along task execution, greatly reducing the ambiguity beginning with observation 16.

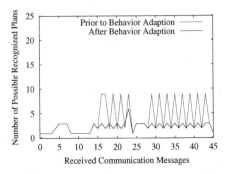

Fig. 6. Adaptive monitoring: adpating behavior.

We have also conducted preliminary experiments to evaluate the suitability of our models of the reliability and cost of different communication channels. The results on cost are shown in Figure 7 (the results on reliability are similar and not shown). Here, the users received a series of hypothetical messages and then provided the feedback required for the reinforcement learning. Most of the parameters converged monotonically to an equilibrium value, while the cost of the user's screen remained very low. In these preliminary experiments, the system appeared to make the correct *decisions* about which communication channels to use and when to use them.

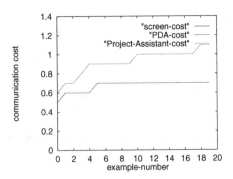

Fig. 7. Learning costs of communication channels.

We may also attempt to evaluate the benefits of Teamcore proxy's in-built teamwork capabilities. One key alternative to such an in-built teamwork model is reproducing all of Teamcore's capabilities via domain-specific coordination plans. In such a domain-specific implementation, about 10 separate domain-specific coordination plans would be required for each of the 40 team plans in Teamcore[9]. That is, 100s of domain-specific coordination plans could potentially be required to reproduce Teamcore's capabilities to coordinate among each other, just for this domain. In contrast, with Teamcore, no coordination plans were written for inter-Teamcore communication. Instead, such communications occurred automatically from the specifications of team plans. Thus, it would appear that Teamcores have significantly alleviated the coding effort for coordination plans.

5   Related Work

In terms of related work, Jennings's GRATE*[3] integration architecture is similar to Teamcore, in that distributed proxies, each containing a cooperation module integrate heterogeneous agents. One major difference is that GRATE* proxies do not adapt to individual agents, a critical capability if architectures are to integrate an increasingly heterogeneous, complex agent set. Also, GRATE* cooperation module is arguably weaker than Teamcore's Steam, e.g., Steam enables role substitution in repairing team activity, which is not available in GRATE*. The Open Agent Architecture (OAA) [5] provides centralized facilitators to enable agents to locate each other, and a blackboard architecture to communicate with each other, but not teamwork capabilities, or adaptation, as in Teamcore. Also, Teamcore's distributed approach avoids a centralized processing bottleneck, and a central point of failure.

One other related system is the RETSINA[8] multi-agent framework. While the goal of this frameworks is somewhat similar to ours, its development appears complementary to Teamcore. For instance, RETSINA is based on three types of agents: (i) interface agents; (ii) task agents; and (iii) information agents. Middle agents allow these various agents to locate each other. Thus, as Section 2 discusses, Karma can use RETSINA middle agents for locating relevant agents, while adaptive, infrastructural teamwork in our Teamcores may enable the different RETSINA agents to work flexibly in teams.

6   Conclusion

With software agents, smart hardware devices and diverse information appliances coming into wide-spread use, integration infrastructures that allow such diverse systems to work together are becoming increasingly important. The need to identify key design principles underlying such infrastructures is therefore critical. This paper investigates some of these principles through an integrated, adaptive architecture, Teamcore, which is evaluated in two different domains. A key lesson learned from our work is that despite the heterogeneity of agents integrated, sound principles of multi-agent interactions—in our case a principled teamwork model— can serve as a principled foundation for rapid development of robust integrated systems. Another key novel lesson is adaptive capabilities are critical in the integration architecture to adapt to the requirements of heterogeneous agents. Adaptation is necessary in different ways, which we demonstrate in four areas: (i) adaptive autonomy; (ii) adaptive execution; (iii) adaptive monitoring; and

(iv) adaptive information delivery. There are several avenues for future work, including enhancing the learning mechanisms for quicker and more accurate adaptation.

Acknowledgements

This research was supported by DARPA Award no. F30602-98-2-0108. We thank Phil Cohen, Katia Sycara and Steve Minton for contributing agents used in the work described here.

References

1. J. Hendler and R. Metzeger. Putting it all together – the control of agent-based systems program. *IEEE Intelligent Systems and their applications*, 14, March 1999.
2. M. N. Huhns and M. P. Singh. All agents are not created equal. *IEEE Internet Computing*, 2:94–96, 1998.
3. N. Jennings. Controlling cooperative problem solving in industrial multi-agent systems using joint intentions. *Artificial Intelligence*, 75, 1995.
4. N. Jennings. Agent-based computing: Promise and perils. In *Proceedings of the International Joint Conference on Artificial Intelligence (IJCAI-99)*, August 1999.
5. David L. Martin, Adam J. Cheyer, and Douglas B. Moran. The open agent architecture: A framework for building distributed software systems. *Applied Artificial Intelligence*, 13(1-2):92–128, 1999.
6. J. R. Quinlan. *C4.5: Programs for machine learning*. Morgan Kaufmann, San Mateo, CA, 1993.
7. S. Rogers, C. Fiechter, and P. Langley. An adaptive interactive agent for route advice. In *Third International Conference on Autonomous Agents*, Seattle,WA, 1999.
8. K. Sycara, K. Decker, A. Pannu, M. Williamson, and D. Zeng. Distributed intelligent agents. *IEEE Expert*, 11:36–46, 1996.
9. M. Tambe. Towards flexible teamwork. *Journal of Artificial Intelligence Research (JAIR)*, 7:83–124, 1997.

RoboCup Soccer Server and CMUnited: Implemented Infrastructure for MAS Research

Itsuki Noda[1] and Peter Stone[2]

[1] Electrotechnical Laboratory, JAPAN
[2] AT&T Labs – Research, NJ, USA

Abstract. The RoboCup Soccer Server and associated client code is a growing body of software infrastructure that enables a wide variety of multiagent systems research. This paper describes the current Soccer Server and the champion CMUnited soccer-playing agents, both of which are publically available and used by a growing research community. It also describes the ongoing development of FUSS, a new, flexible simulation environment for multiagent research in a variety of multiagent domains.

1 Introduction

The Robot Soccer World Cup, or RoboCup, is an international research initiative that uses the game of soccer as a domain for artificial intelligence and robotics research. Annual international RoboCup events involve technical workshops as well as software and robotic competitions.

The RoboCup Soccer Server [5, 4] and associated client code is a growing body of software infrastructure that enables a wide variety of multiagent systems research. It is used as the substrate for the RoboCup software competitions. Originally released in 1995, Soccer Server has an international user community of over 1000 people.

Soccer Server is a multiagent environment that supports 22 independent agents interacting in a complex, real-time environment. The server embodies many real-world complexities, such as noisy, limited sensing; noisy action and object movement; limited agent stamina; and limited inter-agent communication bandwidth. AI researchers have been using the Soccer Server to pursue research in a wide variety of areas, including real-time multiagent planning, real-time communication methods, collaborative sensing, and multiagent learning [2].

As such, this infrastructure is appropriate for a wide variety of multiagent systems research, with algorithms developed for the Soccer Server likely to apply to other domains. Indeed, such research has been applied to other domains including disaster rescue [3], helicopter fighting [11], and network routing [8], among others.

In addition to the server itself being publicly available in an open-source paradigm, users have contributed several clients that can be used as starting points for newcomers to the domain. One example is the CMUnited-98 simulated soccer team, champion of the RoboCup-98 robotic soccer competition. After winning the competition, much of the CMUnited-98 source code became publicly

T. Wagner and O.F. Rana (Eds.): Infrastructure for Agents, LNAI 1887, pp. 94–101, 2001.
© Springer-Verlag Berlin Heidelberg 2001

available, and several groups used it as a resource to help them create new clients for research and as entries in the RoboCup-99 competition.

Based on the success of Soccer Server and its associated client code, we are now in the process of creating a new flexible utility for simulation systems (FUSS) that will be designed to support simulations of multiple domains. For example, we plan to use the same underlying simulation for an improved simulator of the game of soccer as well as a disaster rescue simulator for use in the RoboCup Rescue initiative [3]. FUSS will also be available as infrastructure for the MAS research community.

The remainder of the paper is organized as follows. Section 2 gives an overview of the RoboCup Soccer Server. Section 3 presents the CMUnited simulated soccer clients for use with Soccer Server. Section 4 motivates and presents the current state of the development of FUSS and Section 5 concludes.

2   The RoboCup Soccer Server

Soccer Server enables a soccer match to be played between two teams of player-programs (possibly implemented in different programming systems). A match using Soccer Server is controlled using a form of client-server communication. Soccer Server provides a virtual soccer field and simulates the movements of players and a ball. A client program can provide the 'brain' of a player by connecting to the Soccer Server.

A client controls only one player. It receives visual ('see') and verbal ('hear') sensor information from the server and sends control commands ('turn', 'dash', 'kick' and 'say') to the server. Sensor information tells only partial situation of the field from the player's viewpoint, so that the player program must make decisions using these partial and incomplete information. Limited verbal communication is also available, by which the player can communicate with each other to decide team strategy.

Soccer Server has been used by researchers to examine multi-agent systems (MAS). The biggest reason why it is used widely is that it simulates *soccer*, which is known widely in the world. As same as the case of chess, well-known-ness is an important factor for example applications of research.

The second reason is that it uses the middle-level abstraction for representing the client commands and the sensor information. If we used a low-level, physical description, it was felt that such a representation would concentrate users' attention too much on the actual control of a players' actions. On the other hand, if we used tactical commands such as pass-ball-to and block-shoot-course, it would produce a game in which the real-world nature of soccer becomes obscured. Thus, our representation, turn, dash, and kick, is a compromise. To make good use of the available commands, clients will need to tackle both the problems of real-world and MAS.

3   The CMUnited Client

Soccer Server clients interact with the Soccer Server via an ASCII string protocol. The server supports low-level sensing and acting primitives. However, there are several basic tasks left up to the clients, including

- Managing socket communication with the server;
- Parsing the sensory commands;
- Handling asynchronous sensation and action cycles;
- Maintaining a model of the world; and
- Combining the low-level actions primitives useful skills.

Depending on one's research focus, a newcomer to the domain may not be interested in solving each of these tasks from first principles. Instead, one can look to the growing body of publicly available client code available at `http://medialab.di.unipi.it/Project/Robocup/pub/rc1999.html`.

While there are many possible solutions to each of these tasks, it is often difficult to evaluate them independently. The CMUnited client code [10] offers robust solutions to these tasks that have been successfully tested in competitive environments: CMUnited won both the RoboCup-98 and RoboCup-99 simulator competitions. It has already been successfully used by others. For example, the 3rd place finisher in the RoboCup-99 competition, was partially adapted from the CMUnited-98 simulator team code.

The remainder of this sections gives an overview of the CMUnited client code.

3.1   Agent Architecture Overview

CMUnited agents are capable of perception, cognition, and action. By perceiving the world, they build a model of its current state. Then, based on a set of behaviors, they choose an action appropriate for the current world state.

At the core of CMUnited agents is what we call the locker-room agreement [9]. Based on the premise that agents can periodically meet in safe, full-communication environments, the locker-room agreement specifies how they should act when in low-communication, time-critical, adversarial environments.

Individual agents can capture locker-room agreements and respond to the environment, while acting autonomously. Based on a standard agent paradigm, our team member agent architecture allows agents to sense the environment, to reason about and select their actions, and to act in the real world. At team synchronization opportunities, the team also makes a locker-room agreement for use by all agents during periods of limited communication. Fig. 1 shows the functional input/output model of the architecture.

The agent keeps track of three different types of state: the *world state*, the *locker-room agreement*, and the *internal state*. The agent also has two different types of behaviors: *internal behaviors* and *external behaviors*. See [10] for further details.

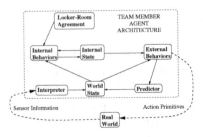

Fig. 1. A functional input/output model of CMUnited's team member agent architecture.

3.2 World Modeling

When acting based on a world model, it is important to have as accurate and precise a model of the world as possible at the time that an action is taken. In order to achieve this goal, CMUnited-98 agents gather sensory information over time, and process the information by incorporating it into the world model immediately prior to acting.

There are several objects in the world, such as the goals and the field markers which remain stationary and can be used for self-localization. Mobile objects are the agent itself, the ball, and 21 other players (10 teammates and 11 opponents).

Each agent's world model stores an instantiation of a stationary object for each goal, sideline, and field marker; a ball object for the ball; and 21 player objects. Since players can be seen without their associated team and/or uniform number, the player objects are not identified with particular individual players. Instead, the variables for team and uniform number can be filled in as they become known.

Mobile objects are stored with confidence values within [0,1] indicating the confidence with which their locations are known. The confidence values are needed because of the large amount of hidden state in the world: no object is seen consistently.

3.3 Agent Skills

Once the agent has determined the server's world state as accurately as possible, it can choose and send an action to be executed at the end of the cycle. In so doing, it must choose its local goal within the team's overall strategy. It can then choose from among several low-level skills which provide it with basic capabilities. The output of the skills are primitive movement commands.

The skills available to CMUnited players include kicking, dribbling, ball interception, goaltending, defending, and clearing.

The common thread among these skills is that they are all *predictive, locally optimal skills* (PLOS). They take into account predicted world models as well as predicted effects of future actions in order to determine the optimal primitive action from a local perspective, both in time and in space.

3.4 Layered Disclosure

A perennial challenge in creating and using complex autonomous agents is following their choices of actions as the world changes dynamically, and understanding why they act as they do. To this end, we introduce the concept of *layered disclosure* [6] by which autonomous agents include in their architecture the foundations necessary to allow them to disclose to a person upon request the specific reasons for their actions. The person may request information at any level of detail, and either retroactively or while the agent is acting.

A key component of layered disclosure is that the relevant agent information is organized in *layers*. In general, there is far too much information available to display all of it at all times. The imposed hierarchy allows the user to select at which level of detail he or she would like to probe into the agent in question.

The CMUnited layered disclosure module is publicly available and has been successfully used by other researchers to help them in their code development.

4 Next Generation Infrastructure

While Soccer Server is used widely for research, several problems have become clear. (1) **Generality**: Many researcher are interested in simulations of other kind of games and phenomenas like *rescue*. However, the current structure of Soccer Server make it difficult to apply it for such a purpose. (2) **Network Traffic**: Soccer Server communicates with various types of clients directly. This often makes the server a bottle-neck. The server should be re-designed to enable distributed processing easily. (3) **Legacy**: Soccer Server uses version control of protocol for keeping upper compatibility. It makes the server code comlicated.

A hint to overcome these problems is "modular structure over network". In Soccer Server, the monitor module is separated from the simulation module. This modularity evolves various research activities to develop 3D viewers, comentary systems, and game analyzers [7, 1, 12]. We are now applying a similar technique to other part of the simulator.

4.1 Overview

FUSS (Framework for Universal Simulation System) is a collection of programs and libraries to develop distributed simulation systems. It is designed to help development of systems that simulate complex environments like MAS.

A simulation system on FUSS consists of a few modules, each of which simulates individual factor or phenomena. For example, a soccer simulator on FUSS may consist of a field simulation module, a referee module, and multiple player simulation modules. The modules are combined into a system by a kernel and libraries. Fig. 2 shows a brief structure of an example of a simulation system built on FUSS.

FUSS itself consists of the following items:

- **fskernel**: provides services of module database, shared memory management, and synchronization control.

- FUSS library (libfuss): consists of `FsModule` (module interface), `ShrdMem` (shared memory) and `PhaseRef` (synchronization) libraries.

FUSS uses CORBA for the communication layer. This makes users free from selection of platform and programming languages to develop simulation modules. While the current implementation of FUSS uses C++, we can develop libraries in other languages that have CORBA interface.

4.2   Shared Memory and Time Management

In development of distributed systems, there are two major issues, *shared data management* and *time management*. As an infrastructure for distributed simulation systems, FUSS provides two frameworks, *shared memory* and *phase control*, to realize these management.

Each shared data in a FUSS simulation system must be defined by IDL of CORBA. The definitions are converted into C++ classes and included by all related modules. The shared data is defined as a sub-class of `ShrdMem`, the *shared memory* class, in each module. A module calls the `download` method before using the shared memory, and calls the `upload` method after modifying the memory. Then the FUSS library maintain the consistency of the memory among modules.

In order to make an explicit order of execution of multiple simulations, FUSS modules are synchronized by *phase control*. A *phase* is a kind of an event that have joined modules. When a module is plugged into the simulation system, the module tells `fskernel` to joins phases in which it executes a part of simulation. When a phase starts, the kernel notifies the beginning of the phase to all joined modules. Then, a user-defined `cycle` method of the phase is called in each modules. The kernel waits until all joined modules finish the `cycle` operations, and moves to the next phase. In other words, executions of simulation modules are serialized according to sequential order of phases.

The kernel can handle two types of phases, *timer phase* and *adjunct phase*. A *timer phase* starts every specified interval. For example, a **field simulation phase** in soccer simulation may occur every 100ms.

An *adjunct phase* is invoked before or after another phase adjunctively. For the example of soccer simulation, a **referee phase** will be registered as an adjunct phase after a **field simulation phase**. Then the kernel starts the **referee phase** immediately after the **field simulation phase** is achieved.

A phase can have multiple adjunct phases before/after it. To arrange them in an order explicitly, each adjunct phase has its own tightness factor. The factor is larger, the phase occurs more tightly adjoined to the mother phase.

4.3   Implementation of Soccer Simulator on FUSS

We implemented Soccer Simulator using FUSS. In the implementation, we divided the functions of Soccer Server into the following modules: **Field Simulator** is a module to simulate the physical events on the field respectively. **Referee Simulator** is a privileged module to control a match according to rules. This

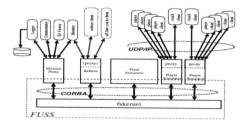

Fig. 2. Plan of Design of New Soccer Server

module may override and modify the result of field simulator. **Player Simulators/Proxies** are modules to simulate events inside of player's body, and communicate with player and on-line coach clients. **Monitor Proxy** provides a facility of multiple monitors, commentators, and saving a log.

The implementation of the referee module is the key of the simulator. Compared with other modules, the referee module should have a special position, because the referee module needs to affect behaviors of other modules directly rather than via data. For example, the referee module restricts movements of players and a ball, that are controlled by the field simulator module, according to the rules of the game. In order to realize it, the referee module should be invoked just before and after the simulator module and check the data. In other words, the referee module works as a 'wrapper' of other modules. Phase control described in Sec. 4.2 enables this style of implementation. **Referee phase** is an adjunct phase to **field phase** with a large tightness. Therefore, the referee module can affect the result of the field phase directly. This means the referee module regulates execution of the field module by modifying the result of the simulation.

The advantage of this feature becomes clear when we think of adding a coach module, which will regulate the result of the field simulation in weaker manner than the referee module. In this case, a user defines **coach phase** as an adjunct phase to the field phase, whose tightness is intermediate between ones of the referee phase and the publish phase. As a result, the coach phase is invoked after the referee phase and before the publish phase, where the coach module can modify the result of simulation after the referee module.

5   Conclusion

Soccer Server and CMUnited client code provide a robust infrastructure for MAS research using the game of soccer as the underlying domain. A large community has been successfully using it for several years.

Building on the lessons learned via the Soccer Server, FUSS will provide a utility for creating simulations in a wide variety of multiagent domains. Its modular facilities enable incremental and distributed development of large simulation systems. By using FUSS, Soccer Server's problems are solved as follows:

- Generality: Actually, FUSS provides general facilities for distributed modular simulation system.
- Huge Traffic: Compared to Soccer Server, communications with clients are dealt with multiple modules separately. Therefore, we can distribute the network traffic by invoking these modules on different machines.
- Legacy: Communication with player clients is localized into by player proxies. So, we can handle multiple protocol by providing multiple player proxies for each protocol.

Further information about FUSS is available from
http://ci.etl.go.jp/~noda/soccer/fuss/.

References

1. E. Andrè, G. Herzog, and T. Rist.   Generating multimedia presentations for RoboCup soccer games. In H. Kitano, editor, *RoboCup-97: Robot Soccer World Cup I*, pages 200–215. Lecture Notes in Artificial Intelligence, Springer, 1998.
2. M. Asada and H. Kitano, editors. *RoboCup-98: Robot Soccer World Cup II*. Lecture Notes in Artificial Intelligence 1604. Springer Verlag, Berlin, 1999.
3. H. Kitano, S. Takokoro, I. Noda, H. Matsubara, T. Takahashi, A. Shinjou, and S. Shimada. RoboCup rescue: Search and rescue in large-scale disasters as a domain for autonomous agents research. In *Proceedings of the IEEE International Conference on Man, System, and Cybernetics*, 1999.
4. I. NODA and I. FRANK. Investigating the complex with virtual soccer. In J.-C. Heudin, editor, *Virtual Worlds*, pages 241–253. Ppringer Verlag (LNAI-1434), Sep. 1998.
5. I. Noda, H. Matsubara, K. Hiraki, and I. Frank. Soccer server: A tool for research on multiagent systems. *Applied Artificial Intelligence*, 12:233–250, 1998.
6. P. Riley, P. Stone, and M. Veloso. Layered disclosure: Revealing agents' internals. In *Submitted to the Sixth Pacific Rim International Conference on Artificial Intelligence (PRICAI 2000)*, 2000.
7. A. Shinjoh and S. Yoshida. The intelligent three-dimensional viewer system for robocup. In *Proceedings of the Second International Workshop on RoboCup*, pages 37–46, July 1998.
8. P. Stone. TPOT-RL applied to network routing. In *Proceedings of the Seventeenth International Conference on Machine Learning*, 2000.
9. P. Stone and M. Veloso. Task decomposition, dynamic role assignment, and low-bandwidth communication for real-time strategic teamwork. *Artificial Intelligence*, 110(2):241–273, June 1999.
10. P. Stone, M. Veloso, and P. Riley. The CMUnited-98 champion simulator team. In M. Asada and H. Kitano, editors, *RoboCup-98: Robot Soccer World Cup II*. Springer Verlag, Berlin, 1999.
11. M. Tambe. Towards flexible teamwork. 7:81–124, 1997.
12. K. TANAKA-Ishii, I. NODA, I. FRANK, H. NAKASHIMA, K. HASIDA, and H. MATSUBARA.   MIKE: An automatic commentary system for soccer. In Y. Demazeau, editor, *Proc. of Third International Conference on Multi-Agent Systems*, pages 285–292, July 1998.

An Agent Infrastructure to Build and Evaluate Multi-Agent Systems: The Java Agent Framework and Multi-Agent System Simulator *

Regis Vincent, Bryan Horling, and Victor Lesser

Dept of Computer Science,
University of Massachusetts,
Amherst MA 01003
USA
{vincent,bhorling,lesser}@cs.umass.edu

Abstract. In this paper, we describe our agent framework and address the issues we have encountered designing a suitable environmental space for evaluating the coordination and adaptive qualities of multi-agent systems. Our research direction is to develop a framework allowing us to build different type of agents rapidly, and to facilitate the addition of new technology. The underlying technology of our Java Agent Framework (JAF) uses a component-based design. We will present in this paper, the reasons and the design choices we made to build a complete system to evaluate the coordination and adaptive qualities of multi-agent systems.
Abbreviation:
- JAF Java Agent Framework;
- MASS Multi-Agent System Simulator

1 Introduction

Agent technology, in one form or another, is gradually finding its way into mainstream computing use, and has the potential to improve performance in a wide range of computing tasks. While the typical commercial meaning of the word agent can refer to most any piece of software, we believe the real potential of this

---

* Effort sponsored by the Defense Advanced Research Projects Agency (DARPA) and Air Force Research Laboratory Air Force Materiel Command, USAF, under agreement number #F30602-97-1-0249 and #F30602-99-2-0525. The U.S. Government is authorized to reproduce and distribute reprints for Governmental purposes notwithstanding any copyright annotation thereon. This material is based upon work supported by the National Science Foundation under Grant No.IIS-9812755. The views and conclusions contained herein are those of the authors and should not be interpreted as necessarily representing the official policies or endorsements, either expressed or implied, of the Defense Advanced Research Projects Agency (DARPA), Air Force Research Laboratory or the U.S. Government.

paradigm lies with more sophisticated, autonomous entities. In general, our definition of an *agent* is an autonomous entity capable of reacting to its environment, determining its most appropriate goals and actions in its world, and reasoning about deadlines and tradeoffs arising from those determinations. To correctly develop such autonomous, intelligent, reactive pieces of software, we must have good ways of implementing, debugging and evaluating them. Many researchers have realized this, and have begun to develop the required infrastructure [2, 10, 16, 20, 3, 19]. Our research has done the same, but with a different approach. Our direction is to develop a framework allowing us to build different type of agents rapidly, and to facilitate the addition of new technologyt-

The underlying technology of our Java Agent Framework (JAF) uses a component-based design. Developers can use this plug and play interface to build agents quickly using existing generic components, or to develop new ones. For instance, a developer may require planning, scheduling and communication services in their agent. Generic scheduling and communication components exist, but a domain-dependent planning component is needed. Additionally, the scheduling component does not satisfy all the developer's needs. Our solution provides the developer with the necessary infrastructure to create a new planning component, allowing it to interact with existing components without unduly limiting its design. The scheduling component can be derived to implement the specialized needs of their technology, and the communication component can be used directly. All three can interact with one another, maximizing code reuse and speeding up the development process. We also respect the fact that researchers require flexibility in the construction of their software, so in general, our solution serves as simple scaffolding, leaving the implementation to the developer beyond a few API conventions.

Much of the generality available in existing JAF components is derived from their common use of a powerful, domain-independent representation of how agents can satisfy different goals. This representation, called TÆMS [4, 5], allows complex interactions to be phrased in a common language, allowing individual components to interact without having direct knowledge of how other components function. Implemented components in JAF are designed to operate with relative autonomy. Coincidentally, a reasonable analogy for a JAF agent's internal organization is a multi-agent system, to the degree that each has a limited form of autonomy, and is capable of interacting with other components in a variety of ways. They are not sophisticated agents, but within the agent, individual components do provide specific, discrete functionality, and may also have fixed or dynamic goals they try to achieve. This functionality can be requested by components via direct method invocation, or it may be performed automatically in response to messages or events occurring in the agent.

Our objective was to allow developers to implement and evaluate systems quickly without excessive knowledge engineering. This way, one can avoid working with domain details, leaving more time and energy to put towards the more critical higher level design. We have also focused on more precise and controlled methods of agent evaluation technologies. Together with the agent framework, we

have built a simulation environment for the agents to operate in. The motivation
for the Multi-Agent System Simulator (MASS) is based on two simple, but potentially conflicting, objectives. First, we must accurately measure and compare
the influence of different multi-agent strategies in an deterministic environment.
At the same time, it is difficult to model adaptive behavior realistically in multi-
agent systems within a static environment, for the very reason that adaptivity
may not be fully tested in an environment that does not substantively change.
These two seemingly contradictory goals lie at the heart of the design of MASS
- we must work towards a solution that leads to reproducible results, without
sacrificing the dynamism in the environment the agents are expected to respond
to.

In this paper, we describe our agent framework and address the issues we have
encountered designing a suitable environmental space for evaluating the coordination and adaptive qualities of multi-agent systems. In the following sections,
we will describe both the JAF framework and the MASS simulation environment. To describe how these concepts work in practice, we will also present an
example implemented system, the Intelligent Home (IHome) domain testbed.
Lastly, we present an example of the how a JAF-based multi-agent system can
run in an alternate simulated environment, and also how it was migrated to
a real-time, hardware-based system. We conclude with a brief overview of the
future directions of this project.

2   Java Agent Framework

An architecture was needed for the agents working within the MASS environment
which effectively isolated the agent-dependent behavior logic from the underlying
support code which would be common to all of the agents in the simulation. One
goal of the framework was therefore to allow an agent's behavioral logic to perform without the knowledge that it was operating under simulated conditions,
e.g. a problem solving component in a simulated agent would be the same as in a
real agent of the same type. This clean separation both facilitates the creation of
agents, and also provides a clear path for migrating developed technologies into
agents working in the real world. As will be shown later, this has been recently
done in a distributed sensor network environment, where agents were migrated
from a simulated world to operating on real hardware [15]. The framework also
needed to be flexible and extensible, and yet maintain separation between mutually dependent functional areas to the extent that one could be replaced without
modifying the other. To satisfy these requirements, a component-based design,
the Java Agent Framework (JAF) [12], was created[1].

Component based architectures are relatively new arrivals in software engineering which build upon the notion of object-oriented design. They attempt to
encapsulate the functionality of an object while respecting interface conventions,

---

[1] This architecture should not be confused with Sun's agent framework of the same
name.

thereby enabling the creation of stand alone applications by simply plugging together groups of components. This paradigm is ideal for our agent framework, because it permits the creation of a number of common-use components, which other domain-dependent components can easily make use of in a plug-and-play manner. Note that the agents produced with this scheme act as small multi-agent systems in and of themselves, where components function as partially autonomous entities that communicate and interact to achieve their individual goals. For instance, our system has a scheduling component, whose goal it is to schedule activities as best as possible, respecting quality, time and resource constraints. It can operate in several ways, the most common being to respond to events describing new tasks needing to be performed. On receiving such an event, the scheduler attempts to integrate these actions into the existing schedule, which in turn will be used by an execution component to determine when to perform the actions. Thus, the scheduling component operates autonomously, reacting to changes and requests induced by other components. This arrangement is key to the flexibility of JAF. Because other components for the most part do not care how or where in an agent an operation is performed, the designer is free to add, modify or adapt components as needed.

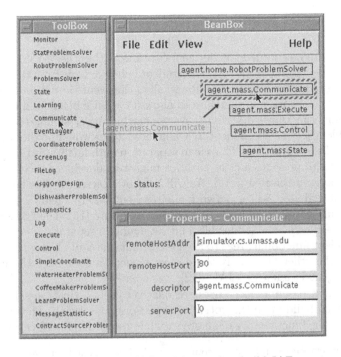

Fig. 1. Sun Beanbox, which can be used to build JAF agents.

JAF is based on Java Beans, Sun Microsystem's component model architecture. Java Beans supplies JAF with a set of design conventions, which provides behavior and naming specifications that every component must adhere to. Specifically, the Java Beans API gives JAF a set of method naming and functional conventions which allow both application construction tools and other beans to manipulate a component's state and make use of its functionality easily. This is important because it provides compatibility with existing Java Beans tools, and facilitates the development process by providing a common implementation style among the available components. JAF also makes heavy use of Java Bean's notion of event streams, which permit dynamic interconnections to form between stream generating and subscribing components. For instance, we have developed a causal-model based diagnosis component [13] which tracks the overall performance of the agent, and makes suggestions on how to optimize or repair processes performed by, or related to, the agent. The observation and diagnosis phase of this technology is enabled by the use of dynamic event streams, which the diagnosis component will form with other components resident in the agent. The component will begin by listening to one or more components in the agent, such as the local coordination component. This stream could tell the diagnosis component when coordination attempts where made, who the remote agents were, whether the coordination succeeded or not, and if the resulting commitment was respected. Events arising from this component are analyzed, and used to discover anomalous conditions. In the case of the coordination component, a series of similar failed coordination attempts could indicate that a particular remote agent has failed, or that it no longer provides the desired service. More proactive analysis into the current state of the coordination component could then yield further information. By both monitoring the events the components produce, and the state they are currently in, the diagnosis component can determine if the components are performing correctly, and generate potential solutions to the problems it finds. Our experience with the diagnosis component was that we did not have to modify other components in order to integrate its functionality.

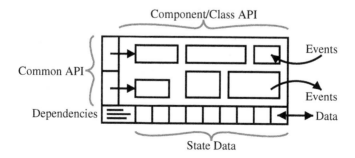

Fig. 2. Abstract view of a typical JAF component.

JAF builds upon the Java Beans model by supplying a number of facilities designed to make component development and agent construction simpler and more consistent. A schematic diagram for a typical JAF component can be seen in figure 2. As in Java Beans, events and state data play an important role in some types of interactions among components. Additional mechanisms are provided in JAF to specify and resolve both data and inter-component dependencies. These methods allow a component, for instance, to specify that it can make use of a certain kind of data if it is available, or that it is dependent on the presence of one or more other components in the agent to work correctly. A communications component, for example, might specify that it requires a local network port number to bind to, and that it requires a logging component to function correctly. These mechanisms were added to organize the assumptions made behind flexible autonomy mentioned above - without such specifications it would be difficult for the designer to know which services a given component needs to be available to function correctly. More structure has also been added to the execution of components by breaking runtime into distinct intervals (e.g. initialization, execution, etc.), implemented as a common API among components, with associated behavioral conventions during these intervals. Individual components will of course have their own, specialized API, and "class" APIs will exist for families of components. For instance a family of communication components might exist, each providing different types of service, while conforming to a single class API that allows them to easily replace one another.

The goal of a designer using JAF is to use and add to a common pool of components. Components from this pool are combined to create an agent with the desired capabilities (see Figure 1). For instance, rather than regenerating network messaging services for each new project, a single Communicate component from the pool can be used from one domain to the next. This has the added benefit that once a component has been created, it may be easily swapped out of each agent with one that respects the original class API, but offers different services. Later in this paper we will describe the MASS simulation environment, which provides simulation and communication services to agents. Messages sent from an agent working in this environment must be routed through MASS, which requires a specialized Communication component which is "aware" of MASS and how to interact with it. In our pool of components we thus have a simple Communicate which operates in the conventional sense using TCP, and a MASS Communicate which automatically routes all messages through the simulation controller. Components using communication need not be aware of the internal delivery system being used, and can therefore be used without modification in both scenarios. Revisiting the hybrid simulation issue raised earlier, we can have an agent which conforms to the MASS communication specification, or uses real world messaging as needed by just exchanging these two components. Analogously, one could have a MASS Execute component, which uses the simulator to perform all executable actions, or one which actually performed some actions locally, and reported the results to the MASS controller when completed. In this latter case, the consistency of the simulation environment is maintained through the notification, but real data may be still generated by the agent.

The organization of a JAF agent does not come without its price. The autonomous nature of individual components can make it difficult to trace the thread of control during execution, a characteristic exacerbated by the use of events causing indirect effects. It can also be difficult to implement new functionalities in base components, while respecting conventions and APIs in derived ones. However, we feel the flexibility, autonomy and encapsulation offered by a component oriented design makes up for the additional complexity.

To date, more than 30 JAF components have been built. A few of these are explained below.

- **Communicate** This component serves as the communication hub for the agent. TCP based communication is provided through a simple interface, for sending messages of different encodings (KQML, delimited or length-prefixed). It also serves as both a message receiver and connection acceptor. Components interact with Communicate by listening for message events, or by directly invoking a method to send messages. Derived versions exist to work with MASS and other simulation environments.
- **Preprocess Taems Reader** TÆMS is our task description language, which will be covered later in this article. This component allows the agent to maintain a library of TÆMS structure templates, which can be dynamically instantiated in different forms, depending on the needs of the agent. For example, the designer may update method distributions based on learned knowledge, or add in previously unrecognized interactions as they are discovered. This is important because it facilitates the problem solving task by allowing the developer to condition generated task structures with respect to current working conditions. Data manipulation capabilities exist which permit mathematical and conditional operations, along with TÆMS structure creation and manipulation. Simple routines can then be written with these tools to use information given to the preprocessor to condition the structure. The ability to perform these operations within the TÆMS file itself allows the problem solving component to be more generic. A derived version of the component also exists which reads simple static task structure descriptions.
- **Scheduler** The scheduling component, based on our Design-To-Criteria (DTC) scheduling technology [22], is used by other components to schedule the TÆMS task structures mentioned above. The resulting schedule takes into account the cost and quality of the alternative solutions, and their durations relative to potential deadlines. The scheduler functions by both monitoring state for the addition of new TÆMS structures, for which it will produce schedules, and through direct invocation.
- **Partial Order Scheduler** A derived version of the Scheduler component, the partial-order scheduler provides the agent with a more sophisticated way of managing its time and resources [21]. Replacing the Scheduler with this component allows the agent to correctly merge schedules from different structures, exploit areas of potential parallelism, and make efficient use

of available resources. Functionally, it provides a layer on top of the DTC Scheduler component, first obtaining a conventional schedule as seen above. It then uses this to reason about agent activity in a partially-ordered way - concentrating on dependencies between actions and resources, rather then just specifying times when they may be performed. This characteristic allows agents using the partial order scheduler to more intelligently reason about when actions can and can not be performed, as well as frequently speeding up failure recovery by avoiding the need to replan.

- **State** The state component serves as an important indirect form of interaction between components by serving as a local repository for arbitrary data. Components creating or using common information use State as the medium of exchange. Components add data through direct method calls, and are notified of changes through event streams. Thus one component can react to the actions of another by monitoring the data that it produces. For instance, when the problem solving component generates its task and places it in State, the scheduler can react by producing a schedule. This schedule, also placed in State, can later be used by the execution component to perform the specified actions.

- **Directory Services** This component provides generic directory services to local and remote agents. The directory stores multi-part data structures, each with one or more keyed data fields, which can be queried through boolean or arithmetic expressions. Components use directory services by posting queries to one or more local or remote directories. The component serves as an intermediary for both the query and response process, monitoring for responses and notifying components as they arrive. This component can serve as the foundation to a wide variety of directory paradigms (e.g. yellow pages, blackboard, broker).

- **FSM Controller** The FSM component can be used as a common interface for messaging protocols, specifically for coordination and negotiation interactions. It is first used to create a finite state machine describing the protocol itself, including the message types, when they can arrive, and what states a particular message type should transition the machine to. This scaffolding, provided by the FSM and used by the FSM Controller at runtime, is then populated by the developer with code to send and process the different messages. This clean separation between a protocol and its usage allows protocols to be quickly migrated from one environment to the next.

Other components provide services for logging, execution, local observation, diagnosis, and resource modeling, as well as more domain dependent functions. Examples of agents implemented with JAF will be covered later in this article.

3   Evaluation Environment for Multi-Agent Systems

Numerous problems arise when systematic analysis of different algorithms and techniques needs to be performed. If one works with a real-world MAS, is it possible to know for certain that the runtime environment is identical from one run to the next? Can one know that a failure occurs at exactly the same time in two different runs when comparing system behavior? Can it be guaranteed that inter-agent message traffic will not be delayed, corrupted, or non-deterministically interleaved by network events external to the scenario?

If one works within a simulated environment, how can it be known that the system being tested will react optimally a majority of the time? How many different scenarios can be attempted? Is the number is large enough to be representative?

Based on these observations, we have tried to design an environment that allows us to directly control the baseline simulated environment (e.g. be deterministic from one run to the next) while permitting the addition of "deterministically random" events that can affect the environment throughout the run. This enables the determinism required for accurate coordination strategy comparisons without sacrificing the capricious qualities needed to fully test adaptability in an environment.

Hanks et al. define in [11] several characteristics that multi-agent system simulators should have:

- **Exogenous events**, these allow exogenous or unplanned events to occur during simulation.
- **Real-world complexity** is needed to have a realistic simulation. If possible, the simulated world should react in accordance with measures made in the real world. Simulated network behavior, for instance, may be based on actual network performance measures.
- **Quality and cost of sensing and effecting** needs to be explicitly represented in the test-bed to accurately model imperfect sensors and activators. A good simulator should have a clear interface allowing agents to "sense" the world.
- **Measures of plan quality** are used by agents to determine if they are going to achieve their goal, but should not be of direct concern to the simulator.
- **Multiple agents** must be present to simulate inter-agent dependencies, interactions and communication. A simulator allowing multiple agents increases both its complexity and usefulness by adding the ability to model other scenarios, such as faulty communications or misunderstanding between agents, delay in message transfer.
- **A clean interface** is at the heart of every good simulator. We go further than this by claiming that the agents and simulator should run in separate processes. The communication between agents and simulator should not make any assumptions based on local configurations, such as shared memory or file systems.
- **A well defined model of time** is necessary for a deterministic simulator. Each occurring event can be contained by one or more points in time in the simulation, which may be unrelated to real-world time.
- **Experimentation** should be performed to stress the agents in different classes of scenarios. We will also add **deterministic experimentation** as another important feature of a simulator. To accurately compare the results separate runs, one must be sure that the experimental parameters are those which produce different outcomes.

We will show in this section how MASS addresses these needs. One other characteristic, somewhat uncommon in simulation environments, is the ability to have agents perform a mixture of both real and simulated activities. For instance, an agent could use the simulation environment to perform some of its actions, while actually performing others. Executable methods, sensor utilization, spatial constraints and even physical manifestations fall into this category of activities which an agent might actually perform or have simulated as needed. An environment offering this hybrid existence offers two important advantages: more realistic working conditions and results, and a clear path towards migrating work from the laboratory to the real world. We will revisit how this can be implemented in later sections.

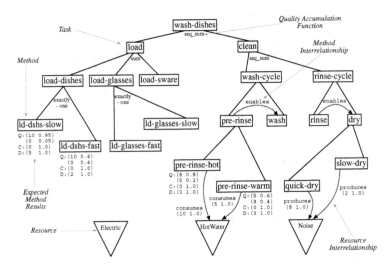

Fig. 3. TÆMS task structure for the IHome Dishwasher agent

4   Multi Agent System Simulator

MASS is a more advanced incarnation of the TÆMS simulator created by Decker and Lesser in 1993 [7]. It provides a more realistic environment by adding support for resources and resource interactions, a more sophisticated communication model, and mixed real and simulated activity. It also adds a scripting language, a richer event model, and a graph-like notion of locations and connectors in which agents can move about (e.g. rooms and doorways, or towns and roads). The new MASS simulator is completely domain independent; all domain knowledge is obtained either from configuration files or data received from agents working in the environment,

Agents running in the MASS environment use TÆMS [14, 6], a domain-independent, hierarchical representation of an agent's goals and capabilities (see Figure 3), to represent their knowledge. TÆMS , the Task Analysis, Environmental Modeling and Simulation language, is used to quantitatively describe the alternative ways a goal can be achieved [9, 14]. A TÆMS task structure is essentially an annotated task decomposition tree. The highest level nodes in the tree, called task groups, represent goals that an agent may try to achieve. The goal of the structure shown in figure 3 is `wash-dishes`. Below a task group there will be a set of tasks and methods which describe how that task group may be performed, including sequencing information over subtasks, data flow relationships and mandatory versus optional tasks. Tasks represent sub-goals, which can be further decomposed in the same manner. `clean`, for instance, can be performed by completing `wash-cycle`, and `rinse-cycle`. Methods, on the other hand, are terminal, and represent the primitive actions an agent can perform. Methods are quantitatively described, in terms of their expected quality, cost and duration. `pre-rinse-warm`, then, would be described with its expected duration and quality, allowing the scheduling and planning processes to reason about the effects of selecting this method for execution. The quality accumulation functions (QAF) below a task describes how the quality of its subtasks is combined to calculate the task's quality. For example, the `sum` QAF below `load` specifies that the quality of `load` will be the total quality of all its subtasks - so only one of the subtasks must be successfully performed for the `sum` task to succeed. Interactions between methods, tasks, and affected resources are also quantitatively described as interrelationships. The `enables` between `pre-rinse` and `wash`, for instance, tells us that these two must be performed in order. The curved lines at the bottom of figure 3 represent resource interactions, describing, for instance, the different consumes effects method `pre-rinse-hot` and `pre-rinse-warm` has on the resource `HotWater`.

One can view a TÆMS structure as a prototype, or blueprint, for a more conventional domain-dependent problem solving component. In lieu of generating such a component for each domain we apply our technologies to, we use a domain independent component capable of reasoning about TÆMS structures. This component recognizes, for instance, that interrelationships between methods and resources offer potential areas for coordination and negotiation. It can use the quantitative description of method performance, and the QAFs below tasks, to reason about the tradeoffs of different problem solving strategies. The task structure in figure 3 was used in this way to implement the washing machine agent for the intelligent home project discussed later in this article. Figure 6 shows how an agent in the distributed sensor network domain (also discussed later), can initialize its local sensor. With this type of framework, we are essentially able to abstract much of the domain-dependence into the TÆMS structure, which reduces the need for knowledge engineering, makes the support code more generic, and allows research to focus on more intellectual issues.

Different *views* of a TÆMS structure are used to cleanly decouple agents from the simulator. A given agent will make use of a *subjective* view of its structure, a local version describing the agent's beliefs. MASS, however, will use an *objective* view, which describes the true model of how the goals and actions in the structure would function and interact in the environment. Differences engineered between these two structures allow the developer to quickly generate and test situations where the agent has incorrect beliefs. We will demonstrate below how these differences can be manifested, and what effects they have on agent behavior. This technique, coupled with a simple configuration mechanism and robust logging tools, make MASS a good platform for rapid prototyping and evaluation of multi-agent systems.

The connection between MASS and JAF is at once both strong and weak. A JAF agent running within a MASS environment uses the simulator for the vast majority of its communication and execution needs, by employing "MASS-aware" components which route their respective data and requests through the simulation controller. The agent also provides the simulator with the objective view of its task structure, as well as the resources it provides and its location. The simulator in turn gives the agent a notion of time, and provides more technical information such as a random number generator seed and a unique id. Despite this high level of interconnection, the aspects of a JAF agent performing these actions are well-encapsulated and easily removed. Thus, an agent can be run outside of MASS by simply replacing those MASS-aware components with more generic ones. Outside of MASS, an agent would use conventional TCP/IP based communication, and would perform its actions locally. It would, for instance, use the local computer's clock to support its timeline, and read the random seed from a configuration file. An example of how this type of separation can be achieved will be covered in section 5.2, where we will show JAF agents running both in a different simulation environment, and independently on real hardware.

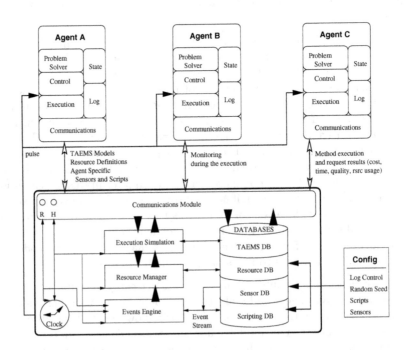

Fig. 4. Architecture of the MASS and agent systems.

Figure 4 shows the overall design of MASS, and, at a high level, how it interacts with the agents connected to it. On initialization, MASS reads in its configuration, which defines the logging parameters, random seed, scripts (if any) and global sensor definitions. These are used to instantiate various subsystems and databases. While the simulator itself is not distributed, connections to the simulator are made with standard TCP-based sockets, so agents can be distributed among remote systems. When connected, agents will send additional information to be incorporated into this configuration, which allows environmental characteristics specific to the agent to be bundled with that agent. For instance, an agent might send a description of a sensor which it needs to function, or a resource which it makes available to the environment. Arguably the most important piece of data arising from the agents is their TÆMS task structures, which are assimilated into the TÆMS database shown in figure 4. This database will be used by the execution subsystem during simulation to quantify both the characteristics of method execution and the effects resource and method interactions have on that method. The resource manager is responsible for tracking the state of all resources in the environment, and the event engine manages the queue of events which represent tangible actions that are taking place. The last component shown here, the communications module, maintains a TCP stream connection with each agent, and is responsible for routing the different kinds of messages between each the agent and their correct destination within the controller.

The MASS controller has several tasks to perform while managing simulation. These include routing message traffic to the correct destination, providing hooks allowing agents to sense the virtual environment and managing the different resources utilized by the agents. Its primary role, however, is to simulate the execution of methods requested by the agents. Each agent makes use of its partial, subjective view of the environment, typically describing its local view of a goal and possible solutions, which determines the expected values resulting from such an execution. As mentioned above, the simulator also has the true, objective view of the world which it uses to compute the results of activities in the environment. The distributions from the objective view are used when computing the values for a method execution, and for determining the results of method or resource interactions. This probabilistic distribution describes the average case outcomes; the simulator will degrade or improve results as necessary if, for instance, required resources are not available, or other actions in the environment enable or facilitate the method's execution in some way. For example, consider what would happen if the `enables` interrelationship between `rinse` and `dry` were absent in the subjective view of figure 3. During scheduling, the agent would be unaware of this interdependency, and thus would not enforce an ordering constraint between the two actions. If the agent were to perform `dry` first, the simulator would detect that its precondition `rinse` had not been performed, and would report that the `dry` method failed. In this case, the agent would need to detect and resolve the failure, potentially updating its subjective view with more accurate information.

MASS is also responsible for tracking the state and effects of resources in the environment. Figure 3 shows three such resources: `Electricity`, `HotWater`, and `Noise`. Two types of resources are supported - consumable and non-consumable. The level of a consumable resource, like `HotWater` is affected only through direct consumption or production. A non-consumable resource, like `Noise`, has a default level, which it reverts back to whenever it is not being directly modified. MASS uses the objective view from each agent to determine the effects a given method will have on the available resources. Also present in the objective view is a notion of bounds, both upper and lower, which the resource's level cannot exceed. If an agent attempts to pass these bounds, the resource switches to an error state, which can affect the quality, cost and duration of any action currently using that resource. At any given time, MASS must therefore determine which methods are affecting which resources, what effects those actions will have on the resources' levels, if the resource bounds have been exceeded, and what quantitative repercussions there might be for those violations.

Another responsibility consuming a large portion of the simulator's attention is to act as a message router for the agents. The agents send and receive their messages via the simulator, which allows the simulation designer to model adverse network conditions through unpredictable delays and transfer failures. This routing also plays an important role in the environment's general determinism, as it permits control over the order of message receipt from one run to the next. Section 4.1 will describe this mechanism in more detail.

4.1   Controllable Simulation

In our simulated experiments, our overriding goal is to be able to compare the behavior of different algorithms in the same environment under the same conditions. To correctly and deterministically replicate running conditions in a series of experiments, the simulator should have its own notion of time, "randomness" and sequence of events. Two simulation techniques exist which we have exploited to achieve this behavior: discrete time and events. Discrete time simulation segments the environmental time line into a number of slices. In this model, the simulator begins a time slice by sending a pulse to all of the actors involved, which allows them to run for some period of (real) CPU time. In our model, a pulse does not represent a predefined quantity of CPU time, instead, each agent decides independently when to stop running. This allows agent performance to remain independent of the hardware it runs on, and also allows us to control the performance of the technique itself. To simulate a more efficient scheduling algorithm, for instance, one could simply reduce the number of pulses required for it to complete. Since the agent dictates when it is finished its work, this can be easily accomplished by performing more work before the response is sent. This allows us to evaluate the potential effects of code optimization before actually doing it. The second characteristic of this simulation environment is its usage of events, which are used to instigate reactions and behaviors in the agent. The MASS simulator combines these techniques by dividing time into a number of slices, during which events are used to internally represent actions and interact with the agents. In this model, agents then execute within discrete time slices, but are also notified of activity (method execution, message delivery, etc.) through event notification.

In the next section we will discuss discrete time simulation and the benefits that arise from using it. We will then describe the need for an event based simulation within a multi-agent environment.

Discrete time simulation Because MASS utilizes a discrete notion of time, all agents running in the environment must be synchronized with the simulator's time. To enable this synchronization, the simulator begins each time slice by sending each agent a "pulse" message. This pulse tells the agent it can resume local execution, so in a sense the agent functions by transforming the pulse to some amount of real CPU time on its local processor. This local activity can take an arbitrary amount of real time, up to several minutes if the action involves complex planning, but with respect to the simulator, and in the perceptions of other agents, it will take only one pulse. This technique has several advantages:

1. A series of actions will always require the same number of pulses, and thus will always be performed in the same amount of simulation time. The number of pulses is completely independent of where the action takes place, so performance will be independent of processor speed, available memory, competing processes, etc...
2. Events and execution requests will always take place at the same time. Note that this technique does not guarantee the ordering of these events within the time slice, which will be discussed later in this section.

Using this technique, we are able to control and reproduce the simulation to the granularity of the time pulse. Within the span of a single pulse however, many events may occur, the ordering of which can affect simulation results. Messages exchanged by agents arrive at the simulator and are converted to events to facilitate control over how they are routed to their final destination. Just about everything coming from the agents, in fact, is converted to events; in the next section we will discuss how this is implemented and the advantages of using such a method.

Event based simulation *Events* within our simulation environment are defined as actions which have a specific starting time and duration, and may be incrementally realized and inspected (with respect to our deterministic time line, of course). Note that this is different from the notion of event as it is traditionally known in the simulation community, and is separate from the notion of the "event streams" which are used internally to the agents in our environment.

All of the message traffic in the simulation environment is routed through the simulator, where it is instantiated as a message event. Similarly, execution results, resource modifiers or scripted actions are also represented as events within the simulation controller. We attempt to represent all activities as events both for consistency reasons and because of the ease with which such a representation can be monitored and controlled.

The most important classes of events in the simulator are the *execution* and *message* events. An *execution* event is created each time an agent uses the simulator to model a method's execution. As with all events, execution events will define the method's start time, usually immediately, and duration, which depends on the method's probabilistic distribution as specified in the objective TÆMS task structure (see section 3). The execution event will also calculate the other qualities associated with a method's execution, such as its cost, quality and resource usage. After being created, the execution event is inserted into the simulator's time based event queue, where it will be represented in each of the time slots during which it exists. At the point of insertion, the simulator has computed, but not assigned, the expected final quality, cost, duration and resource usage for the method's execution. These characteristics will be accrued (or reduced) incrementally as the action is performed, as long as no other events perturbate the system. Such perturbations can occur during the execution when forces outside of the method affect its outcome, such as a limiting resource or interaction with another execution method. For example, if during this method's execution, another executing method overloads a resource required by the first execution, the performance of the first will be degraded. The simulator models this interaction by creating a limiting event, which can change one or more of the performance vectors of the execution (cost, quality, duration) as needed. The exact representation of this change is also defined in the simulator's objective TÆMS structure.

As an example, we can trace the lifetime of an action event in the MASS system - the `pre-rinse-hot` method from figure 3. The action begins after the agent has scheduled and executed the action, which will typically be derived from a TÆMS task structure like that seen in the figure. The Execute component in the agent will redirect this action to MASS, in the form of a network message describing the particular method to be executed. MASS will then resolve this description with its local objective TÆMS structure, which will contain the true quantitative performance distributions of the method. When found, it will use these distributions to determine the resulting quality, cost and duration of the method in question, as well as any resource effects. In this case, MASS determines the results of `pre-rinse-hot` will have a quality of 8, a cost of 0 and a duration of 3. In addition, it also determines the method will consume 10 units of `HotWater` for each time unit it is active. An action event is created with these values, and inserted into MASS's action queue. Under normal conditions, this event will remain in the queue until its assigned finish time arrives, at which point the results will be sent to the agent. Interactions with other events in the system, however, can modify the result characteristics. For instance, if the `HotWater` resource becomes depleted during execution, or if a conflicting method is invoked, the duration of the action may be extended, or the quality reduced. These effects may change the performance of the action, and thus may change the results reported to the agent.

Real activities may be also incorporated into the MASS environment by allowing agents to notify the controller when it has performed some activity. In general, methods are not performed by MASS so much as they are approximated, by simulating what the resulting quality, cost and duration of the action might be. Interactions are simulated among methods and resources, but only in an abstract sense, by modifying those same result characteristics of the target action. The mechanism provided by MASS allows for mixed behavior. Some actions may be simulated, while others are performed by the agent itself, producing the actual data, resources or results. When completed, the agent reports these results to the simulator, which updates its environmental view accordingly to maintain a consistent state. For example, in section 5.2 we will see how agents fuse sensor data from disparate sources to produce a estimated target position. This position is needed to determine how and when other agents subsequently gather their data. A simulated fusion of this data would be inadequate, because MASS is unable to provide the necessary domain knowledge needed to perform this calculation. An agent, however, could do this, and then report to the simulator its estimated quality, cost and duration of the analysis process. Both parties are satisfied in this exchange - the agent will have the necessary data to base its reasoning upon, while the simulator is able to maintain a consistent view of the results of activities being performed. Using this mechanism, agents may be incrementally improved to meet real world requirements by adding real capabilities piecemeal, and using MASS to simulate the rest.

The other important class of event is the message event, which is used to model the network traffic which occurs between agents. Instead of communicating directly between themselves, when a message needs to be sent from one agent to another (or to the group), it is routed through the simulator. The event's lifetime in the simulation event queue represents the travel time the message would use if it were sent directly, so by controlling the duration of the event it is possible to model different network conditions. More interesting network behavior can be modeled by corrupting or dropping the contents of the message event. Like execution events, the message event may also may be influenced by other events in the system, so a large number of co-occurring message events might cause one another to be delayed or lost.

To prevent non-deterministic behavior and race conditions in our simulation environment, we utilize a kind of "controlled randomness" to order the realization of events within a given time pulse. When all of the agents have completed their pulse activity (e.g. they have successfully acknowledged the pulse message), the simulator can work with the accumulated events for that time slot. The simulator begins this process by generating a a unique number or hash key for each event in the time slot. It uses these keys to sort the events into an ordered list. It then deterministically shuffles this list before working through it, realizing each event in turn. This shuffling technique, coupled with control over the random function's initial seed, forces the events to be processed in the same order during subsequent runs without unfairly weighting a certain class of events (as would take place if we simply processed the sorted list). This makes our simulation completely deterministic, without sacrificing the unpredictable nature a real world environment would have. That's how we control the simultaneity problem.

5   Experiences

5.1   Intelligent Home project

The first project developed with MASS was the Intelligent Home project [18]. In this environment, we have populated a house with intelligent appliances, capable of working towards goals, interacting with their environment and reasoning about tradeoffs. The goal of this testbed was to develop a number of specific agents that negotiate over the environmental resources needed to perform their tasks, while respecting global deadlines on those tasks. The testbed was developed to explore different types of coordination protocols and compare them. The goal was to compare the performance of specialized coordination protocols (such as seen in [17]) against generic protocols (like Contract-Net[1] and GPGP[8]). We hoped to quantitatively evaluate how these techniques functioned in the environment, in terms of time to converge, the quality and stability of the resulting organization, and the time, processing and message costs.

JAF and TÆMS were used extensively, to develop the agents and model their goal achievement plans, respectively. MASS was used to build a "regular day in the house" - it simulates the tasks requested by the occupants, maintains the status of all environmental resources, simulates agent interactions with the house and resources, and manages sensors available to the agents. MASS allowed us to that events occurred at the same time in subsequent trials, and the only changes from one run to the next were due to changes in agent behavior. Such changes could be due to different reasoning activities by the agents, new protocols or varied task characteristics.

The Intelligent Home project includes 9 agents (dishwasher, dryer, washing machine, coffee maker, robots, heater, air conditioner, water-heater) and were running for 1440 simulated minutes (24 hours). Several simulations were run with different resource levels, to test if our *ad-hoc* protocols could scale up with the increasing number of resource conflicts. Space limitations prevent a a complete report of the project here, more complete results can be found in [17]. Instead, we will give a synopsis of a small scenario, which also makes use of diagnosis-based reorganization [13].

A dishwasher and waterheater exist in the house, related by the fact that the dishwasher uses the hot water the waterheater produces. Under normal circumstances, the dishwasher assumes sufficient water will be available for it to operate, since the waterheater will attempt to maintain a consistent level in the tank at all times. Because of this assumption, and the desire to reduce unnecessary network activity, the initial organization between the agents says that coordination is unnecessary between the two agents. In our scenario, we examine what happens when this assumption fails, perhaps because the owner decides to take a shower at a conflicting time (i.e. there might be a preexisting assumption that showers only take place in the morning), or if the waterheater is put into "conservation mode" and thus only produces hot water when requested to do so. When this occurs, the dishwasher will no longer have sufficient resources to perform its task. Lacking adaptive capabilities, the dishwasher could repeatedly progress as normal but do a poor job of dishwashing, or do no washing at all because of insufficient amounts of hot water. We determined that using a diagnostics engine the dishwasher could, as a result of poor performance observed through internal sensors or user feedback, first determine that a required resource is missing, and then that the resource was not being coordinated over - the dishwasher did not explicitly communicate its water requirements to the waterheater. By itself, this would be sufficient to produce a preliminary diagnosis the dishwasher could act upon simply by making use of a resource coordination protocol. This diagnosis would then be used to change the organizational structure to indicate that explicit coordination should be performed over hot water usage. Later, after reviewing its modified assumptions, new experiences or interactions with the waterheater, it could also refine and validate this diagnosis, and perhaps update its assumptions to note that that there are certain times during the day or water requirement thresholds when coordination is recommended. The MASS simulator allowed us to explore and evaluate this new approach to adaptation without the need for a tremendous investment in knowledge engineering to create a realistic environment.

5.2 Distributed Sensor Network

A distributed sensor network (DSN) stresses a class of issues not addressed in the IHome project. We are presented in this research with a set of sensor platforms, arranged in an environment. The goal of the scenario is for the sensors to track one or more mobile targets that are moving through that environment. No one sensor has the ability to precisely determine the location of a target by itself, so the the sensors must be organized and coordinated in a manner that permits their measurements to be used for triangulation. In the abstract, this situation is analogous to a distributed resource allocation problem, where the sensors represent resources which must be allocated to particular tasks at particular times. Additional hurdles include a lack of reliable communication, the need to scale to hundreds or thousands of sensor platforms, and the ability to reason within a real time, fault prone environment. In this section we will show how JAF was migrated to new simulation and hardware environments.

Several technical challenges to our architectures are posed by this project. It operates in real-time, it must work in both a foreign simulation environment (called Radsim) and on an actual hardware implementation, it must function in a resource-constrained environment, and handle communication unreliability. We were provided with Radsim as a simulator, obviating the need for MASS[2]. Radsim is a multi-agent simulation environment operating in the DSN domain. One or more agents inhabit its environment, each attached to a sensor node.

---

[2] Radsim is developed and maintained by Rome Labs

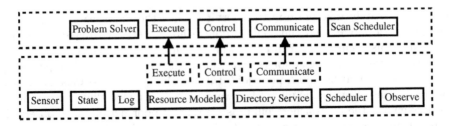

Fig. 5. Organization of a DSN JAF agent. Upper bounds contain the domain dependent components, the lower bounds the independent.

Radsim models the communication between agents, the capabilities and action results of the individual sensors, and the position and direction of one or more mobile targets. Radsim differs from MASS in several significant ways. Because it is domain-specific, Radsim simulates a finite number of predefined actions, returning actual results rather than the abstract quality value returned by MASS. It's timeline is also continuous - it does not wait for pulse acknowledgement before proceeding to the next time slice. This, along with the lack of a standard seeding mechanism, causes the results from one run to the next to be non-deterministic. Our first challenge, then, was to determine what changes were required for JAF to interface with this new environment. This was done by deriving just three JAF components: Control, Communicate and Execute, as shown in figure 5. The new Control component determines the correct time (either in Radsim or hardware), the Communicate component funnels all message traffic through the radio-frequency medium provided in the environment, and additions to Execute provide the bridge allowing JAF actions to interface with the sensor. These changes were made with around 1,000 lines of code, the remainder of the JAF worked unchanged, allowing us to reuse roughly 20,000 lines of code. A domain dependent problem solver, which reasons about the various goals an agent should pursue, and scan scheduler, which produces scanning pattern schedules, were also implemented.

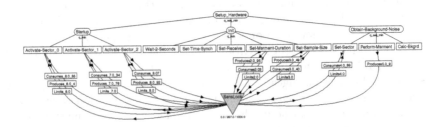

Fig. 6. TÆMS task structure for initializing a DSN agent.

To address real-time issues, the partial-order scheduler (mentioned in section 2) was used to provide quick and flexible scheduling techniques. A resource modeling component was used to track both the availability of the local sensor, and the power usage of the sensor. This component was used by the scheduler to determine when resources were available, and to evaluate the probability that a given action might fail because of unexpected resource usage. The Communicate component was enhanced to add reliable messaging services (using sequence numbers, timeouts and retransmits), enabling other components to flag their messages as "reliable", if needed. Several new components were added to address the domain-specific tasks of scheduling the target detection scans, managing the track generation and performing the negotiation. In all cases there was a high degree of interaction between the new components and the generic domain-independent ones. Much of the necessary domain dependent knowledge was added with the use of TÆMS task structures, such as seen in figure 6. Here we see the initialization structure, which dictates how the agent should initialize its local sensor, perform background measurements, and contact its regional manager.

In our solution to this problem, a regional manager negotiates with individual sensors to obtain maximal area coverage for a series of fast target-detection scans. Once a target is found, a tracking manager negotiates with agents to perform the synchronized measurements needed for triangulation. Our technology enables this, by providing fine grained scheduling services, alternative plan selection and the capacity to remove or renegotiate over conflicting commitments. Two of the metrics used to evaluate our approach are the RMS error between the measured and actual target tracks, and the degree of synchronization achieved in the tracking tasks themselves.

After successfully demonstrating JAF in a new simulation environment, we were then challenged with the task of migrating it to the actual sensor hardware. In this case, JAF agents were hosted on PCs attached to small omnidirectional sensors via the serial and parallel ports. Our task was facilitated by the development of a middle layer, which abstracted the low level sensor actions into the same API used to interface with Radsim[3]. The actual environment, however, differed from Radsim in its unpredictable communication reliability, extreme measurement noise values and varied action durations. It also lacked the central clock definition needed to synchronize agent activities. In this case, the agents were modified to address the new problems, for instance by adding a reliable communication model to Communicate, and a time definition scheme to the control component. These JAF agents have been successfully tested in this new hardware environment, and we are currently in the process of developing better negotiation and scaling techniques to apply to this interesting domain [15].

5.3   Producer Consumer Transporter

The JAF/MASS architecture has also been used to prototype an environment for the to the producer, consumer, transporter (PCT) domain [13]. In this domain, there are conceptually three types of agents: producers, which generate resources;

---

[3] Middle layer API and sensor drivers were implemented by Sanders.

consumers, which use them; and transporters, which move resources from one place to another. In general, a producer and consumer may actually be different faces of a factory, which consumes some quantity of resources in order to produce others. There are several characteristics of this domain where alternatives exist for the factories and transporters - the choices made at these points by or for the PCT agents make up the organizational structure of the system.

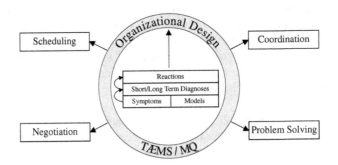

Fig. 7. Role of organizational knowledge within a PCT agent.

This particular system differs from the previous two in that it used the TÆMS representation as an organizational design layer, in addition to describing the local goals and capabilities of the agent. For instance, the subjective view would describe which agents in the system a consumer could obtain resources from, or identify the various pathways a transporter could take. It also made use of a third view of TÆMS - the *conditioned* view. The agent's conditioned TÆMS view is essentially the subjective view, modified to better address current runtime conditions. In figure 8, we see a subjective view which provides three potential candidates capable of producing X. Instead of specifying all producers a consumer could coordinate with, the conditioned view might identify only those which were most promising or cheap or fast, depending on the current goals of the agent. On the right side of the figure, we can see an example of this, where P1 and P3 have been removed from consideration. The idea is to constrain the search space presented by the task structure, to both speed up the reasoning and selection process, and increase the probability of success. The conditioned view was used as the organizational design for the agent - since the majority of decision making was based on this structure, changes in the organization could be made there to induce change in the agent's behavior.

In addition to local reasoning, a diagnosis component was used to generate the conditioned view. As mentioned earlier, the diagnosis component made use of a causal model, which served as a road map from symptom to potential diagnoses. The component itself would monitor the state of the agent, by listening to event streams and monitoring state, to detect aberrant behavior.

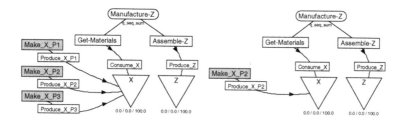

Fig. 8. Subjective and conditioned task structures for PCT

Once detected, the causal model would be used to identify potential causes of the problem, which would result in a set of candidate solutions. These solutions would be induced by making changes to the organizational design in the agent, through modification to the local conditioned view, as shown in figure 7. The JAF architecture facilitated this sort of technology, by providing the common mechanisms for interaction among components. The diagnosis component was integrated by simply plugging it into the agent, and no modifications to other components were necessary.

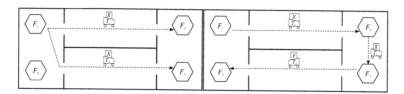

Fig. 9. Experimental solutions in the PCT environment.

Experiments in this environment focused on the convergence time of various diagnosis techniques to stable organizations, and the efficiency of those organizations. For instance, in figure 9, initial conditions in the environment on the left included transporters T_1 and T_2 bringing resource X from producer F_1 to consumers F_2 and F_3. Later in the scenario, the needs of F_4 change, such that it now requires Y. Several different organizations are possible, not all of them functional and efficient. Different diagnosis techniques were applied to situations like this to evaluate the characteristics of the individual organizations, and eventually converging on a solution like that shown on the right side of the figure. More details on the results of these experiments can be found in [13], and more sophisticated PCT environments are currently being tested and evaluated with the help of Dr. Abhijit Deshmukh and Tim Middelkoop.

6   Conclusions

The key idea in this article is the ability of the JAF/MASS architecture to quickly and easily prototype and explore different environments. Varied coordination, negotiation, problem solving and scheduling can all be implemented and tested, while retaining the ability to reuse code in future projects or migrate it to an actual implemented solution.

The JAF component-based agent framework provides the developer with a set of guidelines, conventions and existing components to facilitate the process of agent construction. We have seen in several examples how generic JAF components can be combined with relatively few domain specific ones to produce agents capable of complex reasoning and behaviors. The use of TÆMS as a problem solving language further extends the usefulness of this framework by providing a robust, quantitative view of as agent's capabilities and interactions. Of particular importance is JAF's demonstrated ability to easily work in a wide range of environments, including the discrete time MASS simulator, the real-time Radsim simulator, and on actual hardware, while making use of existing, generic components.

The MASS simulation environment was built to permit rapid modeling and testing of the adaptive behavior of agents with regard to coordination, detection, diagnosis and repair mechanisms functioning in a mercurial environment. The primary purpose of the simulator is to allow successive tests using the same working conditions, which enables us to use the final results as a reasonable basis for the comparison of competing adaptive techniques.

In the Intelligent Home project, we showed how a heterogenous group of agents were implemented in JAF and tested using MASS. Different coordination and problem solving techniques were evaluated, and the TÆMS language was used extensively to model the domain problem solving process. In the distributed sensor network project, JAF agents were deployed onto both a new simulation environment, and real hardware. Agents incorporated complex, partial-ordered scheduling techniques, and ran in real-time. Finally, in the producer/consumer/transporter domain, notions of organizational design and conditioning were added, and adapted over time by a diagnosis component.

We feel the main advantages of the JAF framework are its domain independence, flexibility, and extensibility. Our efforts in MASS to retain determinism without sacrificing unpredictability also make it well suited for algorithm generation and analysis.

7   Acknowledgements

We wish to thank the following individuals for their additional contributions to the research described in this paper. Thomas Wagner contributed the Design-To-Criteria scheduler and to extensions to the TÆMS formalization. Michael Atighetchi, Brett Benyo, Anita Raja, Thomas Wagner, Ping Xuan and Shelley XQ. Zhang contributed to the Intelligent Home project. The DSN project was

implemented by Raphen Becker, Roger Mailler and Jiaying Shen, and Sanders
and Rome Labs provided background, simulation and hardware expertise. Brett
Benyo contributed to our work in the PCT domain.

References

1. Martin Andersson and Tumas Sandholm. Leveled commitment contracts with myopic and strategic agents. In *Proceedings of the Fifteenth National Conference on Artificial Intelligence*, pages 38–44, 1998.
2. K. S. Barber, A. Goel, and C. E. Martin. Dynamic adaptive autonomy in multi-agent systems. *Journal of Experimental and Theoretical Artificial Intelligence*, 2000. Accepted for publications. Special Issue on Autonomy Control Software.
3. Deepika Chauhan. *A Java-based Agent Framework for MultiAgent Systems Development and Implementation*. PhD thesis, ECECS Department, University of Cincinnati, 1997.
4. K. Decker. *Environment Centered Analysis and Design of Coordination Mechanisms*. PhD thesis, Department of Computer Science, University of Massachusetts, Amherst, 1995.
5. Keith Decker and Victor Lesser. Generalizing the partial global planning algorithm. *International Journal of Intelligent Cooperative Information Systems*, 1(2):319–346, 1992.
6. Keith Decker and Victor Lesser. Quantitative modeling of complex environments. Technical report, Computer Science Department, University of Massachusetts, 1993. Technical Report 93-21.
7. Keith S. Decker. Task environment centered simulation. In M. Prietula, K. Carley, and L. Gasser, editors, *Simulating Organizations: Computational Models of Institutions and Groups*. AAAI Press/MIT Press, 1996. Forthcoming.
8. Keith S. Decker and Victor R. Lesser. Generalizing the partial global planning algorithm. *International Journal of Intelligent and Cooperative Information Systems*, 1(2):319–346, June 1992.
9. Keith S. Decker and Victor R. Lesser. Quantitative modeling of complex environments. *International Journal of Intelligent Systems in Accounting, Finance, and Management*, 2(4):215–234, December 1993. Special issue on "Mathematical and Computational Models of Organizations: Models and Characteristics of Agent Behavior".
10. Keith S. Decker and Victor R. Lesser. Coordination assistance for mixed human and computational agent systems. In *Proceedings of Concurrent Engineering 95*, pages 337–348, McLean, VA, 1995. Concurrent Technologies Corp. Also available as UMASS CS TR-95-31.
11. Martha E. Pollack Hanks, Steven and Paul R. Cohen. Benchmarks, testbeds, controlled experimentation, and the design of agent architectures. *AI Magazine*, 14(4):pp. 17–42, 1993. Winter issue.
12. Bryan Horling. A Reusable Component Architecture for Agent Construction. UMASS Department of Computer Science Technical Report TR-1998-45, October 1998.
13. Bryan Horling, Brett Benyo, and Victor Lesser. Using Self-Diagnosis to Adapt Organizational Structures. Computer Science Technical Report TR-99-64, University of Massachusetts at Amherst, November 1999. [http://mas.cs.umass.edu/ bhorling/papers/99-64/].

14. Bryan Horling et al. The tæms white paper, 1999. http://mas.cs.umass.edu/research/taems/white/.
15. Bryan Horling, Régis Vincent, Roger Mailler, Jiaying Shen, Raphen Becker, Kyle Rawlins, and Victor Lesser. Distributed sensor network for real time tracking. Submitted to Autonomous Agents 2001, 2001.
16. Lyndon Lee Hyacinth Nwana, Divine Ndumu and Jaron Collis. Zeus: A tool-kit for building distributed multi-agent systems. *Applied Artifical Intelligence Journal*, 13(1):129–186, 1999.
17. Victor Lesser, Michael Atighetchi, Bryan Horling, Brett Benyo, Anita Raja, Regis Vincent, Thomas Wagner, Ping Xuan, and Shelley XQ. Zhang. A Multi-Agent System for Intelligent Environment Control. Computer Science Technical Report TR-98-XX, University of Massachusetts at Amherst, October 1998.
18. Victor Lesser, Michael Atighetchi, Bryan Horling, Brett Benyo, Anita Raja, Regis Vincent, Thomas Wagner, Ping Xuan, and Shelley XQ. Zhang. A Multi-Agent System for Intelligent Environment Control. In *Proceedings of the Third International Conference on Autonomous Agents*, Seattle,WA, USA, May 1999. ACM Press.
19. Nelson Minar, Roger Burkhart, Chris Langton, and Manor Askenazi. The swarm simulation system: A toolkit for building multi-agent simulations. Web paper: http://www.santefe.edu/projects/swarm/, Sante Fe Institute, 1996.
20. Nortel Networks. Fipa-os web page. Web, 2000. http://www.nortelnetworks.com/products/announcements/fipa/.
21. Régis Vincent, Bryan Horling, Victor Lesser, and Thomas Wagner. Implementing soft real-time agent control. Submitted to Autonomous Agents 2001, 2001.
22. Thomas Wagner, Alan Garvey, and Victor Lesser. Criteria-Directed Heuristic Task Scheduling. *International Journal of Approximate Reasoning, Special Issue on Scheduling*, 19(1-2):91–118, 1998. A version also available as UMASS CS TR-97-59.

Design-to-Criteria Scheduling:
Real-Time Agent Control [*]

Thomas Wagner[1] and Victor Lesser[2]

[1] Computer Science Department
University of Maine
Orono, ME 04469
wagner@umcs.maine.edu
[2] Computer Science Department
University of Massachusetts
Amherst, MA 01003
lesser@cs.umass.edu

Abstract. Design-to-Criteria builds custom schedules for agents that meet hard temporal constraints, hard resource constraints, and soft constraints stemming from soft task interactions or soft commitments made with other agents. Design-to-Criteria is designed specifically for online application – it copes with exponential combinatorics to produce these custom schedules in a resource bounded fashion. This enables agents to respond to changes in problem solving or the environment as they arise.

1   Introduction

Complex autonomous agents operating in open, dynamic environments must be able to address deadlines and resource limitations in their problem solving. This is partly due to characteristics of the environment, and partly due to the complexity of the applications typically handled by software agents in our research. In open environments, requests for service can arrive at the local agent at any time, thus making it difficult to fully plan or predict the agent's future workload. In dynamic environments, assumptions made when planning may change, or unpredicted failures may occur[1]. In most real applications,

---

[*]   This material is based upon work supported by the National Science Foundation under Grant No. IIS-9812755, by the Department of the Navy and Office of the Chief of Naval Research, under Grant No. N00014-97-1-0591, and by the Defense Advanced Research Projects Agency (DARPA) and AFRL under Grant No. F30602-99-2-0525. This work is also funded by the National Defense Center of Excellence for Research in Ocean Sciences (CEROS). CEROS is a part of the Natural Energy Laboratory of Hawaii Authority (NELHA), an agency of the Department of Business, Economic Development & Tourism, State of Hawaii. CEROS is funded by DARPA through grants to and agreements with NELHA. The content of the information does not necessarily reflect the position or the policy of the Government, NSF, ONR, DARPA, AFRL, or CEROS, and no official endorsement should be inferred.
[1] This differs from states that are explicitly recognized and *planned for* [1] as software agents may be required to perform a different set of tasks, as well as having to react to changes in the environment.

T. Wagner and O.F. Rana (Eds.): Infrastructure for Agents, LNAI 1887, pp. 128–143, 2001.
© Springer-Verlag Berlin Heidelberg 2001

Fig. 1. Modeling and Online Scheduling for Real Time and Resource Boundedness

deadlines or other time constraints are present on the agent's problem solving [16, 8]. For example, in an anti-submarine warfare information gathering application [3], there is a deadline by which the mission planners require the information. Resource limitations may also stem from agents having multiple different tasks to perform and having bounded resources in which to perform them. Temporal constraints may also originate with agent interactions – in general, in order for agent β to coordinate with agent α, the agents require mutual temporal information so that they can plan downstream from the interaction.

In this paper, we focus on the issue of resource bounded agent control. We use the term *resource bounded* to denote the existence of deadlines and of other constraints like cost limitations or application specific resource limitations (e.g., limited network bandwidth). Where it is important to differentiate hard and soft deadlines from these other constraints, we refer to them explicitly.

For agents to adapt rationally to their changing problem solving context, which includes changes in the environment[2] and changes to the set of duties for the agent to perform, they must be able to:

1. Represent or model the time and resource constraints of the situation and how such constraints impact their problem solving. We believe this must be done in a quantified fashion as different constraints have different degrees of effect on problem solving.
2. Plan explicitly to address the resource limitations. In our work, this may imply performing a different set of tasks, using alternate solution methods, or trading-off different resources (or quality), depending on what is available.
3. Perform this planning online – in the general case, this implies coping with exponential combinatorics online in soft real time.

While the first two requirements obviously follow from the domain, the third requirement is less obvious. Agents must be able to perform real time control problem solving online because of the dynamics of the environment. If it is difficult to predict the future and there is a possibility of failure, or new tasks arriving, agents will, by necessity, have to react to new information and replan online.

The Design-to-Criteria (DTC) agent scheduler and the TÆMS task modeling framework are our tools for addressing these requirements and achieving resource-bounded agent control (Figure 1). TÆMS provides agents with the framework to represent and reason about their problem solving process from a quantified perspective, including

---

[2] Including resources uncontrollably becoming more or less constrained. For example, network latency increasing due to some activity other than the agent's problem solving.

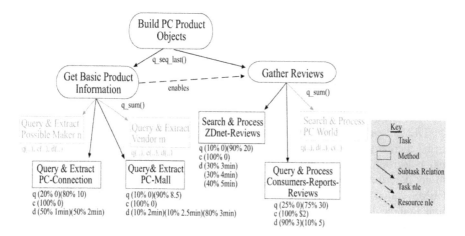

Fig. 2. Conceptual Information Gathering Task Structure of the BIG Agent

modeling of interactions between tasks and resource consumption properties. Design-to-Criteria performs analysis of the processes (modeled in TÆMS) and decides on an appropriate course of action for the agent given its temporal and resource constraints. Design-to-Criteria both produces resource-aware schedules for the agent, and, does this reasoning process online in a resource bounded fashion.

While the output of Design-to-Criteria is real time in the sense that the schedules address hard and soft deadlines, and resource constraints, the schedules are not hard real time and are not fault tolerant in the sense that they may contain uncertainty and known potential failure points. Because DTC is applied in domains where failure is expected, and modeled, and rescheduling is expected, it may often be prudent to choose a schedule that contains some probability of failure, but, also some probability of higher returns. The issue of uncertainty, and its role in addressing hard deadlines, is covered in greater detail later. For situations in which a mid-stream schedule failure leads to catastrophic system-wide failure, we have developed an offline variant of DTC that uses contingency analysis [17, 24] to explore and evaluate recovery options from possible failure points.

This paper is organized as follows: in Section 2 we present TÆMS and describe its role in our domain independent approach to agent control. In Section 3 we describe how DTC reasons about the agent's context and makes control decisions to produce resource bounded schedules. In Section 4, DTC's approximate online solution strategy is presented and in Section 5 we discuss limitations, open questions, and future work.

2   TÆMS Task Models

TÆMS (Task Analysis, Environment Modeling, and Simulation) [6] is a domain independent task modeling framework used to describe and reason about complex problem solving processes. TÆMS models are used in multi-agent coordination research [25, 11] and are being used in many other research projects, including: cooperative-information-gathering [14], hospital patient scheduling [5], intelligent environments [13], coordination of software process [12], and others [21]. Typically, in our domain-independent agent architecture, a domain-specific problem solver or planner translates its problem solving options in TÆMS, possibly at some level of abstraction, and then passes the TÆMS models on to agent control problem solvers like the multi-agent coordination modules or the Design-to-Criteria scheduler. The control problem solvers then decide on an appropriate course of action for the agent, possibly by coordinating and communicating with other agents (that also utilize the same control technologies).

TÆMS models are hierarchical abstractions of problem solving processes that describe alternative ways of accomplishing a desired goal; they represent major tasks and major decision points, interactions between tasks, and resource constraints but they do not describe the intricate details of each primitive action. All primitive actions in TÆMS, called *methods*, are statistically characterized via discrete probability distributions in three dimensions: quality, cost and duration. Quality is a deliberately abstract domain-independent concept that describes the contribution of a particular action to overall problem solving. Duration describes the amount of time that the action modeled by the method will take to execute and cost describes the financial or opportunity cost inherent in performing the action. Uncertainty in each of these dimensions is implicit in the performance characterization – thus agents can reason about the certainty of particular actions as well as their quality, cost, and duration trade-offs. The uncertainty representation is also applied to task interactions like *enablement, facilitation* and *hindering* effects, [3] e.g., "10% of the time facilitation will increase the quality by 5% and 90% of the time it will increase the quality by 8%."

The quantification of actions and interactions in TÆMS is not regarded as a perfect science. Task structure programmers or problem solver generators *estimate* the performance characteristics of primitive actions. These estimates can be refined over time through learning and reasoners typically replan and reschedule when unexpected events occur.

To illustrate, consider Figure 2, which is a conceptual, simplified sub-graph of a task structure emitted by the BIG [14] resource bounded information gathering agent; it describes a portion of the information gathering process. The top-level task is to construct product models of retail PC systems. It has two subtasks, *Get-Basic* and *Gather-Reviews*, both of which are decomposed into actions, that are described in terms of their expected quality, cost, and duration. The *enables* arc between *Get-Basic* and *Gather* is a non-local-effect (NLE) or task interaction; it models the fact that the review gathering actions need the names of products in order to gather reviews for them. Other task interactions modeled in TÆMS include: *enablement, facilitation, hindering, bounded facilitation, disablement, consumes-resource* and *limited-by-resource*. Task interactions are important to scheduling because they denote points at which a task may be affected, either positively or negatively, by an outcome elsewhere in the task structure (or at another agent).

---

[3] Facilitation and hindering task interactions model soft relationships in which a result produced by some task may be beneficial or harmful to another task. In the case of facilitation, the existence of the result generally increases the quality of the recipient task or reduces its cost or duration.

Returning to the example, *Get-Basic* has two actions, joined under the *sum()* quality-accumulation-function (*QAF*), which defines how performing the subtasks relate to performing the parent task. In this case, either action or both may be employed to achieve *Get-Basic*. The same is true for *Gather-Reviews*. The QAF for *Build-PC-Product-Objects* is a *seq_last()* which indicates that the two subtasks must be performed, in order, and that the quality of *Build-PC-Product-Objects* is determined by the resultant quality of *Gather-Reviews*. There are nine alternative ways to achieve the top-level goal in this particular sub-structure.[4] In general, a TÆMS task structure represents a family of plans, rather than a single plan, where the different paths through the network exhibit different statistical characteristics or trade-offs. The process of deciding which tasks/actions to perform is thus an *optimization* problem rather than a *satisfaction* problem.

TÆMS also supports modeling of tasks that arrive at particular points in time, parallelism, individual deadlines on tasks, earliest start times for tasks, and non-local tasks (those belonging to other agents). In the development of TÆMS there has been a constant tension between representational power and the combinatorics inherent in working with the structure. The result is a model that is non-trivial to process, coordinate, and schedule in any optimal sense (in the general case), but also one that lends itself to flexible and approximate processing strategies. This element of choice and flexibility is leveraged both in designing resource-bounded schedules for agents and in performing online scheduling in a resource bounded fashion.

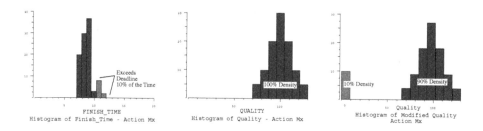

Fig. 3. Reflecting Probability of Missing Deadline in Method Quality

3   Modeling and Reasoning about Temporal and Resource Constraints

TÆMS tasks may have both soft and hard constraints that must be considered when scheduling. In terms of hard temporal constraints, any TÆMS task may have a hard deadline, by which some quality must be produced (or it is considered a failure), as well

---

[4] While it might appear per the *seq_last()* QAF that there are only two possible resultant quality distributions, the enables interaction between *Build* and *Gather* affects the possible quality values for *Gather*.

as an earliest-start-time, before which the task may not be performed (or zero quality will result). These hard constraints may also be caused by hard commitments[5] made with other agents or hard delays between task interactions. The constraints may also be inherited from nodes higher in the structure – thus a client may specify a hard deadline on the *Build-PC* task that applies to all subtasks, or a deadline may be specified on the process of *Gathering-Reviews*. If multiple temporal constraints are present, the tightest or most conservative interpretation applies.

Recall that actions in TÆMS are characterized using discrete probability distributions. Because durations may be uncertain, and because actions are sequenced in a linear fashion,[6] the implication of duration uncertainty is that there is generally uncertainty in both the start and finish times of tasks – even tasks that do not have duration uncertainty of their own. When each TÆMS action is added to a schedule, or considered for a particular schedule point, a data structure called a *schedule element* is created and the start, finish, and duration distributions for the schedule element are computed as a function of the characteristics of the previous schedule element and the action being scheduled. The constraints associated with the action (and higher level task) are then examined and compared to the characteristics that will result if the action is performed at the "current" time or point in the schedule.

One approach for determining whether or not a given action will violate a hard deadline, for example, is to look at some single statistic (median, mean, max, min) of the action and to compare that statistic to the deadline, e.g., if $(mean($ $finish\_time($ $action_x$ $))$ $>$ $hard\_deadline($ $action_x$ $))$
$then$ $violated$. This approach is used during some of the approximation processes of the scheduling algorithm. Another reasonable approach is to compute the probability that the action will violate its hard constraint and compare the probability to a predetermined threshold, e.g., P $=$ $Pr($ $finish\_time($ $action_x$ $)$ $>$ $hard\_deadline($ $action_x$ $))$. if P $>$ $Threshold_P$ $then$ $violated$.

However, TÆMS provides us with a better tool for reasoning about constraint violation. Because zero quality reflects failure, and in TÆMS an action that violates its hard deadline produces zero quality, we can reason about the probability that a given action violates its hard deadline simply by reflecting said probability in the quality distribution of the action and then treating it like any other TÆMS action.[7] Enforcing hard deadline constraints on the agent's entire process (analogous to imposing a deadline on the task structure root) is handled in the same way. For example, as shown in Figure 3, if M_x has a 10% chance of exceeding its deadline (and thus failing), the densities of all the members of its quality distribution are multiplied by 90% (thus re-weighting the entire distribution) and a new density / value pair is added to the distribution to reflect the 10% chance of returning a result after the deadline. The leftmost histogram describes M_x's

---

[5] In contrast to commitments that are soft or relaxable, possibly through a decommitment penalty mechanism.

[6] While DTC supports scheduling of specialized parallel activities, even when activities are scheduled in parallel, they may inherit uncertainty from prior activities.

[7] Professor Alan Garvey, developer of a forerunner to Design-to-Criteria, Design-to-Time, first used a similar technique in Design-to-Time. The technique presented here was developed independently in the DTC research.

expected finish time, the middle histogram describes M_x's unmodified quality distribution, and the rightmost figure shows the modified quality distribution after re-weighting and merging with the new (10%, 0 *quality*) pair. Through this solution approach, the scheduler may actually select a course of action for the agent that has some probability of failure, however, the probability of failure is reflected directly in solution quality so that if the risk is not worthwhile (relative to the other solution paths available to the agent) it will not be taken. In other words, a path containing a possible deadline violation will only be chosen if it has a higher quality than the other solutions on an expected value basis.

On the surface, this model is not appropriate for hard real time applications in which the failure of the action results in no solution for the agent. However, if this is the case, the action will serve a key role in the task structure or will interact with (e.g., enable) other actions in the structure and thus the failure will result in the quality of the affected actions also being decreased and further lower solution quality. The view presented here, if modeled appropriately, gives the scheduler a very powerful tool for reasoning about the implications of possible failures and their impact on overall problem solving.

In addition to hard temporal constraints, TÆMS also models hard resource constraints. For example, a given task may require the use of a network connection and without this connection, the task may produce zero quality (fail). In TÆMS, the effects of resource constraints are modeled using a *limits* NLE from the resource to the task where the NLE describes a multiplier relationship between the resource and the task. For example, running out of a resource may cause the task to take 1.5 times as long to execute, or it may cause the quality to decrease by 50%, or it may cause the cost to increase, or it may simply cause failure. As with violating a hard temporal constraint, if a resource constraint causes action failure, it is reflected in the quality of the action and any actions or tasks that are acted-upon (e.g., by an enables from the affected action) will also have their qualities adjusted to reflect the effects of the resource problem.

Soft constraints in TÆMS take the form of soft commitments made with other agents and soft interactions between tasks. For example, if task α *facilitates* β, performing α before β will positively affect β, possibly by shorting β's duration, but the facilitation does not need to be leveraged to perform either task. When scheduling for soft constraints associated with actions, the scheduler attempts to utilize them when possible (or avoid the in the case of a soft negative interaction, e.g., *hinders*). However, whenever a soft constraint is violated, either on the positive or negative side, the quality distributions of the involved actions are modified to reflect the situation and thus the scheduler can again reason directly about the impact of constraint violation on the agent's process.

The scheduler also supports soft constraints on overall problem solving. In addition to setting hard temporal constraints, the scheduler client may specify an overall soft deadline, soft cost limit, or soft quality requirement. These soft constraints are members of a package of client preferences called *design criteria* that describes for the scheduler the client's objective function. The scheduler then works to produce a schedule (or set of schedules) to suit the client's needs. The criteria mechanism is soft because, due to the combinatorics of reasoning about TÆMS task structures, it is often difficult to predict what types of solutions are possible. Instead, the client describes the

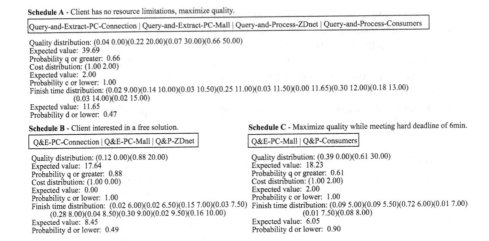

Schedule A - Client has no resource limitations, maximize quality.

| Query-and-Extract-PC-Connection | Query-and-Extract-PC-Mall | Query-and-Process-ZDnet | Query-and-Process-Consumers |

Quality distribution: (0.04 0.00)(0.22 20.00)(0.07 30.00)(0.66 50.00)
Expected value: 39.69
Probability q or greater: 0.66
Cost distribution: (1.00 2.00)
Expected value: 2.00
Probability c or lower: 1.00
Finish time distribution: (0.02 9.00)(0.14 10.00)(0.03 10.50)(0.25 11.00)(0.03 11.50)(0.00 11.65)(0.30 12.00)(0.18 13.00)
            (0.03 14.00)(0.02 15.00)
Expected value: 11.65
Probability d or lower: 0.47

Schedule B - Client interested in a free solution.

| Q&E-PC-Connection | Q&E-PC-Mall | Q&P-ZDnet |

Quality distribution: (0.12 0.00)(0.88 20.00)
Expected value: 17.64
Probability q or greater: 0.88
Cost distribution: (1.00 0.00)
Expected value: 0.00
Probability c or lower: 1.00
Finish time distribution: (0.02 6.00)(0.02 6.50)(0.15 7.00)(0.03 7.50)
    (0.28 8.00)(0.04 8.50)(0.30 9.00)(0.02 9.50)(0.16 10.00)
Expected value: 8.45
Probability d or lower: 0.49

Schedule C - Maximize quality while meeting hard deadline of 6min.

| Q&E-PC-Mall | Q&P-Consumers |

Quality distribution: (0.39 0.00)(0.61 30.00)
Expected value: 18.23
Probability q or greater: 0.61
Cost distribution: (1.00 2.00)
Expected value: 2.00
Probability c or lower: 1.00
Finish time distribution: (0.09 5.00)(0.09 5.50)(0.72 6.00)(0.01 7.00)
    (0.01 7.50)(0.08 8.00)
Expected value: 6.05
Probability d or lower: 0.90

Fig. 4. Different Schedules for Different Clients

desired solution space in terms of relaxable, relative, design criteria (in quality, cost, duration, uncertainty in each dimension, and limits and thresholds on these) and the scheduler makes trade-off decisions as needed to best address the client's needs. The criteria metaphor is based on importance sliders for quality, cost, duration, limits and thresholds on these, and certain in each of these dimensions. The metaphor, the formal mathematics of the criteria mechanism, and the scheduler's trade-off computations have been fully documented in [23, 22].

Let us revisit BIG's process, shown in Figure 2, and illustrate DTC's creation of custom, resource bounded, schedules and the role of task interaction in modeling the effects of failure. Even this simple task structure gives DTC room to adapt BIG's problem solving. Figure 4 shows three different schedules constructed for different BIG clients that have different objectives. For brevity, the detailed distributions associated with each action are omitted, however, the aggregate schedule statistics are shown. Schedule A is constructed for a client that has both time and financial resources – he or she is simply interested in maximizing overall solution quality. Schedule B is constructed for a client that wants a free solution. Schedule C meets the needs of a client interested in maximizing quality while meeting a hard deadline of 6 minutes. Note that schedule C is actually preferred over a schedule that includes action *Query-and-Extract-PC-Connection* even though said action has a higher expected quality than *Query-and-Extract-PC-Mall*. This is because the *PC-Connection* action also has a higher probability of failure. Because of the enables NLE from the task of getting product information to retrieving reviews, this higher probability of failure also impacts the probability of being able to query the Consumer's site for a review. Thus, though the local choice would be to prefer *PC-Connection* over *PC-Mall* for this criteria, the aggregate effects lead to a different decision. Note also that schedule C also exceeds its deadline 10% of the time. The deadline over-run and the enablement from *PC-Mall* contribute to the probability of failure exhibited by the schedule (probability of returning a zero quality result), i.e., Consumer's fails 25% of the time without considering these other constraints. When considering the other constraints, probability of failure is: $(((25\% * .90) + 10\%) * .90) + 10\% = 39.25\%$.

4 Online Scheduling - Coping with Exponential Combinatorics

As TÆMS task structures model a family of plans, the DTC scheduling problem has conceptually certain characteristics in common with planning and certain characteristics of more traditional scheduling problems, and it suffers from pronounced combinatorics on both fronts. The scheduler's function is to read as input a TÆMS task structure (or a set of task structures) and to 1) decide which set of tasks to perform, 2) decide in what sequence the tasks should be performed, 3) to perform the first two functions so as to address hard constraints and balance the soft criteria as specified by the client,[8] and 4) to do this computation in soft real time (or interactive time) so that it can be used online.

Meeting these objectives is a non-trivial problem. In general, the upper-bound on the number of possible schedules for a TÆMS task structure containing n actions is given in Equation 1. Clearly, for any significant task structure the brute-strength approach of generating all possible schedules is infeasible – offline or online. This expression contains complexity from two main sources. On the "planning" side, the scheduler must consider the (unordered) $O(2^n)$ different alternative different ways to go about achieving the top level task (for a task structure with n actions). On the "scheduling" side, the scheduler must consider the $m!$ different possible orderings of each alternative, where m is the number of actions in the alternative.

$$\sum_{i=0}^{n} \binom{n}{i} i! \tag{1}$$

In general, the types of constraints present in TÆMS, and the existence of interactions between tasks (and the different $QAFs$ that define how to achieve particular tasks), prevent a simple, optimal solution approach. DTC copes with the high-order combinatorics using a battery of techniques. Space precludes detailed discussion of these, however, they are documented in [23]. From a very high level, the scheduler uses:

Criteria-Directed Focusing The client's goal criteria is not simply used to select the "best" schedule for execution, but is also leveraged to focus all processing activities on producing solutions and partial solutions that are most likely to meet the trade-offs and limits/thresholds defined by the criteria.

Approximation Schedule approximations, called *alternatives*, are used to provide an inexpensive, but coarse, overview of the schedule solution space. One alternative models one way in which the agent can achieve the top level task. Alternatives contain a set of unordered actions and an estimation for the quality, cost, and duration

---

[8] Because there may be alternative ways to perform a given task, and some of the options may not have the same associated deadlines, the scheduler actually balances both meeting hard constraints and the design criteria.

characteristics that will result when the actions are sequenced to form a schedule. This, in conjunction with criteria-directed focusing enables DTC to address the "planning" side complexity.

Heuristic Decision Making To address the scheduling side complexity, DTC uses a superset of the techniques used in Design-to-Time [8], namely an iterative, heuristic, process of sequencing out the actions in a given alternative. These action rating heuristics rate each action and the ratings (in DTC) are stratified so that certain heuristics and constraints dominate others. The net effect is a reduction of the $O(n!)$ ($\omega(2^n)$ and $o(n^n)$ by Stirling's Approximation) complexity to polynomial levels in the worst case.

Heuristic Error Correction The use of approximation and heuristic decision making has a price – it is possible to create schedules that are suboptimal, but, repairable. A secondary set of improvement [28, 19] heuristics act as a safety net to catch the errors that are correctable.

The Design-to-Criteria scheduling process falls into the general area of flexible computation [9], but differs from most flexible computation approaches in its use of multiple actions to achieve flexibility (one exception is [10]) in contrast to *anytime algorithms* [4, 18, 26]. We have found the lack of restriction on the properties of primitive actions to be an important feature for application in large numbers of domains. Another major difference is that in DTC we not only propagate uncertainty [27], but we can work to reduce it when important to the client. DTC differs from its predecessor, Design-to-Time[8], in many ways. From a client perspective, however, the main differences are in its use of uncertainty, its ability to retarget processing at any trade-off function, and its ability to cope with both "scheduling" and "planning" side combinatorics.

Design-to-Criteria is not without its limitations; when adapting the DTC technology for use in potentially time critical domains, such as the CEROS anti-submarine warfare information gathering task, shown in Figure 5, we encountered an interesting problem. The satisficing focusing methodology used in Design-to-Criteria leads to poor solutions when combined with hard deadlines and certain classes of very large task structures. Without delving into exhaustive detail, the problem is that in order to cope with the high-order combinatorics in these particular situations, the scheduling algorithm must prune schedule approximations, or alternatives, and develop only a subset of these. Herein lies the problem.

Alternatives are constructed bottom-up from the leaves of the task hierarchy to the top-level task node, i.e., the alternatives of a task are combinations of the alternatives for its sub-tasks. Figure 6 shows the alternative set generation process for a small task structure. Alternatives are generated for the interior tasks T_1 and T_2, and these alternatives are combined to produce the alternative set for the root task, T. The complexity of the alternative generation process is pronounced. A task structure with n actions leads to $O(2^n)$ possible alternatives at the root level. We control this combinatorial complexity by focusing alternative generation and propagation on alternatives that are most likely to result in schedules that "best" satisfice to meet the client's goal criteria; alternatives that are less good at addressing the criteria are pruned from intermediate level alternative sets. For example, a criteria set denoting that certainty about quality is an important issue will result in the pruning of alternatives that have a relatively low degree of quality

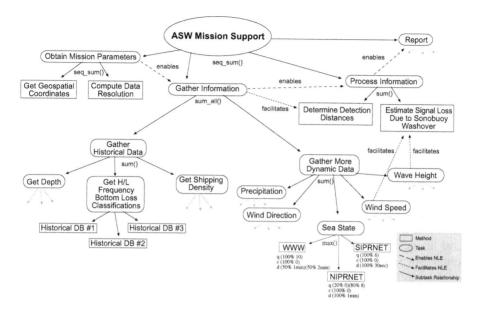

Fig. 5. Partial TÆMS Task Structure for Gathering and Processing ASW Mission Information

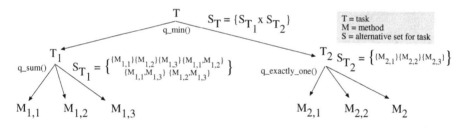

Fig. 6. Alternative Sets Lead to Cumbersome Combinatorics

certainty. After the alternative set for the high-level task is constructed, a subset of the alternatives are selected for scheduling.

For situations in which there is no overall hard deadline, or in which shorter durations are also preferred, the focusing mechanism works as advertised. However, in the CEROS project, we are also interested in meeting real-time deadlines and other hard resource constraints (in contrast to those that are relaxable), and often these preferences are not accompanied by a general preference for low duration or low cost. In these cases, the problem lies in making a *local* decision about which alternatives to propagate (at an interior node) when the decision has implications to the local decisions made at other nodes – the local decision processes are interdependent and they interact over a shared resource, e.g., time or money. Casting the discussion in terms of Figure 6: assume T has an overall deadline of 5 minutes and T_1's alternatives require anywhere from 2 minutes to 20 minutes to complete, and T_2's alternatives are similarly characterized. Assume that quality is highly correlated with duration, thus the more time spent problem solving, the better the result. If the criteria specifies maximum quality within the deadline, the alternatives propagated from T_1 to T will be those that achieve maximum quality (and also have high duration). Likewise with the alternatives propagated from T_2. The resulting set of alternatives, S_T at node T will contain members characterized by high quality, but also high duration, and the scheduler will be unable to construct a schedule that meets the hard deadline. The optimal solution to this problem is computationally infeasible ($\omega(2^n)$ and $o(n^n)$) as it amounts to the general scheduling problem because of task interactions and other constraints.

Two approximate solutions are possible. One approach is to preprocess the task structure, producing small alternative sets at each node that characterize the larger alternative population for that node. Then examining the ranges of alternatives at each node and heuristically deciding on an allocation or apportionment of the overall deadline or cost limitation to each of the interior nodes. This local-view of the overall constraint could then be used to focus alternative production on those that will lead to a root-level set that meets the overall constraint. The other approach, which we have employed, is to detect when the local-view of the decision process is problematic and in those cases sample from the population of alternatives, producing a subset that exhibits similar statistical properties, and propagating these alternatives. This leads to a less-focused set of root level alternatives than the prior approach, but it saves on the added polynomial level expense of the first approach.

5   Conclusion, Future Work, and Limitations

We have discussed a class of issues in DTC that pertain to modeling and scheduling for hard and soft temporal constraints, resource constraints, and task interactions. Space precludes a full enumeration of the different aspects of DTC that relate to addressing resource limitations – the issue is ubiquitous to the design of the DTC algorithm, the TÆMS modeling framework, and the decisions made by the DTC scheduler. From a very high level, possibly the most important features that relate to resource boundedness is the detailed quantified view of actions, and task interactions, afforded by the TÆMS modeling framework. This, combined with the element of choice present in TÆMS families of plans, sets the foundation for DTC's reasoning about the implications of failures, failing to acquire resources, and violating hard constraints.

In terms of limitations, DTC's approximate solution approach is clearly not optimal in many circumstances. As discussed, this is particularly true when the alternative sets must be severely pruned (focused) to produce solutions. Additionally, in some applications, in which only very specific subsets of the features afforded by TÆMS are employed, custom schedulers may do a better job of balancing the different concerns and finding good solutions. In terms of optimality, it is difficult to compare the performance of DTC to optimal as found via exhaustive generation simply because it is not feasible to generate all possible schedules for realistic task structures. Members of our group are currently working on an MDP-based TÆMS scheduling tool [17, 24] and we plan to measure DTC's performance on smaller applications through this tool.

It is important to note that though DTC takes great pains to produce schedules quickly, the scheduler is not hard real time itself. We cannot make performance guarantees [15, 20] for a given problem instance, though it would be possible to produce such guarantees by classifying similar task structures and measuring scheduling performance offline. At issue is the constraints present in an arbitrary TÆMS task structure. For certain classes of task structures, guarantees without an in-depth preclassification are possible. In practice, the scheduler (implemented in 50,000 lines of C++) is fast and capable of scheduling task structures with 20-40 primitive actions in under 7 seconds on a 600mhz Pentium III machine running Redhat Linux 6.0. A sampling of applications and runtimes are shown in Table 1.

In the table, the first column identifies the problem instance, the second column identifies the number of primitive actions in the task structure, the third column (*UB # R-Alts*) indicates the upper bound on the number of root-level alternatives, the fourth column identifies the upper bound on the number of schedules possible for the task structure ("N/C" indicates that the value is too large for the variable used to compute it). The fifth column (*# Alts R / Total*) identifies the number of alternatives actually produced during the scheduling run – the first number is the number of alternatives produced at the root note and the second number is the total number of alternatives produced during scheduling. The first number is comparable to the upper-bounds expressed in column three. The sixth column shows the number of schedules actually produced. The column labeled *# D Combines* indicates the number of distribution combination operations performed during scheduling – this is particularly informative because nearly all aspects of the scheduling process involve probability distributions rather than expected values. The last three columns pertain to the time spent (in whole seconds) doing different activities, namely producing the set of root-level alternatives, creating schedules from the alternatives, and the total scheduler runtime (which includes some final sorting and other output-related operations). Due in part to the scheduler's use of a particular set of clock functions, which are integer based, there is no variance when the experiments are repeated because the variance pertains to less than whole seconds.

Most of the task structures produced 15 schedules – this is the system default. When fewer schedules are produced it indicates that there are not sufficient alternatives at the root level to produce more schedules. When more than 15 schedules are produced, it indicates that the scheduler's termination criteria was not met – generally caused by a large percentage of zero quality schedules or by there being alternatives that appear better than any schedules generated thus far per the design criteria. The scheduler will work beyond its preset number under these conditions but only to some multiple of the preset. The JIL_translated structure, for example, contains some modeling problems that produce a very large number of zero quality schedules and DTC scheduled up to 4*15 and then halted with a small set of viable schedules.

With respect to scheduler computation overhead and online performance, the time required to schedule these task structures is reasonable given that the grainsize of the structures themselves is much larger than the seconds required to perform the scheduling operation (generally, scheduler overhead is at most 1% of the total runtime of the agent's application). That being said, however, being "appropriately fast" is not necessarily the long term objective and performance guarantees and performance estimates are important research avenues for the future.

Task Structure	# Methods	UB # R-Alts	# UB Schedules	# Alts R / Total	# Sched. Prod.	# D Combines	T Prod. Alts	T Prod. Sched.	T Total
Simple Plan Trip	10	1,023	9,864,100	53 / 91	15	8,686	0	1	1
HotWaterHeater1.0	6	63	1,956	45 / 108	19	7,831	0	1	2
DishWasher1.0	14	16,383	N/C	100 / 1018	15	47,136	0	1	2
IHomeRobot	186	2,147,483,647	N/C	50 / 665	15	46,140	0	2	3
Transport_v0	9	511	986,409	48 / 167	15	13,032	0	1	1
BIG_v1.2	26	67,108,863	N/C	50 / 4540	15	273,283	2	3	6
JIL_translated	25	33,554,431	N/C	139 / 3526	60	334,393	2	3	7

Table 1. Scheduler Performance on an Assortment of Different Applications

One promising area of DTC related research is an offline contingency analysis tool [17, 24] that uses DTC to explore an approximation of the schedule space for a given TÆMS task structure. The use of DTC as an oracle enables the contingency analysis tool to cope with the combinatorics of the general scheduling problem. The contingency analysis methodology determines the criticality of failures within a schedule and for critical points, evaluates the statistical characteristics of the available recovery options. The analysis, while expensive, is appropriate for mission-critical hard deadline situations in which a solution must be guaranteed by a particular time. With DTC's approach, it is possible to start down a solution path (that is appealing even with the possibility of failure) for which there is no mid-stream recovery option that will enable the agent to still produce some result by the hard deadline. DTC will always recover and find whatever options are available, but, because it does not plan for contingency and recovery a priori, in hard deadline situations in which solutions must be guaranteed, there is some possibility of unrecoverable failure.

DTC has many different parameter settings not discussed here and it can be made to avoid failure if possible. However, while this covers a certain class of the functionalities offered by the contingency analysis tool, the two are not equivalent. Whereas the best DTC can do is avoid failure if possible, or work to minimize failure, it can only do this for a single line of control. Using the contingency analysis tool, the agent can select a high risk plan of action that also has some potential of a high pay off, but, it can also reason a priori about the ability to recover from a failure of the plan. While DTC can be extremely conservative, it cannot plan for both high-risk and recovery concurrently. The choice between DTC and the contingency analysis approach is dependent on the application. For online, responsive control to unplanned events, DTC is most appropriate. For mission-critical situations combined with time for a priori offline planning, the contingency approach is most appropriate.

6 Acknowledgments

We would like to acknowledge the Design-to-Time work of Professor Alan Garvey; said work made this and other developments in TÆMS scheduling possible. We would also like to thank Garvey for his assistance in understanding the details of Design-to-Time when implementing the first stages of Design-to-Criteria. The deadline over-run technique discussed in this paper, where over-run is reflected in a method's quality, is similar to a technique developed and deployed by Garvey in Design-to-Time. The technique was independently developed and deployed in Design-to-Criteria.

Anita Raja also deserves credit for pushing on the issue of recovery in mission critical environments. Her work in contingency analysis via Design-to-Criteria encouraged a clear distinction between situations in which a deeper analysis is worthwhile or required and situations in which online responsiveness is appropriate.

References

1. Ella M. Atkins, Edmund H. Durfee, and Kang G. Shin.   Detecting and Reacting to Unplanned-for World States. In *Proceedings of the Fourteenth National Conference on Artificial Intelligence*, July 1997.
2. Mark Boddy and Thomas Dean. Solving time-dependent planning problems. In *Proceedings of the Eleventh International Joint Conference on Artificial Intelligence*, pages 979–984, Detroit, August 1989.
3. Ceros-related information gathering project – in progress.   Organization url is http://www.ceros.org.
4. T. Dean and M. Boddy. An analysis of time-dependent planning. In *Proceedings of the Seventh National Conference on Artificial Intelligence*, pages 49–54, St. Paul, Minnesota, August 1988.
5. Keith Decker and Jinjiang Li. Coordinated hospital patient scheduling. In *Proceedings of the Third International Conference on Multi-Agent Systems (ICMAS98)*, pages 104–111, 1998.
6. Keith S. Decker. *Environment Centered Analysis and Design of Coordination Mechanisms*. PhD thesis, University of Massachusetts, 1995.
7. E. H. Durfee. A cooperative approach to planning for real-time control. In *Proceedings of the Workshop on Innovative Approaches to Planning, Scheduling and Control*, pages 277–283, November 1990.
8. Alan Garvey and Victor Lesser. Design-to-time real-time scheduling. *IEEE Transactions on Systems, Man and Cybernetics*, 23(6):1491–1502, 1993.
9. Eric Horvitz, Gregory Cooper, and David Heckerman. Reflection and action under scarce resources: Theoretical principles and empirical study. In *Proceedings of the Eleventh International Joint Conference on Artificial Intelligence*, August 1989.
10. Eric Horvitz and Jed Lengyel. Flexible Rendering of 3D Graphics Under Varying Resources: Issues and Directions. In *Proceedings of the AAAI Symposium on Flexible Computation in Intelligent Systems*, Cambridge, Massachusetts, November 1996.
11. David Jensen, Michael Atighetchi, Regis Vincent, and Victor Lesser. Learning Quantitative Knowledge for Multiagent Coordination. *Proceedings of AAAI-99*, 1999. Also as UMASS CS Technical Report TR-99-04.
12. David Jensen, Yulin Dong, Barbara Staudt Lerner, Eric K. McCall, Leon J. Osterweil, Stanley M. Sutton Jr., and Alexander Wise. Coordinating agent activities in knowledge discovery processes. In *Proceedings of Work Activities Coordination and Collaboration Conference (WACC) 1999*, 1999. Also available as UMASS Tech Report UM-CS-1998-033.
13. Victor Lesser, Michael Atighetchi, Bryan Horling, Brett Benyo, Anita Raja, Regis Vincent, Thomas Wagner, Ping Xuan, and Shelley XQ. Zhang. A Multi-Agent System for Intelligent Environment Control. In *Proceedings of the Third International Conference on Autonomous Agents (Agents99)*, 1999.

14. Victor Lesser, Bryan Horling, Frank Klassner, Anita Raja, Thomas Wagner, and Shelley XQ. Zhang. BIG: An agent for resource-bounded information gathering and decision making. *Artificial Intelligence*, 118(1-2):197–244, May 2000. Elsevier Science Publishing.

15. David J. Musliner, Edmund H. Durfee, and Kang G. Shin. CIRCA: A cooperative intelligent real-time control architecture. *IEEE Transactions on Systems, Man and Cybernetics*, 23(6), 1993.

16. David J. Musliner, James A. Hendler, Ashok K. Agrawala, Edmund H. Durfee, Jay K. Strosnider, and C. J. Paul. The Challenge of Real-Time Artificial Intelligence. *Computer*, 28(1):58–66, January 1995.

17. Anita Raja, Thomas Wagner, and Victor Lesser. Reasoning anout Uncertainty in Design-to-Criteria Scheduling. Computer Science Technical Report TR-99-27, University of Massachusetts at Amherst, March 2000. To appear in the 2000 AAAI Spring Symposium on Real-Time Systems.

18. Stuart J. Russell and Shlomo Zilberstein. Composing real-time systems. In *Proceedings of the Twelfth International Joint Conference on Artificial Intelligence*, pages 212–217, Sydney, Australia, August 1991.

19. Wolfgang Slany. Scheduling as a fuzzy multiple criteria optimization problem. *Fuzzy Sets and Systems*, 78:197–222, March 1996. Issue 2. Special Issue on Fuzzy Multiple Criteria Decision Making.

20. John A. Stankovic and Krithi Ramamritham. Editorial: What is predictability for real-time systems? *The Journal of Real-Time Systems*, 2:247–254, 1990.

21. Regis Vincent, Bryan Horling, Thomas Wagner, and Victor Lesser. Survivability simulator for multi-agent adaptive coordination. In *Proceedings of the First International Conference on Web-Based Modeling and Simulation*, 1998.

22. Thomas Wagner, Alan Garvey, and Victor Lesser. Complex Goal Criteria and Its Application in Design-to-Criteria Scheduling. In *Proceedings of the Fourteenth National Conference on Artificial Intelligence*, pages 294–301, July 1997. Also available as UMASS CS TR-1997-10.

23. Thomas Wagner, Alan Garvey, and Victor Lesser. Criteria-Directed Heuristic Task Scheduling. *International Journal of Approximate Reasoning, Special Issue on Scheduling*, 19(1-2):91–118, 1998. A version also available as UMASS CS TR-97-59.

24. Thomas A. Wagner, Anita Raja, and Victor R. Lesser. Modeling Uncertainty and its Implications to Design-to-Criteria Scheduling. Under review, Special issue of the AI Journal, 1998. Also available as UMASS CS TR#1998-51.

25. Ping Xuan and Victor R. Lesser. Incorporating uncertainty in agent commitments. In N.R. Jennings and Y. Lespérance, editors, *Intelligent Agents VI (Proceedings of ATAL-99)*, Lecture Notes in Artificial Intelligence. Springer-Verlag, Berlin, 2000.

26. S. Zilberstein and S. J. Russell. Optimal composition of real-time systems. *Artificial Intelligence*, 82(1):181–214, December 1996.

27. Shlomo Zilberstein. Using anytime algorithms in intelligent systems. *AI Magazine*, 17(3):73–83, 1996.

28. M. Zweben, B. Daun, E. Davis, and M. Deale. Scheduling and rescheduling with iterative repair. In M. Zweben and M. Fox, editors, *Intelligent Scheduling*, chapter 8. Morgan Kaufmann, 1994.

Integrating Conversational Interaction and Constraint Based Reasoning in an Agent Building Shell

Mihai Barbuceanu and Wai-Kau Lo

Enterprise Integration Laboratory
University of Toronto
4 Taddle Creek Road, Rosebrugh Building
Toronto, Ontario, Canada, M5S 3G9
{mihai, wklo}@eil.utoronto.ca

Abstract. In this paper we identify several types of specific services that agent infrastructures must support, including complex interaction, decision making for individual utility maximization, team formation in organizations and multi-attribute negotiation. We describe each of these services in part and show how they are supported in an integrated manner to provide abstract functionality related to complex interaction and unified individual and social reasoning in multi-agent settings. We show that this range of services can be achieved by combining conversational technology at the interaction level with constraint satisfaction and optimization as a common reasoning infrastructure supporting the required reasoning services. All services are provided by generic components packaged into a Java written Agent Building Shell.

1 Introduction

As the connectivity provided by the Internet reaches more people and organizations, each with their own goals and resources, the ability to effectively coordinate the actions of the participants takes over as the most critical requirement for the successful operation of the system. Global systems for manufacturing and service provisioning for example, connecting suppliers, producers, distributors and customers all over the world need to coordinate the activities of agents inside their different component organizations and the organizations themselves on the global market place to provide value for all participants.

In this paper we articulate a multi-level view of coordination and we provide solutions for an integrated agent architecture that addresses all the levels. We adopt the view that full coordination requires a range of services from intentional communication based on speech acts to complex models of individual and social reasoning determining how agents can achieve their goals by using their own resources, by teaming-up with other agents in their organization and finally by negotiating deals on the market place. We cover all these requirements by integrating two main technologies. First, we use conversational mechanisms to support long running, complexly structured intentional communication based on speech acts. Second, we develop new constraint based representations of action and behavior that allow agents to plan their behavior by integrating their own goals with the organizational structures they belong to and by using market

T. Wagner and O.F. Rana (Eds.): Infrastructure for Agents, LNAI 1887, pp. 144–156, 2001.

place negotiation with other agents and organizations. For all of these issues we develop generic solutions that we package into our Java written Agent Building Shell.

2   The Agent Building Shell

We believe that many of the concerns related to interaction and reasoning can be addressed in generic and reusable ways by means of an Agent Building Shell (ABS). The ABS is a collection of reusable software components and interfaces providing support for application independent agent services. Using these services, developers can build on a high level infrastructure whose abstractions provide a conceptual framework that helps designing and understanding agent systems, eliminate work duplication and offer guarantees about the services provided by the tool.

Figure 1 shows the current architecture of the ABS. The coordination layer, reviewed in section 3, provides a full coordination language (named COOL in the initial version, JCOOL in the current Java version) based on the conversation metaphor. Conversations are able to model peer-to-peer interactions in which autonomous agents make requests, volunteer information, react to events, update their state etc. Conversations express the shared conventions that stand at the basis of coordination and are used as the basic abstraction for capturing coordination knowledge and social know-how [6]. The shell supports a full range of conversational abstractions and constructs - conversation plans, conversation rules, actual conversations etc - in terms of which complex interactions are described, as well as the programming tools and interfaces required for use in applications [2].

The second layer of the shell deals with the ways in which agents plan their behavior and execute the planned activities. This is based on a *common, constraint based representation and reasoning infrastructure* that represents an agent's goals, constraints and utilities and provides the solvers used to perform planning and decision making - all described in section 4.

Three levels of planning and decision making are currently supported. At the *individual agent level* (section 5), we address the decision making problem faced by individual agents that need to discover their highest utility goals and the plans to achieve them. Individual behaviors normally contain goals that the agent can't achieve without the collaboration of other agents in the organization. At the *organization level*, organization models are dynamically generated for these goals. These novel models, based on the Steiner-tree problem [5], are compiled into a form solvable by the same constraint optimization solver used at the individual level, determining the structure of the teams that can achieve the goals with minimal cost (section 6). Individual and organizational reasoning both rely on knowing the utilities of the goals. In many cases, these are not given in advance but have to be discovered dynamically by market interaction. At the *market level* (section 7), we use Multi-Attribute Utility Theory (MAUT) [10] to evaluate and negotiate the optimal exchanges between agents or organizations, given their multiple interdependent objectives and their preferences. This is done by giving a constraint optimization formulation to the MAUT problem and by using the same constraint optimization solver to find the best offerings or responses in negotiation.

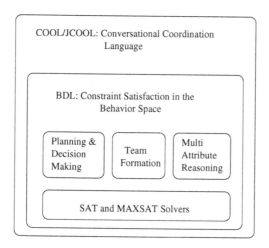

Fig. 1. The Agent Building Shell.

3   BDL: The Common Reasoning Infrastructure

We support the range of individual and social reasoning tasks that agents must perform with a language for describing and reasoning about agent behavior, the Behavior Description Language (BDL). A behavior consists of partially ordered goal achieving activities that satisfy given constraints. In our representation there are two kinds of goals, *composed* and *atomic*. Composed goals consist of other (sub)goals, while atomic goals do not. We allow three kinds of compositions.

Sequential compositions, $a = seq(a_1, a_2, ...a_n)$ denote that all component goals a_i must be executed in the given order.

Parallel compositions, $a = par(a_1, a_2, ...a_m)$ denote that all component goals must be executed, but without imposing any order.

Choice compositions, $a = choice(a_1, a_2, ...a_p)$ denote execution of only a non-empty subset of sub-goals, also without imposing any order. *Exclusive choices* (*xchoice*) require the execution of exactly one component sub-goal.

From the execution viewpoint, choices have *or* (*xor* for xchoices) semantics in that a choice g is 'on' - meaning will be executed and written $On(g)$ - iff at least one component is on (exactly one for xchoices) and 'off' - meaning will not be executed and written $Off(g)$ - iff all components are off. Sub-goals can occur negated within choices and parallels, but not within sequences. Thus, $c = choice(a, -b)$ denotes a choice between achieving a and not achieving b. Sequences and parallels both have *and* semantics - 'on' iff all components are on, and 'off' otherwise. The difference is that sequences also require *ordered* execution of subgoals, while parallels don't. At the planning level we address this by enforcing specific constraints for sequences. For example, $On(seq(a_i, a_{i+1})) \supset Off(seq(a_{i+1}, a_i))$. From this we derive that if a sequence is 'on', all its sub-sequences are also 'on', and if a subsequence is 'off' then all its super-sequences are also 'off'. E.g., $Off(seq(a_1, a_3)) \supset Off(seq(a_1, a_2, a_3))$.

From an agent's viewpoint, a goal is *individually achievable* if the agent acting alone can achieve it. A goal is *collectively achievable* if a coalition of agents must be put together and coordinated in order to achieve the goal. Often, one or more collectively achievable goals are part of an agent's plans. In such cases, the agent has to determine the best set of agents to collaborate with to achieve these goals. This is addressed later on.

Planning Behavior. Let $G = \{g_1, ...g_n\}$ be a set of goals, or a goal network. An on-off labeling of the network is a mapping $L : G \rightarrow \{on, off\}$ associating either 'on' or 'off' labels to each goal in G. A labeling is *consistent* iff the labels of each composed node and of its subgoals are consistent with the node's execution semantics. E.g. if a sequence goal is 'on', then all its subgoals are 'on' and no other contradictory sequences are 'on'. If a sequence is 'off', either some subgoal is 'off' or else the ordering of the sequence is not implied by the current 'on' sequences. Consistent labelings thus define *executable* behaviors.

Let $C = \{c_1, ...c_m\}$ be a set of constraints, where each c_i is either a simple constraint of the form $On(g_j)$ or $Off(g_k)$, or an implication on both sides of which there are conjunctions of simple constraints.

Let $U = \{(g_1, u_{on}(g_1), u_{off}(g_1))...(g_l, u_{on}(g_l), u_{off}(g_l))\}$ be a utility list, that is a set of goals with their associated utilities. $u_{on}(g)$ is the utility obtained if g is achieved. $u_{off}(g)$ is the utility obtained if g is not achieved. Given a utility list U and a consistent labeling L of G, the total utility of the labeling, $Util(L, U)$, is the sum of on-utilities for the 'on' labeled goals plus the sum of off-utilities for the 'off' labeled goals.

Finally, a behavior planning problem is a tuple $P =< G, C, U, criterion >$ where $criterion \in \{max, min\}$. A problem specifies a goal network, a set of constraints, a utility list and an optimization criterion, either max or min. A solution to a problem P is a labeling L such that $Util(L, U)$ is either maximal or minimal, according to the $criterion$.

The Solver. The problem of finding a consistent labeling (without enforcing the sequencing constraints) is equivalent to satisfiability (SAT). The problem of finding a labeling that maximizes (minimizes) utility is a form of MAXSAT. The Solver we provide integrates an incomplete random search procedure based on the WSAT method of [15], and a systematic (complete) branch and bound procedure, both operating over the same representation of goal networks. In both cases enforcing the sequencing constraints is done polynomially each time the main loop of the algorithm finds a solution. As known, the random search method is not guaranteed to find a solution, but performs very well on large scale problems.

The branch and bound procedure maintains the utility of the current best solution such that if the partial solution currently explored can not be extended to one with better utility than the current best, then it is dropped and a new one is explored. The procedure uses the variable selection heuristic of selecting the most constrained goal first (the one with most subgoals assigned) and forward checks any proposed assignment to ensure it is not inconsistent with past assignments. The solver provides API-s for the integration of the two methods, for example by using random search first for a number of runs and then taking the utility of the best solution produced as the bound for branch and bound.

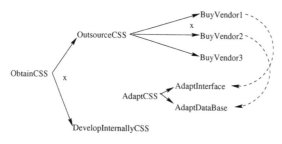

Constraints: {On(ObtainCSS), On(BuyVendor1) => On(AdaptInterface),
                    On(BuyVendor2) => On(AdaptDataBase)}
Utilities: {(BuyVendor1, 3, 0)(BuyVendor2, 4, 0) (BuyVendor3, 3, 0)
                    (AdaptInterface, -1, 0) (AdaptDataBase, -2, 0) (DevelopInternally 4, 0)}
Best Solution: {On(ObtainCSS), On(DevelopInternallyCSS), Off(BuyCSS), Off(AdaptCSS)...}

Fig. 2. Individual reasoning about the Make or Buy problem.

4 The Individual Level

Let us now introduce the example that will be used throughout rest of the paper to
illustrate the reasoning components of our architecture. The problem is that of an organization that needs to decide whether to make or buy a certain type of Customer Service
Software (CSS). Figure 2 shows the goal network, the constraints and the best solution
individual level solution, as viewed by the member of the organization who has the
leading role in solving it, agent VP-Sam. In the figure, ObtainCSS and BuyCSS are
both xchoices, while the other goals are choices.

5 The Organizational Level

Several of the goals in figure 2 can only be achieved by *groups* of agents working
together: DevelopInternallyCSS, AdaptInterface and AdaptDataBase.
The organization will need to assemble *teams* for developing the software internally, or
for adapting a vendor solution. Because of that, the utility of any behavior involving the
goals in figure 2 can only be computed after considering the cost of the teams that can
be formed for achieving the collective goals.

Determining these teams and selecting the min-cost one is the purpose of our organizational reasoning method. The key to the method is the use of *organization models*.
Figure 3 shows such an organization model, a graph representation of the agents that can
take part in achieving the collective goal DevelopInternallyCSS. The upper part
of the figure contains all agents and groups that can be involved. Individual agents (like
ProjectMgr-Cindy) and groups (like DevTeam2) are shown as nodes. Encircled
nodes without outgoing arcs (like SoftDev and QA) represent the goals achievable by
agents. Directed edges between an agent (or a group) and a goal node signify that the
agent (group) will achieve the goal with the cost attached to the edge. Directed edges
between two agents (groups) signify that the source node has *authority* to manage the
target node for achieving some goal, according to the *social contract* that agents have

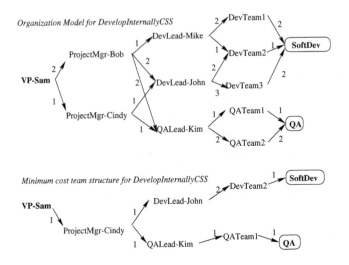

Fig. 3. Organization model with team structure.

agreed to abide by. These edges are labeled with the total cost of involving the target
agent (group). Thus, ProjectMgr-Cindy has authority to manage both DevLead-
John and QALead-Kim, at a cost of 1 each, to achieve the SoftDev and QA goals
respectively. If a target agent can achieve several goals, we allow a different cost for
each goal (this is not shown in the figure). Finally, we also require that any agent (group)
must be on a path ending in a goal node - anybody contributes to some goal - and that
an organization model is directionally acyclic.

An organization model represents the views of one agent. Each agent has a number of such models representing its beliefs about how authority is distributed, what
itself and others can do and what the costs of doing things are. We use the notation
$O = < a, A, E, G >$ to denote organization models representing agent a's viewpoint
and containing agents (or groups) A ($a \in A$), labeled edges E and goals G. Given an
organization model O, a team structure (or a coalition) T led by a and able to achieve
the set of goals G is a tree rooted in a and spanning all goals G. In other words, it is
a group of agents that a believes it can manage at the top, with specified management
and goal execution roles that ensure that a set of goals will be achieved. The cost of a
team structure T, $cost(T)$, is the sum of all costs of all edges in T.

A minimal cost team structure is a team structure that has the minimum cost in O.
Figure 3 (lower part) shows a minimal cost team structure that achieves both the Soft-
Dev (software development) and QA (quality assurance) goals for developing internally
the CSS software.

Finding the Minimal Cost Team Structure. As defined above, the problem of finding a minimal cost team structure in an organization graph is equivalent to the Steiner
tree problem studied in operations research [5]. Recently, [8] have shown that this
NP-complete problem can be very competitively solved by a stochastic satisfiability
method. They have reported very good time performance (sometimes orders of mag-

nitude better than specialized OR methods) as well as scalability to complex problems with thousands of nodes. Based on these results, we have adopted their method for use in our architecture.

Given an organization model $O =< a, A, E, G >$, the method first pre-computes the best (least cost) k paths in the graph between the leader a and each of the nodes in G. The intuition is that the tree structured best team can be composed by assembling some of these paths together. By computing a maximum of k paths between the leader and every goal, as opposed to *all* such paths, we guarantee a propositional encoding with size linear in the number of edges in O (otherwise the encoding would be quadratic). This approximation works well in practice and there exists empirical evidence about the best values for k for various sizes of E and G (see [8] for details).

Second, we create a new MAXSAT problem P_O and a new goal network for it, according to the method of [8]. For each edge between two nodes in O we create an atomic goal. The on-utility of this goal is the cost of the edge in O. For each path between the leader and a goal in G (there are at most k such paths) we create another atomic goal. After creating all k such goals, we define a constraint imposing that exactly one of these goals can be true. That is only one path between the leader and each goal in G will be allowed. Finally, for each path goal created above, we add a constraint stating that if the goal is 'on' then all goals associated with the edges will be 'on'.

The Steiner tree problem P_O thus created is solved for minimizing the sum of utilities. The result is the set of 'on' edges such that the total cost is minimal and there is a path between the leader and each organization graph goal. The elements of the tree (except for the leaves) are the agents (or groups) that need to be involved in the team. This team structure not only has minimal cost, but it also describes a number of aspects related to teamwork: what goal each agent is supposed to achieve, which agents are coordinators and whom they coordinate, the costs associated with every goal achievement or coordination relation. In general, the costs can be interpreted as containing the *pay-offs* to be paid to the team agents to obtain their commitment to the joint work.

In the end, to determine an agent's best behavior we have to combine the previous individual behavior planning with the organizational planning method presented here. Assuming S is a solution to the individual planning problem, there will be $S_c \subset S$ collective goals which are 'on'. For each goal in S_c the agent has to use its corresponding organization model to generate and solve the min cost team formation problem. Then the final utility of a behavior S is $util_f(S) = util_i(S) - \sum_{c \in S_c} cost(t_c)$.

If branch and bound is used, we can generate the best solution wrt $util_f()$, by using $util_f(S)$ as the bound, because always $util_f(S) \leq util_i(S)$. This requires that the min cost team formation problem be solved at each iteration of branch and bound. Research is needed to find more efficient ways of integrating these methods in this case.

Once the min-cost team determined, the commitments of the agents composing it are obtained through negotiation. The negotiation protocol used is shown in detail as a conversation plan in figure 4. The agent first determines its best behavior S_1 and team structures T_1 (by creating and solving the MAXSAT problems - states 1, 2). Then the agent tries to obtain the commitments of the agents involved in the T_1 teams (state 3). If an agent A's commitment can not be obtained for some goal, the agent determines the maximum pay-off increase that it can afford to offer to A (state 5). This is done by finding the best behavior S_2 and team structure T_2 in a model that does not contain A for the given goal. The difference $util_f(S_1) - util_f(S_2)$ represents how much A's pay-off can be increased before the agent has to give up including A in its plans. The pay-off increase is offered incrementally (in a 2 agents auction)(state 6). If this does not result in A's commitment, then A is eliminated from the organization models for the given goal and the process is restarted (state 7). For better efficiency, the availability of potential team members can be checked prior to team formation.

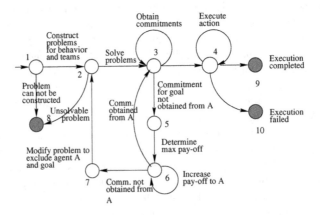

Fig. 4. Protocol integrating reasoning with interaction.

6   The Market Level

If our agent knew the utilities of buying the CSS software from the three vendors in figure 2, then the previous methods would have been enough to decide how to achieve its goals. In reality however, the utilities are not given in advance, they have to be discovered dynamically by interaction on the market. The utility of an offer for the CSS depends on how the offer satisfies a number of relevant and interdependent objectives, including e.g. the price, the overall quality, the level of support offered, the warranties, etc. We address this problem by using Multi-Attribute Utility Theory (MAUT) [10] in a constraint optimization formulation that allows the use of our MAXSAT solvers for determining the best offering and supports agent interaction by means of Pareto optimal negotiation protocols.

Encoding attributes. Let $A = a_1, a_2, ...a_n$ be a set of attributes shared by a number of agents. In our example, interesting attributes include the *price*, the overall *quality*, the level of *support* etc. The domain of an attribute a_i, D_{a_i} is an interval $[l, h]$ where l and h are integers or reals. The domain describes the range of values that the attribute can take. Each value in the domain is assumed to be measured in a unit specific to the attribute. E.g., for *price* a domain can be $D_{price} = [5, 100]$ measured in dollars. Agents

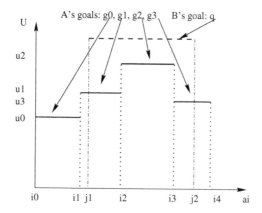

Fig. 5. Representing and encoding attributes.

interact by exchanging multi-attribute specifications formed by means of a shared set of attributes that have shared domain specifications.

An agent's utility function is approximated in the form shown in figure 5. The domain of the attribute is decomposed into a set of disjoint sub-intervals that cover the entire domain, such that on each sub-interval the utility is constant. Let $D_{a_i} = [i_0, i_1) \cup [i_1, i_2) \cup ...[i_{n-1}, i_n]$ be a decomposition of D_{a_i} into n subintervals such that $i_0 = l$, $i_n = h$ and for any $x \in [i_l, i_{l+1})$ we have $U_{a_i}(x) = u_l$ (figure 5). For each domain sub-interval $[i_l, i_{l+1}]$ we create an atomic goal $g^l_{a_i}$ which is 'on' iff the value of a_i is in the subinterval $[i_l, i_{l+1})$. As the subintervals cover the domain and are disjoint, in any situation only one of these goals can be 'on'. This is enforced by posting, for each attribute a_i, the constraint $On(xa_i)$ where $xa_i = xchoice(g^0_{a_i}, g^1_{a_i}, ...g^{n-1}_{a_i})$ (we call these attribute encoding constraints). The utility function of a_i is translated into a utility list where $u_{on}(g^l_{a_i}) = u_l$ and $u_{off}(g^l_{a_i}) = 0$.

Agents may add their own constraints about what attribute values or combinations of values are acceptable. For example, an agent may only accept *support* $\in \{4, 5\}$, where support levels range between 0 and 5. Or an agent may accept to pay more than $50 only if the quality is greater than some given limit. A proposal from another agent will not be accepted unless all these acceptability constraints are satisfied.

Using the common BDL infrastructure, we encode a MAUT problem as a behavior planning problem whose goals are all the goals generated for all attributes of interest, whose constraints are all the attribute encoding constraints plus all the acceptability constraints and whose utility list is obtained by merging the utility lists of each encoded attribute. A solution of a MAUT problem is an on-off assignment to the goals of the problem that satisfies all constraints. The optimal solution is the solution that has maximum utility.

Let S be a solution to agent A's MAUT problem and a_i an attribute of the problem. Because of the attribute encoding constraint, one and only one of the goals associated with the subintervals of the attribute will be 'on' in S. The subinterval associated with

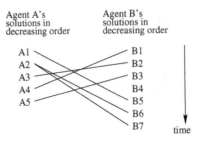

Agent A's
solutions in
decreasing order

Agent B's
solutions in
decreasing order

Connections define intersecting pairs of solutions of A and B.
(A3, B2) is the Pareto optimum.

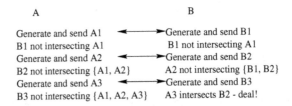

A   B

Generate and send A1   ◄────────►Generate and send B1
B1 not intersecting A1   B1 not intersecting A1
Generate and send A2   ◄────────►Generate and send B2
B2 not intersecting {A1, A2}   A2 not intersecting {B1, B2}
Generate and send A3   ◄────────►Generate and send B3
B3 not intersecting {A1, A2, A3}   A3 intersects B2 - deal!

Fig. 6. The negotiation process.

this goal defines the acceptable set of values for the attribute in the given solution in the sense that any value in the set is equally acceptable to the agent. Let now S_A and S_B be solutions to A's, respectively B's MAUT problem. The two solutions intersect iff for each attribute a_i the acceptable sets of values for the two agents have a non-empty intersection. In figure 5 $[i_3, j_2]$ is the intersection of A's goal g^3 and B's goal q for the represented attribute. If an intersection exists for each attribute, then the two solutions intersect. The existence of intersecting solutions represents a possible agreement between the agents, because each solution contains non-empty ranges of values for each attribute which are acceptable to each agent.

The Negotiation Process. Assume we have two negotiating agents A and B. For each agent, an acceptable solution specifies, for each attribute in part, an interval of acceptable values that the attribute can take. The branch and bound solver allows an agent to generate its solutions in decreasing order of utility. The first (best) solution is obtained by running the solver on the original constraints. The next best solution is obtained by logically negating the previous best solution, adding it as a constraint and solving the resulting more constrained problem. This allows each agent to generate all its acceptable solutions in decreasing order of utility. Figure 6 shows an interaction protocol allowing two agents to determine the best deal they can achieve given their valuations and acceptability constraints. Each agent generates its solutions in decreasing order of utility, and sends each solution to the other agent. If any agent discovers an intersection between the current solution received from the other agent and one of its own past solutions, then this is the Pareto optimal deal (no other pair of solutions can be better for both agents).

In figure 7, this negotiation protocol is shown in more detail as a conversation plan. Each agent generates its current best solution for as long as it has solutions to generate (state 1). Each solution is saved locally. The solution is also sent to the other agent (state 2). Then the process waits for a message from the interlocutor (state 3). If the message is an acceptance (state 6), it signals that the sent solution is consistent (has a non-empty intersection) with one of the interlocutor's past solutions, making it a mutually acceptable deal, which terminates the negotiation successfully. If the received message is "NoMoreSolutions", the other agent has run out of solutions to generate. If the same is true for this agent as well, then the negotiation ends unsuccessfully. Otherwise the agent that still has solutions will continue to generate them. Finally, if the message contains a proposed solution from the interlocutor, this solution is checked for compatibility (intersection) with any of the past solutions generated by this agent (state 4). If an intersection is found (state 5), it represents a mutually acceptable deal, which terminates the negotiation successfully. Otherwise the top loop is resumed. The process ends when either a deal acceptable to both parties is found or when both agents have run out of solutions.

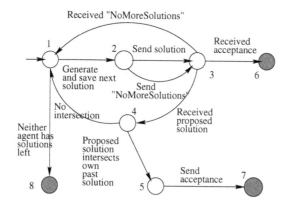

Fig. 7. Negotiation protocol as a conversation plan.

Going back to the situation in figure 2, we see that by representing the attributes of interest and the associated utility functions, our agent (the buyer) can negotiate with each of the three vendors the best deal for the CSS system. The utility of each deal can then be used as the utility of the BuyVendor1..3 goals. Knowing these, the agent can use the integrated individual and organizational reasoning method to discover its best course of action in the given situation.

7   Conclusions

We believe that multi-agent applications require new, higher level services from the infrastructures they will be built on. We have identified several classes of such services, including complex interaction, decision making for individual utility maximization, team formation in organizations and multi-attribute negotiation. For each of these services, we have shown how generic components can be devised and packaged into an agent infrastructure. From these components, the conversational system has been used in the largest number of applications, from puzzles to supply chain simulation [3], auctions and service provisioning in telecommunications [1]. Our experience to date shows that the conversational model of interaction is natural and expressive and can reduce the development time for multi agent applications, especially when supported by appropriate programming tools. Some of our users have been persons without a computer background who were still able to quickly build complex multi-agent applications in their domain of interest.

The other components are newer and their evaluation in applications is underway. Besides being generic elements of the infrastructure, these components also extend the current research on teamwork, coalition formation and negotiation. Current teamwork research is illustrated by the logical models of [11] and the practical architectures developed by [17] and [7]. These models and systems address the issue of *teamwork execution*, for example stipulating when and how an agent should quit the team. Our organizational reasoning model complements this work by addressing the *team design* problem as part of a single optimization problem whose solution specifies the individual goals to adopt, the plans to execute and the collaborations to pursue in order to maximize the agent's utility.

With respect to coalition formation, this generally includes three activities [14]. Coalition generation is the partitioning of the set of agents into sets (coalitions), usually disjoint and exhaustive. Solving the coalition problem is done by joining together the work and resources of member agents. Finally, the value generated by the activity of the coalition has to be divided among its members. [13] presents an anytime algorithm for coalition generation with worst case performance guarantees. This solution produces flat (unstructured) coalitions which specify neither what work will be done by each agent nor what pay-offs will they receive. Our Steiner tree based solution produces *structured coalitions* where the roles and goals of every agent are specified and the pay-offs to be received are determined. In [9] a coalition formation algorithm is presented which uses a two-agent auction method to determine the pay-off division and to introduce a limited structure inside a coalition (with one agent being the manager of the coalition and the others receiving an agreed pay-off).

Finally, the markel level negotiation component provides a new tool, integrating MAUT, constraint satisfaction and conversational interactions, that leads to automating multi-objective negotiation. MAUT has previously been used in negotiation by [16] and [4] has suggested that a combination of MAUT and constraint satisfaction could be used in multi-objective e-commerce negotiation. Our work is the first concrete technical solution we have seen to using MAUT and constraint satisfaction in a practical (we believe) negotiation system.

The next step on the application side is the integration of all levels into a significant application. We are developing a supply chain system where market level interaction determines what to buy from which suppliers, team formation determines the teams of contractors to be involved in manufacturing an order and individual level planning decides on the best course of action for each team member. To integrate an application on this scale, we are extending our infrastructure in a number of necessary directions. First, at the market level we are generalizing the one-to-one negotiation method presented to a many-to-many method able to support continuous double auctions. Second, behavioral specifications are being extended with temporal and resource constraints by including a scheduler and a temporal execution system, turning BDL into a more complete agent behavior planning and execution infrastructure.

References

[1] Barbuceanu, M. Negotiating Service Provisioning. In *Multi-Agent Systems Engineering*, Francisco J. Garijo and Magnus Boman (eds), Lecture Notes in Artificial Intelligence 1647, Springer Verlag (Proceedings of MAAMAW'99), Valencia, Spain, July 1999, 150-162.

[2] Barbuceanu, M. and Fox, M. S. 1997. Integrating Communicative Action, Conversations and Decision Theory to Coordinate Agents. *Proceedings of Automomous Agents'97*, 47-58, Marina Del Rey, February 1997.

[3] Barbuceanu, M., R. Teigen, and M. S. Fox. Agent Based Design And Simulation of Supply Chain Systems. *Proceedings of WETICE-97*, IEEE Computer Press, Cambridge, MA, pp 36-43.

[4] Gutman, R., Moukas,A., and Maes, P. Agent Mediated Electronic Commerce: A Survey. *Knowledge Engineering Review*, June 1998.

[5] Hwang, F.K, Richards, D.S. and Winter, P. The Steiner Tree Problem. North-Holland (Elsevier Science Publications), Amsterdam 1992.

[6] Jennings, N.R. Towards a Cooperation Knowledge Level for Collaborative Problem Solving. In Proceedings 10-th European Conference on AI, Vienna, Austria, pp 224-228, 1992.

[7] Jennings, N. R. Controlling Cooperative Problem Solving in Industrial Multi-Agent Systems Using Joint Intentions. Artificial Intelligence, 75 (2) pp 195-240, 1995.

[8] Jiang, Y., Kautz, H. and Selman, B. Solving Problems with Hard and Soft Constraints Using a Stochastic Algorithm for MAXSAT. *First International Joint Workshop on Artificial Intelligence and Operations Research*, Timberline, Oregon, 1995.

[9] Ketchpel, S. Forming Coalitions in the Face of Uncertain Rewards. *Proc. of AAAI-94* vol1, 414-419, Seattle, WA, July 1994.

[10] Keeney,R. and Raiffa, H. Decisions with Multiple Objectives: Preferences and Value Tradeoffs. *John Willey & Sons*, 1976.

[11] Levesque, H., Coehn, P., Nunes, J. On acting together. *Proc. of AAAI-90*, Boston. MA, 1990, 94-99.

[12] Pearl, J. Probabilistic Reasoning in Intelligent Systems, *Morgan Kaufmann*, 1988.

[13] Sandholm, T.V., Larson, K., Andersson, M., Shehory, O., and Tohme, F. Anytime Coalition Structure Generation with Worst Case Guarantees. *Proc. of AAAI-98*, Madison, WI, July 1998, 46-53.

[14] Sandholm, T. V. and Lesser, V.R. Coalitions among computationally bound agents. *Artificial Intelligence* 94, 1997, 99-137.

[15] Selman, B., H.J. Levesque and D. Mitchell. 1992. A new method for solving hard satisfiability problems. *Proceedings of AAAI-92* San Jose, CA, pp. 440446.

[16] Sycara, K. The PERSUADER. In *The Encyclopedia of Artificial Intelligence*, D. Shapiro (ed), JohnWilley & Sons, January 1992.

[17] Tambe, M. Towards flexible teamwork. *Journal of Artificial Intelligence Research* 7, 1997, 83-124.

An Enabling Environment for Engineering Cooperative Agents

Soe-Tsyr Yuan

Information Management Department, Fu-Jen University
Taipei, Taiwan, R.O.C.
E-mail: yuans@tpts1.seed.net.tw

Abstract: This paper presents a tool that enables the bottom-up design of multi-agent systems. The tool has two parts. The first part is a wrapper that wraps each agent so that it exempts the designers from the careful detailed deployment of the inter-relationships between cooperation knowledge and task knowledge inside the agent. This wrapper should be independent of the functions of agents. The second part is an environment that can support the wrapper to automate the cooperation process in behalf of agents.

1. Introduction

It has been predicted that agents will be pervasive in every market by the year 2000 [1]. However, with the passing of the 20th century, there is still some way to go before the multi-agent technology hits its success of critical mass. Therefore, it is time to broaden the concepts and seek infrastructures in the search for successful factors in reaching the critical mass of the multi-agent technology. Accordingly, one successful factor, the bottom-up design of multi-agent systems, should be addressed.

The bottom-up design aims to make it possible that given agents as function entities, agents are reassembled into multi-agent systems and agents can be easily reused as needed, resulting in a great amount of reduced effort in the development of multi-agent systems. However, in the traditional bottom-up design of multi-agent systems, various *inter-relationships between cooperation knowledge and task knowledge* has to be customizedly deployed for each agent and thus making it difficult for agents to be reused. For example, in the traditional multi-agent system design [2, 3, 4, 5, 6], with the designated relations between agents, cooperation knowledge has to be mingled with task knowledge within agents, where the mingling work is not that simple. The necessary steps of their designs include the following:

- The initial objective planning of the whole multi-agent system, the necessary agents and their functions, the necessary relations between the agents, and the necessary cooperation knowledge within each agent.
- The implementation of agents, each of which requires the careful deployment of inter-relationships between the task knowledge (agent's functions) and the required cooperation knowledge, which could be stored in a library and duplicated inside each agent as in [6].

T. Wagner and O.F. Rana (Eds.): Infrastructure for Agents, LNAI 1887, pp. 157–165, 2001.

The drawbacks of these multi-agent system designs are two-fold:

- In the worst case, a multi-agent system with n agents, each of which has designated relations with the rest of $n-1$ agents, multi-agent system developers have to expend $O(n^2)$ efforts in the customized deployment of the inter-relationships between the task knowledge and the cooperation knowledge of the n agents.

- Agents in one multi-agent system can not be reused by another multi-agent system because the contents of an agent body is not pure task knowledge anymore.

A fully bottom-up design aims to make it possible that, given agents as function entities, agents are assembled into multi-agent systems and can be easily reused as needed, resulting in a great amount of reduced effort in the development of multi-agent systems.

However, what do we need to fully support the bottom-up design? The key is a wrapper that wraps each agent so that it exempts the designers from the careful detailed deployment of cooperation knowledge inside the agent. Of course, this wrapper should be independent of the functions of agents. We name this wrapper the **Unified Agent Cooperation Interface (Interface)***. On the other hand, this interface needs an environment that can support the interfaces to automate the cooperation process in behalf of the agents. We name this environment an* **Agent Reuse Master (ARM)***.* This paper aims to present a novel building environment using these two parts for the bottom-up design of multi-agent systems.

This paper is organized as follows: Sections 2, 3 present a tool to the bottom-up design of multi-agent systems, providing descriptions for each part of the tool – the Agent Reuse Master and the Unified Agent Cooperation Interface. The conclusion is then made in Section 4.

2. The Environment - ARM

In this section we describe how the ARM supports the interfaces to automate the cooperation process on behalf of the agents. We describe the elements of the environment for understanding the way ARM supports the interfaces.

2.1 The Elements of the ARM

Fig. 1 shows the elements of the ARM and the interactions between the ARM and the interfaces. Below are the descriptions of the three elements:

- Agent Name Sever: It provides the mapping between the names of agents and their Internet address so that agents are able to address each other by name only.

- Relationship Panel: The panel records the functions of agents and their inter-relationships represented by the name of cooperation protocols involved. Subsequently, agents do not need to have these relationships in mind and thus are able to be independent of the cooperation protocol involved.

- Protocol Mapping Facilitator: In order to automate the cooperation with each other, the cooperation knowledge the Unified Agent Cooperation Interface needs on behalf of the agents is obtained from the Protocol Mapping Facilitator. The Protocol Mapping Facilitator is designed as a collection of mapping tables. An example of the mapping table for the protocol of CNP with counter proposal is shown in Table 1. In Table 1, Field *Client/Server* represents the role of the agent where 'Client' is for agents that initiate request conversations and 'Server' is for agents that follow the conversation, Field *Protocol* is the inter-relationship between the initiator agent and the counter-part agent, Field *Current State* is the initial state of the initiator agent, Field *Performative Received* is the incoming message received by the initiator agent, Field *Reaction* is the decision made by the initiator agent in correspondence to the incoming message received, Field *Performative* is the appropriate feedback, and Field *Next State* is the new reached state, reflective of the feedback of the initiator agent.

Without loss of generality, the reactions of agents are categorized into three classes, Accept, Reject, and Counter Propose regardless of the protocols involved. As a result, the cooperation knowledge the Interface requires at different stages of cooperation can be acquired by the acknowledgement of the protocol involved through the Panel, the current state of agent through the Interface, the incoming message, and the final reaction determined by the task knowledge of agents.

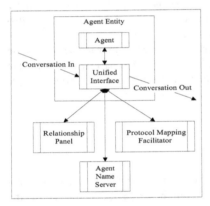

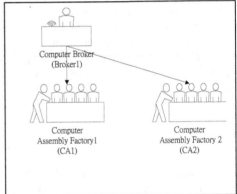

Fig. 1. Various factors that affect next-generation multiagent-based software.

Fig. 2. A Web-based computer broker example.

For the example of Web-based computer broker shown in Fig. 2, Fig. 3 depicts the interactions between ARM and the Unified Interface of agents. From the Relation Panel, the Interface of the agent Broker, whose role is *Client*, in the *Current State* of Start, knows the suitable service-provider agents are Agent CA1 and Agent CA2 and sends a request (TaskAnnouncement) to the Agent CA1 and the Agent CA2. The Interfaces of these two agents acquire the proper acts (either Bid, Reject, or Counter) in reply to the request sent by the agent Broker through the help of the Protocol Mapping Facilitator.

Client Or Server	Protocol	Current State	Performative Received	Reaction	Performative	Next State
Client	CNP-C	announced	Counter	yes	Award	awarded
Client	CNP-C	announced	Counter	no	Reject	rejected
Client	CNP-C	announced	Counter	counter	Counter	countered
Client	CNP-C	countered	Counter	yes	Award	awarded
Client	CNP-C	countered	Counter	no	Reject	rejected
Client	CNP-C	countered	Counter	counter	Counter	countered
Client	CNP-C	announced	Reject			received reject
Client	CNP-C	countered	Reject			received reject
Client	CNP-C	start			TaskAnnounce	announced
Client	CNP-C	announced	Bid	yes	Award	awarded
Client	CNP-C	announced	Bid	no	Reject	rejected
Client	CNP-C	countered	Bid	yes	Award	awarded
Client	CNP-C	countered	Bid	no	Reject	rejected
Client	CNP-C	announced	Bid	counter	Award	awarded
Client	CNP-C	countered	Bid	counter	Award	awarded
Server	CNP-C	countered	Reject			received reject
Server	CNP-C	start	TaskAnnounce	yes	Bid	bidden
Server	CNP-C	start	TaskAnnounce	no	Reject	rejected
Server	CNP-C	start	TaskAnnounce	counter	Counter	countered
Server	CNP-C	countered	Counter	yes	Bid	bidden
Server	CNP-C	countered	Counter	no	Reject	rejected
Server	CNP-C	countered	Counter	counter	Counter	countered
Server	CNP-C	bidden	Award			received award
Server	CNP-C	bidden	Reject			received reject

Table 1. The mapping table for the CNP Protocol in the Protocol Mapping Facilitator.

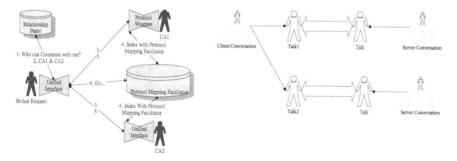

Fig 3. The picture of the interactions between ARM and the Unified Interface of agents.

Fig. 4. The relationships between Conversation Session and Talk Session.

3. The Unified Cooperation Interface

The Unified Cooperation Interface is a wrapper of agents that enables each wrapped agent communication and cooperation. In other words, the designers are exempted from the communication-enabling know-how and the careful customized deployment of the inter-relationships between agent's task knowledge and various cooperation knowledge inside the agents regardless of the cooperation protocols involved in different multi-agent systems. In this section, we only describe how the cooperation capability is accomplished by the Interface, via introducing the internal process of the Interface in the following subsections. As for communication-enabling know-how, the

Interface is equipped with the KQML package we've implemented, WinKQML, and please see [7] for details.

*Without loss of generalization, the essence of cooperation between agents can be either service requesting or service supplying. Therefore, the detailed deployment of inter-relationships between task knowledge and various cooperation knowledge for agents (this may involve a succession of interactions with the other multiple agents for a single requested service) can be reduced down to simply **voicing out** the service the agent requests or the feedback of the service the agent supplies.*

This section gives the description of the internal process of the Unified Cooperation Interface and its implementation. First, the description of the process of the Interface and its rationale are given below, then the descriptions of the data structure that implements such processing follows, and in summary a simple scenario demonstrates this internal process.

3.1 The Process of the Unified Cooperation Interface

The Interface aims to exempt the designers from the careful detailed deployment of the inter-relationships between the task knowledge and the cooperation knowledge within a delegating agent regardless of the functions of the agent. As we know, the purpose of the deployment of such inter-relationships essentially is two-fold:

- Requesting service that is in the form of the type of information to be requested or the commitments to be requested from a variety of potential agents, each of which has a cooperation relation to the delegating agent.
- Providing service that is in the form of the information delivered or commitments granted to a variety of agents, each of which has a cooperation relation to the delegating agent.

Therefore, the functions of the Interface should comprise of the automatic processing of requesting service and providing service from/to multiple agents in order to exempt the designers from the detailed deployment of inter-relationship between task knowledge and cooperation knowledge. Below shows the internal process of the Interface that can automate the handling of service request and service provision:

The Processing of the Interface:
Case 1: Service-Request Handling (Out-Going Message)

(1) Initialize the conversation environment by inquiring the Relation Panel about the agents that provide the service and the relationships between these potential agents and the delegating agent.

(2) Create a *Conversation Session* that covers the interactions between the delegating agent and the potential agents.

(3) For the *Conversation Session*, create as many *Talk Sessions* as required, each of which handles only the interactions between the delegating agent and a potential agent as shown in the left-hand side of Fig. 4.

(4) A *Talk Session* acquires the appropriate protocol verb with respect to the protocol involved with a potential agent through the help of the Protocol Mapping Facilitator, composes the complete message, and then sends it out.

Case 2: Service-Feedback Handling (In-Coming Message)

(1) Initialize the conversation environment by inquiring the Relation Panel about the delegating agent and the service-requesting agent.

(2) Create a *Conversation Session* that covers the interactions between the delegating agent and the service-requesting agent.

(3) In the Conversation Session, create one *Talk Session* that handles the interactions between the delegating agent and the service-requesting agent as shown in one branch of the right-hand side of Fig. 4.

(4) The *Talk Session* separates the in-coming message into two parts: the communication part that specifies the sender, receiver, and so on; the content part that encompasses the feedback the delegating agent needs.

The *Talk Session* activates an event at the delegating agent that processes the content and determines the response (Accept, Reject, or Counter Propose), acquires the appropriate protocol verb with the help of the Protocol Mapping Facilitator, composes the complete message, and then sends it out.

The above description demonstrates the basic flow of process inside the Interface. In summary,

• Both service request and service provision can take on the form of the Conversation establishment of the macro level and the Talk establishment of the micro level. Both levels of processes account for the machinery behind the automation of the handling of service request and service provision.

• The Conversation level acquires the information of cooperative agent counterparts from the Relation Panel of the ARM environment.

• The Talk level acquires the information of how to react from the Protocol Mapping Facilitator of the ARM environment.

• The Talk level packages and transmits the exchanged message for the delegating agent.

Another point that needs to be addressed is that each Conversation Session can be extended to a space of hierarchical conversations, which will be explained in Section 3.2.

3.2. The Implementation

Following the above explanation of the internal process of the Interface, we shall now provide brief descriptions of the data structure that implements such processing: (Currently, the Interface is implemented with ActiveX. Please refer [8] for details.)

Data Structure:

For simplicity, we describe the data structure that is necessary for the CNP protocol, and Fig. 5(a) shows this structure. There are a few underlying assumptions:

• Each agent offers a set of services, each of which (*Service*) can be represented by a set of internal resources (*Resource*) inside the agent as shown in Fig. 5(b). For example, the major service of a computer-assembly factory is 'Sell Computer', with the resources of this service comprising of the CPU, Monitor, *etc.*

• While an agent offers services or requests services to/from other agents, the Interface should bookkeep all the information as shown in Fig. 5(c). *ServiceOut* is a record of service provision offered by the agent, which records the internal resources used (ResourceUsed) for this service and the records of service request (*ServiceIn*) made by the agent when the internal resources are not enough.

The following are descriptions of the data structure employing the Web-based computer broker example in Fig. 2:

- *Service*: a service provided by an agent, for instance a Computer Assembly Factory, in which *ServiceName*, *'Sell Computer'*, represents its name, *Countable* indicates if the service can be quantified (for example, computers are countable), *ServiceCount* represents the available number of computers, and *BidCount* is the number of computers currently under negotiation.

- *Resource*: an internal resource to be used by an agent, for instance a Computer Assembly Factory, in which *ResourceName*, 'CPU', represents one such resource to be used by the factory, *Countable* indicates if the resource can be quantified (for example, CPU are countable), *ResourceCount* as the available number of CPUs, and *BidCount* is the number of CPUs involved in the undergoing negotiation.

- *ResourceForService*: the amount (*CountNeeded*) of a resource (*ResourceName*) required for an unit of service (*ServiceName*), for instance, a unit of service 'Sell Computer', i.e., a computer, requires one unit of resource Monitor.

- *ServiceOut*: a record of a service provision, in which *ServiceOutID* and *ServiceName* represent the identification number and the name of this service provision, *Countable* indicates if the service can be quantified, *ServiceCount* refers to the units of service to be consumed by a service provision, *TaskFinished* indicates if the service provision is accomplished, *ClientName* is the name of the agent which is requesting the service, and *Ontology, Language, Content* refer to the underlying ontology and language used in expressing the communicated content.

- *ResourceUsed*: the amount (*CountUsed*) of a resource (*ResourceName*) used for a service provision (*ServiceOutID*).

- *ServiceIn*: a record about a service request, in which *ServiceInID* is the identification number of this service request, *ServiceOutID* and *ServiceName* indicates the identification number and the service name of a service which initiates this service request, *ServerName* is the name of the agent which provides the requested service, *ServiceCount* is the amount of service under request, *TaskFinished* indicates if the service request is accomplished, and *Ontology, Language, Content* refer to the underlying ontology and language used in expressing the communicated content.

A Scenario:

With the data structure and the process described above, we are able to show a scenario about how the Interface enables the automatic processing of requesting service and providing service as shown in Fig. 6, in which the Server Talk 1-1 can start another session of conversation. For the details of the hierarchical approach, please refer [8]:

- The client Broker attempts to request for 100 computers.

- The Interface of the Broker creates a *Client Conversation Session* for handling all of the subsequent communication and cooperation processes.

- The *Client Conversation1 Session* inquires the Relationship Panel about the possible cooperation partners, and obtains two agents, CA1 and CA2, which provide the service of 'Sell Computer'.

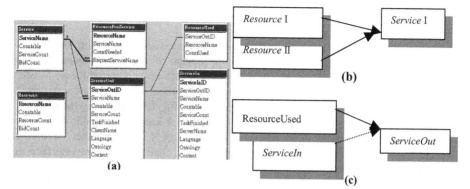

Fig. 5. The data structure and the conceptual structures used by the Interface for the CNP protocol, in which (a) is the data structure and (b) & (c) are the conceptual structures.

- The *Client Conversation1* generates two *Client Talk Sessions, Client Talk 1-1 and Client Talk 1-2,* each of which is responsible for a cooperation process between the Broker and CA1/CA2.

- When receiving this service request, the Interface of CA1/CA2 creates a *Server Conversation1 Session/Server Conversation2 Session,* which in turn generates *a Server Talk1-1/Server Talk 1-2.*

- Suppose CA1 only has 80 assembled computers, 10 Monitors, 10 CPUs, *etc.* in stock, This would be represented by data captured inside the Interface as follows: *ServiceCount* of *Service* equals 80, both *ResourceCount* of *Resource* CPU and *Resource* Monitor equal 90, and both *CountNeeded* of *ResourceForService* for CPU and Monitor are 1. In an attempt to serve the request of 100 computers, the Interface of CA1 creates a Client Conversation out of *Server Talk1-1,* S*ub Client Conversation1-1 Session,* which subsequently makes requests from upstream partners for the supply of extra CPUs, Monitors, *etc.* This would subsequently be represented by data captured inside the Interface as follows: *ServiceCount* of *ServieOut* equals 100, both *CountUsed* of *ResourceUsed* for resource CPU and resource Monitor are 90, and both *ServiceCount* of *ServiceIn* from the CPU supplier and the Monitor supplier are 10.

- The Interfaces of the agents continues their cooperation process till the end.

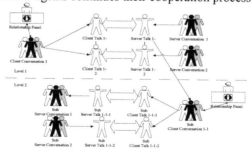

Fig. 6. A picture view of hierarchical Conversation Sessions.

4. Conclusion

The main contribution of this paper is to present an enabling tool for engineering cooperative agents economically, the bottom-up design of multi-agent systems. This tool comprises of a Unified Agent Cooperation Interface and an Agent Reuse Master supporting environment. The Unified Agent Cooperation Interface can wrap each agent so that it exempts the designers from the careful detailed deployment of the inter-relations between cooperation knowledge and task knowledge inside the agent. This Interface is independent of the functions of agents. On the other hand, the Interface needs the Agent Reuse Master environment that supports the Interface to automate the cooperation process on behalf of the agents. In summary, our tool aims to raises agent reusability, simple human-computer interaction, and to improve the multi-agent enabling environment. Currently we are building a business-business open e-marketplace for matching supplies and demands based with the tool. In this open e-marketplace, any business can engage or terminate its participation dynamically. We believe there will be more positive views about the tool especially for E-Commerce applications or systems in the near future.

Reference

1. P.C. Janca: Pragmatic application of information agents. BIS Strategic Report (1995)
2. Belakhdar and J. Ayel: COOPLAS - Cooperation Protocols Specification Language. First International Workshop on Decentralized Intelligent and Multi-Agent Systems (1995)
3. Jeffrey M. Bradshaw: KaoS - an Open Agent Architecture – Supporting Reuse, Interoperability, and Extensibility.   Knowledge Acquisition Workshop (1996)
4. K. Kuwabara, T. Ishida, and N. Osata, AgentTalk: Describing Multi-agent Coordination Protocols with Inheritance. Proceedings of Tools for Artificial Intelligence (1995)
5. Omar Belakhdar: Using Ontology-Sharing to Designing Automated Cooperation in Protocol-Driven Multi-Agent Systems. Proceedings of the Second International Conference on the Practical Application of Intelligent and Multi-Agent Technology (1997)
6. M. Barbuceanu and M. S. Fox: COOL: A Language for describing coordination in multi-agent systems. In Lesser, V., ed., Proceedings of the first International Conference on Multi-Agent Systems, 17-25. San Francisco, CA: MIT Press (1995)
7. AI Lab of Fu-Jen: WinKQML ActiveX Control. Information Management Department, Fu-Jen University, Taipei, Taiwan (1997)
8. Soe-Tsyr Yuan and Zeng-Lung Wu: Automatic Agent Cooperation Wrapper. Tech. Report, Information Management Department, Fu-Jen University (1999)

Agent Mobility and Reification of Computational State: An Experiment in Migration

Werner Van Belle, Theo D'Hondt

Vrije Universiteit Brussel (VUB), Departement Informatica (DINF), Programming
Technology Lab (PROG), Pleinlaan 2, B1050 Belgium
{werner.van.belle@vub.ac.be, tjdhondt@vub.ac.be}

Abstract. This paper describes an experiment with mobility in multi-agent
systems. The setting is a virtual machine that supports reification of the
computational state of a running process. The objective is to investigate how
this feature facilitates telescripting and to speculate on how languages like Java
should evolve to include the resulting notion of strong migration

1   Introduction: Mobile Agent Systems

An agent is a persistent and autonomous software component. It can be thought of as
a process executed by some virtual machine but it is mainly intended to provide a
particular service. Viewed as processes, agents run concurrently on one or more
machines and have their own data space and computational state.

We talk about multi agents if two or more agents, represented by processes, are able
to communicate with each other. Depending on the agent system this communication
can be performed by means of the available technology (*Remote Procedure Call,
Remote Method Invocation*, etc.). In our particular setup, we will require our
communication mechanism to support asynchronous remote message passing.

A mobile agent is an agent which is able to move between different machines, or in a
more abstract sense, between *locations*. We will discuss migration in the following
section.

A mobile multi agent system is a software artefact specified in   a language that
provides sufficient expressiveness and flexibility to allow the construction of multiple
interacting mobile agents. This includes routing of messages between agent systems
and providing an interconnection with other systems. The agent system has to take
care of migration of agents, serialization of messages and scheduling of processes.
This should, of course, have a minimum of direct impact on the agents themselves.
This definition of mobile multi agents differs from others which view an agent as an
intelligent entity that interacts with some user on a creative basis: it should learn
about its environment and adapt to it as needed. In this paper we are more interested
in the architectural support, so we will focus on the design and implementation of
mobile multi agent systems. Particular attention is paid to the migration aspect.

T. Wagner and O.F. Rana (Eds.): Infrastructure for Agents, LNAI 1887, pp. 166–173, 2001.
© Springer-Verlag Berlin Heidelberg 2001

2   Migration

In this paper, migration denotes the act of transferring a running agent to another location. After migration, the agent should continue and proceed seamlessly with what it was performing before its move. In order to obtain this result, three actions should be undertaken to prepare, guide and complete the actual migration. First we have to encapsulate the agent's complete state; next, we need to transfer this capsule and finally, we need to restore and re-activate the agent in its new environment. With the wide availability of standard communication networks we can safely say that transfer itself is no longer a problem. The challenging aspect in migration is the wrapping and unwrapping of the agent in order to restore it to its full powers.

An encapsulated agent should not carry the complete agent system in its wrapping. We therefore need to make an inventory of those features that determine the working of an agent. Conceptually, an agent consists of

- A data section which contains the environment needed by the agent;
- A (shared) code section which describes the behavior of the agent
- One or more runtime structures which describe the computational state of the processes
- Connections to resources and to the underlying agent system

Today, almost no mobile multi agent system (except 0 and 0), encapsulates and transfers the computational state of the agent's process. Typically, the agent program is duplicated on the receiving location and after migration the agent is reinitialized from data saved before the move. This is because it is a major challenge to the builder of a virtual machine to provide a mechanism for capturing the computational state, as will be shown later.

This difficulty led to two kinds of migration models.

The first kind, called *weak migration* (aka as the *looping model)* 0, transfers all of the agent's constituent parts except for the computational state. This means that the only way to encapsulate an agent correctly is to ensure that the computational state is empty. Consequently, the agent has to stop voluntarily prior to migration and afterwards start up again. As such this model *loops* between sequences of computation that start up and stop completely.
   In our view this approach to migration is flawed. First of all, the looping model has a nefarious impact on how the agent's program is engineered, making the program code difficult to manage. Migration therefore becomes too difficult to use and as such will be avoided unless absolutely needed. Second, the agent itself is sole master of the migration process; it is impossible for some external agency to capture the agent's full state and direct migration from the outside. This prohibits the use of manager agents which send out agents to other machines as needed.

The second model of migration is called *strong migration* 0, also called *telescripting*. When an agent systems supports telescripting it allows the agent to move at all times to other locations, without the need of restarting the entire computation. As can be inferred, in this model the agent's computational state is transferred correctly.

3   Scripting an Agent

Before starting out on the fundamentals of building a virtual machine that supports reification of computation, we shall describe the experimental setting of this report.

In our approach we have started from an existing virtual machine called Pico [7] which features open semantics. Pico is accessible via an extremely simple language yet its expressiveness is very high, comparable to e.g. Scheme. Pico semantics are defined by a set of nine evaluation functions that are supported by a storage model and a computational model. The storage model features full storage management and reclamation; the computational model is based on a pushdown automaton that manages expressions and continuations on a double stack. Continuations, inspired by *continuation passing style* 0, are thunks that are sequenced in order to support computation. Pico requires less than twenty continuations to implement the complete semantics of the language.

In order to support our experiment, Pico semantics were extended to support objects and multi threading. The result, called *Borg* is a prototype-based language. Objects can specified and cloned in a very simple but effective way. In the transcript below makecircle denotes a mixin method which extends the basic point to become a circle:

```
createpoint(x,y)::
  { getx()::  x;
    gety()::  y;
    setx(nx)::  x:=nx;
    sety(ny)::  y:=ny;
    makecircle(r)::
              { setr(nr)::  r:=nr;
                getr()::  r;
                clone()  };
    clone()  }            -> <closure createpoint>
a:createpoint(1,2)        -> <dictionary>
b:a.makecircle(900)       -> <dictionary>
b.getx()                  -> 1
b.setx(8)                 -> 8
b.getx()                  -> 8
a.getx()                  -> 1
```

Another abstraction layer we needed to support our experiment is routing of messages and naming of agents. The problem with existing distributed systems is that whenever an object changes its place (insofar as possible) its name changes to reflect its new position. *Borg* has an original naming service built into it so that we have a location transparent naming scheme and a hierarchical interconnection network. 0

4   Uniform Message Sending

On top of this all we have installed a serializer to store and retrieve subgraphs of the data store. The serializer differentiates between two kinds of serialization. The first concerns expressions handled as messages sent to another location. The second concerns expressions handled as complete agents which should be sent to a remote host.

When a message is serialized, we traverse the data graph and store everything that we encounter on a stream. This process stops at leaves and at dictionaries which will be serialized as references to remote dictionaries. In this way, an agent can send a local dictionary to another agent without having to send the entire dictionary content to the communication partner.

Uniform Message Sending: We use this messages serializer as a means for sending messages to other agents in the same way we would send a message to an object. There is only one difference: the caller will not receive a return value and the execution will continue immediately. The expressions given as arguments to a remote function will be serialized and deserialized automaticaly. If there are too many expressions for an agent to evaluate, the agent will store them in a queue and evaluate them one by one.

Below is an example of two *Borg* programs that communicate with each other. The first program is the receiving agent which will do a callback to the second agent. After having installed a callback procedure the second agent calls the first one.

To all intents and purposes we have introduced asysnchronous message passing, very similar to an actor system [8].

```
Agent Tecra/ses1
calculate(…,callback)::
   {  <some calculation>;
      callback.Answeris(…)  }

Agent Tecra/ses2
Answeris(result)::
   display("The answer is: " + result);
agent:agent("Tecra/ses1");
agent.calculate(…,agentself()) }
```

We can see that this way of working has a number of advantages over standard distributed systems:

- We don't have to generate and compile stubs beforehand. (in comparison to Java and CORBA this is definitely a strong advantage, particularly when we transfer code to other locations)
- The code is interpreted which guarantees small and powerful pieces of code (compiled code is much larger than interpreted code)

- We don't have to take location of an agent into account, since an agent's name doesn't change after migration.
- Sending messages between agents is similar to sending messages between objects, with automatic serialization of messages.

5   Virtual Machine

A standard virtual machine for a simple language such as *Borg* consists of:

- A language processor which, given a program text, generates an instance of some abstract grammar (called expression). In *Borg* for example, the program

```
setr(nr):: r:=nr
```

will be translated into the following expression:

[DEF [APL setr [TAB [REF nr]]][ASS r [REF nr]]]

Expressions can be externally stored as a sophisticated kind of *bytecode* or they can be kept as executable code in some datastructure. *Borg* is very close to for instance *Scheme*, in that language and execution model practically coincide.
- A dictionary (or symboltable) to store identifiers and their values. The values are either inline, or are references to a subset of possible expressions (actually, values are expressions that have identity for the evaluation function). A *Borg* dictionary is effectively a stack of frames so as to support the notion of *scope*.
- An evaluation loop that unites the evaluation functions that make up *Borg* semantics; this loop accepts a sequence of expressions and evaluates them.

In the more general case, the complete process will take program text, convert it into an expression which will be dispatched to a specialised interpreter. For instance:

```
apply(exp)::
  if(exp.operand = '-',
     { par: evaluate(exp.par(1));
       number(-par.value) },
     if(exp.operand = '+',
        { a: evaluate(exp.par(1));
          b: evaluate(exp.par(2));
          number(a.val+b.val) },
     error()))
```

then, for example an evaluation of will result in a growing of the runtime stack of the evaluator. The expressions used during this computation are typically stored on a stack, which in general coincides with the run-time stack of the program that implements the interpreter. Which is something we don't want because we cannot migrate it as such.

6   Reification of the runtime stack

We will now describe a very straightforward way to reify the runtime stack of the agent interpreter, thus making the agent runtime stack a first order entity in the interpreted language. We will not describe full reification because it not needed for our application (strong migration of code), but we nevertheless need some way to capture the runtime stack and to handle it as if it were yet another object in the interpreted language and not only in the language the interpreter is written in. We view the computational model as a paired expression/continuation stack. Below are the rules which should be kept in thought when changing an existing interpreter.

- Whenever the interpreter is required to evaluate an expression it should not call other functions to divide the given expression and conquer a result.
- To retrieve the parameters passed to a function it has to take a peek at the expression stack and pop these parameters by itself.
- When another function has to be called (e.g. a function such as evaluate) it has to store the function to be called and the expression accompanying the function on the continuation stack.
- At the end of a given function it has to proceed with the next function on the continuation stack. In a tail recursive language this can be done by applying the result of contstack.pop() at the end of the function. If we don't have a tailrecursive language we need to return control and hope there will be an outerstackloop available.

The above interpreter code will be converted to

```
Minus()::
    { par: expstack.pop();
      expstack.push(number(-par.value))  }

Apply()::
    { exp: expstack.pop();
      if(exp.operand = '-',
          { contstack.push(minus);
            contstack.push(evaluate);
            expstack.push(exp.par(1))  },
        if(exp.operand = '+',
            { par1: exp.par(1);
              par2: exp.par(2);
              contstack.push(addfinal);
              contstack.push(addaux);
              expstack.push(par2);
              contstack.push(evaluate);
              expstack.push(par1)  },
          error())))  }
```

```
Addaux () ::
  { result1: expstack.pop();
    exp2: expstack.pop();
    expstack.push(result1);
    expstack.push(exp2);
    contstack.push(evaluate)  }

Addfinal () ::
  { result1: expstack.pop();
    result2: expstack.pop();
    expstack.push(number(result1.value+result2.value))
```

Implications of this conversion are obvious:

– We can easily garbage collect the system, because we can put the running stacks in
  some root-table.
– We have an extra indirection which could lead to a suboptimal performance.
– We can easily implement stack optimizations because we have the stack under
  control. For example, implementing tail recursion is no problem if we change the
  apply somewhat: An application consists of changing the current dictionary,
  evaluating an expression and returning a value. If we check that there is already a
  return-result continuation we won't have to push a new one.

7   Migration revisited

An interpreter written in this way, i.e.with (a) the capability of serializing the data
store and (b) the ability to reify the computational state, can easily be used to
implement strong migration. Even if an agent process is in the midst of being
evaluated, we simply interrupt the process, serialize the state of the entire
computation, which also includes its computational state, and send it to another
location while removing the proces from interpreter control. At the receiving end we
deserialize the agent and start a process which uses the freshly deserialized
computational state.

The above steps should be taken at a moment at which the stack is consistent, neither
while a continuation thunk is executing, nor when there are global variables which are
not saved in the data store. With only these things to think of we can state that we
have implemented strong migration without too much difficulty.

Serializing agents consists of traversing the data graph and storing everything we
encounter, including local dictionaries. The one exception to this is the root
environment which is simply marked as being the root environment. In this way we
can integrate agents in their new agent environment upon their arrival at a new
location.

The example below illustrates how migration can be exploited. We see that we can
call the agentmove native function at any time. When the agent arrives at its new

location it will print 'after moving' without the need for restarting it at its main entry point.

```
Calcul(pars)::
  { <some calculation>;
    display("before moving");
    agentmove(remotedict("otherplace.tecra"));
    display("after moving") }

main(pars,callback)::
  callback.Answeris(calcul(pars))
```

8   Conclusion

In this paper we have reported on an experiment in mobility of software agents. In particular, we investigated the reification of the computational state of an agent's underlying process, as a basis for the actual migration scheme. We extended a simple, experimental virtual machine with first-class computations and we proceeded by using these to transmit an active agent from one location to another without direct impact on the agent's specification. In order to make migration of code really useball we need strong migration and reification of the computational state. Without this, mobile applications are doomed to remain complex artefacts, well outside of the mainstream of software engineering.

9   References

1. Jim White, *Mobile Agents White Paper*, General Magic
2. Robert S. Gray, *Agent TCL: A flexible and secure mobile-agent system*, Department of Computer Science, Dartmouth College
3. Gian Pietro Picco, *Understanding Code Mobility*, Politecnico di Torino, Italy, Tutorial at ECOOP98, 22 July 1998
4. Gerald Jay Sussman, Guy Lewis Steele Jr, *Scheme, An Interpreter for Extended Lambda Calculus*, Massachusetts Institute of Technology, Artificial Intelligence Laboratory. December 1975
5. Werner Van Belle, Reinforcement Learning as a Routing Technique for Mobile Multi Agent Systems, April 1997
6. Ad Astra, *Jumping Beans, a white paper* , 1 september 1998
7. Online documentation on http://pico.vub.ac.be
8. Agha G. Actors: A Model of Concurrent Computation in Distributed Systems, AI Tech Report 844, MI

As Strong as Possible Agent Mobility

Tim Walsh, Paddy Nixon, Simon Dobson

Dept. Of Computer Science,
Trinity College
Dublin 2
{tim.walsh, paddy.nixon, simon.dobson}@cs.tcd.ie

Abstract. A major challenge for distributed applications working in mobile contexts is to provide application developers with a method of building stable systems whose elements may change across time. We introduce the concept of As Strong As Possible mobility that uses a combination of data space management and thread state capture so that objects and threads can migrate in a manner that has not been properly explored yet. The ultimate goal is to provide a mechanism for mobility where an object will be migrated using strong mobility techniques where possible and using rebinding mechanisms when it is not advantageous to simply 'grab' a thread's state.

Introduction

Research into agent technology is providing many potential application domains. One such domain is that of e-commerce. This is a perfectly natural arena for agents to operate in. The issue then remains on what type of underlying architecture they should execute in. We attempt to introduce a methodology to allow agents free to roam remote hosts while continuing thread execution.

Issues in Mobility

The primary difference between mobile objects and mobile agents is one of autonomy. Mobile objects, like mobile agents, migrate between remote address spaces, typically separate physical nodes. Mobile agents migrate and then restart execution. This requires a server or daemon at the destination that will act as a docking station or 'sandbox' for the agent. The sandbox should provide the 'needs' of the agent.

The area of mobile agents is still in its infancy. It has had no strict rules or standards placed upon it, unlike the client server paradigm. This allows us the opportunity to mould a standard for this emerging technology which is sure to form an important element in future networking applications. As global communications become more accessible to all, and Internet usage becomes ubiquitous, the need to use agents to represent physical entities becomes more evident.

T. Wagner and O.F. Rana (Eds.): Infrastructure for Agents, LNAI 1887, pp. 174–176, 2001.

Migration strength

An agent executing on a node invariably requires the services of other agents and system resources. Should this single agent need to be migrated, procedures need to be developed to allow the migration of the agent to be as resourceful as possible. High level abstractions prescribe the capture of all code and state of the agent, packaging it, and moving it to some destination node where it can be restarted and allowed to continue.

Upon closer examination we discover that there are numerous obstructions. Protocols need to be established to address what happens to resources the agent utilises and also how the agent itself gets captured. Analysis by Fuggetta [1] demonstrates that mobile execution units, be they mobile objects or mobile agents, have two forms of migration.

Weak mobility is the ability to allow code transfer across nodes; code may be accompanied by some initialisation data, but no migration of execution state is involved.

Strong mobility allows migration of both the code and the execution state to a remote host. Strong mobility has been chiefly fixed in the domain of scripting languages and proprietary systems such as Emerald [3]. These systems were specifically designed to run on small LAN's and clusters.

Advantages and Disadvantages

One of the advantage of strong mobility is that long-running or long-lived threads can be suddenly move or be moved from one host to another. In principle, such a transparent mechanism would allow continued thread execution without any data loss in their ongoing execution. Such an approach is useful in building distributed systems with complex load balancing requirements. Threads that are not 'location-sensitive' are ideal candidates. Should a thread be executing without specifically using data outside its closure, it is unaffected by changes in its location.

Unfortunately large distributed networks are inappropriate sites to run systems which require inherently coherent coupling to other nodes. This is based upon the assumption that an agent, with bindings to host resources, retains those binding (via a proxy) after migration.

Waldo [2] argues this case in point. To attempt location transparency over large distant networks is attempting to ignore latency, memory access into different address spaces and partial failure. Clusters and high speed networks offer a better platform to run these systems.

Weak mobility does not involve any migration of execution state. A modern day instance is the Java serialisation mechanism. When an object is serialised, all the instance variables of the object are packaged into an output stream. No execution state gets transferred.

As Strong as Possible Agent Mobility

In Java, threads and the objects that created them are separate entities. A Java thread can be created from object's methods but it then becomes an abstract entity onto itself. The state of the object is retained separately. Executing threads hold all local variables generated as methods are invoked. The section of memory they occupy is referred to as the working memory. All objects have state encapsulated in the shared main memory, which is split between static and dynamic memory.

The standard Java API does not provide mechanisms to achieve strong migration. There is no way to access these thread objects directly. We wish to investigate whether this is feasible using Java's Just In Time (JIT) Compiler API. This API gives hooks into the virtual machine that can be used, amongst other things, to extract the execution environment for particular threads. The JIT appears to be sufficient to allow access to the thread stacks. The second stage will require reseeding this captured data into a foreign virtual machine.

Java threads, like operating system threads, can be pre-empted to allow others access to the processor. By extending the virtual machine we intend to re-seed thread data into a virtual machine and place it on the scheduler's waiting queue, thus allowing Java to restart the thread naturally.

This approach to extending the virtual machine has been accomplished before [4] but we intend to build upon the idea in an attempt to create a more formal framework. If an abstraction of a container is created it allows threads and objects to be grouped in a single logical unit which can be migrated.

Conclusions

Existing system used in mobile agent architectures follow either weak or strong migration behaviour. Container abstractions allow agents to execute several threads and store passive data objects. Self contained threads within the container can be strongly migrated while others require that their bindings to resources are replaced on the destination node with local equivalents. This allows an agent freedom of movement without the constraints of remote bindings which can result in instability and latency problems.

References
[1] A. Fuggetta, G.P. Picco, G. Vigna, "Understanding Code Mobility" IEEE Trans of Software Eng., vol 24, no. 5, pp. 342-361, May 1998.
[2] Jim Waldo, Geoff Wyant, Ann Wollrath, Sam Kendall, "A Note on Distributed Computing", Technical Report TR-94-29, Sun Microsystems Laboratories, Inc, November 1994.
[3] E. Jul, H. Levy, N. Hutchinson, A. Black, "Fine-Grained Mobility in the Emerald System" ACM Trans. On Computer Systems, Vol. 6, no. 1, pp. 109-133, February 1988.
[4] S. Bouchenak. "Pickling threads state in the Java system", Third European Research Seminar on Advances in Distributed Systems (ERSADS'99), Madeira Island - Portugal. 23rd-28th April 1999.

An Architecture for Adaptive Web Stores

Giovanna Petrone

Dipartimento di Informatica, University of Torino
{giovanna}@di.unito.it

1   Introduction

In the last three years, we have developed SETA, a prototype toolkit for the creation of Web stores personalizing the interactions with users, focusing on the design of the front-end of on-line stores and on the development of a flexible interface. We have exploited knowledge representation techniques and agent-based technologies to improve the configurability of the toolkit and its scalability [2, 3]. Moreover, we have organized the overall architecture as a multiagent one, where specialized agents fill the main roles for the management of personalized interactions with customers [8]. An on-line demo of a prototype store created using SETA is available at the following URL: http://www.di.unito.it/~ seta. This store presents telecommunication products, like phones and switchboards, and will be used throughout the rest of the paper as a concrete example to describe the functionalities of our system.

In the design of the SETA architecture, we identified a number of functionalities that an adaptive Web store should offer while interacting with a user; then, we isolated the activities necessary to obtain the desired system behavior. The result of this analysis is the identification of a set of basic roles: for instance, the maintenance of the user models containing the customers' preferences and needs, the application of personalization strategies to tailor the generation of the hypertextual pages and the personalization of the suggestion of items. The identified roles are necessary to offer a personalized navigation of a Web catalog, but are not exhaustive: depending on the requested system functionalities, the architecture might need to be further extended; for instance, we did not include the management of orders and payment transactions in the set of basic roles we have developed. Indeed, the exploitation of agent-based technologies has been very useful for the design of our architecture, and for the implementation of our Web store shell, for the following reasons:

- Components filling different roles have to be coordinated in a single architecture and this fact may create serious organizational problems: the components may use heterogeneous knowledge sources and technologies; still, they must cooperate with one another to offer the overall service to the user.
- Some roles fit well in a traditional Object-Oriented programming paradigm [7]; however, others require that the components filling them are proactive and may initiate tasks although their methods are not explicitly invoked.

T. Wagner and O.F. Rana (Eds.): Infrastructure for Agents, LNAI 1887, pp. 177–179, 2001.

- For efficiency purposes, the activity of the agents has to be performed in parallel whenever possible. Therefore, a sequential interaction model has difficulties in scaling up. On the other hand, agent-based technologies offer different types of communication, including synchronous and asynchronous messages, that enhance the parallelism in the execution of tasks.
- Although we have developed the architecture of a single marketplace, an interesting extension is the possibility to provide broker agents with information about the items available in the Web store. This scenario raises interoperability issues, that can be faced thanks to the exploitation of agent communication languages and, at a lower level, of the facilities to interact in heterogeneous communication platforms (CORBA, RMI), offered by several tools to build multiagent systems.
- The exploitation of agent-based technologies facilitates the extension of complex systems with new components.
- Other technical reasons have influenced our design decisions. For instance, the seamless distribution facilities offered by many agent-based technologies: in fact, given a complex system, the distribution of its components on several computers may be desirable and our experience showed that the exploitation of agent-based communication techniques and specific tools to build multiagent systems allows the developer to distribute agents easily and efficiently.

The system architecture, described in detail in [2], is a parallel architecture where synchronous, asynchronous and multicast messages can be exchanged and handled by the agents. We described the messages as performatives in a speech-act based agent communication language [5].

We have implemented this architecture by exploiting Objectspace Voyager [6], a tool for developing multiagent systems which provides system components with basic agent capabilities, such as distribution and communication protocols. The agents of our system are Java objects offering the services necessary to carry on the personalized interactions with customers; moreover, we have exploited Voyager's facilities to allow the distribution of agents over different computers and their communication. While synchronous messages are handled by the main thread of an agent, the multithread environment supported by Voyager enables the agents to spawn for handling the asynchronous messages; in this way, they can also manage the active user contexts in parallel. Thus, we can handle in a homogeneous way an almost complete parallelization of the activity of the various agents within a user session, as well as different sessions.

2   Infrastructures for Developing Multi-agent Systems

We have considered several tools for building multiagent systems in a Java-based environment: all these tools offer communication and distribution facilities, and introduce an abstraction level with respect to the communication protocol, which might be RMI, DCOM, CORBA, or other. We have selected ObjectSpace Voyager [6], which best suited the needs of our architecture, allowing a convenient object distribution: objects created by the Voyager compiler can be remotely executed. Moreover, Voyager supports an almost seamless transformation of a Java object, which can only exchange synchronous messages, into an agent able to send and receive various types of messages: Voyager offers synchronous, oneWay, oneWayMulticast and "future" messages ("future" messages correspond to asynchronous messages, which do not involve the sender and the receiver in a rendez-vous). While synchronous communication corresponds to traditional Java method invocation, the other types of messages can be delivered by objects by invoking specific Voyager methods.

As we need flexibility in agent communication, we excluded other well known agent building tools, specifically focused on the management of agent mobility, which handle agent communication at a rather low level: e.g., IBM Aglets. At the same time, other tools for building open multiagent systems, which also provided negotiation and coordination primitives to enable an active cooperation between the agents, proved to exceed our needs: for instance, the Agent Building Shell [4]. In fact, in our system, the agents offer fixed services, and there is no need to dynamically distribute tasks among them.

It should be noticed that SETA is based on a well-established architecture for complex Web-based systems. In particular, the most recent research has triggered the development of other frameworks for the creation of these types of systems. For instance, the Jackal agent building shell [1] supports a rich, KQML-based communication among agents; moreover, the Java 2 Enterprise Edition by Sun Microsystems provides the developer of a distributed, Web-based system with all the facilities for the management of parallel user sessions and also supports a transactional access to databases. Such frameworks were not available when we developed SETA; however, our approach is compatible with the one adopted by these tools; thus, the SETA system could be updated to exploit such environments, if needed.

References

1. IBM alphaWorks. Jackal. http://jackal.cs.umbc.edu/.
2. Ardissono L., Barbero C., Goy A., and Petrone G. An agent architecture for personalized web stores. In *Proc. 3rd Int. Conf. on Autonomous Agents (Agents '99)*, pages 182–189, Seattle, WA, 1999.
3. Ardissono L., Goy A., Meo R., Petrone G., Console L., Lesmo L., Simone C., and Torasso P. A configurable system for the construction of adaptive virtual stores. *World Wide Web*, 2(3):143–159, 1999.
4. Barbuceanu M. and Teigen R. Higher level integration by multi-agent architectures. In P. Bernus, editor, *Handbook of Information System Architectures*. Springer Verlag.
5. Finin T.W., Labrou Y., and Mayfield J. KQML as an agent communication language. In J. Bradshaw, editor, *Software Agents*. MIT Press, Cambridge, 1995.
6. ObjectSpace. Voyager. http://www.objectspace.com/index.asp.
7. Petrie C.J. Agent-based engineering, the web, and intelligence. *IEEE Expert*, December:24–29, 1996.
8. Sycara K.P., Pannu A., Williamson M., and Zeng D. Distributed intelligent agents. *IEEE Expert*, December:36–45, 1996.

A Performance Analysis Framework for Mobile Agent Systems

Marios D. Dikaiakos   George Samaras

Department of Computer Science
University of Cyprus, CY-1678 Nicosia, Cyprus
{mdd,cssamara}@ucy.ac.cy

Abstract. In this paper we propose a novel performance analysis approach that can be used to gauge quantitatively the performance characteristics of different mobile-agent platforms. We materialize this approach as a hierarchical framework of benchmarks designed to isolate performance properties of interest, at different levels of detail. We identify the structure and parameters of benchmarks and propose metrics that can be used to capture their properties. We present a set of micro-benchmarks, comprising the lower level of our hierarchy, and examine their behavior when implemented with commercial, Java-based, mobile agent platforms.

1 Introduction

Quantitative performance evaluation is crucial for performance "debugging," that is the thorough understanding of performance behavior of systems. Results from quantitative performance analyses enhance the discovery of performance and scalability bottlenecks, the quantitative comparison of different platforms and systems, the optimization of application designs, and the extrapolation of properties of future systems. The quantitative performance evaluation of mobile-agent systems is much harder than the analysis of more traditional parallel and distributed systems. To study MA-system performance, one should take into account issues such as [4]: the absence of global time, control and state information; the complicated architecture of MA platforms; the variety of distributed computing (software) models applicable to mobile-agent applications; the diversity of operations implemented and used in MA-based applications; the constinuously changing resource configuration of Internet-based systems, and the impact of issues affecting the performance of Java, such as interpretation versus compilation, garbage collection, etc.

In this context, we focus on the *quantitative performance evaluation* of mobile agents. In particular, we introduce a performance analysis approach that can be used to gauge the performance characteristics of different mobile-agent platforms used for the development of systems and applications on Internet. This approach defines a "hierarchical framework" of benchmarks designed to isolate performance properties of interest, at different levels of detail. We identify the

T. Wagner and O.F. Rana (Eds.): Infrastructure for Agents, LNAI 1887, pp. 180–187, 2001.

structure and parameters of benchmarks and propose metrics that can be used to capture their properties. We implement these benchmarks with a number of Java-based, mobile agent platforms (IBM's Aglets [3], Mitsubishi's Concordia [6], ObjectSpace's Voyager [5], and IKV's Grasshopper [2]) and run various experiments. Experimental results provide us with initial conclusions that lead to further refinement and extension of benchmarks and help us investigate the performance characteristics of the platforms examined. The remaining of this paper is organized as follows: Section 2 describes our performance analysis framework. Section 3 introduces the hierarchy of benchmarks we defined to implement this framework, and presents our experimental results from the lower layer of benchmarks, the *micro-benchmarks*. We conclude in Section 4.

2 A Performance Analysis Framework

Basic Elements

To analyze the performance of mobile-agent platforms, we need to develop an approach for capturing basic performance properties of these platforms. These properties should be defined independently of the various ways each particular mobile-agent API can be used to program and deploy applications and systems on Internet. To this end, our approach focuses on *basic elements* of MA platforms that implement the functionalities commonly found and used in most MA environments. Also, it seeks to expose the performance behavior of these functionalities: how fast they are, what is their overhead, if they become a performance bottleneck when used extensively, etc. For the objectives of our work, the basic elements of MA platforms are identified from existing, "popular" implementations [2,5,6] as follows:

- *Agents*, which are defined by their state, implementation (bytecode), capability of interaction with other agents/programs (interface), and a unique identifier.
- *Places*, representing the environment in which agents are created and executed. A place is characterized by the virtual machine executing the agent's bytecode (the *engine*), its network address (location), its computing resources, and any services it may host (e.g., a database gateway or a Web-search program).
- *Behaviors* of agents within and between places, which correspond to the basic functionalities of a MA platform: creating an agent at a local or remote place, dispatching an agent from one place to another, receiving an agent that arrives at some place, communicating information between agents via messages, multicasts, or messenger agents, synchronizing the processing of two agents, etc.

Application Kernels

Basic elements of MA environments are typically combined into *application kernels*. Application kernels define scenarios of MA-usage in terms of a set of places participating in the scenario, a number of agents placed at or moving between these places, a set of interactions of agents and places (agent movements, communication, synchronization, resource use). Essentially, application kernels describe solutions common to various problems of agent design. These solutions implement known models of distributed computation on particular application domains [8]; they represent widely accepted and portable approaches for addressing typical agent-design problems [1]. Typically, application kernels are the building blocks of larger applications; their performance properties affect the performance behavior of applications.

The performance traits of an application kernel depend on the characteristics of its constituent elements, and on how these elements are combined together and influence each other. For example, an application kernel could involve an agent residing at a place on a fixed network and providing database-connectivity services to agents arriving from remote places over wireless connections. This kernel may exist within a large digital library or e-commerce application. It may, as well, belong to the "critical path" that determines end-to-end performance of that application. To identify how the kernel affects overall performance, we need to isolate its performance characteristics: what is the overhead of transporting an agent from a remote place to a database-enabled place, connecting to the database, performing a simple query, and returning the results over a wireless connection. Interaction with the database is kept minimal, is we are trying to capture the overhead of this kernel and not to investigate the behavior of the database.

Investigating the performance of "popular" application kernels can help us explain the behavior of full-blown applications built on top of these kernels. Consequently, a study of application kernels has to be included in our performance analysis framework and should focus on simple metrics capturing basic performance measurements, overheads, bottlenecks, etc. For performance analysis purposes, we define application kernels corresponding to the Client-Server model of distributed computing and its extensions: the Client-Agent-Server model, the Client-Intercept-Server model, the Proxy-Server model, and variations thereof that use mobile agents for communication between the client and the server. More details on these models are given in [7, 8]. Besides the Client-Server family of models, we define application kernels that correspond to the *Forwarding* and the *Meeting* agent design patterns, defined in [1, 3]. We choose the *Forwarding* and *Meeting* patterns, because they can help us quantify the performance traits of agents and places in terms of their capability to re-route agents and to host inter-agent interactions.

Parameterization

To proceed with performance experiments, measurements and analyses, after the identification of basic elements and application kernels, we need to specify the *parameters* that define the context of our experimentation, and the *metrics* measured. Parameters determine: a) The *workload* that drives a particular experiment, expressed as the number of invocations of some basic element or application kernel. Large numbers of invocations correspond to intensive use of the element or kernel during periods of high load. b) The *resources* attached to participating places and agents: the channels connecting places, the operating system and hardware resources of each place, and the functionality of agents and places.

The exact definition of parameters and parameter-values depend on the particular aspects under investigation. For example, to capture the intrinsic performance properties of basic elements, we consider agents with limited functionality and interface, which carry the minimum amount of code and data needed for their basic behaviors. These agents run within places, which are free of additional processing load from other applications. Places may correspond either to agent servers with full agent-handling functionality or to agent-enabled applets. The latter option addresses situations where agents interact with client-applications, which can be downloaded and executed in a Web browser. Participating places may belong to the same local-area network, to different local-area networks within a wide-area network, or to partly-wireless networks. Different operating systems can be considered.

Parameters become more complicated when studying application kernels. For instance, when exploring the Client-Server model, we have to define the resources to be incorporated at the place which corresponds to the server-side of the model. Resources could range from a minimalistic program acknowledging the receipt of an incoming request, to a server with full database capabilities.

Application Frameworks

Following an investigation of intrinsic performance properties of application kernels, it is interesting to examine how these kernels behave when employed in a real application. To this end, we need to enhance application kernels with the full functionality required by application domains of interest, such as database access, electronic auctions, etc. We call these adapted kernels, *application frameworks*. To experiment with application frameworks, we need to use realistic rather than simple workloads. Such workloads can be derived either from traces of real applications or from models of real workloads.

A Hierarchical Performance Analysis Approach

In view of the above remarks, we propose the analysis of MA-performance at four layers of abstraction as follows: At a first layer, exploring and characterizing performance traits of Basic Elements of MA platforms. At a second layer, investigating implementations for popular Application Kernels upon simple workloads. At a third layer, studying Application Frameworks, that is, implementations of application kernels which realize particular functionalities of interest and run on realistic workloads. Last but not least, at a fourth layer, studying full-blown Applications running under real conditions and workloads.

This hierarchical approach has to be accompanied by proper metrics, which may differ from layer to layer, and parameters representing the particular context of each study, i.e., the processing and communication resources available and the workload applied. It should be noted that the design of our performance analyses in each layer of our conceptual hierarchy should provide measurements and observations that can help us establish causality relationships between the conclusions from one layer of abstraction to the observations at the next layer in our performance analysis hierarchy.

We propose three layers of benchmarks for the implementation of the hierarchical Performance Analysis Framework introduced in the previous sections. These benchmarks correspond to the first three levels of the hierarchy described earlier:

- **Micro-benchmarks:** short loops designed to isolate and measure performance properties of basic behaviors of MA systems, for typical system configurations.
- **Micro-kernels:** short, synthetic codes designed to measure and investigate the properties of Application Kernels, for typical applications and system configurations.
- **Application Kernels:** instantiations of micro-kernels for real applications. Here, we involve places with full application functionality and employ realistic workloads complying to the *TPC-W* specification (see http://www.tpc.org

3   Micro-benchmarks and Experimentation

We present in more details the suite of proposed micro-benchmarks and a summary of experimental results derived by these benchmarks. Further information about micro-kernels, application kernels and experimental results can be found in [7, 4]. The basic components we are focusing on are: a) mobile agents, used to materialize modules of the various distributed computing models and agent patterns; b) messenger agents used for flexible communication, and c) messages used for efficient communication and synchronization. Accordingly, we define the following micro-benchmarks:

- AC-L: Captures the overhead of agent-creation locally within a place.
- AC-R: Captures the overhead of agent-creation at a remote place.
- AL: Captures the overhead of launching agents towards a remote place.
- AR: Captures the overhead of receiving agents that arrive at a place.
- MSG: Captures the overhead of point-to-point messaging.
- MULT: Captures the overhead of message multicasting.
- SYNCH: Captures the overhead of synchronizing two agents with message-exchange.
- ROAM: Captures the agent-travelling overhead.

These micro-benchmarks involve two places located at different computing nodes, agents with the minimum functionality that is required for carrying out the behaviors studied, and messages carrying very little information between agents. Table 1 presents the parameters and metrics for our benchmarks: "Loop size" defines the number of iterations included in each benchmark. "Operating System" and "Place Configuration" represent the resources of each place involved in our experimentation. We have conducted experiments on PCs running Windows 95 and Windows NT. In most experiments, places were agent servers. We also conducted experiments where one of the places was an agent-enabled Java

Table 1. Micro-benchmark Parameters and Metrics

Name	Parameters						Metrics		
	Loop Size	Operating System	Place Config.	Channel Config.	Agent Size	Msg. Size	Total Time	Average Time	Peak Rate
AC-L	√	√	√	-	√	-	√	√	√
AC-R, AL, AR	√	√	√	√	√	-	√	√	√
MSG, SYNCH, MULT	√	√	√	√	-	√	√	√	√
ROAM	√	√	√	√	√	-	√	√	√

applet. Channel configuration specifies whether the two places involved reside at the same LAN, at two different LANs, or if one of the places gets connected to the other via a wireless link.

As shown in Table 1, we measure three different metrics. Total time to completion is a raw performance metric, which can provide us with some insight about the performance characteristics of the basic element studied by each benchmark. It can also help us identify bottlenecks as the load (loop size) is increased, and test the robustness of each particular platform. Average timings provide estimates of the overhead involved in a particular behavior of a MA system, i.e., the cost of sending a short message, of dispatching a light agent, etc. Finally, peak rates provide a representation of the performance capacity of MA platforms, based on the sustained performance of their basic elements.

The number of parameters involved in our micro-benchmarks lead to a very large space of experiments, many of which may not be useful or applicable. We have experimented with four commercial platforms: IBM's Aglets, Mitsubishi's Concordia, ObjectSpace's Voyager and the Grasshopper by IKV. We tried various parameter settings before settling to a small set of micro-benchmark configurations that provide useful insights. Fig. 1 displays the average times for micro-benchmarks **AC** and **AL** (in msec). AC was executed on a PC running Windows 95. AL was executed on two PCs running Windows 95 and residing at the same LAN, with a small traffic-load. From these figures we can easily see that, in terms of performance, Concordia and Voyager are more optimized than Aglets and Grasshopper. For Concordia, Voyager and Grasshopper, the average time it takes to create and dispatch an agent varies greatly with loop size. This can be attributed to the fact that MA platforms cache the bytecodes of classes loaded during agent creation and dispatch. Therefore, repeated invocations of the same primitive cost less than the initial ones. As the loop size increases beyond a certain point, however, the agent servers hosting the benchmark start facing overloading problems (shortage of memory, higher book-keeping overheads, etc.), leading to a degradation in performance. Behavior changes from one platform to the other, since some systems employ different techniques to cope with overloading.

Similar remarks can be driven from Figure 2, which presents the average times extracted for micro-benchmarks **MSG** and **SYNCH**. These benchmarks were executed on PCs running Windows 95 and residing at the same LAN. From

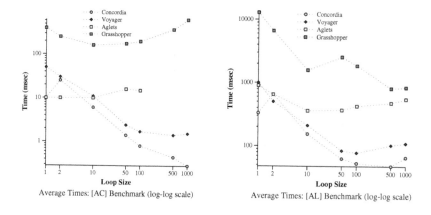

Fig. 1. Average timings for agent creation and launching.

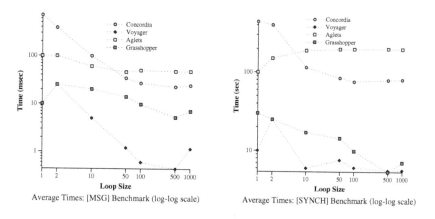

Fig. 2. Average timings for MSG and SYNCH micro-benchmarks.

these diagrams we can easily see that the time to send and exchange messages in Voyager is much shorter than in other platforms. Average message dispatch and exchange times are leveling off with loop size, due to caching of the classes that comprise the message data structures. If loop size exceeds a certain level, the messaging subsystems in all platforms start facing overloading problems (Grasshopper and Voyager). Both Concordia and Voyager, however, prove to be quite robust even under heavy load of agent or message transmissions. It should be noted that, although not shown in the diagrams of Figures 2, messaging is more robust and efficient under Windows NT, for all platforms tested.

Table 2 presents the peak rate of agent creation, agent dispatch, and message dispatch for the MA platforms studied. From these numbers, we can easily see that Concordia is a clear winner when it comes to the number of agents that can be created at and dispatched from a particular agent server. Voyager, on

Table 2. Peak Rates (Windows95)

Benchmark	Concordia	Voyager	Aglets	Grasshopper
Agent Creation (agents/sec)	3571.43	649.3	10.67	1.59
Agent Dispatch (agents/sec)	21	9.07	10.67	1.187
Message Dispatch (msg/sec)	40.9	869.56	20.7	141.44

the other hand, provides more than an order of magnitude higher capacity in message dispatch than other platforms.

4   Conclusions

To our knowledge, our Performance Analysis Framework provides the first structured approach for analyzing the performance of mobile-agent systems quantitatively, by focusing at the different layers of a MA-based system's architecture. Experiments with our micro-benchmark suite provide a corroboration of this approach. Experimental results help us isolate the performance characteristics of MA platforms examined, and lead us to the discovery and explanation of basic performance properties of MA systems. Furthermore, they provides a solid base for the assessment of the relative merits and drawbacks of the platforms examined from a performance perspective.

Acknowledgements: The authors wish to thank C. Spyrou and M. Kyriacou for helping out with experiments.

References

1. Y. Aridov and D. Lange. Agent Design Patterns: Elements of Agent Application Design. In *Proceedings of Autonomous Agents 1998*, pages 108–115. ACM, 1998.
2. M. Breugst, I. Busse, S. Covaci, and T. Magedanz. Grasshopper – A Mobile Agent Platform for IN Based Service Environments. In *Proceedings of IEEE IN Workshop 1998*, pages 279–290, Bordeaux, France, May 1998.
3. D. Lange and M. Oshima. *Programming and Deploying Java Mobile Agents with Aglets*. Addison Wesley, 1998.
4. M. Dikaiakos and G. Samaras. Quantitative Performance Analysis of Mobile-Agent Systems: A Hierarchical Approach. Technical Report TR-00-2, Department of Computer Science, University of Cyprus, June 2000.
5. G. Glass. Overview of Voyager: ObjectSpace's Product Family for State-of-the-Art Distributed Computing. Technical report, ObjectSpace, 1999.
6. R. Koblick. Concordia. *Communications of the ACM*, 42(3):96–99, March 1999.
7. G. Samaras, M. D. Dikaiakos, C. Spyrou, and A. Liverdos. Mobile Agent Platforms for Web-Databases: A Qualitative and Quantitative Assessment. In *Proceedings of the Joint Symposium ASA/MA '99. First International Symposium on Agent Systems and Applications (ASA '99). Third International Symposium on Mobile Agents (MA '99)*, pages 50–64. IEEE-Computer Society, October 1999.
8. C. Spyrou, G. Samaras, E. Pitoura, and P. Evripidou. Wireless Computational Models: Mobile Agents to the Rescue. In *2nd International Workshop on Mobility in Databases & Distributed Systems. DEXA '99*, September 1999.

A Layered Agent Template for Enterprise Computing

Carmen M. Pancerella and Nina M. Berry[1]

Sandia National Laboratories, P.O. Box 969, MS 9012, Livermore, CA, 94551-0969 USA
{carmen, nmberry}@ca.sandia.gov

Abstract. The development of agent systems based on layered agent templates has expanded the development and deployment of agent applications. We are developing an agent template to support the integration of a wide range of enterprise applications. In particular, we are targeting existing enterprises, such that agents can manage enterprise resources and reason across these resources. This agent template has five functional layers. Software developers can plug-and-play layers and customize features in each layer. We have discovered infrastructure requirements and design issues for employing layered agent designs into existing enterprises. In this brief paper we describe some requirements of our agent template. In general, we believe these same issues are relevant to system designers who are building multi-agent systems for use in large scale enterprise computing.

1 Layered Agent Templates

An agent template or agent shell is a common approach to developing agent systems [1,2]; this methodology allows for scalability in both developing and managing agents. Designers can easily generate collections of agents. Agent templates generally have components for basic activities, e.g., message transport, messaging generation/validation, and problem-solving/control. Optionally they may include advanced components for conversation development, negotiation, security, learning, human-agent interactions, and planning. A layered agent template expands this concept of conjoined and interacting components by grouping related functionality into a single layer with well-defined interfaces between layers. This allows developers to customize layers for individual project needs. The layers should be orthogonal and encapsulate related functionality. Furthermore, the template must be designed so as not to compromise agent autonomy.

We have created the Agent-Based enhanced Integration (ABeI) architecture [3], where agents are created from a common agent template design; this template facilitates the creation of new agents. Our template is suitable for developing a small number (i.e. less than 30) of large-grained agents which interact via messages in order to solve enterprise problems.

The ABeI template has five pre-defined layers. The developer can choose to replace or in some cases eliminate a layer. However, the replacement or removal of a

---

[1] This work was supported by Sandia Corporation under Contract No. DE-AC04-94-AL85000 with the U.S. Department of Energy.

T. Wagner and O.F. Rana (Eds.): Infrastructure for Agents, LNAI 1887, pp. 188–191, 2001.

layer requires the implementation of the default interfaces to ensure the flow of information between existing and phantom layers. The *transport layer* provides for the sending/receiving of agent messages. In the *message layer* the agent communication language (ACL) is implemented. *The conversation protocol layer* is where agent conversations and negotiations take place. The *agent control layer* contains the problem solving unit, planner, scheduler and knowledge base for an agent. Finally, the *detailed agent layer* is unique for each agent. This is where application-specific functionality is implemented.

Unlike agent toolkits that are typically geared to the novice agent developer, our agent template is perhaps more appealing to agent researchers. This allows developers to create heterogeneous agents. The ability to interchange layers provides an opportunity for experimentation.

2 Infrastructure Requirements for Using Templates in Enterprises

Using our layered approach to developing agents, we have been able to incorporate agents into existing enterprise frameworks. To accomplish this task some infrastructure requirements must be resolved. Unlike traditional agent architectures, the ABeI transport layer is most often directly linked to the underlying enterprise infrastructure. This is the only layer at which the enterprise framework is visible. In our case, we are using PRE [4] as the enterprise architecture, with CORBA the actual transport mechanism. All enterprise details are hidden from the end-user of the template. We have also implemented a transport layer which uses email to deliver ACL messages. Email is attractive because it allows messages to be sent across firewalls.

We assume that the transport layer handles most of the problems associated with distributed computing. This layer provides reliable message transport across a variety of hardware platforms, provides message integrity, allows for large binary data blobs to be transported, delivers messages in order between sender-receiver pairs, and provides the required security that the application demands. Other layers assume these properties of the transport layer. Also, we assume that there is some way of discovering new enterprise applications and locating enterprise applications. The agent control layer will need this functionality in order to build resource agents and broker agents as described in [3]. If a new transport layer is implemented, it must provide these services to the agent.

3   Agent Communication and Conversations in Agent Templates

The AbeI message layer allows agents to exchange messages in a machine readable ACL. At this layer, the syntax of all messages is checked to ensure that only valid message are sent and received. The semantics of the message is ignored at this layer.

In the conversation protocol layer a legal set of performatives or communicative acts is generated for the current conversation sequence. The agent control layer or detailed agent layer determines which performative will ultimately be used. At the protocol layer, new conversation sequences can be added, and an incoming or outgoing message is checked to ensure that the ongoing conversation is valid.

Both of these layers are simple and deterministic. Neither the message layer nor the protocol layer affect the overall autonomy of the agent. Autonomy and proactivity must be implemented in the agent control and detailed agent layers.

4 Some Control Issues for Using Agent Templates

Perhaps the greatest challenge is developing an agent control layer. To date there is no general-purpose agent problem-solving unit. The flow of control in the agent directly influences how the overall agent template must be designed. Like most agents, ABeI uses a rule-based problem-solving mechanism that is incorporated in a larger agent control layer. The control layer incorporates control issues needed to run general agent tasks (i.e., sending/receiving messages, accessing knowledge base, initiating proactive behaviors, scheduling of tasks, etc.). The control layer does not determine which performative to use in a message nor does it manipulate the content of a message.

We have made a number of design decisions to support design autonomy [5] within the template. Our initial design of the agent template assumed that all information would flow between layers in a hierarchy: transport, message, protocol, agent control, and detailed agent. This design was too restrictive for the creation of a collection of communicating autonomous agents because the agent control layer needed to interact with other layers. We have adapted our interfaces accordingly. The second decision was to select either a single thread of control or multiple threads of control for the different layers. Like Jade[6], the ABeI architecture has a single thread of control directed by the agent control layer. However, the control layer may spawn additional threads to initiate certain predefined behaviors.

There are a number of open research problems dealing with autonomy, proactivity and control in agent-based systems. We are continuing to develop our agent template and explore many of these issues for large scale enterprise computing.

References

1. Jeon, H., Petrie, C., Cutkosky, M. R.: JATLite: A Java Agent Infrastructure with Message Routing. In IEEE Internet Computing 4:2(March/April 2000)
2. Bayardo, R., Bohrer, W., Brice, R., et. al.: InfoSleuth: Semantic Integration of Information in Open and Dynamic Environments. In Proceedings of the 1997 ACM International Conference on the Management of Data (SIGMOD). May 1997
3. Berry, N. M., and Pancerella, C. M.: Agent-Based Enterprise Integration. In Proceedings of the Fourth International Conference and Exhibition on The Practical Application of Intelligent Agents and Multi-Agents (PAAM 99). April 1999

4. Whiteside, R. A., Friedman-Hill, E. J. and Detry, R. J.: PRE: A framework for enterprise integration. In Proceedings of Design of Information Infrastructure Systems for Manufacturing 1998 (DIISM '98). May 1998
5. Singh, M. P.: Agent Communication Languages: Rethinking the Principles. In IEEE Computer 31:12(December 1998)
6. Bellifemine, F., Poggi, A., and Rimassa, G.: JADE – A FIPA-compliant agent framework. In Proceedings of the Fourth International Conference and Exhibition on The Practical Application of Intelligent Agents and Multi-Agents (PAAM 99). April 1999

A Community of Agents
for User Support
in a Problem-Solving Environment

Line Pouchard[1] and David W. Walker[1]

Computer Science and Mathematics,
Oak Ridge National Laboratory, P. O. Box 2008,
Oak Ridge TN 37831-6414, USA
{pouchardlc, walkerdw}@ornl.gov

Abstract. A community of agent system is proposed for administration and control of remote instrumentation in the Materials Microcharacterization Collaboratory (MMC). The MMC is a joint-project between national laboratories, academia and industrial collaborators in the US. The community of agents makes use of software agents for user authorization and authentication, training, scheduling instrumentation, and responding to user queries. A methodology providing for agent responsibilities and an interaction model is being used. Scalability issues discussed include raising the number of instruments and of users in the system. The authorization and authentication agent creates a bottleneck.

1 Introduction

The Materials Microcharacterization Collaboratory (MMC) is a joint project between national laboratories, academia, and industrial collaborators across the US [1]. We use the example of the MMC to propose a multi-agent architecture for the support of scientific users in a problem-solving environment. In this architecture, a community of agents interacts to provide users of the MMC with intelligent services such as dynamic scheduling, query handling, training, and authentication and access control. The system is expected to scale up to 100 users; this represents the expected maximum user population in the MMC. The methodology used to design the system provides for its extensibility. This paper describes an agent-oriented architecture for solving the problem of user support in a collaborative problem-solving environment. It is currently being implemented and will be the topic of future papers.

2 Background

A "Collaboratory" has been defined as a research "center without walls, in which the nation's researchers can perform their research without regard to geographical location - interacting with colleagues, accessing instrumentation, sharing data

T. Wagner and O.F. Rana (Eds.): Infrastructure for Agents, LNAI 1887, pp. 192–198, 2001.

and computational resources, and accessing information in digital libraries." [2] Scientists in a Collaboratory perform experiments, share data across distributed sites, analyze and record results across geographical and organizational boundaries. The purpose of collaboration within the MMC is to characterize the microstructure of material samples using techniques such as electronic microscopy, and x-ray and neutron diffraction. Observation, data acquisition, and analysis are performed using instruments such as transmission and scanning electronic microscopes, and a neutron beam line. An important aspect of the MMC project is the computer co-ordination and control of remote instrumentation, data repositories, visualization platforms, computing power, and expertise that are distributed over a national scale. In the MMC's first phase, instruments operational at individual laboratories with varying capabilities were brought online and broadcast on the Web; synchronous observation and data analysis for purposes of comparison can be performed over the Internet [3]; other functionality is also provided with DeepView [4]. DeepView is a collaborative framework for distributed microscopy providing CORBA-based services for the remote control of instrumentation.

In the MMC, collaborators from academia and industry are invited to send a proposal for having their samples examined with an instrument at one of the labs [5]. Once cost and research method have been agreed upon, the user sends the sample for experiment. Two options are possible: a) the user travels to the site and interacts directly with the instrument under the supervision of expert instrument staff; b) the user connects to the instrument with a secure network connection and observes the experiment on his desktop while an expert onsite manipulates instrument and sample for him. In certain cases, the user is remotely connected to the instrument through DeepView, and, depending on his individual access level, the user can remotely control some instrument controls, such as magnification and focus.

3 Analysis

The MMC owns about 50 instruments spread across the U.S. and a dozen of them is available for remote collaboration. This year's focus is to provide users with support tools that enable effective and efficient use of the MMC facilities. The goal of the Community of Agents is to provide seamlessly integrated intelligent services to users of the MMC. The community of agents provides an adaptive framework for a wide range of intelligent services for supporting resource discovery, remote data acquisition, and analysis.

3.1 Why use an agent-based system for the MMC?

An agent-based architecture such as the one proposed in this paper is appropriate to the type of problem to be solved here. The tasks performed by each component in our system can be solved independently by object-oriented software. But an agent-based system provides users with capabilities beyond that of any single component such as: concurrency (several agents can execute simultaneously); a common interface for separate components; proper workflow between tasks performed by the agents (e.g. complete training before scheduling time on an instrument); and appropriate levels of access. With independently implemented OO components, the user or a staff member would have the responsibility of launching separate applications, ensuring proper workflow between tasks, and controlling access to the instruments.

An agent-based system is also desirable because it provides a good abstraction for representing communication between people. The agents' ability to represent users make it intuitive for utilizing the system (user point of view) and modeling the problem (developers' point of view). Agents representing various groups of users and entities in the system (e.g. instrument, schedule, etc..) are designed. These agents can have various degrees of autonomy according to users or expert staff's preferences. Such a system requires high level cooperation and negotiation between the components.

Another reason for the choice of an agent-oriented architecture is the geographical distribution of resources, expertise, and instruments. Information, resources and instruments are distributed across the nation at various facilities. Scientists with expertise on each resource act independently; the use of these resources, the parameters of experiments and the interpretation of data are also independent. Thus, the role played by a community of agents in bringing resources and expertise together for the benefit of a single user may not be achieved independently by a single component.

3.2   Methodology

We have designed an agent-oriented architecture model using the methodology for agent-oriented analysis and design proposed in [6]. Our multi-agent system makes use of software agents for user authorization and training, scheduling instrumentation, and responding to user queries. The different agents in the system are distinguished according to their roles and responsibilities. An interaction model is built on the protocols of interaction between agents. The agents interact with each other and with human users, experts, technicians, and controllers. A User Agent (UA) coordinates the distribution of tasks to the other agents. The Authorization and Control Agent (CA) is of central importance, and is responsible for checking what actions, if any, a given user is permitted to perform on a particular instrument. Access permissions are based on the user's level of experience (human experts may override the agents), prior training on a particular instrument, payment of fees if any, and security clearance level. The ACA also interacts with the Scheduling Agent (SA), the Training Agent (TA), and the Query Agent (QA). The SA responds to user requests to use an instrument according to the user's authorization status, the instrument usage rules, and its availability. The TA supervises on-line training of users. The QA responds to queries based on on-line knowledge repositories, and when necessary human expertise. The QA (Query Agent) may operate without obtaining prior authorization from the Control Agent for some queries (such as FAQ, and initial information requests). Additional agents for authorization, queries, and scheduling are associated with each instrument and are activated when an instrument is actually used.

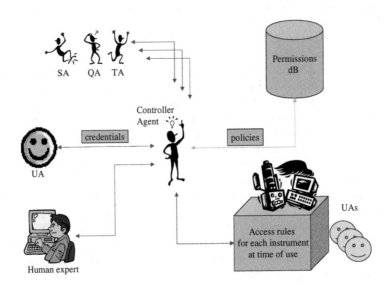

Fig. 1. Interaction model from the perspective of the Controller Agent (*CA*). This view shows all the agents in the system because the CA interacts with all the other agents: the Scheduling Agent (*SA*), the Query Agent (*QA*), and the Training Agent (*TA*). The CA receives access policies from a Permissions database, and credentials from a User Agent (*UA*). The CA also receives sub-type of agents and access rules from each instrument (*IA*).

4   Implementation plan

4.1   Use of agent design environments

We are considering two options. The first is the Zeus Agent toolkit [7] and plain Java for implementation. An agent communication language is used to enable communication between agents. Zeus provides a TCP/IP-based message passing mechanism and transmits messages obeying the 1997 FIPA ACL specification [8]. The Zeus toolkit uses 20 performatives. FIPA ACL provides the advantage of promised standardization. Zeus includes an Agent Generator and standard agent utilities (a facilitator, a visualizer, a name server).

The second is Voyager from ObjectSpace [9]. Voyager is designed to support mobile agents with a system of proxies. It supports CORBA, RMI, and DCOM, includes a naming service, a directory service, an activation framework and publish-subscribe messages.

4.2   Scalability issues

The system includes 5 main agents: Control (CA), Query (QA), Training (TA), Scheduling (SA), and User Agent (UA). There are sub-types of agents associated with instruments (1 per instrument). These verify authorizations at time of use. No agent is associated with databases, and knowledge repositories. User Agents run on clients' machines. The Query and Training Agent may also run on clients, depending on the type of interaction. The total number of agents depend on the number of instruments and the number of users active in the system. In practice, the expert staff available for assisting users limits these numbers.

The methodology allows adding a new role or a new interaction to the existing system. However, we anticipate that adding a new user (by instantiating the User Agent) is easier than adding a new agent with new functionality. Adding a new role may occur when a new type of interaction between a user and the system emerges. For instance, if the user needs to manipulate the control of an instrument remotely, a new role is created that provides the interaction between the system and DeepView. In this case, a new agent role is added to the architecture and its protocols of interaction with existing components defined.

4.3   Ontologies

Domain and task ontologies may be developed for providing common semantics to agent messages. One ontology per domain corresponding to the types of measurements, such as microscopy, diffraction, high temperature measurements, and x-rays may be necessary. For example, in microscopy an ontology may reduce the confusion introduced in instrument controls by different microscope vendors. An ontology of users, where user groups and their profiles are defined may also be required as user profiles determine levels of access. Zeus includes an ontology editor.

4.4   Databases

Agents communicate with databases and convey information to the user browser using XML. Ontologies may also provide a metadata scheme for developing XML DTDs. The re-use of existing DTDs will be investigated.

5   Discussion

We have designed the architecture using the methodology proposed in [6]. We find that this methodology served our purposes well for defining the various roles and responsibilities of agents, and the protocols by which these agents interact. In particular, the need for a User Agent that manages the interaction between the individual user and each agent became apparent while using the method. As the abstract roles, responsibilities, and protocols are well defined before agent types are defined, aggregated and instantiated, the method permits extensibility of the system.

The methodology does not ensure any means for the scalability of the resulting architecture. For this scalability, we can scale the number of agents, replacing single agents with multiple agents for the UA, SA, TA, and QA, each running on the user client. As the number of users increases, so does the processing power of the system. However, the CA may create a bottleneck since the CA authorizes access control for all other agents and instruments.

Further development will show whether parallel execution of code is required in addition to the existing concurrent execution of agents on various user clients. MMC users require advanced visualization components in order to remotely observe experiments and acquire raw data, but few computationally intensive calculations are currently performed on this data.

Task and domain ontologies must be developed to formally define and constrain the use of concepts relevant to instrument manipulation, and the attributes of such concepts. The literature emphasizes the need for ontologies in agent-based systems, and re-affirms the importance of tasks and domain ontologies for inter-operability and for content exchange in context [10, 11]. Without such ontologies, the confusion introduced by instrument vendors who need to maintain a competitive advantage will pervade the agent-based system. This confusion will render the system difficult to use for evaluation of parameters and interpretation of results by users. This in turn may result in the support system not being used at all.

Finally, the idea of a Community of Agents must be emphasized. Several agents in our system are proposed to perform various actions and act towards the common goal of efficient and effective user support for MMC users. The Community of Agents provides capabilities beyond the scope of any single agent. However, we do not have a Multi-Agent System (MAS), in the strict sense defined by Nwana [10]. A MAS is defined as a system interconnecting agents developed by different developers. Provision is made for a DeepView agent in our system; this introduces development by separate developers. But until DeepView is integrated, all agents are being developed by the same developers and do not include communication with any legacy code.

6   Summary and future work

We proposed a multi-agent system for supporting users of a scientific environment. The system is expected to scale up to 100 users. User Agents representing each user, Scheduling Agents representing each instrument, and Query and Training Agents run on the user client. These agents communicate with each other using a java-based agent communication language, and with databases using XML. The Authorization and Control Agent may present an obstacle to scalability.

Our system can be used for user support, administration and control in other collaboratories and in collaborative problem-solving environments. These environments typically involve geographically distributed resources and users for solving scientific applications. Another interesting future development is the integration of intelligence in the agents. Agents with access to knowledge repositories and some decision-making capabilities may guide scientists about the choice of resources and offer help on how to run scientific applications.

References

1. The Materials Microcharacterization Collaboratory. Available at
   http://tpm.amc.anl.gov/MMC/HomePage.html
2. Kouzes, R.T., Myers, J.D., Wulf, W.A.: Collaboratories: Doing Science on the Internet. IEEE Computer **29:8** (August 1996)
3. The Advanced Analytical Electron Microscope (AAEM) TelePresence Microscopy Site. Available at http://tpm.amc.anl.gov/TPMLVideo.html
4. Parvin, B., Taylor, J., Cong, G., O'Keefe, M., Barcellos-Hof, M.H.: DeepView: A Channel For Distributed Microscopy And Informatics. Proceedings of the ACM/IEEE SC99 Conference. Portland, OR. (November 1999)
5. MMC Resource Request. Available at
   http://tpm.amc.anl.gov/MMC/MMCResourceRequest.html
6. Wooldridge, M, Jennings, N.R., and Kinny, D. L.: A Methodology for Agent-Oriented Analysis and Design. Proceedings of Autonomous Agents 99. Seattle, WA. (June 1999)
7. The Zeus Agent toolkit. Available at
   http://www.labs.bt.com/projects/agents/zeus/index.htm
8. FIPA ACL. Available at http://drogo.cselt.it/fipa and http://www.fipa.org
9. Voyager. Available at http://www.objectspace.com
10. Nwana, H. S., Ndumu, D. T.: A Perspective on Software Agents Research. The Knowledge Engineering Review **14:2** (February 1999) 125-142
11. Huhns, M., Singh M. P.: Ontologies for Agents. IEEE Internet Computing, **1:6** (November-December 1997) 81-88

Scalable Mobile Agents Supporting Dynamic Composition of Functionality

In-Gyu Kim[1], Jang-Eui Hong[1], Doo-Hwan Bae[1], Ik-Joo Han[1], and
Cheong Youn[2]

[1] Dept. of Electrical Engineering & Computer Science, KAIST,
373-1, Kusong-dong, Yusong-gu, Taejon 305-701, Korea
{igkim, jehong, bae, ijhan}@salmosa.kaist.ac.kr
[2] Dept. of Computer Science, Chung-Nam National University,
220, Kung-dong, Yusong-gu, Taejon 305-764, Korea
cyoun@cs.chungnam.ac.kr

Abstract. Mobile agents are increasingly used in various Internet-based
applications such as electronic commerce, network management, and information retrieval. If mobile agents can dynamically add, delete, and
change their functionalities at run-time, they can sufficiently satisfy characteristics such as scalability, dynamicity, robustness, and performance,
which are important in Internet-based applications. In this paper, we
introduce Dynamic Composition of Functionality (DCF) based on code
mobility, which enables mobile agents to dynamically compose their functionalities at run-time. In order to realize DCF based on code mobility,
we propose necessary language constructs and implement a platform for
scalable mobile agents, called DC-AOP. We also present a case study
using DC-AOP to show the usefulness of our proposal.

1 Introduction

As the Internet has grown explosively, the demand of Internet-based applications
is growing rapidly. Some of Internet-based applications such as electronic commerce, network management, and information retrieval are developed by using
mobile agents, which are mobile objects that are capable of navigating through
the network autonomously and performing tasks at the nodes they visit.

Since these Internet-based applications often need to be scalable and are operational on dynamic and unreliable Internet environments, they are required to
possess characteristics such as scalability, dynamicity, robustness, performance,
etc.

Mobile agents supporting DCF based on code mobility give us a great benefits for satisfying these characteristics. Dynamic Composition of Functionality[1]
(DCF) for mobile agents means the capability of adding, deleting, and changing
dynamically functionalities at run-time. DCF based on code mobility is capable

---

[1] Functionality means a unit of computation such as a method or an object

T. Wagner and O.F. Rana (Eds.): Infrastructure for Agents, LNAI 1887, pp. 199–213, 2001.

of adding functionalities in remote nodes into their own behaviors by code mobility at run-time. How mobile agents supporting DCF based on code mobility satisfy the characteristics of Internet-based applications, is shown as follows.

- Scalability: Since scalable mobile agents can add their functionalities at run-time, they can expand their functionalities. For example, when a scalable mobile agent does not have a functionality for printing as it visits a node and needs to print a message at the node, it can add a functionality for printing in a remote node into its behavior and use the functionality at run-time.
- Dynamicity: Each node in the Internet has different environments (for example, memory size and CPU power). Since scalable mobile agents are able to add or change their functionalities at run-time, they can provide services at each node in different ways according to the characteristics of each node.
- Robustness: When faults occur in a node, scalable mobile agents can add functionalities for exception handling in remote nodes into their behaviors and use the functionalities to overcome the faults at run-time. Thus, scalable mobile agents can continue their works robustly.
- Performance: Scalable mobile agents do not need to have all functionalities initially which are used by them. They can initially have only necessary functionalities at first time. And when they need to use other functionalities such as exception handling functionalities, they can add the functionalities at run-time. In addition, when they do not use existing functionalities any more, they can delete the functionalities and move fast to other nodes. Thus, scalable mobile agents can reduce network traffic and enhance their performance by adding or deleting functionalities at run-time.

In order to satisfy above characteristics, there are many aspects to consider. However, we satisfy the characteristics only in aspect of DCF based on code mobility.

There exists some research on DCF based on code mobility for mobile agents [1, 14, 16]. However, they only partially address DCF based on code mobility. For example, mobile agents in existing researches lack the capability of adding functionalities in remote nodes by code mobility. Thus, they do not provide all benefits obtained through code mobility [5].

This paper addresses DCF based on code mobility for mobile agents. We, first, introduce DCF based on code mobility in detail. Second, in order to realize DCF based on code mobility, we propose the language constructs and introduce a platform for scalable mobile agents, called DC-AOP. Third, we present a case study to show the usefulness of our proposal.

The rest of this paper is organized as follows: In Section 2, we give related works and show features of each work. We also evaluate DCF based on code mobility of each work and compare the related works with respect to various features. In Section 3, we show the motivation of DCF based on code mobility and describe DCF based on code mobility in detail. In Section 4, in order to realize DCF based on code mobility, we propose the language constructs and introduce a platform for scalable mobile agents. In Section 5, we provide a case study using DC-AOP to show the usefulness of our proposal. In Section 6, we conclude our research with further works.

2   Related Work

There exist many researches on mobile agents [6, 12–16, 18, 19, 22]. In this section, four works, which are closely related to our work among them, are presented. For each work, we survey various features and evaluate DCF based on code mobility. We compare these works with a platform DC-AOP which we implement for DCF based on code mobility.

2.1   MESSENGERS

MESSENGERS [6–9], which was developed at the University of California, Irvine, is a distributed computing system based on autonomous objects, and aims at general-purpose distributed applications. Autonomous objects are mobile entities capable of navigating autonomously through nodes in the network and performing tasks at the nodes they visit.

MESSENGERS is implemented in C and is operational on a LAN environment. Autonomous objects which are programmed in a script language, are interpreted by daemons on nodes in the network.

Autonomous objects in MESSENGERS, called Messengers, navigate a logical network which is composed of logical nodes and edges. They can change the logical network by using navigational statements (`create(node, link, weight, daemon)`, `delete(node, link, weight, daemon)`, `hop(node, link, daemon, NODE, LINK, WEIGHT)`). They, at each node, perform tasks by invoking the ordinary C functions resident in the nodes.

Messengers can add functions in other nodes into their own behaviors not by code mobility but by Network File System (NFS) and call the functions in the current node. In other words, currently the MESSENGERS language specification only supports carrying function specifications with Messengers. When a Messenger invokes a function with a given function specification, the MESSENGERS daemon loads the corresponding shared library by NFS, dynamically links it to itself, and calls it. Hence, MESSENGERS does not fully support DCF based on code mobility.

2.2   AGLETS

Aglets Software Development Kit (ASDK) [13], which was developed at IBM's Tokyo Research Laboratories, is a platform for building network based applications based on mobile agents called aglets. ASDK aims at a uniform platform for mobile agents in heterogeneous environments such as the Internet. Thus, ASDK provides Aglet API which is an agent development kit - a set of Java classes and interfaces that allows you to create mobile Java agents.

ASDK is implemented in Java and is operational on the Internet environment. Because mobile agents in ASDK are programmed in Java, they can exploit various characteristics of Java language: Simple, Portable, Dynamic, and so on [3, 10, 21]. Especially, Java can support dynamic-binding of remote classes by the customized class loader. If mobile agent platforms provide such customized class loader, mobile agents in the mobile agent platforms can support the dynamicity: they can dynamically perform tasks by dynamic-binding of remote classes at runtime. However, ASDK does not provide customized class loader supporting dynamic-binding of remote classes. Thus, ASDK does not support DCF based on code mobility.

2.3   Java-To-Go

Java-To-Go [14], which was developed at the University of California, Berkeley, is a framework for developing agent-based applications for itinerative computing (itinerative computing: the set of applications that requires site-to-site computations). It aims at providing tool and environment to experiment with agents and agent-based applications.

Java-To-Go is implemented in Java and is operational on the Internet environment. Java-To-Go provides a customized class loader called RemoteClassLoader. RemoteClassLoader enables agents to load classes in predefined remote nodes (previous node, agent home node). Because RemoteClassLoader cannot load classes in other remote nodes rather than the predefined remote nodes, Java-To-Go partially supports DCF based on code mobility.

2.4   Voyager

Voyager [16], which was developed at ObjectSpace is the Agent ORB for Java. Voyager combines the features of ORB with those of mobile agents. It provides the ability for programmers to create and use objects on remote systems as if those objects were in the same Java virtual machine. It also enables general objects to have mobility feature. It enables general objects to move to other nodes by using `Mobility.of()` and `Agent.of()`.

Voyager is implemented in Java and in operational on the Internet environment. Voyager provides a customized class loader called VoyagerClassLoader which enables agents to load explicitly classes from another node. Voyager also supports the concept of dynamic aggregation, which allows an agent to extend its own behavior at run time. This means that an agent in Voyager extends its own behavior by adding to itself new functionality called *facet* at run time. When agents move to other nodes, the facets which was dynamically aggregated move together with them. However, agents in Voyager search facets in the current local node and cannot delete the added facets. Thus, Voyager partially supports DCF based on code mobility.

2.5   Comparison of Related Works

Table 1 compares the related works and our work with respect to various features which are related to DCF based on code mobility. The comparing features shown in Table 1 mean that:

- Loading functionalities from other nodes: Mobile agents can load (add) functionalities from other nodes by code mobility.
- Moving together with the added functionalities: A mobile agent can add functionalities into its own behavior at run time and move together with the added functionalities.
- Changeability of the added functionalities: A mobile agent can delete the added functionalities at run-time. Thus, it can change the added functionalities.

We implemented a platform for scalable mobile agents supporting DCF based on code mobility, which is called DC-AOP. Only DC-AOP satisfies all the above features. We address more details about DC-AOP in Section 4.2.

Table 1. Comparison of related works and our work (DC-AOP)

Features	Mobile agent platforms					
	MESSENGERS	AGLETS	Java-To-Go	Voyager		DC-AOP
				class	facet	
Loading functionalities from other nodes	Yes (Partially)	No	Yes (Partially)	Yes	No	Yes
Moving together with the added functionalities	No	No	No	No	Yes	Yes
Changeability of the added functionalities	-	-	-	-	No	Yes

3   Dynamic Composition of Functionality Based on Code Mobility

In order to satisfy the characteristics of Internet-based applications such as scalability, dynamicity, robustness, and performance, it is important that mobile agents support DCF based on code mobility. In this section, we show the motivation of DCF based on code mobility and describe DCF based on code mobility in detail.

3.1   Motivation

Bic, et al. who developed MESSENGERS, defined that DCF for mobile agents[2] means a capability of dynamically incorporating functions into their own behav-

---

[2] In [1], they used "autonomous objects" term instead of "mobile agents" term

iors at run time [1]. "incorporating" means that mobile agents can add functions into their behaviors and call the functions. Bic, et al. categorized levels of DCF such as follows [1].

– None level: Mobile agents have no ability to invoke functions or to interact with processes. Thus, mobile agents supporting this level cannot dynamically incorporate functions into their own behaviors.
– Process-based level: Mobile agents can invoke a function by spawning a new process on the receiving node. This means that mobile agents can dynamically incorporate functions into their own behaviors by spawning new processes on the current node.
– Resident-function-based level: Mobile agents can invoke and execute node-resident functions not only as separate child processes but also by dynamically linking them into the currently running process. Thus, mobile agents can dynamically incorporate functions in the current node into their own behaviors.
– Carried-function-based level: Mobile agents can carry a function specification in some form (as source code or native code, for example) and invoke it at the receiving node. Such carrying of function specification and invoking of functions support that mobile agents can dynamically incorporate functions in other nodes into their own behaviors.

In Carried-function-based level, mobile agents carry only with function specifications, link functions corresponding to the function specifications at the receiving node, and invoke the functions. However, they do not carry the linked functions, which means that MESSENGERS does not fully address DCF based on code mobility which enables mobile agents to add functions in remote nodes and carry with the added functions. Mobile agents can obtain many benefits from DCF based on code mobility, which are explained in Section 1. Thus, in this paper, we focus on DCF based on code mobility, which enables mobile agents to scale their functionalities.

3.2   DCF Based on Code Mobility

DCF based on code mobility for mobile agents means the capability of adding functionalities in remote nodes dynamically into their own behaviors by code mobility, and deleting and changing the added functionalities at run-time.

Functionalities which mobile agents supporting DCF based on code mobility can use are shown as follows [11].

– Built-in functionality: Mobile agents can use functionalities within themselves as if objects use methods within themselves. Built-in functionalities are added into the behaviors of mobile agents at compile-time. Mobile agents in all existing platforms support built-in functionalities.
– Resident functionality: Mobile agents can use functionalities in the current node as if objects use library functions (for example, System.out.println()) in the current node. Resident functionalities are added at run-time. If mobile

agents want to use any other functionality rather than built-in functionality at run-time, the current node has to provide the functionality. Otherwise, the mobile agents cannot use the functionality at run-time. In order to fully support mobile agents using resident functionalities, nodes have to provide all resident functionalities which are used by the mobile agents.

- Carried functionality: Mobile agents can add functionalities in remote nodes into their behaviors by code mobility and use the functionalities at run-time. When they move to other nodes, they can carry the added functionalities. And they can use the added (carried) functionalities at the nodes.

The behaviors of a mobile agent supporting DCF based on code mobility are shown as follows.

- A mobile agent can use built-in functionalities.
- A mobile agent can use resident functionalities.
- A mobile agent has functionality specifications.
- When a mobile agent needs a functionality corresponding to a functionality specification, it adds the functionality in a remote node into its behavior by code mobility.
- A mobile agent uses the added functionality.
- When a mobile agent moves to other nodes, it moves together with the added functionality.
- A mobile agent can delete the added functionality.

Figure 1 shows a mobile agent MA1 performing some of above behaviors. At compile-time, MA1 has three built-in functionalities (Analysis, Travel, Calculate) and the functionality specification of Display. In node A, MA1 uses a built-in functionality Analysis [numbered with (1) in Figure 1]. MA1 moves to node B only with the functionality specification [(2)]. In node B, MA1 loads (adds) functionality Display corresponding to the functionality specification from node E by code mobility [(3)] and uses the loaded functionality [(4)] as well as built-in functionality Calculate [(5)]. MA1 moves to node C together with both the loaded functionality and the functionality specification [(6)]. In node C, MA1 uses the loaded functionality [(7)] as well as built-in functionality Travel [(8)]. Then, MA1 disposes (deletes) the loaded functionality [(9)]. MA1 moves to node D only with the functionality specification[(10)].

4   Realizing DCF Based on Code Mobility

In this section, in order to realize DCF based on code mobility, we propose the language constructs for DCF based on code mobility and introduce a platform for mobile agents supporting DCF based on code mobility, which is called DC-AOP.

4.1   Language Constructs

For DCF based on code mobility, we propose the following language constructs.

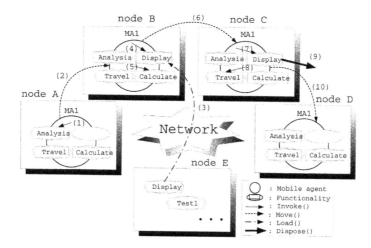

Fig. 1. Behaviors of a mobile agent supporting DCF based on code mobility

- cafLoad(RemoteNodeLocation rnl, FunctionalitySpec fs): loads the functionality corresponding to functionality specification fs from remote node location rnl.
- cafDispose(FunctionalitySpec fs): disposes the loaded functionality corresponding to functionality specification fs out of the mobile agent's behavior.
- cafInvoke(FunctionalitySpec fs, Args args): invokes (calls or uses) the functionality corresponding to functionality specification fs with arguments args as input.
- cafMove(RemoteNodeLocation rnl): Mobile agents move to the node which is located in rnl together with the functionalities loaded by cafLoad().

A simplified example program of a mobile agent MA1 in Figure 1, is shown as follows.

```
(1)      public class MA1 extends MA
(2)      {
(3)          ...
(4)          public int do_work()
(5)          {
(6)              ...
(7)              Analysis(float_arg);
(8)              cafMove(nodeB);
(9)              ...
(10)             cafLoad(nodeE, fs_Display);
(11)             cafInvoke(fs_Display, Display_args1);
(12)             Calculate(int_arg);
(13)             ...
```

```
(14)                    cafMove(nodeC);
(15)                    ...
(16)                    cafInvoke(fs_Display, Display_args2);
(17)                    Travel();
(18)                    cafDispose(fs_Display);
(19)                    cafMove(nodeD);
(20)                    ...
(21)              }
(22)              public int Analysis(float x){ ... }
(23)              public String Travel(){ ... }
(24)              public int Calculate(int x){ ... }
(25)              ...
(26)        }
```

MA1 uses built-in functionality `Analysis` with `float_arg` as input [line numbered with (7)]. MA1 moves to `nodeB` [(8)]. MA1 loads the functionality corresponding to functionality specification `fs_Display` from `nodeE` [(10)]. MA1 uses the loaded functionality corresponding to the functionality specification `fs_Display` with `Display_args1` as input [(11)]. MA1 uses built-in functionality `Calculate` with `int_arg` as input [(12)]. MA1 moves to `nodeC` together with both the loaded functionality and the functionality specification [(14)]. MA1 uses the loaded functionality corresponding to the functionality specification `fs_Display` with `Display_args2` as input [(16)]. MA1 uses built-in functionality `Travel` [(17)]. MA1 disposes the loaded functionality corresponding to the functionality specification `fs_Display` [(18)]. MA1 moves to `nodeD` only with the functionality specification [(19)]. MA1 has built-in functionalities `Analysis`, `Travel`, and `Calculate` [(22), (23), (24)].

4.2   DC-AOP: A Platform for Mobile Agents Supporting DCF Based on Code Mobility

We implemented a platform for mobile agents supporting DCF based on code mobility, which is called DC-AOP[3]. In this section, we show an architecture of DC-AOP and explain the techniques with which we implemented DC-AOP.

Architecture of DC-AOP DC-AOP consists of engines and autonomous objects[4]. A high level architecture of engines and autonomous objects is shown in Figure 2. Each node (computer) in our DC-AOP consists of an operating system and Java virtual machine and Engine. Engine plays a role of a server for autonomous objects. Engines receive autonomous objects from other nodes and send the autonomous objects to other nodes. Then, they provide environments where autonomous objects can work.

---

[3] DC-AOP stands for Autonomous Object Platform supporting Dynamic composition of functionality based on Code mobility

[4] Autonomous objects and mobile agents are used interchangeably

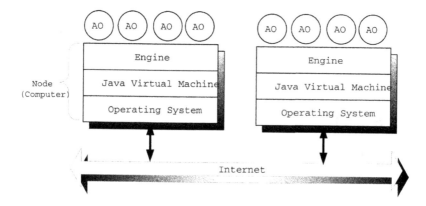

Fig. 2. High level architecture of DC-AOP

DC-AOP is programmed in Java. It operates on the Internet environment. DC-AOP is composed of 4 packages and 5 sub-packages and 21 classes. The size of DC-AOP's source code is 2561 lines of Java code. For more detail information on our platform, "http://salmosa.kaist.ac.kr/~igkim/DC-AOP/" is available.

Techniques Used to Support DCF Based on Code Mobility In order to implement DCF based on code mobility, we used the following techniques provided by Java.

- Dynamic Loading and Binding: ClassLoader is an abstract class that can be used to define policies for loading Java classes into the runtime environment [2].
  DC-AOP provides a subclass of ClassLoader: AOClassLoader. AOClass-Loader provides methods for customized class loading such as loadClass(). DC-AOP also provides a class for sending requested classes to requesters: RemoteClassServer. RemoteClassServer provides (sends) classes which are requested by autonomous objects in remote nodes. RemoteClassServer plays a role of class provider.
- Reflection: Java (java.lang.reflect) provides classes and interfaces for obtaining reflective information about Java classes and objects. Reflective information includes information about the members that a class has, the signatures of a class's constructors and members, and the types of its fields. With it, you also can create new objects, access and change an object's fields, and invoke an object's methods [2].
  Reflection is used when autonomous objects invoke the loaded functionality. Autonomous objects load objects from remote nodes and invoke methods in the loaded objects by reflection methods such as Method.invoke() and Class.getDeclaredMethod(), which are provided by Java.
- Serialization: Serializing an object means to convert its state into a byte stream in such a way that the byte stream can be reconverted back into a copy of the object [2].

Serialization is used for DCF based on code mobility as well as for sending and receiving autonomous objects. When autonomous objects move to other nodes, autonomous objects move together with loaded functionality. Loaded functionality is serialized into byte code and carried to other nodes and deserialized into functionality.

5   Case Study

In this section, we present web-based *dynamic component testing example* to show the capability of our suggestions.

5.1   Overview

In general, software components are developed by various vendors in different ways (for examples, performance, robustness, compatibility-focused implementation). In this example, an autonomous object called *DynamicComponentTestAO* moves to various nodes and at each node, tests a software component called *componentA* in the node by using a test functionality (first testing). After the first testing, DynamicComponentTestAO selects the nodes having componentA of good quality from the visited nodes. Then, it moves to the selected nodes and tests componentA again in the node by using another test functionality (second testing). Finally, it reports the node which has componentA of the best quality.

The typical scenario of DynamicComponentTestAO is as follows.

1. `DynamicComponentTestAO` is inserted into the engine in medusa by `AOStarter` which is used when autonomous objects are inserted into engines.
2. `DynamicComponentTestAO` loads a test functionality Test1 from boa.
3. `DynamicComponentTestAO` tests `componentA` in medusa by using the test functionality Test1.
4. `DynamicComponentTestAO` moves to other nodes (adam, salmosa, boa, se70, se59) and tests `componentA` in the node sequentially.
5. When `DynamicComponentTestAO` arrives at medusa, it changes the test functionality Test1 into another test functionality Test2 in boa.
6. `DynamicComponentTestAO` moves to the selected nodes (medusa, salmosa, se59) and tests `componentA` in the node sequentially by using the new test functionality Test2.
7. After `DynamicComponentTestAO` finishes its second testing at se59, it moves to medusa and reports the name of the node which has the component of the best quality.

Figure 3 shows graphically the above scenario. The test functionality is an object that has a method `test`. `DynamicComponentTestAO` with a test functionality Test1 moves to medusa, adam, salmosa, boa, se70, se59, and medusa sequentially (thin dotted line). `DynamicComponentTestAO` with the new test functionality Test2 moves to medusa, salmosa, se59, and medusa sequentially (bold dotted line).

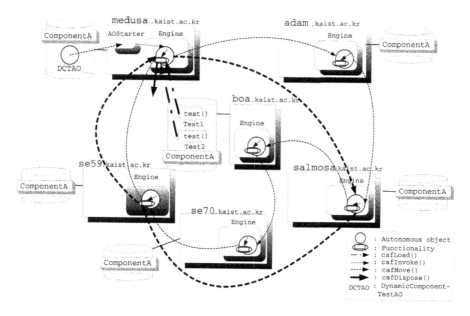

Fig. 3. Overview of dynamic component testing example

This example shows that autonomous objects supporting DCF based on code mobility satisfy scalability, dynamicity, and performance. After `DynamicComponent-TestAO` performs the first testing, it performs the second testing. Thus, it needs to change the functionality (`Test1`) into another functionality (`Test2`); Scalability & Dynamicity are enhanced. If autonomous objects do not support DCF based on code mobility, they have to add all functionalities for testing (`Test1`, `Test2`) at compile-time. Thus, for the first testing, they move carrying with `Test2` as well as `Test1`, which increases network traffic. Since `DynamicComponentTestAO` moves with only necessary a functionality (i.e., `Test1`), it can reduce the network traffic; Performance is enhanced. This example also shows that autonomous objects can be programmed by the concept of *separation of concerns*. `Dynamic-ComponentTestAO` is programmed by combining functionalities such as `Test1`, `Work`, `Travel`, etc. Autonomous objects supporting DCF based on code mobility can be programmed by combining functionalities as if we made toys by combining lego blocks.

5.2   Result

DynamicComponentTestAO prints messages at each node. The result of this example at each node is shown as follows.

– medusa

```
!!! Engine Ready !!!
###-------- First Travel: DynamicComponentTestAO arrives in medusa.kaist.ac.kr -------###
###-------- Second Travel: DynamicComponentTestAO arrives in medusa.kaist.ac.kr -------###
```

```
###@@@@@ host name having the best component is salmosa.kaist.ac.kr @@@@@###
DynamicComponentTestAO --- Success : do_work()
```

— adam

```
!!! Engine Ready !!!
###-------- First Travel: DynamicComponentTestAO arrives in adam.kaist.ac.kr -------###
```

— boa

```
!!! Engine Ready !!!
###-------- First Travel: DynamicComponentTestAO arrives in boa.kaist.ac.kr -------###
```

— salmosa

```
!!! Engine Ready !!!
###-------- First Travel: DynamicComponentTestAO arrives in salmosa.kaist.ac.kr -------###
###-------- Second Travel: DynamicComponentTestAO arrives in salmosa.kaist.ac.kr -------###
```

— se70

```
!!! Engine Ready !!!
###-------- First Travel: DynamicComponentTestAO arrives in se70.kaist.ac.kr -------###
```

— se59

```
!!! Engine Ready !!!
###-------- First Travel: DynamicComponentTestAO arrives in se59.kaist.ac.kr -------###
###-------- Second Travel: DynamicComponentTestAO arrives in se59.kaist.ac.kr -------###
```

The engine at each node prints the ready message (!!! Engine Ready !!!). DynamicComponentTestAO starts at medusa and moves to adam, boa, salmosa, se70, and se59 sequentially. At each node, it prints an arrival message and tests componentA at the node. After it finishes the first testing at the final node (se59), it selects nodes for the second testing and moves to the nodes (medusa, salmosa, se59) sequentially. It again tests componentA at each node by another functionality for testing (Test2). After the second testing, it moves to medusa and prints the name of the node having componentA of the best quality. It ends its work and prints the end message.

6 Conclusion and Further Work

Scalable mobile agents are mobile agents supporting DCF based on code mobility. Scalable mobile agents can sufficiently satisfy the characteristics of Internet-based applications that are scalability, dynamicity, robustness, and performance.

In this paper, we addressed DCF based on code mobility for mobile agents. Although some existing works about mobile agents have mentioned about DCF, they lack consideration for the extension of functionality by code mobility. In open system environments such as the Internet, code mobility is one of the important characteristics for scalable mobile agents. DCF based on code mobility provides rich functionalities more flexibly to Internet-based applications. Thus, DCF based on code mobility will contribute to enhancement of capabilities such as customizing services, reducing network traffic, and fault-tolerance (exception handling), which are needed in the development of mobile agent systems for Internet-based applications. In order to realize DCF based on code mobility, we designed the language constructs and implemented a platform (DC-AOP) for scalable mobile agents. We also applied DC-AOP to a system, which needs scalability, dynamicity, and performance.

While our research offers improvement in DCF based on code mobility, there are some issues that are worth to talk about further research. First, since the granularity of the functionality of existing general software systems is generally a set of objects (components), we need to extend the granularity of the functionality, which mobile agents add into their behaviors, to a set of objects (components) [20]. Second, in order to search functionalities needed by mobile agents, we could use the trader service for functionalities like CORBA trader service or exploit JINI technique that provides systematic search mechanisms such as lookup services [4, 17].

References

1. L. Bic, M. Fukuda, and M. Dillencourt. "Distributed Computing Using Autonomous Objects". *COMPUTER*, 29(8):55–61, August 1996.
2. P. Chan, R. Lee, and D. Kramer. *The Java Class Libraries Second Edition Volume 1*. Addison-Wesley, 1998.
3. G. Cugola, C. Ghezzi, G. Picco, and G. Vigna. "Analyzing Mobile Code Languages". *Mobile Object Systems: Towards the Programmable Internet, J. Vitek and C. Tschudin, eds., LNCS 1222. Springer-Verlag*, pages 93–109, April 1997.
4. W. Edwards. *Core JINI*. Prentice-Hall PTR, 1999.
5. A. Fuggetta, G. Picco, and G. Vigna. "Understanding Code Mobility". *IEEE Transactions on Software Engineering*, 24(5):342–361, May 1998.
6. M. Fukuda. *MESSENGERS: A Distributed Computing System Based on Autonomous Objects*. PhD thesis, Information and Computer Science, University of Carifornia, Irvine, 1997.
7. M. Fukuda, L. Bic, M. Dillencourt, and J. Cahill. "Messages versus Messengers in Distributed Programming". *Journal of Parallel and Distributed Computing*, 57(2):188–211, May 1999.
8. M. Fukuda, L. Bic, M. Dillencourt, and F. Merchant. "MESSENGERS: Distributed Programming Using Mobile Autonomous Objects". *Journal of Information Sciences*, 1997.
9. M. Fukuda, L. Bic, M. Dillencourt, and F. Merchant. "Distributed Coordination with MESSENGERS". *Science of Computer Programming Journal, Special Issue on Coordination Models, Languages, and Applications*, 31(2):291–311, July 1998.
10. J. Gosling and H. McGilton. The Java Language Environment: A White Paper. Technical report, Sun Microsystems, May 1996.
11. I. Kim. Dynamic Composition of Functionality using Code Mobility for Autonomous Objects. Master's thesis, Department of Computer Science, Korea Advanced Institute of Science and Technology, 2000.
12. J. Kiniry and D. Zimmerman. "A hands-On Look at Java Mobile Agents". *IEEE Internet Computing*, 1(4):21–30, 1997.
13. D. Lange and M. Oshima. *Programming and Deploying Java Mobile Agents With Aglets*. Addison-Wesley, 1998.
14. M. Li and D. Messerschmitt. Java-To-Go. Technical report, University of California, Berkeley, 1996.

15. W. Lugmayr. *Gypsy: A Componenet-Oriented Mobile Agent System*. PhD thesis, Distributed System Group, Technical University of Vienna, Austria, 1999.

16. ObjectSpace. ObjectSpace Voyager ORB 3.1 Developer Guide. Technical report, ObjectSpace Inc., 1999.

17. J. Siegel. *CORBA Fundamentals and Programming*. John Wiley & Sons, 1996.

18. A. Silva, M. Silva, and J. Delgado. "An Overview of AgentSpace: A Next-Generation Mobile Agent System". In *Proceedings of the Mobile Agents'98, K. Rothermel and F. Hohl, eds., LNCS 1477. Springer-Verlag*, pages 148–159, Sep. 1998.

19. M. Straßer, J. Baumann, and F. Hohl. "Mole - A Java Based Mobile Agent System". In *Special Issue Object-Oriented Programming: Workshop Reader of the 10th European Cof. Object-Oriented Programming ECOOP'96*, pages 327–334, dpunkt, July 1996.

20. C. Szyperski. *Component Software Beyond Object-Oriented Programming*. Addison-Wesley, 1998.

21. D. Wong, N. Paciorek, and D. Moore. "Java-based Mobile Agents". *Communicaions of the ACM*, 42(3):92–105, March 1999.

22. D. Wong, N. Paciorek, T. Walsh, J. DiCelie, M. Young, and B. Peet. "Concordia: An Infrastructure for Collaborating Mobile Agents". *Mobile Agents: First Int'l Workshop MA'97, K. Rothermel and R. Popescu-Zeletin, eds., LNCS 1219. Springer-Verlag*, pages 86–97, April 1997.

A Formal Development and Validation Methodology Applied to Agent-Based Systems [*]

Giovanna Di Marzo Serugendo

CERN/IT Division
CH-1211 Geneva 23, Switzerland
Giovanna.Di.Marzo@cern.ch
http://www.cern.ch/Giovanna.Di.Marzo

Abstract. This paper presents first a formal development methodology that enables a specifier to add complexity progressively into the system design, and to formally validate each step wrt client's requirements. Second, the paper describes the application of this methodology to agent-based systems, as well as development guidelines that help the specifier during the development of such systems. The methodology and the development guidelines are presented through an agent market place example.

1 Introduction

Multi-agent systems need, as any other system, to be supported by a proper development methodology. The need for such a methodology is more crucial in the case of agent-based systems, since the composition of independently developed agents may lead to unexpected emergent behaviour. In addition, agent-based systems are complex, and it is difficult for a specifier or a programmer to put every details immediately into his design.

This paper presents a *formal development methodology* that enables the designer to add complexity progressively into the system: problems are solved one after the other, and design decisions are formally validated at each step. The methodology follows the two languages framework, i.e., it advocates the joint use of a model-oriented specifications language for expressing the system's behaviour, and a property-oriented specifications language (logical language) for expressing properties. The proposed methodology is general enough and can be applied to any model-oriented formal specifications language. A particular application has been realised for a special kind of synchronized Petri nets, called CO-OPN/2 [1].

This paper describes as well *development guidelines for agent-based systems* within the proposed methodology. Agent decomposition, interactions between agents (composition, coordination, message passing, blackboard), as well as implementation constraints (e.g., actual communication using RMI, CORBA, etc.) are progressively added during the development process.

---

[*] Part of this work has been performed while the author was working at the University of Geneva and at the Swiss Federal Institute of Technology in Lausanne (EPFL).

T. Wagner and O.F. Rana (Eds.): Infrastructure for Agents, LNAI 1887, pp. 214–225, 2001.

The structure of this paper is as follows. Section 2 describes the formal development methodology, and presents the formal specifications language CO-OPN/2. Section 3 provides the development guidelines for agent-based systems. Section 4 illustrates the methodology and guidelines through a simple agent market place example. Section 5 presents related works.

2   Development Methodology

The proposed methodology addresses the three classical phases of the development process of distributed applications: the analysis phase, the design phase, and the implementation phase. This section presents the design phase, explains the necessity of development guidelines, and briefly describes CO-OPN/2.

2.1   Design by Contracts

The analysis phase produces informal requirements that the system has to meet. The design phase consists of the stepwise refinement of model-oriented specifications. Such specifications explicitly define the behaviour of a system, and implicitly define a set of properties (corresponding to the behaviour defined by the specification). During a refinement step it is not always necessary, desirable or possible, to preserve the whole behaviour proposed by the specification. Therefore, essential properties expected by the system are explicitly expressed by means of a set of logical formulae, called *contract*. A contract does *not* reflect the whole behaviour of the system, it reflects only the behaviour part that must be preserved during all subsequent refinement steps. A refinement is then defined as the replacement of an abstract specification by a more concrete one, which respects the contract of the abstract specification, and takes into account additional requirements.

The implementation phase is treated in a similar way as the design phase. At the end of the design phase, a concrete model-oriented specification is reached, it is implemented, and the obtained program is considered to be a correct implementation if it preserves the contract of the most concrete specification.

Figure 1 shows the three phases. On the basis of the informal requirements, an abstract specification $Spec_0$ is devised. Its contract $Contract_0$ formally expresses the requirements. During the design phase, several refinement steps are performed, leading to a concrete specification $Spec_n$ and its contract $Contract_n$. The implementation phase then provides the program Program and its contract Contract. A refinement step is correct if the concrete contract contains the abstract contract.

This methodology is founded on a general theory defined in [4]. The particularity of this methodology wrt traditional ones using the two languages framework is that it goes a step further, since the contracts explicitly point out the essential properties to be verified. Indeed, the specifier can freely refine the formal specifications, without being obliged to keep all the behaviour.

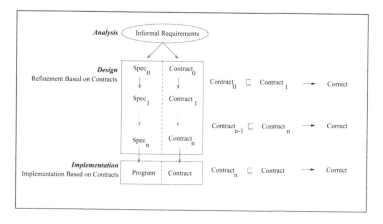

Fig. 1. Development Methodology

This methodology is well-suited for agent-based systems, since complexity is introduced progressively, and emergent behaviour can be controlled by the means of contract.

2.2 Development Guidelines

The theory of refinement and implementation based on contracts provides the basis to formally prove that a refinement step and the implementation phase are correct. However, the theory cannot help the specifier in establishing a contract, and in choosing a more concrete specification. Therefore, we suggest the use of *development guidelines*, i.e., a sequence of refinement steps that a specifier should follow when developing an application. Development guidelines depend on the kind of application being developed. They should be seen as refinement patterns, since, after having identified the system to develop, the specifier applies a dedicated series of design steps.

Development guidelines have already been defined for client/server applications [3], as well as for dependable applications [5].

2.3 CO-OPN/2 and HML

The above general theory has been applied to a high-level class of Petri nets, called CO-OPN/2, using the Hennessy-Milner logic (HML) as logical language. Examples of this paper will be illustrated using CO-OPN/2 and HML.

CO-OPN/2 [1] is an object-oriented formal specifications language. An object is defined as an encapsulated algebraic net in which places compose the internal state and transitions model the concurrent events of the object. Transitions are either methods (callable from other objects), or internal transitions (describing the internal behaviour of an object). Objects can be dynamically created. Each object has an identity that can be used as a reference. When an object requires a service, it asks to be synchronised with the method of the object provider (with). The synchronisation policy is expressed by means of a synchronisation expression, which can involve many partners joined by three synchronisation operators (simultaneity (//), sequence (..), and alternative (+)).

An HML formula, expressed on CO-OPN/2 specifications is a sequence (or a conjunction ($\wedge$), or an alternative (+)) of observable events (firing of a single method or parallel firing of several methods). An HML formula is satisfied by the model of a CO-OPN/2 specification if the sequence of events defined by the formula corresponds to a possible sequence of events of the model of the specification.

3   Agent-Based Systems

There is currently no general consensus on the definition of an agent. Therefore, this section first presents some preliminary definitions of what we think are an agent, and an agent-based system. Second, it describes the development guidelines identified for these systems.

3.1   Definitions

From a software engineering point of view, we consider an agent-based system in the following manner:

- the system performs some *functionality* to some final user (another software system, human being, etc.);
- the system is made of one or more *collections* of agents, together with *relationships* among collections (negotiation techniques, cooperation protocols, coordination models). Agents engage in collections, that can change at runtime (joint intentions, teams);
- agents in a collection *interact together* to solve a certain goal (message passing, blackboard, etc). They may have some social knowledge about their dependencies (peers, competitors);
- an agent is a *problem-solving entity*. It performs a given algorithm to reach its goal.

3.2   Development Guidelines

The development steps identified in the case of agent-based applications are the following:

1. *Informal Requirements:* a set of informal application's requirements including validation objectives is defined;
2. *Initial contractual specification: System's functionality.*
   Based on the informal requirements, the initial specification provides an abstract view of the system where the problem is *not* agent based. The contract reflects the functionality of the application;

3. *First refinement step: System's collections.* This step leads to a view of the system made of several collections of agents, together with the relationship among the collections (e.g. joint intentions, teams, etc.). The contract is extended to the functionality of each collection, and to the properties of their composition;
4. *Second refinement step: Collections design.* Each collection is specified as a set of agents together with their interactions (message passing, blackboard, dependencies). The contract describes the functionality of each agent in the collection, as well as the desired properties of the agents interactions;
5. *Third refinement step: Agent design.* The internal behaviour of each agent is fully described (algorithm used for solving its goal, action decision upon knowledge processing, etc.). The contract is extended to the properties expected by the internal behaviour of each agent;
6. *Fourth refinement step: Actual communications means.* The previous steps define the high-level communication means employed by the agents. This step integrates the low-level communications means upon which high-level communications can be realised (RMI, CORBA, etc.). The contract contains the characteristics of the chosen communication;
7. *Implementation.* Step 6 is implemented using the chosen programming language. The contract of step 6 is expressed on the program.

These guidelines enable the macro-level part (identification of collections of agents) to be followed by a micro-level part (design of collections, design of agents). In addition, the micro-level part can be done independently for every collection (steps 4. to 7.).

4   Market Place Example

We consider a simple market place example based on [2]. This section describes the development of this system according to the guidelines given above.

4.1   Informal Requirements

This step corresponds to guideline 1. The market place application offers some operations to buyers and sellers that have to respect the following requirements:

- A new buyer can register itself at any moment to the market place system;
- A new seller can register itself at any moment to the market place system;
- A registered buyer can propose a price for a given item that he wants to buy, and specifies the highest price that he is ready to pay for the item;
- A registered seller can make an offer for a given item that he wants to sell, and specifies the lowest price at which he is ready to sell the item;
- Buyers and sellers can consult the system to know if they have been involved in a transaction. The price reached during the transaction must be less or equal to the highest price specified by the buyer, and greater or equal to the lowest price specified by the seller.

4.2   Initial Specification: Functional View

The initial specification corresponds to development guideline 2. It is given by CO-OPN/2 specification made of `MarketPlace` class of Fig. 2.

Class MarketPlace

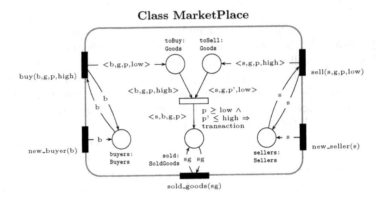

Fig. 2. Market Place System

This class offers five methods, corresponding to the five system operations identified in the previous design step (Section 4.1):

- the `new_buyer(b)` method is used by a buyer whose identity is b for registering itself to the system. The system simply enters identity b into place `buyers`;
- the `new_seller(s)` method is used by a seller, called s, for registration. The system simply enters identity s into place `sellers`;
- the `buy(b,g,p,high)` method enables an already registered buyer b to inform the system that he wants to buy an item g at a desired price p. The highest price he is ready to pay for the item is `high`. The system then enters this information into place `toBuy`;
- the `sell(s,g,p,low)` method enables an already registered seller s to propose the item g, with a starting price p, and a minimum price `low`. The offer is entered in place `toSell`.
  As soon as there is a request for buying item g and an offer concerning the same item g, with a buying price compatible with the lowest selling price, and a selling price compatible with the highest buying price, the transaction occurs. The request for buying and the offer are removed from the system by transition `transaction`, and the transaction is entered into place `sold`;
- the `sold_goods(sg)` method enables a buyer (or seller) to consult the system for occurred transactions.

Contract. In order to remain concise, we present a contract $\phi_{\mathbf{I}}$, expressed on this initial specification, made of only two HML formulae: $\phi_{\mathbf{I}_1}$ and $\phi_{\mathbf{I}_2}$. It is obvious that a larger contract is necessary to ensure all the informal requirements.

Assuming variables such that $l \leq p1 \leq h$, $p2 \leq l$ and $p3 \geq h$:

$$\phi_{\mathbf{I}_1} = <MP.\,\text{create}><MP.\,\text{new\_buyer}(b)><MP.\,\text{new\_seller}(s)>$$
$$<MP.\,\text{buy}(b,g,p,h)><MP.\,\text{sell}(s,g,p',l)><MP.\,\text{sold\_goods}(s,b,g,p1)>$$
$$\phi_{\mathbf{I}_2} = <MP.\,\text{create}><MP.\,\text{new\_buyer}(b)><MP.\,\text{new\_seller}(s)>$$
$$<MP.\,\text{buy}(b,g,p,h)><MP.\,\text{sell}(s,g,p',l)>$$
$$(\neg <MP.\,\text{sold\_goods}(s,b,g,p2)> \wedge \neg <MP.\,\text{sold\_goods}(s,b,g,p3)>) \,.$$

Formula $\phi_{\mathbf{I}_1}$ states that once the market place MP has been created, a buyer b, and a seller s can register themselves to the system. They can respectively make a request to buy item g, and an offer to sell item g. Then, the transaction occurs for prices $p1$ compatible with the lowest selling price, and with the highest buying price, i.e., such that $l \leq p1 \leq h$.

Formula $\phi_{\mathbf{I}_2}$ is similar to $\phi_{\mathbf{I}_1}$, but it states that for prices $p2$ such that $p2 \leq l$ and prices $p3$ such that $p3 \geq h$, then the transaction does *not* occur.

Contract $\phi_{\mathbf{I}}$ is actually satisfied by the model of the initial specification. Indeed, transition **transaction** is guarded by condition $p \geq low \wedge p' \leq high$. This condition prevents the firing of this transition whenever it does not evaluate to true.

4.3   Refinement R1: Agent Decomposition and Interactions

This step corresponds to development guideline 4. (In this example, step 3. is skipped, because the system contains only one collection of agents.)

The specification is made of three classes: the MarketPlace class, given by Fig. 3, the BuyerAgents class of Fig. 4, and the SellerAgents class of Fig. 5.

The MarketPlace class stands for the homonymous class of the initial specification. It offers the same interface as before to the actual buyers and sellers, enriched with some more methods:

- the new_buyer(b) and new_seller(s) methods enable a new buyer b, or a new seller s to enter the system. A dedicated agent b_agent, respectively s_agent is created. The system stores pairs, made of a buyer's identity and the identity of its dedicated agent, into place buyers; and pairs of seller's identity and agent's identity into place sellers;
- the buy(b,g,p,high) and sell(s,g,p,low) methods are used by buyer b, respectively seller s, to enter a request to buy an item, respectively an offer to sell an item into the system. The market place forwards this information to the agent that works on behalf of the buyer or the seller. It retrieves the identity of the corresponding agent, and calls the method new_good(g,p,high), respectively new_good(g,p,low);
- the sold_goods(sg) method enables buyers and sellers to consult the list of transactions;
- the get_buyers(l) and get_sellers(l) methods return the list of all buyer agents, and seller agents respectively. Method get_buyers(l) is used by seller agents to know the identities of buyer agents, in order to ask them

Class MarketPlace

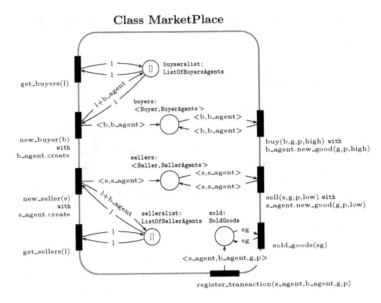

Fig. 3. Refinement R1: Market Place System

some services. Similarly, method `get_sellers(l)` is used by buyer agents to know identities of seller agents;

- the `register_transaction(s_agent,b_agent,g,p)` method is used by seller or buyer agents to inform the system about the transactions that have occurred.

The `BuyerAgents` class, given by Fig. 4, specifies buyer agents, while the `SellerAgents` class, given by Fig. 5, specifies seller agents. These classes are very similar, and behave almost in the same manner.

- the `create` constructor of the `BuyerAgents` class enables to create new instances of buyer agents;
- the `new_good(g,p,high)` method is called by the market place whenever the buyer (for whom the agent is working) enters a request to buy an item into the system. The agent stores the request into place `toBuy`. As soon as the request is stored in this place, transition `makeOffers` first contacts the market place in order to obtain the current list of sellers (this list changes when the system evolves, since new sellers can enter the system at any moment). Second, the transition informs every seller of this list (broadcast) that there is a new request for buying item `g`, by calling method `sendOffer` of each seller agent. If after some time, no transaction concerning this request has occurred, transition `timeout` increases the price from one unit (provided that the highest price condition is not violated);
- the `sendOffer(s_agent,g,p)` method is used by a seller agent, whose identity is `s_agent`, to inform the buyer agents that it sells item `g` at price `p`. As soon as the there is an offer for item `g` at a price `p`, which is the same as the

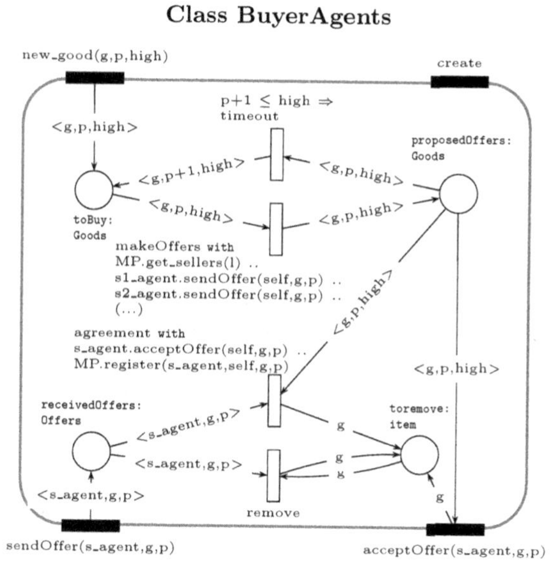

Class BuyerAgents

Fig. 4. Refinement R1: Buyer Agent

current price offered by the buyer agent, the transaction occurs. Transition `agreement` fires: it calls method `acceptOffer` of the corresponding seller agent (`s_agent`), and informs the market place. Due to the CO-OPN/2 semantics, transition `agreement` can fire only if method `acceptOffer` of the corresponding seller agent can fire. In that manner, only one agreement can be reached for a given offer (the seller does not sell two times the same item). Indeed, if the seller agent has already reached an agreement with another buyer, then its method `acceptOffer` cannot fire, and consequently transition `agreement` of the current buyer cannot fire;

– the `acceptOffer(s_agent,g,p)` method is called by a seller agent, whose identity is `s_agent`, when an agreement is reached with the buyer agent.

The **SellerAgents** class is similar to the **BuyerAgents** class, except that these agents decrease their prices when there is no corresponding buyer.

Contract. The contract for refinement R1 is made of three formulae. Considering, as before, variables such that: $l \le p1 \le h$, $p2 \le l$ and $p3 \ge h$, the contract is made of the three formulae below:

$\phi_{R1_1} = \phi_{I_1}, \phi_{R1_2} = \phi_{I_2}$

$\phi_{R1_3} = <MP. \text{create}><s\_agent. \text{create}><b1\_agent. \text{create}><b2\_agent. \text{create}>$
  $<s\_agent. \text{sendOffer}(b1\_agent, g, p)><s\_agent. \text{sendOffer}(b2\_agent, g, p)>$
  $<b1\_agent. \text{sendOffer}(s\_agent, g, p)><b2\_agent. \text{sendOffer}(s\_agent, g, p)>$
  $((<b1\_agent. \text{acceptOffer}(s\_agent, g, p)> + <b2\_agent. \text{acceptOffer}(s\_agent, g, p)>) \land$
  $\neg (<b1\_agent. \text{acceptOffer}(s\_agent, g, p)><b2\_agent. \text{acceptOffer}(s\_agent, g, p)>) \land$
  $\neg (<b1\_agent. \text{acceptOffer}(s\_agent, g, p)> // <b2\_agent. \text{acceptOffer}(s\_agent, g, p)>))$.

Formulae ϕ_{R1_1}, and ϕ_{R1_2} are the same as ϕ_{I_1} and ϕ_{I_2}. Formula ϕ_{R1_3} states that once the market place has been created, it is possible to create a seller agent

s_agent, and two buyer agents $b1\_agent$ and $b2\_agent$. The seller agent offers item g at price p, and the two buyer agents are ready to pay the same price p for g. The formula then states that either buyer agent $b1\_agent$ or $b2\_agent$ accepts the offer (+), but *not* both (neither in sequence, nor simultaneously (//)).

The three formulae of the contract are satisfied by the specification. Indeed, formulae ϕ_{R1_1} and ϕ_{R1_2} are true, because of the guarded transition `timeout`. There is no request (nor offer) that violates the condition $p + 1 \leq high$ (respectively $p - 1 \geq low$).

Formula ϕ_{R1_3} is true because transition `agreement` can fire only once per transaction: either transition `agreement` of the buyer agent fires, or that of the seller agent fires, but not both. The firing of transition `agreement` requires the firing of the method `acceptOffer` of the other agent involved in the transaction. The firing of these methods causes the removal of token `<g,p,high>` from place `proposedOffers` of the buyer agent, and `<g,p,low>` from place `proposedOffers` of the seller agent. In that manner, transition `agreement` and method `acceptOffer` cannot fire more than once for each offer.

Although the internal behaviour of the initial specification and the first refinement are different (the agreement is reached on a different basis), the specification of the first refinement is actually a correct refinement of the initial specification. Indeed, the contract of the initial specification is preserved by the refinement R1.

Class SellerAgents

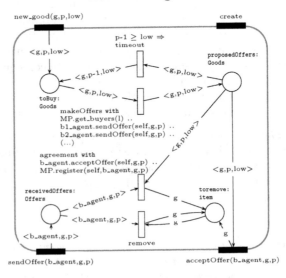

Fig. 5. Refinement R1: Seller Agent

4.4 Refinement R2: Actual Communications

This step corresponds to development guideline 6. (Step 5 is skipped, since, in this example, we do not want a more sophisticated agent algorithm).

In the case of an electronic market place, communications among agents occur through the Internet. Therefore, mechanisms such as RMI, CORBA, sockets, etc. have to be considered, and chosen.

In the case of our example, an RMI mechanism (based on TCP/IP) has been considered. The market place acts as a server: it provides some RMI object to the agents so that they access the market place through this object as if it was local. Agents are specified as RMI objects, thus remote invocation may occur from the market place to the agents and between agents. The specification is made of 5 classes: the market place (acting as a server); an RMI class for accessing the market place; two RMI classes for the buyer agents, and the seller agents respectively; and an additional class representing the RMI registry.

Contract. The contract of section 4.3 is extended to take into account RMI features.

4.5 Implementation

This step corresponds to development guideline 7. A Java program is derived from the previous step. Each CO-OPN/2 class is implemented in Java.

Contract. The contract contains the same formulae as the contract of the previous step, but expressed on the Java program, instead of the CO-OPN/2 specification, e.g., the creation of the system is represented by the call to the `main` method of the program (Java Class `MarketPlace`). Description of such translation is given in [4].

5 Related Works

Agent-oriented software engineering is currently a subject of increasing research. Jennings [6] describes agent-based systems under a software engineering point of view: agents, high-level interactions, and organisational relationships. Gaia [8] is a methodology defined for agent-oriented analysis and design. It enables to develop a system increasingly. The specifier describes the system using several models: requirements, roles models, interactions models (for the analysis); and agent model, services model, acquaintance model (for the design).

The verification that a program is correct wrt system specifications is a problem similar to the one of verifying that system specifications are correct wrt the requirement specifications. Meyer [7] advocates that, in order to face the problem of correctness, every program operation (instruction or routine body) should be systematically accompanied by a pre- and a post-condition.

6 Summary

This paper presents a methodology for developing agent-based systems that enables progressive system design and formal validation of each step. The paper presents as well development guidelines, that help the specifier to introduce complexity into the design. A small agent market place system is described: starting from informal requirements a Java implementation is reached, and every step is formally proved.

References

1. O. Biberstein, D. Buchs, and N. Guelfi. CO-OPN/2: A concurrent object-oriented formalism. In *Proc. Second IFIP Conf. on Formal Methods for Open Object-Based Distributed Systems (FMOODS)*. Chapman and Hall, 1997.
2. A. Chavez and P. Maes. Kasbah: An agent marketplace for buying and selling goods. In *Proceedings of the First International Conference on the Practical Application of Intelligent Agents and Multi-Agent Technology*, 1996.
3. G. Di Marzo Serugendo. A formal development and validation methodology for system design. In *5th International Conference on Information Systems Analysis and Synthesis (ISAS'99)*, 1999.
4. G. Di Marzo Serugendo. *Stepwise Refinement of Formal Specifications Based on Logical Formulae: from CO-OPN/2 Specifications to Java Programs*. PhD thesis, Swiss Federal Institute of Technology in Lausanne, 1999.
5. G. Di Marzo Serugendo, N. Guelfi, A. Romanovsky, and A. F. Zorzo. Formal development and validation of Java dependable distributed systems. In *Fifth IEEE International Conference on Engineering of Complex Computer Systems (ICECCS'99)*. IEEE Computer Society Press, 1999.
6. N. Jennings. On agent-based software engineering. *Artificial Intelligence*, 117(2000):277–296, 2000.
7. B. Meyer. *Object-Oriented Software Construction*. Prentice Hall, 1997.
8. M. Wooldridge, N. Jennings, and D. Kinny. The Gaia methodology for agent-oriented analysis and design. *Journal of Autonomous Agents and Multi-Agent Systems*, 3(2000), 2000.

A Proposal for Meta-learning through a MAS (Multi-agent System)

Juan A. Botía * and Antonio F. Gómez-Skarmeta *, Juan R. Velasco + and Mercedes Garijo +

Departamento de Informática, Inteligencia Artificial y Electrónica. Universidad de Murcia. •
{juanbot, skarmeta}@um.es
Departamento de Ingeniería Telemática. Universidad Politécnica de Madrid. +
{juanra, mga}@gsi.dit.upm.es

Abstract. The meta-learning problem has become an important issue in the recent years. This has been caused by the growing role of datamining applications in the global information systems of big companies which want to obtain benefits from the analysis of its data. It is necessary to obtain faithfull application rules that guide the datamining process in order to achieve the best possible models that explain the databases. We follow an inductive approach to discover these kind of rules. This paper explains the MAS-based information system we use for mining and meta-learning, and how the scalability problem is solved in order to support a community of many software agents.

1 Introduction

The problem we tackle in the present work has become very important the last years. This is the problem of automating the process of deciding the most suitable learning algorithm for a concrete intelligent data analysis task. We call it the *Meta-learning problem*. Maybe, the most important reason for the ocurrence of this fact is a certain stability situation in both machine learning and datamining reseach fields. Concerning the machine learning discipline, lots of algorithms have been developed that try to create approximated theories from a number of observed examples (for a good introduction to the field you can see [6]). In the other hand, algorithms coming from the former discipline have been successfully applied in many real world datamining applications. But a very important problem still remains open and that is that of the lack of methodollogies to guide the process of the correct design of a intelligent data analyisis experiment.

In a typical datamining session, once we are familiar with the problem domain, and have the data ready to get it automatically analised, two important decissions have to be taken by the data miner and these are (1) choosing a data mining task and then (2) deciding which data analysis algorithm to apply to the data. Those decission have to be taken sequentially as (2) strongly depends on decission (1).

The data mining phase is the closest to the concrete applicability of the KDD (Knowledge Discovery in Databases) process because it answers the question of *"What do we want to do with our customer's data?"* Some datamining tasks could be **classification** (i.e. learning a function that maps a data example into one of several predefined classes), **regression** (i.e. learning a function that maps a data item to a real-value variable), **clustering** (i.e. grouping behaviours not known a priori in data), etc. Others are summarization, dependency modeling and change and/or deviation detection.

To model the possible relations between a concrete datamining task and a learning algorithm is not easy. In order to get deeper into the problem, we shall introduce the factors that influence decission labeled as (1). Choosing a data mining task depends on three factors:

1. User requeriments: we have clearly identified three dimensions on user requiremets, the user's primary goal (i.e. why is he using a data analysis tool), its interactivity needs, and the dessired quality level of the final data model.
2. Nature of the source data: meta-data parameters of source data like number of available tuples, number of features, nulls percentaje, etc. have to be taken into account in order to obtain a data theory with an optimun quality.
3. Type of model to obtain: in some cases, obtainning a model that the user can easily understand and interpretate is an important thing. However, in other cases the user is more interested in accuracy of the model. Besides, the data mining expert could have more skills with certain types of models than with others so he could introduce a bias in the use of the application.

Hence, the problem of choosing the datamining task is reduced to the selection of one or a few of the above introduced types of mining techniques.

There are many automatic learning approaches and each one owns its own pletora of automatic learning algorithms. However, all of those can be featured in terms of three concrete parameters. The first parameter,

T. Wagner and O.F. Rana (Eds.): Infrastructure for Agents, LNAI 1887, pp. 226–233, 2001.

model representation, is defined by the manner in which knowledge is represented. The second, model evaluation, refers to the strategy for evaluating learned models. The third, the search method, is the heuristic that guides the search for the optimal model.

If we found our strategy in searching in a problem space compound of these three dimensions, it is obvious that the objective datamining system will not be very useful if the learning algorithm found as optimal, for a concrete KDD session, were not present in the system. One of the directions of this work is the proposal of a multi-agent architecture that provides a repository of *ready to go* datamining algorithms that are encapsulated into learning agents. Each one of them offering a common interface so all of them can be managed in the same manner no matter the type of datamining algorithm. Besides, these algorithms must be distributed in different machines; perhaps with different operating systems and hardware architectures. In this way we can offer both a powerful datamining tool (in terms of performance) and a scalable scheme of integration of datamining algorithms as the system can be extended through as many hosts as we would need.

The other direction is that this system is being used, at the same time, to study the problem of meta-learning, under an inductive approach. That is, we maintain the idea of using all datamining session results as a feedback for the system in order to automatically learn what sould be done in the next session. In this sense the approach is inductive if we see each datamining session results as a tuple of a meta-learning data set.

Section 2 is dedicated to introduce and explain the part of the multi-agent architecture devoted to offer a repository of intelligent analysis algorithms. The following section, 3 shows our approach to afford scalability. Section 4 gets deeper into the meta-learning issue and give details on the inductive approach we use. In section 5 related works are introduced and both conclusions and future works are pointed out.

2   A Multi-agent Architecture for Intelligent Data Analysis

In this section we will concentrate our attention on the software engineering process of the encapsulation of a machine learning algorithm into a software agent.

In order to better understand what could be a typical scenario of the final system we are propossing, that we call GEMINIS (GEneric MINIng System), in this work we will begin showing a possible configuration of the system, that appears in figure 1. This figure shows a host named A that runs three different data analysis processes. There are two of them that work with decission rules, (i.e. AQ11 and ID3) and another one that is an antificial neural networks that learns with the backpropagation rule. The host named as B is running FOIL that learns first order logic predicates, and C4.5 that generates regression decission trees. At least, in the host named C there is a single algorithm, ANFIS that generates fuzzy rules from data. There are two important issues that must be taken into account after having a look at the figure:

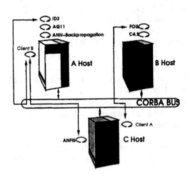

Fig. 1. Typical scenario of GEMINIS. Notice that there is a middleware that works as an IPC (Inter Process Communication) layer and it is based on CORBA.

- All algorithms are seen in the same manner by a possible client (i.e. they offer the same interface in terms of service calls).
- There is a middleware that offers distrution services and holds communication between clients and learning agents based on CORBA (Common Object Request Broker Arquitecture).

2.1 Learning Services Declaration

The set of common services that all algorithms are offering must be specified in a descriptive language. This language is IDL (Interface Definition Language) [7] and it is used to define CORBA based distributed services that could be acceses from anywhere through the CORBA bus.

```
module algorithms{
    interface IMachineLearningService{
    void conf_algorithm();
    void make_learning(in TLearningTimeConstraint mode,in unsigned long time)
        raises (AlgorithmIsNotConfiguredException, BadConfigurationException,
                LearningExperimentDoNotConvergeException,
                BestEffortDoneBeforeTimeException, TimeTooConstrainedException);
    model::IInference make_inference(in data_server::IExample example)
        raises (LearningIsNotDoneException, BadExampleException);
    model::IModelService get_learned_model()
        raises(LearningIsNotDoneException);
    double get_experiment_performance()
        raises (LearningIsNotDoneException);
    void forget_all()
        raises (LearningIsNotDoneException);
    };
};
```

Fig. 2. Common services interface for all learning algorithms

The figure 2 shows a reduced IDL definition of the services that all learning algorithms in GEMINIS should offer.

Inside the algorithms name space, it appears the interface IMachineLearningService that includes all services that must be offered by learning algorithms in GEMINIS. IDL follows an object oriented approach, so inheritance can be used. In this way each particular algorithm can be specified defining its particular interface, and including its configuration parameters as data members so it can be properly configured before learning.

Paying attention to figure 2, services offered by the IMachineLearningInterface are:

- void conf_algoritm(): is used to configurate the initial parameters of the learning algorithm. Initial parameters have a group of general parameters, common for all algorithms (e.g. the data source to learn from) and a group of specific parameters (e.g. for an artificial neural network with the backprop learning rule there are parameters like the learning rate, momentum, topology, etc.)
- void make_learning(): this is, obviously, the most important call and makes the algorithm to learn a new theory from data. The algorithm must be configured (i.e. its parameters must be setted) before learning. If this is not so, then a AlgorithmIsNotConfiguredException exception must be raised. There are three modes for learnig indicated by the argument of type TLearningTimeConstraint. These are:
  1. FREE_MODE: the algorithm can learn till its process converges to a model acceptable by itself.
  2. BEST_EFFORT: the algorithm is given a time limit and the client must wait for it to learn. If the time limit is passed and the algorithm did not finish learning, it must stop and return the best model obtained at the moment (the client only sees a normal ending of the call). It the dessired model is obtained at time, then a BestEffortDoneBeforeTimeException exception is raised from the server and the learning call finish.
  3. TIME_CONSTRAINED: this time the time limit is severe and the model is only accepted if the learning process is realised at time. If not then a TimeTooConstrainedException is raised and the model is destroyed.
- IInference make_inference(IExample): once the dessired model has been obtained, inferences can be done (by the learning server) from a given example.
- double get_experiment_performance(): this call allows the client to obtained a goodness meassure for the obtained model. This meassure depends on the type of error estimation used by the algorithm internals.
- void forget_all: tells the server to forget the learned model and put itself in an idle state.

2.2 Agents Behaviour Modeling

The internal functioning of a typical GEMINIS learning server appears modeled by the deterministic finite automata that appears in figure 3. The simplest interaction between a client and a learning server is one in which first of all, the algorithm is configured, then the learning process is carried out in time. After that the

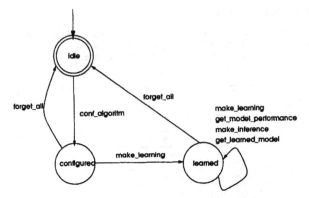

Fig. 3. State transitions (behaviour) of a typical GEMINIS learning server

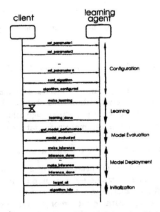

Fig. 4. Simple Interaction : configuration, learning, model evaluation, inferences and reset.

model is evaluated, accepted and inferences done with it. Once the work is done the algorithm goes into an idle state again. The events diagram appearing in figure 4 shows this kind of interaction.

3   Achieving Scalability

In this section we will first define both our characterisation of a learning agent and our characterisation of a learning data set. Then we will justify the use of a X.500 based directory service [2] as a way to centralice the information related to the description of all agents and data. We will see that a directory service is a powerful software mechanism to provide scalability.

3.1   The Learning Agent Information Model

A learning agent in GEMINIS is defined through three different angles:

- **Learning capabilities:** an agent will be enclosed in a concrete machine learning family, and all families are organised in a hierarchical manner. Besides, for each type of family there are common descriptors like the level of visual interpretation of the produced model, the endurance to noisy data that a family shows and the type of data the algorithm works with (i.e. continuous, symbolic or both).
- **Implementation features:** considered as relevant in GEMINIS are the language used to code the agent, the management of data used for learning and the typical algorithm load that is injected to the host by the algorithm when working.

– **Execution environment**: parameters like the hardware architecture of the host (e.g. Sparc, Intel, HP, etc), the operating system used, the typical machine load, available secondary memory space at the moment of execution and main memory used in the host.

Most of the parameters mentioned above take symbolic values (e.g. {LOW, LOW_MEDIUM, MEDIUM, MEDIUM_HIGH, HIGH}). A group of them have fixed values, and others like the one related with available secondary memory could change dinamically. However, at the moment this possibility is not observed. We plan to use JINI technology [9] to keep these parameters upated.

3.2 The Trainning Data Sets Information Model

Trainning data sets features are important in order to choose among available algorithms, the one that best suits to the user requirements. Hence, it is important to characterice them in terms of general parameters and particular parameters of each feature and class (if the tuples are labeled as pertainning to a concrete class).

Following, we will enumerate all important parameters that are considered general:

– Number of examples, number of classes, number of continuous and discrete attributes: those gives an idea of the size the data set has.
– Examples by class, examples by attribute and attributes by class.
– Nulls percentaje
– Data set Entropy: it is calculated as the arithmetic mean of entropy for all attributes in the data set.
– Univar: it is a typical meassure in working with data coming from sensors and estimates the level of separability of the classes in data.

And now, here they come all parameters that are calculated for each attribute of the data set. Parameters for both, continuous and discrete attributes are:

– Attribute entropy, above explained.
– Attribute mode, that is the most frecuent value in the whole attribute data set.

Most important parameters only for continuous attributes are:

– Median, that is the value that can be found in the middle of the set of all values.
– The arithmetic, geometric and armonic mean of an attribute.
– The lower, middle and upper quartiles.
– The skewness of an attribute, that meassures the similarity to a normal-like distribution that the values of the attributes have.
– The kurtosis, that estimates the proportion of attributes that are far to the mean.
– The variance and the variation coefficient, using the mean and variance.

All this parameters, both general for the whole dataset and particular for each attribute are intended to give light to the decission process of meta-learning.

3.3 An X.500 based service as GEMINIS Repository

As we have explain in sections 3.1 and 3.2, there are two important blocks of structured information that results critical for meta-learning. We have decided to use a hierchical information model to represent all this data and an LDAP (Lightweight Directory Access Protocol) [11] based access relational database to store it. In the following two sections, i.e. sections 3.4 and 3.5, we will explain who both agent and trainning data related information is organized in a hierarchical manner.

3.4 Snapshots of Agents DB

In a X.500 based directory, there is a root node from which all the rest of entries of the database can be reached following a path from it, through other entries, to the target node (this node can either or not be leaf). Following the standard X.500 structure that is now working on Internet, we have decided to put our subtree under the path "ou=Geminis, ou=ants, ou=Intelec, o=Universidad de Murcia, c=ES". So, the GEMINIS system X.500 information hangs under our research group (ANTS), that hangs under our department (Intelec), that hangs under our university and so on. This gives us the possibility to put the system in Internet, when it were stable.

Different snapshots of the directory appear in figure 5. You can see, in scheme (a), that under the organizational unit (ou) entry that refers to GEMINIS, there are five others ou's. Each ou under GEMINIS groups

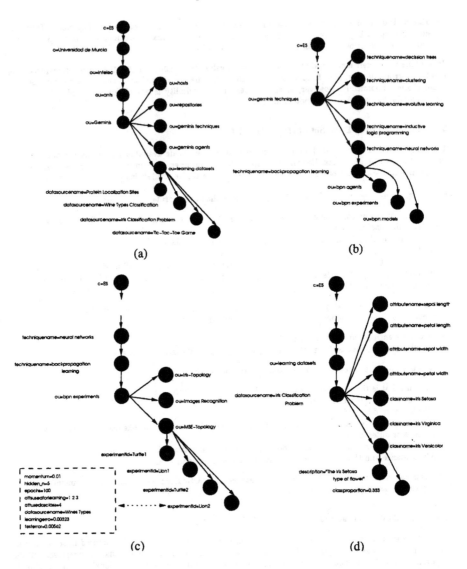

Fig. 5. A non exhaustive representation of the GEMINIS directory contents, related to the intelligent techniques available in GEMINIS.

the most important entities in the systems, like are hosts, data repositories in where an algorithm can get its data, GEMINIS's techniques that refers to learning techniques available, learning support agents like the Directory Service Agent (DSA), and all learning datasets and DBs that are taken into account till now.

Under "ou=geminis techniques, techniquename=neural networks'" it comes another level of specificity as it is depicted in scheme (b). Then each concrete technique has its own three different ou's, one ou for the agents, one ou for holding experiments results and one ou for holding the models for each experiment (i.e. in this concrete case, the model is the topology of the neural network and the arc's weights between nodes). For example, in the (c) scheme, it appears the detail of a concrete relation of experiments, called generically "MSE-Topology" trying to study the effects of topology in the mean squared error in predictions after learning.

This is precisely the basis for meta-learning data. Those results will compound tuples that theirselves will compound a meta-learning data set (see figure 6).

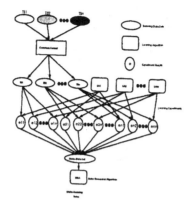

Fig. 6. Our meta-learning scheme.

3.5   Snapshots of Trainning Data Sets

Accounting of experiments is important. For a correct study of the meta-learning problem, all parameters described in 3.2 must be easily accesible from the directory. This is what we show in (d) scheme of figure 5. In this figure it appears the representation of the "Iris Classification Problem". There is a first level of depth in where an entry appears for each attribute and class. This data set has four continuous data attributes, and three different classes which label each tuple. The next level for attributes would show entries for the parameters metioned in section 3.2. Parameters for classes are the same for all classes in all data sets, and those are a description, if available, and the class proportion in the whole dataset.

4   Inductive Meta-Learning

Very little has been mentioned, till now, about our approach on meta-learning. Our approach is inductive, in the sense of trying to discover models of behaviour for the algorithms in the form of rules.
The scheme of inductive meta-learning appears depicted in figure 6. There we have some data sets, that must be converted into a GEMINIS common format. Each learning experiment will be accomplished with a learning algorithm and a learning data set, with a concrete tuple of configuration parameters for the algorithm (e.g. if we are using a neural network, the topology could be a configuration parameter). In this way, each arrow that goes from either an algorithm or a data set, to a result could be actually a potentially infinite number of arrows, each one for each different configuration parameters tuple. With all results we can compound a global meta-learning data set and learning behaviour rules could be extracted from it. This is our main thesis.

5   Conclusions, Related and Future Work

This work focuses mainly on scalability in MAS, although many particular issues are addressed in it. An important development work has been done on the multi-agent system. An interesting project based on Java agents is JAM[8]. In JAM, agents are distributed depending on where the multiple data sources are located. Each agent does its own data mining and then another meta-learning agents combine all results. They are used for fraud and intrusion detection.
Integrating different machine learning tools have been outlined previously at the KEPLER system[10] which introduces the concept of extensibility of a data mining systems, in the sense of integrating any machine learning algorithm. It is based in the concept of *plug-in*, however it does not incorporate decision mechanism to choose among those algorithm for a given data mining session. Related works concerning this topic are those in Statlog[5], MLT(Machine Learning Tool) project(ESPRIT-2154) and MLC++[3]. The Statlog project was intended to compare statistical approaches with machine learning and neural networks in order to obtain some basic guidelines for deciding the algorithm's best possible uses. In the MLT project, a set of machine learning algorithms were developed and compared in performance. MLC++ provides a set of C++ classes for supervised machine learning.

For the engineering of a generic data mining systems being able of integrate any implementation of any machine learning algorithm, both a distributed processing platform and a powerful directory service are needed, in order to assure scalability. CORBA has been signaled here as the most popular framework for object-oriented distributed processing. Besides, LDAP is the most used protocol for accesing X.500 based directory services.

However, there is a lot of work still to be done. The meta-learning software infraestructure is now ready but there are no results until now. However, this GEMINIS system is now being used in other projects [4, 1] in order to do generical intelligent data analysis as is can be a powerful and flexible data analysis tool.

6   Acknowledgements

This work has been supported by the CICYT funding program of the spanish goverment, through the TIC-97-1343C002-02 project and by the FEDER funding of both the European Community and spanish goverment program through the 1FD97-0255-C03-01 project.

References

1. J. Botia-Blaya, A. Gomez-Skarmeta, G. Sanchez, M. Valdes, and J. A. Lopez-Morales. Aplicación de Técnicas Inteligentes a la Mejora de los Procesos de Riego en el Entorno Agrícola de la Región de Murcia. In *CAEPIA'99 TTIA'99 Libro de Actas Volumen II.*
2. ISO/IEC-9594-1, X.501. the Directory: Overview of Concepts, Models and Services.An ISO/ITU-T Standard, 1995.
3. R. Kohavi, G. John, R. Loing, D. Manley, and K. Pfleger. MLC++: A machine learning library in C++. In *Tools with Aritificial Intelligence*, pages 249–271. IEEE Computer Society Press, 1993.
4. H. Martinez-Barbera, A. Gomez-Skarmeta, M. Zamora-Izquierdo, and J. Botia-Blaya. Neural Networks for Sonar and Infrared Sensors Fusion. In *Fussion 2000. Paris, July 2000.*
5. Donald Michie, David J. Spiegelhalter, and CharlesC. Taylor, editors. *Machine Learning, Neural and Statistical Classification.* Ellis Horwood, 1994.
6. Tom M. Mitchell. *Machine Learning.* McGraw-Hill, 1997.
7. OMG. The Common Object Request Broker: Architecture and Specification. Technical report, Object Management Group, July 1995.
8. Salvatore Stolfo, Andreas L. Prodromidis, Shelley Tselepis, Wenke Lee, and Dave W. Fan. JAM:Java Agents for Meta-Learning over Distributed Databases. In David Heckerman, Heikki Mannila, Daryl Pregibon, and Ramasamy Uthurusamy, editors, *The Third International Conference on Knowledge Discovery & Data Mining.* AAAI Press, August 1997.
9. J Waldo. The End of Protocols. JINI White Paper. Technical report, http://java.sun.com.
10. Stefan Wrobel, Dietrich Wettschereck, Edgar Sommer, and Werner Ende. Extensibility in data mining systems. In Jiawei Han Evangelos Simoudis and Usama Fayyad, editors, *The Second International Conference on Knowledge Discovery & Data Mi ning.* AAAI Press, August 1996.
11. W. Yeong, T. Howes, and S. Kille. Lightweight directory access protocol. rfc 1487. Technical report, Performance Systems International, University of Michigan. ISODE Consortium, July 1993.

Scalability Metrics and Analysis of Mobile Agent Systems

Murray Woodside

Dept. of Systems and Computer Engineering
Carleton University, Ottawa K1S 5B6, Canada
1-613-520-5721
cmw@sce.carleton.ca

Abstract. Scalability is a many-sided property which can be captured in a scalability metric that balances cost, volume, timeliness and other attirbutes of value in the system, as a function of its size. Studies of typical metrics can reveal which parts of the agent infrastructure are most critical for scalability. Simple metrics are investigated for systems dominated by agent behaviour. As a system is scaled up, the length of the average tour increases and this has a major effect on performance and scalability limits. Senstivity experiments show that infrastructure improvements can improve scalability but they will not alter the general conclusions.

1 Introduction

A scalability metric was recently defined for continuously and sporadically operating distributed systems [2][4], which generalized previous metrics which had been defined for highly parallel systems running a single computation. In the new metric a scaling plan is introcuced which defines the system configuration at different scale factors. For each scale factor the cost, throughput and performance or quality of service (QoS) are calculated, and the scalability metric depends on a kind of productivity measure:

Productivity P = (Throughput-per-time * Value-per-response-at-QoS) / Cost-per-time

The scalability from $k1$ to $k2$ is then the ratio

Scalability $(k1, k2) = P(k2)/P(k1)$

The performance calculation to predict QoS is the difficult part of this metric; the throughput and cost put it into perspective, as one can often improve QoS by enhancing the system. The metric emphasizes that scalability is an economic concept as well as a echnical challenge. The analysis may include optimization of the configuration at eachscale factor, by adjusting the investment in different factors, the distribution of the load, or any other parameters of the configuration. It is a very general framework, but so far it has been applied only to statically configured layered systems of servers for telecom applications.

The same approach is considered here to analyze scalability issues of systems of mobile agents. Each mobile agent executes a tour to carry out a task on behalf of a

T. Wagner and O.F. Rana (Eds.): Infrastructure for Agents, LNAI 1887, pp. 234–245, 2001.

"user"; a task may require visits to several nodes, in an itinerary determined by the agent itself. Examples include

- agents for searching for data and assembling it,
- commerce agents for negotiating a price and terms for delivery,
- system management agents.

The performance analysis can take advantage of previous work by a number of authors. Strasser and Schwehm [7] developed a model for the delay for a single agent operation which visits several nodes. They considered the sources of delay and of processing steps in some detail, however they did not explicitly model contention. Puliafito et al [5] compared the performance of different kinds of access to remote data, by remote procedures, remote evaluation, and mobile agents. Rana [6], considered the costs of an agent meeting. Here we add the notion of the scaling plan and the scalability metric, and we consider a simple example as an illustration of the method.

2 Model

The scaling plan to be considered here is a particularly simple one; at scale factor k the system has k nodes with facilities for mobile agents, and a flow of Rk agents per sec. entering it. Nodes and agent flows increase together. Each agent follows a sequential tour itinerary of its own, and as k increases the length $I(k)$ of a tour increases also; for the purposes of discussion we assume an average tour length of $I(k) = \sqrt{k}$ nodes and $(1 + \sqrt{k})$ hops. Parallel operation is also possible, either by cloning an agent on entry, or during a tour.

The system cost will be taken as ck, where c is the constant cost per node. With value function $V(k)$ per response, the productivity measure is

Productivity $= P(k) = Rk\ V(k) / ck = R\ V(k) / c$.

Two value functions will be considered here, both based on the average delay T for a tour:

- $Vstep(k)$, defined as 1 if $T(k) < Tmax$, or 0 else. For a given k, if $Rmax$ is the largest R giving $Vstep = 1$, then the productivity is

  $Pstep(k) = Rmax\ k / ck = Rmax / c$.

- $Vsmooth(k) = T(k)/(T(k) + Tmax)$, where $Tmax$ is a target value rather than a hard maximum value. The productivity is

  $Psmooth(k) = R\ k\ Vsmooth(k) / ck = R\ Vsmooth(k) / c$.

A very wide range of evaluation functions could be used, for instance the average value of some function of each individual response time, dropping off as the delay becomes too long.

Each agent visit to a node requires execution resources which average S sec., including communications-related execution, installing the agent, and its operation at the node. There may also be storage operations, which we will not consider here. The amount of data to be communicated may increase over the itinerary, as the agent picks up data at each node. Communications also involves a latency in the network, for each hop in the itinerary, of L sec.

3 Scalability Effects of R, S, and L

Scalability is limited by delay that accumulates over a tour, which is due to work and contention. These three parameters dominate the scalability:

- R = input rate of agent tours at each node,
- S = work demand for a visit to a node,
- L = latency for a single hop.

3.1 No-Contention Evaluation

Without contention, the average delay is just $[I(k) S + (I(k) + 1)L]$ for a purely sequential tour. If $I(k) = \sqrt{k}$ this delay reaches $Tmax$ at the value $k = [(Tmax - L)/(L + S)]^2$. For the value function $Vstep(k)$, this is the scalability limit, without contention effects. The productivity however is unbounded, because without considering contention at the nodes there is no limit on the throughput capability of the system. And for the value function $Vsmooth(k)$ there is no exact scalability limit, just gradually declining productivity (for a given R) as k increases.

3.2 Effect of Contention

Node saturation may limit scalability first. This requires a model of contention, as a function of the traffic.

- Suppose that the computing nodes are all symmetrical, with the utilization level $U0$ for the background traffic (apart from the agent traffic). At scale factor k, the rate of agent arrivals at a node averages $R\sqrt{k}$ per sec, and the node utilization rises to U

  $= U0 + R\sqrt{k} S$.

- A simple queueing network model (see, for instance Jain [3]) of the nodes will give a sufficient illustration of the performance effect of contention. It has exponential service at every node, and an average delay at each node of $S/(1 - U)$. The average itinerary delay is then

$$T = (1 + \sqrt{k})L + \sqrt{k}\, S/(1 - U)$$

$$= (1 + \sqrt{k})L + \sqrt{k}\, S/(1 - U0 - R\sqrt{k}\, S)$$

provided the nodes do not saturate, that is provided that $R\sqrt{k}\, S < 1 - U0$.

We will consider a system with parameter values

- $L = 40$ msec for network latency,
- $S = 30$ msec for the execution at a node,
- $U0 = 0.5$ for 50% utilization of each node by other programs
- $Tmax = 5$ sec

R is the arrival rate at each node, and will first be considered to be fixed. Thus Rk is the system throughput in agent tours/sec. For a fixed value of R below saturation, the delay T depends on k as shown in Figure 1. The no-contention limit for $Vstep$ is calculated as about 5020. . The values of R in the Figure are 2, 3, 4, and 5 agent dispatches

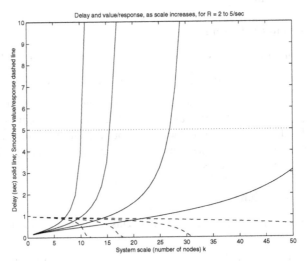

Fig. 1. Delay versus scale factor k for various fixed values of R from 2 to 5. The dashed line is the Vsmooth value function for these delays.

per sec. from each node. As is typical for contention systems, $T(k)$ increases first gradually and then explosively. This makes the smooth value function $Vsmooth(k)$ drop gradually to zero. For each R the limit will occur where T crosses the value of $Tmax$ (for the $Vstep$ value function), or where V becomes too small (for $Vsmooth$).

We can see that for moderate values of R the limit is much smaller than 5020, so contention is important. However, productivity is also proportional to R. Is it more productive to have $R = 4$ and a scale about 15 (where the delay crosses the horizontal line representing the target), or $R = 5$ and $k =$ about 10 (giving about the same delay)? In the former case the overall throughput is about 60 (4 x 15) and in the latter case it is about 50, so $R = 4$ is better.

We can do a more complete analysis by choosing R for each k, so as to maximize the productivity $P(k)$. Taking the cost per node as 1, and value function *Vstep*, we have $Pstep(k) = R$, so it is just a matter of choosing R as large as possible to still satisfy $T <$ *Tmax*. This value *Rmax* is given by

$$Rmax = (1 - U0)/(S \sqrt{k}) - 1/(Tmax - (1 + \sqrt{k})L)$$

With value function *Vsmooth*, R must be found by a function maximization. The

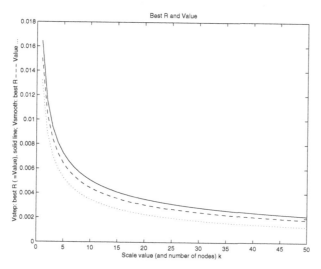

Fig. 2. Best values of R for Vstep and Vsmooth (solid and dashed lines), and best Psmooth obtained (dotted), against scale factor k

values of R which maximize P are shown for both cases in Figure 2, along with the optimal value of *Psmooth(k)*. We can see that the productivity drops off as k increases, essentially because of the inescapable extra delay for visiting additional nodes on a longer tour, in a larger system. The optimization of R means that larger rates can be served, per node, in the smaller systems.

The baseline case for estimating scalability should be a small system with more than a single node, so $k = 5$ was chosen as a baseline system. Then the scalability met-ric $P(k)/P(5)$ was found for both value functions, and is plotted as the lower pair of curves in Figure 3. The decline has the same shape, and is dominated by the average tour length.

However there is more to scalability than just reponse time. A larger system adds value to each tour, by gathering more data from more sites. This could be considered in the productivity function. Either *Tmax* could increase with k, showing willingness to wait for the more valuable results, or a value multiplier could be attached to *V*. For instance, the upper pair of curves in Figure 3 are results for the same system but with a value multiplier proportional to the tour length. In this case:

$Vstep(k) = \sqrt{k}$ for $T < Tmax$, or 0;

$Vsmooth(k) = \sqrt{k}\ Tmax\ /\ (\ Tmax + T(k)\ )$

With value determined this way, the investment in more nodes provides more valuable responses. The upper pair of curves in Figure 3 show that the system seen this way is highly scalable. .

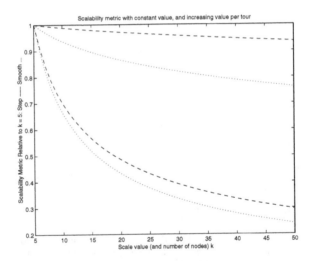

Fig. 3. Scalability metric for the Step (dashed line) and Smooth (dotted) value functions. Lower pair: constant value per tour; upper pair: value proportional to tour length

4   Scalability Impact of Agent Behaviour

In [7] Strasser and Schwehm derived a model to explain the execution demand *S* and the latency *L* for mobile agents, in terms of some factors describing the agent behaviour. The factors were:

- the size of the potential "reply" data that would have to be sent if a mobile agent were not used, and the selectivity σ of the agent (which reduces this size by a factor $(1-\sigma)$);

- the size of the code, state and initial data space of the agent,

- the probability p that the agent code must be transferred (i.e. that it is not cached in the destination node)

They considered that the agent state and basic data must be marshalled, transmitted and unmarshalled at each hop. The code need not be transmiited at all if it is cached at the destination, and if it is not, then it is assumed to already be available in a marshalled form at the origin of the hop, so only transmission and unmarshalling are needed. Applying their approach to our model, we can express the average demand and latency in the form

$$S = s1 + s2(1-\sigma)\sqrt{k} + s3\,p$$

$$L = d1 + d2\,(1-\sigma)\sqrt{k} + d3\,p$$

where $s1$ includes CPU time for communications, marshalling and unmarshalling the state and data, and the agent procedures executed at the node, $s2$ is for handling the "reply" data, which accumulates over the tour, $s3$ is for unmarshalling the code if it has to be sent, $d1$ is a fixed network latency, $d2$ is the "reply" transmission time, and $d3$ is the code transmission time. The analysis in [7] did not consider the procedure execution time at the node as part of the agent workload (because it is a constant across the alternatives they were comparing), but it has been included in the analysis here.

The service-demand parameters used here are a 20-ms execution demand, plus marshal and unmarshal times of 1 ms for state (making $s1 = 21$ ms), 5 ms for reply data ($s2$), and 4 ms for code ($s3$). The latency parameters are a 30-ms pure latency $d1$; 0.5 ms for $d2$, to transmit 50 K bytes/node in the reply, before selectivity reduces it; and $d3 = 0.4$ ms for 40 Kbytes of code. This gives:

$$S = 21 + 5(1-\sigma)\sqrt{k} + 4\,p$$

$$L = 30 + 0.5\,(1-\sigma)\sqrt{k} + 0.4\,p$$

Putting these expressions into T, we see (in Figure 4) that the scalability curves are slightly worse than before. This is because the parameters like S which were constant before, are now increasing with k and further limiting scalability.

5   Sensitivity to Changes

Improved agent infrastructure and agent movement strategies play themselves out as modifications to $I(k)$, L and S. Thus we can study the potential value of improve-

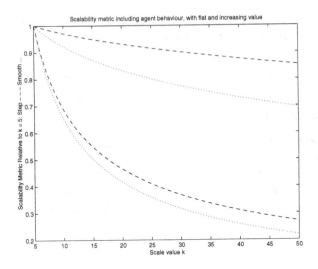

Fig. 4. Scalability metric for the model with agent behaviour and data accumulation (cache miss 0.1, selectivity 0.9). Lower pair: constant value per tour; Upper pair: value proportional to tour length

ments by considering how sensitive the results are to changes in these parameters. There is not space enough here to report extensive sensitivity experiments, but it has been found that:

- latency and the cache miss probability p for agent code made very little difference over the range studied,

- selectivity made an increasing impact at larger scales, so that at scale 50, the difference between $\sigma = 80\%$ and 100% gave a 50% increase in the scalability metric (see Figure 5). More selective agents improve scalability in this analysis mostly by avoiding the marshalling overhead to communicate the accumulated data collected over the itinerary.

- the reply size is similarly extremely important. Going from 50K to 500K bytes reduced the scalability at $k = 50$ by a factor of about 3 (Figure 6). Reply size is also more important at larger scales, because the reply is assumed to accumulate more data.

This last point emphasizes the importance of the design of the application, and the workload imposed by the users, as well as the agent strategies and infrastructure, in influencing scalability. An application that does not flood the agent with data will be better. .

If the value function rewards longer tours proportional to their length, we have already seen that the metric shows much better scalability, in Figure 3. The sensitivities in this case may be different, so they are recalculated in . These two figures corre-

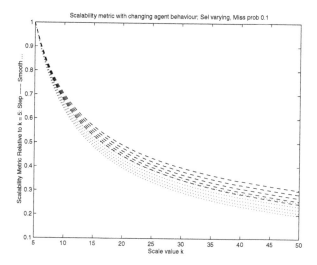

Fig. 5. Sensitivity of the scalability metric to the selectivity of the agent in accumulating data during its tour. Selectivity values of 0.8 to 1.0 gave the five curves for each case (top to bottom). Dashed line for Vstep, dotted for Vsmooth. Tour value was fixed, independent of tour length.

spond to Figure 5 and Figure 6, but with $V(k)$ including a factor $\sqrt{k}$. They show that while the scalability is much better it is still quite sensitive to the selectivity (in Figure 7) and to the size of the reply data, in Figure 8.

6 Generalizations

It is straightforward to use the scalability metric with other models for delay, and with richer descriptions of the system. Agent communications and synchronization, cloning of agents for parallel operations, systems with hot spots, additional node resources besides processors, and network bottlenecks can all be accomodated. Queueing networks are not the only suitable performance model either. Timed Petri net models, as used in [5] and [6], can equally well provide the delay calculations; detailed simulation models or measurements on real systems can also be used. Finally, the value function can express different important attributes of the system responses as well, not just value based on the mean response time.

The way the system is scaled up can also be generalized. The scaling variable k can be taken as an index into a *scaling plan*, as described in [2], [4], which controls not just the number of nodes but also the size of the data at nodes, or the size and complexity of the agent code itself, and the amount of computational effort expended on intelligent operations by the agent.

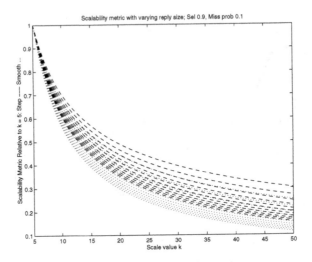

Fig. 6. Sensitivity of the scalability metric to the size of the "reply" data, from 0 to 500 K bytes in steps of 50. Scalability decreases as size increases. Dashed line for Vstep, dotted for Vsmooth. Tour value was fixed, independent of tour length

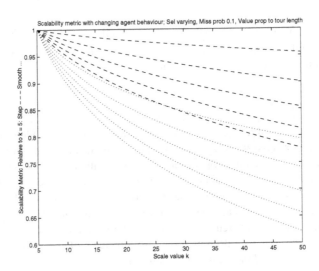

Fig. 7. Sensitivity of the scalability metric to agent selectivity (0.8 to 1.0) with response value proportional to tour length $\sqrt{k}$. Dashed lines for Vstep, dotted for Vsmooth.

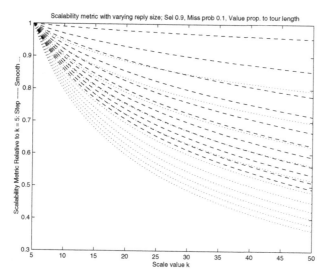

Fig. 8. Sensitivity of the scalability metric to the size of the "reply" data, from 0 to 500 K bytes in steps of 50, with response value proportional to tour length $\sqrt{k}$. Dashed lines for Vstep, dotted for Vsmooth.

7 Conclusions

The scalability metric described here gives a flexible framework for capturing the essence of a scalability problem. It encourages the analyst to capture all the relevant factors, and to balance them together. It has been applied to a class of mobile agent systems, using basic and rather robust models for the workload and delay.

Some very simple models have been analyzed to discover the main features of agent system scalability, at least for independent agents that roam in a system of a given size. If the value of a tour is independent of its length, the results point to a steadily declining scalability measure over a moderate range of scales. However it is possible that a larger system with longer tours gives more valuable responses. For instance, in an e-commerce system with agents that collect data on products, a larger system would offer more selection, and a better chance to find a good match with one's exact requirements, or a good price. If the value of a response is proportional to the length of the tour, the scalability was found to be good up to many tens of nodes.

The analysis can be adapted to different needs. The examples described here have emphasized simplicity in the analysis. However the three aspects of the productivity function (throughput, cost and value per response) can be described in any degree of detail. The throughput can be divided into classes of operations with different values. The value of each completed operation can depend in the scale of the system, the delay in completing the operation, and any other quality factor that might be affected by scale or by a scaling strategy. The cost can include all parts of the system (cost of communications, which was ignored here, and also software, manpower, physical space, etc.). To illustrate this flexibility the value of an operation was changed to reflect the increased value of longer itineraries, which resulted in very different appraisal of scalability.

The examples considered here were also based on a homogeneous system and a queueing network performance model, however any kind of performance estimation could be used, and the system may contain many types of nodes of different capability.

Scalability is a property of a *scaling strategy*. In the present examples, the strategy was to set the number of nodes at k and to adjust the traffic level R per node to give the maximum overall productivity. The strategy could also include modifications to the agents' operational strategy as the system grows, or to the agent size or complexity. Any necessary adaptation to accommodate the increased size can be included in the analysis.

Acknowledgements

This research was supported by NSERC, the Natural Sciences and Engineering Research Council of Canada, through its program of Industrial Research Chairs.

References

[1] C. Ghezzi, G. Vigna, "Mobile code paradigms and technologies: a case study", *Proc. 1st Int Workshop on Mobile Agents,* Berlin, April 1997.

[2] P. Jogalekar and C.M. Woodside, "Evaluating the Scalability of Distributed Systems", *Proc. of Hawaii Int. Conference on System Sciences,* January 1998.

[3] R. Jain, "The Art of Computer Systems Performance Analysis", Wiley, 1991.

[4] P. K. Jogalekar, C. M. Woodside, "Evaluating the scalability of distributed systems", *IEEE Transactions on Parallel and Distributed Systems*, to appear 2000.

[5] A. Puliafito, S. Riccobene, M. Scarpa, "An Analytical Comparison of the client-server, remote evaluation, and mobile agents paradigms", *Proc ASA/MA 99*, Palm Springs, 1999.

6] O. Rana, "Performance of mobile agent systems", Proc MASCOTS 99, Univ of Maryland, Oct. 1999.

7] M. Strasser, M. Schwehm, "A Performance Model for Mobile Agent Systems", *Proc. Int. Conf on Parallel and Distributed Processing Techniques and Applications (PDPTA97),* Las Vegas, 1997.

Improving the Scalability of Multi-agent Systems

Phillip J. Turner and Nicholas R. Jennings

Intelligence, Agents, Multimedia Group. Department of Electronics and Computer
Science, Southampton University, SO17 1BJ. United Kingdom
{pjt,nrj}@ecs.soton.ac.uk

Abstract. There is an increasing demand for designers and developers
to construct ever larger multi-agent systems. Such systems will be composed of hundreds or even thousands of autonomous agents. Moreover,
in open and dynamic environments, the number of agents in the system at any one time will fluctuate significantly. To cope with these twin
issues of scalability and variable numbers, we hypothesize that multi-
agent systems need to be both *self-building* (able to determine the most
appropriate organizational structure for the system by themselves at run-
time) and *adaptive* (able to change this structure as their environment
changes). To evaluate this hypothesis we have implemented such a multi-
agent system and have applied it to the domain of automated trading.
Preliminary results supporting the first part of this hypothesis are presented: adaption and self-organization do indeed make the system better
able to cope with large numbers of agents.

1   Introduction

When designing or building a multi-agent system (MAS), a designer has to
ensure that the agents and overall collective provide the facilities prescribed by
users. However in multi-agent systems that consist of large numbers of agents,
current design methodologies are often unable to ensure such provision. This
is not because these methodologies have inherent limitations, but because the
practice and the theory on which they are based contain very few studies directly
concerned with the scalability of MASs. Yet, MASs for use in open systems
(e.g. the Internet and corporate intranets) are not only likely to require large
numbers of agents, but also present designers with the problem of dynamic agent
numbers too. Even worse, if the expertise to design large MASs was indeed
developed, it may still prove impossible to redesign and upgrade software before
its environment, and thereby the demands on it, evolve. Thus, the current state
of the art is challenged by MASs that are large or where the magnitude or speed
of agent population variability confounds one overall design. To tackle both these
problems we hypothesize that MASs should be *self-building* (able to determine
the most appropriate organizational structure for the system by themselves at
run-time) and *adaptive* (able to change this structure as their environment
changes).

The majority of MAS work deals with systems in which agents are peers
of each other. However, it seems unlikely that such structures are the most

T. Wagner and O.F. Rana (Eds.): Infrastructure for Agents, LNAI 1887, pp. 246–262, 2001.

appropriate when hundreds or thousands of agents are required. For this reason, MAS designers are increasingly using metaphors from human social and economic organizations (e.g. [8])—where we are used to dealing with large numbers of (human) agents—to help structure their systems. Human organizations operate by enforcing avenues of communication and control between individuals in order for the overall grouping to achieve its goals. Of rough equivalence to organizational structure, MASs use acquaintance topologies to perform the same function of defining and constraining interaction. These topologies may be mesh, fully connected, star, hierarchic, etc., or hybrids, and the inter-agent relationships between them may be master, slave or peer, or anything else deemed suitable. Although it is tempting to mirror human socio-economic organizational structures or the roles therein, it is not known if this is the most appropriate way to achieve the goals of MASs. A further disparity between organizational theory and practice for humans and agents arises because the emphasis in MASs may not be on the whole 'organization' achieving its goals at the expense of the goals of individuals if necessary (as in human organizations). In MASs, the achievement of the goals of its users, and thereby their agents, is the prime focus of attention, not the overall emergent behavior. Thus, MASs that have imposed organizational structure, or have the ability to dynamically construct their own, should not be forced to limit (or inherit) their techniques, rationale and structures to those of anthropic organizational theory and practice.

Against this background, the primary focus of this paper is in presenting how a MAS can adapt its structure for various population sizes.[1] In so doing, it is suggested that herein lies a method for: 1) the creation of MASs that can better deal with variable numbers of agents, and 2) compensating for the difficulties of building large-scale MASs by building at a sufficiently manageable small size with reliance upon increased scale tolerance for later scaling to the required size. This work advances the state of the art in the following ways. First, presentation of empiric evidence to support the case for dynamic organizational structure. Second, an implemented method for allowing agents to dynamically change organizational structure. Lastly, evidence to support the proposition that MASs that have fixed organizational structures are less scalable than those that can adapt to population size. (For a discussion of fixed versus flexible form in the context of human organization theory see [11]).

We believe that a MAS that can both operate with different population sizes and deal with dynamic changes to population during operation, is more scalable. To disambiguate *scalable* (noting that the term has several different meanings in computer science), the facets we are concerned with are those that refer to the relationship between the collective computational resource needs of the agents and the population size. However, in order to say that a particular system is scalable, or compare scalability as a property, a measure must be determined. In this case we use a measure of the processing requirements for agents (collectively) which roughly equates to the number of machine instructions they incur when achieving their goals. Despite using a metric to compare several methods of

---

[1] Space limitations prevent us from reporting on the self-building hypothesis.

agent operation, we avoid the pitfalls of defining absolute requirements for a MAS to be termed *scalable*, and instead concentrate on the reduction of growth in computational resource demands whilst maintaining utility. (If a definition of a scalable MAS is to be forced, we would loosely define it as the ability of a MAS operating with given computational resource availability limits to achieve required minimum levels of utility to users for target ranges of population size. Thus, higher scale tolerance implies that larger population sizes may be successfully dealt with.)

The remainder of the paper is structured as follows: section 2 introduces the e-commerce application we have developed for investigating the issues of scalability. Section 3 presents data obtained for a MAS in various organizational forms. Section 4 discusses organizational adaptability. Section 5 covers related research. Finally, section 6 presents our initial conclusions and discusses future work.

2   A Trading Agents Scenario

Electronic commerce is a natural domain for testing hypotheses about scalability. It involves large numbers of end-users and online businesses and it constitutes a highly dynamic environment—both in terms of interactions and in terms of membership. Our particular scenario involves agents that encapsulate the basic needs of the end-user (e.g. automated product location and purchase) and supplier agents (automated query processing and order placement facilities). (See [7] for other goals of the scenario.)

End-users' goals to purchase commodities are presented to the customer agents according to a probability distribution over a specifiable period of simulated time. The specifics of a request include a commodity identifier, the required volume, and a deadline. Generation of these requests is achieved through probability distributions for each request parameter.[2] Customer agents are also capable of dynamically building preferences for suppliers on a per commodity and general basis and propagating information about suppliers and their preferences to other customers (i.e. they can make recommendations), forming co-operative groups to make collective bulk (discounted) purchases, and finally, forming and maintaining models of suppliers' wares and prices.

In contrast to customer agents, suppliers are currently limited in terms of dynamics. Their character within the market is defined in terms of the products they sell and the prices they charge. Although their product ranges do not vary periodically, each supplier has the ability to model and generalize customer commodity requirements, and offer 'good' customers discounts and/or bulk deals. They also monitor the requests they receive and analyze their responses over time. Reaction to such data may be to start selling often requested commodities or drop prices slightly to improve the number of sales of given items.

---

[2] The probability distributions referred to in this paragraph can either be uniform or Poisson. However, the results presented herein were generated with uniform probability distributions for query generation and query parameters.

Both types of agent in this scenario are implemented so that, effectively, they do not have computational or storage resource bounds. That is, the behavior of and interaction between agents are not affected by hardware concerns—neither absolute or relative computational speeds, nor memory requirements (disk space being plentiful). Furthermore, each agent processes each of its goals, its internal models and the messages it receives until no further processing can occur without communication to the other agents. When *all* the agents have reached this state all messages are exchanged. The agents resume processing once all messages have been delivered. These two steps are referred to as a system *tick*, and their repetition provides continuous operation. Note that ticks do not constitute a fixed amount of time, but they do represent the passage of time.

The agents operate in this manner because it means that any variance in the behavior of the individuals, and ultimately the whole MAS (due to the non-deterministic order in which agents are executed or receive and transmit communications) can be eliminated. A further advantage is that since no agent receives information before any other, none can be said to have an advantage over the others. For example, in a MAS where there are too few resources, faster acting agents may gain an unfair advantage over others. We have also found this method of operation provides reproducible MAS behavior.

Moreover, this scheme also fulfills a subtle requirement of these experiments: that the aim is *not* to develop agents whose primary concern is goal prioritization (or any other issues generally dealt with by resource-bounded research), but achievement of the desirable properties of a MAS whilst reducing as far as possible the resource needs. In other words, the experiments do not seek to determine the goal achievement levels possible in a resource bounded environment, but to predict the minimal resource requirements needed to attain a given level of goal achievement. The most important property of this MAS is that of maintaining agents' utility to their users. The agents therefore undertake whatever actions are necessary to ensure that their responsibilities to users are met. (For example, searching all the suppliers for a cheaper deal even when they have already located an acceptable price, or co-operating with other customers to get bulk discount). This is done, however, in a manner which tries to minimize the total computational resource needs of the MAS.

The agents are implemented as interpreted rules with mental and (speech act based) message-content based guards on their firing (similar to agent0 [18]). Upon firing, each rule calls one or more action handlers which are Prolog predicates.

2.1   Performance Measures

The specific metrics used herein to compare scalability are: 1) the number of ticks (process/ communication cycles) that have passed, t, 2) the total number of agents in the system, n, and 3) the sum of the number of (Prologs') logical inferences[3] required for each tick, for all agents (ΣLI_t). (The ratio of the number of customer agents to supplier agents is ten to one, the minimum number of suppliers being five.) Also, as new agents are added to the system, so too are the goals that they receive from their users. Thus, the total of simulated user goals remains at a fixed ratio to the number of agents and therefore there is no need to introduce MAS throughput into the comparisons.

3   Organizational Forms and Agent Interactions

In this section we present several organizational forms of MAS for our trading scenario. These forms can be distinguished by the constraints within which the agents interact with each other. For example, whether they can share information, form co-operative groups or take action to combat inefficiency. The purpose of examining these various forms are firstly to show that different organizational forms place different resource requirements on agents, and secondly, to determine what the relationship between the resource requirements of a given form and the number of constituent agents is.

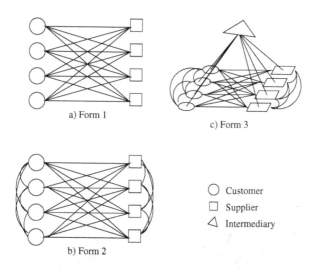

a) Form 1

c) Form 3

○ Customer

□ Supplier

◁ Intermediary

b) Form 2

Fig. 1. Acquaintance topology forms

In the first (and most simple) organization form (figure 1a), each customer agent can reason about and communicate with each supplier (and vice versa). However, customers are unaware of other customers and suppliers are unaware of other suppliers. Consequently, agents cannot form groups, share information, or

---

[3] The number of logical inferences can be equated to a measure of the number of machine instructions the agents execute. More precisely, it is in fact the total number of passes through the Prolog call and redo ports.

undertake co-operative behavior. This form represents a trading scenario where there are multiple intelligent agents— but they do not exhibit properties expected of *MAS agents* since the organizational form forces the agents to be asocial in this respect.

The second form (figure 1b) additionally allows customers to be aware of other customers (and suppliers, other suppliers). Therefore, customer agents are able to form groups with other relevant customer agents, allowing them to co-operate by sharing tasks that are commonly undertaken. For example, sharing information about product availability of suppliers and formation of purchasing groups. Suppliers are similarly enabled. Topologically, this form is a fully connected mesh and represents a standard fully connected peer MAS.

The third form is identical to the second, with the exception that an intermediary agent that undertakes collective tasks is present. For example, centralization of the formation of a supplier-to-product catalogue and modeling and dissemination of user-preferences. This form represents and facilitates intermediary functions (brokerage, matchmaking, recruitment, facilitation, etc [14]). Rather than allowing agents to (s)elect one of their number to take on these tasks (for which its utility to its user may suffer greatly), an extra agent is introduced.

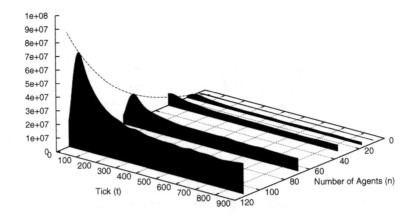

Fig. 2. Logical Inferences versus number of ticks versus number of agents for *Form 1* MAS

3.1   Resource requirements for form 1

Figure 2 shows the relationship between ΣLI_t, t and n.[4] Regardless of the number of agents, the amount of processing resources required can be split into two separate stages. Initially, the agents do not have models of each other so they require higher amounts of processing resources to achieve their goals. This is because they need to locate commodities and services and undertake model formation. As t increases, the completeness of the customers' models of the suppliers increase and they are able to more efficiently achieve their goals. Eventually the initial extra resource requirements needed whilst forming the models lessens sufficiently for the agents to assume a more stable resource requirement. We refer to this first (initial model formation) stage as the *convergence phase*. In the second stage—which we refer to as the *converged phase*— agents require resources to maintain the accuracy of these models (since users may change their buying habits and suppliers may alter product ranges or prices). (In figure 2 the convergence phase ends (and the converged phase begins) at approximately tick 400.) Models are maintained with the aim of preventing (or lessening) agents propagating incorrect information to the other agents (e.g. for recommendations), or wasting time approaching inappropriate acquaintances for group formation.

When using this organizational form, both customer and supplier agent groups have more or less the same functionality and are invariably trying to satisfy goals which are largely common (e.g. forming the same models of each other or buying the same commodities). However, because the acquaintance topology limits them, they cannot co-ordinate their activity, nor share information that could benefit one another.

When viewed from a system's level perspective this is a ridiculous position. There are massive amounts of replicated functionality, data and redundant computation and agents' experiences and discoveries do not benefit others. To this end, it is clear that sharing information and co-operating are necessary to increase efficiency and decrease resource requirements. Therefore, form 2 allows full acquaintance.

3.2   Resource requirements for form two

Figure 3 shows the situation where agents are able to detect and interact with all other agents. Hence, they can and *do* share information and co-operate for common goals. In comparison to the previous graph, we see that the graph is both quantitatively and qualitatively different. In addition to the resource requirements being very much higher, both its growth factor (against agent numbers) and shape differs.

The higher levels of logical inferences required reflect the fact that the agents with the same purpose (purchase/supply) model each other and reason with

---

[4] The graphs in this paper have been smoothed to show their general form. Specifically, they were smoothed with a compound windowed running maximum and windowed running average (in that order). To clarify the relationship between n and the shape of individual MAS runs, we show selected values of n rather than a surface.

Total Logical Inferences

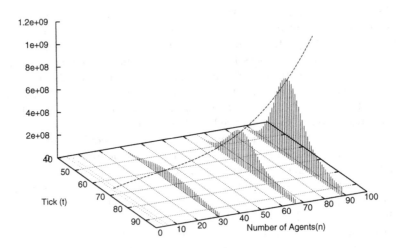

Fig. 3. Logical Inferences versus tick versus number of agents for *Form 2* MAS

these models to form groups. Formation, operation within and disbanding of joint activities is a relatively costly behavior to incorporate, compared to the act of modeling between customers and suppliers for purchasing purposes. However, the number of processing/message delivery cycles that are taken to reach the converged phase is very much reduced (convergence at approximately tick 100 - versus tick 400 for form 1) since the agents *do* share tasks and information. This is manifest by the shape of resource requirements for the convergence phase being roughly parabolic rather than asymptotic. The relationship between ΣLI_t and n remains of the same *order* of complexity (cubic). Any benefits that the agents derive because they co-operate are lost to the overheads of co-operation. (The agents in these tests perform relatively few tasks specific to the scenario compared to those necessary for MAS operation— i.e. most of the complexity and resource needs of the agents resides in general MAS interaction.)

The application scenario also illustrates an important point which can easily be overlooked when using order notation: that its information value is very limited. On paper, the difference between form 1 and form 2 is not great. Equations capturing the maximum of total resource requirements (during the convergence and converged phases) for a range of agent populations (valid only for $5 \le n \le 120$) are given in Table 1. [5]

As implemented systems, however, these minor differences may be crucial. Given a particular computational resource availability **limit**, form one may function perfectly well, whereas form two may not. Conversely, given a system where information changes rapidly, form two may be better (to ensure higher temporal

---

[5] These equations have been numerically derived to reproduce the maxima measured experimentally (correlation co-efficient not less than 0.9999).

Table 1. Growth Functions for Organizational Forms 1 and 2

Max for Convergence Phase
Form 1 $\approx 4 \times 10^5 n - 5000 n^2 + 60 n^3 - 1 \times 10^6$
Form 2 $\approx 5 \times 10^6 n - 1 \times 10^5 n^2 + 1000 n^3 - 3 \times 10^7$

Max for Converged Phase
Form 1 $\approx 2 \times 10^5 n + 3000 n^2 + 25 n^3 - 1 \times 10^6$
Form 2 $\approx 7 \times 10^6 n + 10000 n^2 + 133 n^3 - 2 \times 10^6$

accuracy of the models). It is for this reason that we believe that scalability
studies for MASs should be based on practical observation and measurement.

3.3   Resource requirements for form three

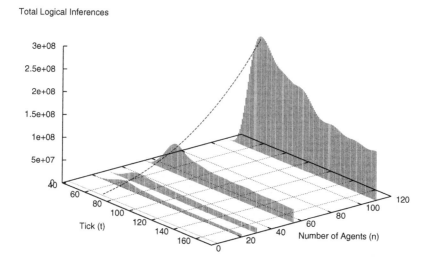

Fig. 4. Logical Inferences versus tick versus number of agents for *Form 3* MAS

Figure 4 shows the resource requirements of agents in the MAS where common tasks are centralized. As an example of a task that can be centralized, and
to illustrate the irregular shape of these resource profiles, consider a common
goal of customer agents: to keep each other updated with supplier commodity
availability and prices. When customers obtain a new piece of information about
a supplier (as a result of buying or failing to buy a commodity), this information
is forwarded to other customer agents for whom it is judged relevant information.
A simple way of determining which other customers will find this information

relevant is to retain statistics on the number of times each other customer attempts to form a collective purchasing group for this item, or alternatively, sent an update (cf [12]). In form one, this behavior was impossible. In form two, each customer maintained a model for every other and reasoned with new pieces of information against these models, finally sending appropriate messages. Since every customer agent undertakes this task, delegating the modeling and reasoning to a single agent will require lower overall resources— instead of n models of n other agents, the intermediary needs only maintain n models. Clearly, the number of messages that need to be sent remains the same (n agents send a message to a maximum of $n - 1$ others, which gives a collective total of $n^2 - n$, conversely, n agents send one message to the intermediary agent who sends a maximum of $n - 1$ in response to each— also resulting in a total of $n^2 - n$). Therefore, the benefit of centralizing this task is a lower total of models (and processing overheads) and customer agents spend more time on other goals. The cost of centralization is that the information update arrives one tick later. This is reflected by the fact that the convergence/converged phase boundary occurs at approximately tick 170 for n=110.[6]

Hence, compared to form 2, collective centralized delegation results in lower overall resource needs, but increased latency in information sharing for those tasks. Therefore form 3 has a higher convergence time than form 2. The number of ticks required to reach convergence remains lower than form 1, but higher than form 2, and the total resource needs of all agents are lower than form 2 but higher than form 1.

4   Achieving adaptable organization

A gross characterization of the relative forms studied to date is shown in Table 2. Based on these generalizations, it would seem natural to select whichever form was pertinent to a given environment. For example, in a domain where the information that is modeled is stable for longer periods of time than is needed to reach the converged state, the form which has the lowest impact on users' agents should be used (form 3). Alternatively, it may be appropriate to select form 2 initially (to converge as quickly as possible) and then revert to a less demanding form (form 3), and so on.

Although the forms shown constrain all the interactions of the agents, it is intuitive that any given form may be inappropriate for a particular shared goal. Therefore agents need to be able to select individual forms for individual shared goals (cf Galbraith's contingency theory [9]). For example, keeping track of the existence of agents (if they have transient membership of the MAS) may be based on detecting a relatively infrequent event, so form 1 may be appropriate. Conversely, modeling suppliers' commodity availability may demand fast (and frequent) updates, so form 2 may be chosen.

---

[6] Unlike form 1, the point at which convergence occurs for forms 2 and 3 (which are co-operative) is a function of the number of co-operating agents. This is most readily seen in form 3 (figure 4).

Table 2. Relative comparison of organizational form attributes

	$LISt$	Ticks for Convergence	Relative Load on (User) Agents
Form 1	Low	High	Mid
Form 2	High	Low	High
Form 3	Mid	Mid	Low

Being able to distinguish these three basic forms sets the foundation for creating self-building and adaptive MASs. With appropriate definitions of acceptable performance specified by designers (such as maximum resources available to individual agents or the collection, or minima for model accuracy), agents can begin to change their organization to meet these demands.

In order to allow agents to dynamically change between organizational forms they have been augmented with several extra abilities: 1) the ability to remove (and add) knowledge of the existence of particular acquaintances to global or specific task data structures, 2) the ability to create intermediaries or destroy them, and 3) the ability to transfer model information and delegate tasks to other agents (and, in turn, become delegatees).

Since changing organization form has repercussions for the collective, it is necessarily a collective choice. For example, a sufficient number need to agree to create an intermediary. Agents therefore need a distributed method for triggering re-organization. In this scenario, triggers for re-organization are related to utility measures and relative resource requirements of tasks per tick. The parameters of agent operation that are appropriate for triggers (and their relative importance) should be dictated by the domain characteristics and application scenario. In this scenario, for example, achieving low purchase costs for commodities (cf utility) has a higher ranking than reducing processing resource requirements (cf efficiency).

As a worked example, consider a group of ten customer agents modeling each other (form 2), and further assume that agents' own models of their users' commodity preferences change rapidly. An agent may find that it has used most of its resources modeling and updating other agents but has benefitted little from doing so. For example, it has spent 8×10^6 logical inferences in the past 100 ticks on this task, but has utilized the resultant models less than 5 times during the same period. The agent therefore notes that this task has a low payoff and increments a counter to reflect the fact. (There being a similar decrease when utility improves.) Each agent has two counters: one being a tally of utility for its own operation, and a second representing the same information from acquaintances. Agents are therefore able to distinguish their own desire for re-organization from that of their acquaintances.[7] The agent then updates the modeled agents with this value. On receipt of this message, each agent updates

---

[7] The private and social counters and their trigger activation functions are used to decide whether to join groups undertaking re-organization.

its 'social' counter (which may trigger the signal to re-organize). If either the social or private trigger reaches its activation level, the agent transmits another message to *its* acquaintances upon receipt of which they take similar action if they also reach this point. If re-organization trigger updates continue to increase or a sufficient number of agents have passed their threshold for reorganization, a cascade of updates occurs between the agents and they enter a group task to reorganize. (Note that not all agents have to agree to re-organize— currently the minimum is at least 50%.)

When re-organization has been triggered and a group has formed for this task, the agents may take several actions based on the identified problem and their current organizational form. *Identifiable problems* for customers (i.e. they each have separate triggers) include 'supplier model errors high' (agent approaches supplier for commodity it does not sell), 'supplier model low coverage' (agent has to broadcast purchase requests to all suppliers and incurs a high amount of resources tracking requests and resultant model updates), and 'ratio of resources for modeling acquaintances to payoff low' (as above example).

In such situations, the actions that the agents can take are a) centralize a task, b) de-centralize a task/create a commitment to share common information/task, or c) end a commitment to share common information/task. Option *a* moves the agents into form 3, *b* moves the agents into form 2, and option *c*, into form 1. The choice of which form to adopt is based on the identified problem (i.e. the trigger that fired), the relative advantages and disadvantages of each form (as in the previous table) and the current form.

CENTRALIZATION OF A TASK

The agents vote to select an intermediary agent or an agent is randomly chosen to create one. (If no intermediary exists, or those that do refuse to take on new tasks, one is created.) When an intermediary agrees to take on another delegated task, the agents take the following actions independently: 1) all agents extract the rules relevant to the task from their Prolog database[8], un-instantiate them, and send them to the intermediary. 2) on receipt of a message to proceed from the intermediary, the agents send all the relevant data from their databases to the intermediary. The intermediary then responds confirming receipt of the rules and data. During this process, the intermediary checks that all the agents have sent the same rules (i.e. verifies that all the agents about to delegate a task to it are going to stop performing the same task), after the success of which, the signal to proceed is sent to each agent in the group. When the intermediary has received all the data from the agents, it removes a guard on the processing of the relevant rules and sends a message to each agent informing them to remove the relevant rules and replace them with another that represents a commitment to undertake that task for them. Additional rules may be sent which cause the agents to forward runtime data to the intermediary. (All the rules the intermediary receives and/or sends back are part of the package of rules that the agents send it.)

---

[8] Additional meta-information is included in the agents which described the rules relevant to particular tasks.

ENDING COMMITMENTS TO SHARED TASKS
A rule for a shared (information) task contains a query to the agents' belief database from which it retrieves the agents to whom it has a commitment to consider forwarding information. Such rules are modified by removing commitment facts from the appropriate belief structures.

ENTERING A COMMITMENT TO A SHARE TASK
Same as for ending commitments, except that commitments are added.

4.1   Resource requirements for form four

Figure 5 shows the resource requirements of agents when utilizing organizational adaption (form 4) as compared to forms one to three. Despite the qualitative difference from the other forms, form 4 initially requires less resources than form 2, but more than forms 1 and 3. Eventually, it requires less resources than form 3.

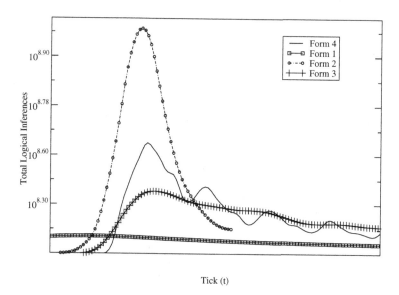

Fig. 5. Total Logical Inferences of Forms 1 to 4. $n = 110$ for forms 1 to 3, $n = 111$ for form 4 (+1 intermediary)

Although form 4 also shows a gradual decline in resource usage (on average), it does have two unique features. First, it undergoes major perturbations, and second, it does not appear to reach a stable resource level (i.e. show signs of being in the converged phase).

The reason that this form does not show the smoothness of forms 1 to 3 is because individual agents do not utilize the same form for all tasks, and not all agents are identical. That is, since the graph is a summation of many agents employing forms 1 to 3 on a per task basis, it is necessarily irregular. The perturbations in the graph and the apparent lack of evidence for convergence show an emergent feature of form 4— that it is periodic. Finally, forms 1 to 3 are isomorphic with regard to n $\geq$10. That is, that any two graphs of resource requirements for any number of agents, $n \geq 10$, can be linearly scaled to fit each other. Form 4 does not have this property. For example, the distance between the perturbation maxima varies with n. Unfortunately this means that accurately projecting the resource requirement curves for higher (untested) numbers of agents is impossible for form 4.

Finally, the figure shows form 4 being a suitable amalgam of forms 1 to 3 in terms of resource requirements. The maximum resources required falls some-way below that of form 2, and it also (eventually) falls below that of form 3. We do not consider the agents of form 1 to constitute a multi-agent system since they are asocial, therefore of the MAS forms presented here, we suggest that form 4 (which is organizationally adaptive) is more scalable than form 2 (because the maxima remain lower) and also form 3 (because the converged phase maxima are lower).

5   Related Research

Publications dealing with scalability and multi-agent systems are relatively few (but gaining in number). In order to place this work in the context of others, we broadly partition MAS scalability research into categories thus: 1) formal and experimental scalability analyses of particular co-operation and resource distribution protocols (e.g. [5] [6]); 2) creation of scalable protocols (e.g. [17]); 3) tools for (pre-implementation) predication of performance and design evaluation (e.g. [16]); 4) clarification of scalability issues (e.g. [15]); 5) scalable architectures and applications (mostly residing in the information retrieval arena); and 6) algorithms and techniques for increasing scalability through change of the MAS environment.

We view this paper as relevant to the last category. Insofar as the research deals with dynamic changes to the structure of the problem solver environment— rather than the protocols they employ. That is, techniques that indirectly affect agents and MASs by altering the agents (but not their mechanisms) or the environment in which they reside. Examples, of this are [1] ("a framework for Dynamic Reorganization"), [13] ("An Organizational Approach to Adaptive Production Systems"), and [10] ("Self-Adaption and Scalability in Multi-Agent Societies").

The creation and destruction of intermediaries as extra (parallel) processing capability is indirectly based on [13]— where not only do Ishida *et al* introduce organization self-design (OSD), but also allow two or more agents to *'compose'* (combine with each other) and *'decompose'* when organizational load is heavy or light respectively. Furthermore, a mechanism is given whereby composition and decomposition can occur at runtime without affecting the operation of the 'agents'. Explicitly included in their scheme is an organization self-designer in each agent (cf [3]). Our approach differs in that lightly loaded agents do not automatically take on extra tasks (since they must maintain a minimal utility for their owners). Also, whereas their agents effectively cease to exist after a composition into a hybrid, our (customer and supplier) agents can not. The equivalent of reduction in total system load occurs because of the centralization/ decentralization of a task, or delimitation (through disbanding and reforming) of a social group which places too large a load on its members.

In [1], André et al refer to dynamic reorganization (DR) through which their centralized MAS (viewed as a hierarchic graph of service decomposition) can swap to alternative decompositions. The new decomposition is retained if the alternative performs worse than the original. The scenario we presented does not allow the agents to form compound services by the combination of existing facilities. In as much as our agents can disband and reform groups, and centralize/de-centralize tasks, no explicit representation of the previous state is retained.

Lastly, in [10], the main thrust of the argument is that the problems of scalability can be managed by changing the relative amounts of processing time and other resources to the various aspects that operate within agents. For example, increasing the amount of time in manipulating knowledge representations. The configuration of the agents is represented as a search space so that when the agents' ability to perform drops below an acceptable level it will move within the search space. The first move in this search space is random. Locally, agents perform hill climbing to achieve local optima of parameters. However, a centralized agent constructs a picture of this search space using the information local to agents (i.e. local agents provide fragments of the picture). The centralized agent uses this information to prevent the agents from settling on local maxima when better solutions are 'nearby'. Viz., the centralized 'monitor' agent is able to direct the agents in their search (e.g. beyond their own fragment of the search space). However, it can not be certain that the search space is smooth and therefore the hill climbing search methods used by the agents and central monitor agent may not be appropriate in all domains. (His approach is presented as a general framework.) Critically, the monitor (as a permanent centralized entity) may constitute a bottle-neck itself and prevent scalability.

Furthermore, Gerber uses the term *Holon* and the notion of abstract resources. Abstract resources are roughly equivalent to the compound services of [1], and holons are essentially, collections of agents (which may be considered as a group or as a single agent) with partially limited autonomy (see [10] for the full extent of his hypothesis). Taken as a whole, Gerber's framework and mechanisms for adaption are both microscopic and macroscopic in nature. Despite having been tested in several application scenarios, none are represented in a form where population size is paramount (so no direct comparison can be made). We suspect that Gerber's framework is better able to fine tune response to small changes in scale than our approach, which we believe may be coarser in comparison. However, we note that our approach is less invasive (since it only requires the ability to change acquaintance topologies and group commitments rather than interfere with internal operation of agents).

Combining our work with that of other researchers, we summarize the approaches that have successfully been employed to achieve organizational adaption thus: a) agent/process de/composition and creation/destruction, b) alternative decomposition/ recomposition of compound abstract resources and dependencies, c) centralization/ decentralization of common goals and alteration of acquaintance (and thus group) topology, and finally d) re-allocation of relative processing power of agents internal processes. Clearly, all these methods could be combined. Moreover, in addition to agents having access to knowledge of their performance and limitations, they could benefit greatly from being able to form and reason with (formal) models of their dynamic organization [4] and [2].

6   Conclusions and Future work

Allowing agents to build and maintain their own organizational structure requires that they are able to decide for themselves what tasks should be shared, delegated, or individually pursued, and which acquaintances are of little benefit. This means they must be aware and be able to meta-reason about their own internal efficiency/efficacy and goals, infer or question that of their acquaintances, and the goals of the system as a whole. It also entails that agents are able to create and annihilate other agents, delegate and surrender tasks and information, modify their own operation and influence that of others (because organizational changes are taken by the collective, not the individual). The algorithm sketched above does show that organizational flexibility has advantages. In summary, although we believe that large scale multi-agent systems should be self-building and self-organizing to allow for a higher degree of scale tolerance, we believe that much greater testing is required in several domains of application. One limitation of the scenario implementation is that the market dynamics is relatively stable. How re-organization copes with fluctuations in user's demands remains unclear, and so too a complete analysis of the influx (and exodus) of population. Secondary in importance to this omission are the effects of the trigger levels for re-organization, and the similarity metrics used by the (customer) agents to decide on group formation. The values to which these are set may have a major effect of the benefit of re-organization. Indeed, determining these values remains a matter of experimentation. Also, relaxation of the synchronized method of operation of agent execution needs to be undertaken since MASs are almost exclusively asynchronous. Answering the questions raised by these issues, constitutes our future work. Finally, we note that creating an algorithm to increase the scalability of a MAS is not the same (and does not imply) that the algorithm is *itself* scalable.

References

1. J.-M. André, J.-M., Mouginot, A., Venet, M.: A Framework for Dynamic Reorganization. Ninth European Conference on Artificial Intelligence (1990) 31–37
2. Baligh, H.H., Damon, W.W.: Foundations for a Systematic Process of Organization Structure Design. Journal of Information & Optimization Sciences $1(2)$ (1980) 133–165
3. Brazier, F.M.T., Jonker, C.M., Treur, J., Wijngaards, N.J.E.: Deliberate Evolution in Multi-Agent Systems. Third Annual International Conference on Autonomous Agents (1999) 356–357
4. Costa, A.C.R., Demazeau, Y.: Toward a Formal Model of Multi-Agent Systems with Dynamic Organization. Second International Conference on Multi-Agent Systems (1996) 431
5. De Wilde, P., Nwana, H.S., Lee, L.C.: Stability, Fairness and Scalability of Multi-Agent Systems. International Journal of Knowledge-Based Intelligent Engineering Systems $3(2)$ (1999) 84–91
6. Foner, L., Crabtree, I.B.: Multi-agent matchmaking. British Telecom Technology Journal $14(4)$ (1996)
7. Foss, J.D., Garcha, K., Turner, P.J., Jennings, N.R.: Brokerage in an Information Economy. INET 2000, 10th Annual Internet Society Conference, Yokohama, Japan (2000)
8. Fox, M.S.: An Organizational View of Distributed Systems. IEEE Transactions of Systems, Man, and Cybernetics $11(1)$ (1981) 70–79
9. Galbraith, J.: Designing complex organizations. Addison-Wesley Publishers (1973)
10. Gerber, C.: Self-Adaption and Scalability in Multi-Agent Societies (PhD thesis). Universität des Saarlandes (1999)
11. De Greene, K.B.:, The Adaptive Organization, anticipation and management of crisis. John Wiley & Sons, Inc. (1982)
12. Huhns, M., Mukhopadhy, U., Stephens, L.M., Bonnel, R.D.: DAI for Document Retrieval: The MINDS Project. Chapter 9 of Distributed AI Volume II, Pitman Publishing Ltd (1987)
13. Ishida, T., Yokoo, M., Gasser, L.: An Organizational Approach to Adaptive Productive Systems. Eighth National Conference on Artificial Intelligence (1990) 52–58
14. Kuokka, D., Harada, L.: Matchmaking for Information Agents. Fourteenth International Joint Conference on Artificial Intelligence (IJCAI) (1995) 672–678
15. Lee, L.C., Nwana, H.S., Ndumu, D.T., De Wilde, P.: The stability, scalability and performance of multi-agent systems. British Telecom Technology Journal $16(3)$ (1998) 94–103
16. Rana, O.F., Stout, K.: What is Scalability in Multi-Agent Systems?. Fourth Annual International Conference on Autonomous Agents (2000)
17. Shehory, O.: A Scalable Agent Location Mechanism. Lecture Notes in Artificial Intelligence, Intelligent Agents VI (2000) 162–172
18. Shoham, Y.: AGENT0: A Simple Agent Language and Its Interpreter. Ninth National Conference on Artificial Intelligence 2 (1991) 704–709

Mobile Agents for Distributed Processing

Penny Noy* and Michael Schroeder

City University, London EC1V 0HB, {p.a.noy,msch}@soi.city.ac.uk

Abstract. In this statement, we sketch how to employ mobile agents for distributed computing and how such a solution compares to traditional approaches.

1 Introduction

In the late 1940s, a British Government report concluded that the demand for computing power in the UK could be satisfied by two or three computers. They turned out to be wrong. Nowadays computers are ubiquitous and demand for computing power is nearly infinite. Although computing power increases by a factor of ten every five years, theoretical results suggest that single processors have their limits. Networking is one way forward beyond these limits. In fact, in the top 500 list of fastest computers [1] a machine with 9152 Pentiums ranks top. The internet adds a new dimension to high-performance computing. Distributed.net, for example, is a distributed system solving a decryption task. It consists of some 100,000 computers connected over the internet.

Given these developments, we address two main questions: How can we design mobile agents for distributed computing? How does this solution compare to traditional approaches such as distributed object computing and message passing libraries? In this statement, we outline answers to these questions.

2 Designing mobile agents for distributed computing: a case study

Millions of computers lie idle for much of the time. How can they be used? One solution (e.g. distributed.net) to use this power is the development of dedicated, static clients, which users install and run on their machines. Can mobile agents provide a more flexible alternative? To answer this question we have developed a collaborative mobile-agent system for distributed computing, implemented its major components with Aglets [1,2], and employed it for prime number computation using PCs in a student lab.

---

* We would like to thank Dr. Keith Mannock, Birkbeck College, London, for his assistance and encouragement in the development of this work, which is supported also by the EPSRC and British Telecom (CASE studentship - award number 99803052).
[1] www.netlib.org/benchmark/top500.html

The system's architecture uses a number of design patterns [1,2] and we list its five main components here:

First, the core of the system is built according to the master-slave pattern with extensions for mobility, scheduling, and load-balancing. Initially, aglets are dispatched to servers on remote computers to carry out a share of the task in parallel.

Second, a dedicated data store saves data persistently. It is used mainly by the master to get information on versions, data, current tasks. The data store is related to the plan pattern.

Third, agents have to find where to move to, a task covered by itinerary patterns. In our case, the location depends on the availability of a server and its work-load. Two structures were developed: (1) Where remote servers are set up as background processes on all machines in the network, a monitor agent examines data on cpu usage of individual machines and recommends dispatch to PCs not heavily loaded. This agent can also initiate the transfer of a slave, if the slave's local cpu becomes busier. (2) Where servers are set up manually on available computers, a server-tester agent sends out scouts to find where they are. The successful dispatch of a Scout confirms the existence of a context and thus a server on that host. Slaves can be moved due to loading as in (1). In either case the master finds out where it is appropriate to send its slaves and dispatches them.

Fourth, a finder agent acts as facilitator. It keeps track of the slaves once they have been dispatched as they move due to cpu monitoring. Registration is used to track the aglet to avoid multicast and forwarding of messages.

Fifth, a timer agent, which is related to task-planning patterns, is activated at the beginning of a task. It contacts the master if an excessive time lapse occurs and coordinates system events (shutdown, power failure).

We have applied this architecture successfully to prime number calculation.

3   Comparison

The next open question is how such a mobile agent solution compares to traditional approaches such as distributed object computing (e.g. Corba, RMI) and message passing (e.g. PVM, MPI). These different approaches can be compared with respect to the following criteria: communication paradigm, capability for load-balancing, advanced services (naming, trading, transactions, etc.), performance, scalability, security, simplicity.

For brevity, we omit a detailed comparison and only outline problem characteristics, which make mobile agent solutions convincing: (1) Decentralize when infrastructure unreliable: A major difference between mobile agents and the other paradigms concerns autonomy. Agents decide when to move where and which tasks to carry out. Autonomy is a desirable feature, when the infrastructure is not reliable. For instance: when the underlying network covers a wide area; when the system is open; when hosts are not permanently connected due to physical failures or as a feature (laptop). (2) Flexible load-balancing: The granularity of parallelization of a task is important in the choice of a platform. While PVM's scheduling and Corba's trading allow for a limited form of load-balancing, they depend hugely on the assumption that the balancing is static, in the sense that once a task is assigned to a host, it does not have to move anymore. This is safe to assume, when dealing with very fine parallelization of the original task, but that increases communication overhead and makes parallelization less efficient in the first place. Therefore, if sub-tasks are still relatively large, it may become necessary to move during processing. A perfect reason to use mobile agents. Typical tasks, which satisfy this property are scientific simulations and decryption.

4 Conclusions

The main aim of this work was to investigate the possibility of utilizing the spare computing power of idle or underused computers using mobile agents. As such, our purpose was not quantitative measurement, but evidence of the practicality of the approach in context. Would mobile agent technology be successful? Would the system be able to do useful work? Would it be possible to choose a host on the basis of how busy its cpu was and could computers be sent tasks whilst other users were logged on to them and using them? These questions were all answered in the affirmative.

Results indicate that the aglet system is capable of doing valuable work and is eminently scalable. This begs the question, why are such systems not more widely employed? The steepness of the learning curve and security are two possible answers. For the general user, the inherent complexity may be the problem. Users tend to rely on simpler solutions: buy more processing power or more memory; use a simpler paradigm. As mobile agent systems emerge that address the security issue more robustly and provide integrated development environments and monitoring tools, more of the complexity will be concealed.

References

1. Yariv Aridor and Danny Lange. Agent design patterns: Elements of agent application design. In *Proceedings of the second Conference on Autonomous Agents*, Minneapolis, USA, 1998. ACM Press.
2. D. Lange and M. Oshima. *Programming and Deploying Java Mobile Agents with Aglets*. Addison Wesley, 1998.

Scalability of a Transactional Infrastructure for Multi-Agent Systems

Khaled Nagi

Institute for Program Structures and Data Organization, Universität Karlsruhe.
Am Fasanengarten 5,
D-76131 Karlsruhe, Germany.
+49-721-608-7336
nagi@ira.uka.de

Abstract. One of the reasons for attending to agent technology is the ever-growing complexity of information systems and the increasing difficulty to foresee and plan for all potentially arising situations. Unfortunately, some pressing issues in practical applications still remain outside the focus of agent research. Chief among them is robustness in environments that are prone to disturbances, failures or uncontrolled interactions. In our research effort, we provide a middleware, based on database transactions, that formally guarantees robustness of execution of agent actions and automates many standard actions carried out in case of disturbances. We built a simulator to test the scalability of the proposed middleware. The simulator also gives us a better understanding of the behavior of the various planning strategies reflected by the transaction trees executed by the middleware and is a valuable tool for evaluating the performance of any multi-agent system before its actual deployment. In this paper, the agent transaction model executed by the middleware is outlined. The simulator is described and the experimental results of simulating a growing number of antagonist agents with collective conflicts over a common database are presented.

1 Introduction

Traditionally, Multi-Agent Systems (MAS) covered the range from the *production domains* with their emphasis on fault-tolerance of repetitive work (see [1] for a good overview) to the *Artificial Intelligence domains* with their attention to planning and solving highly complex problems (see [2] for a good introduction). Today, there is a great tendency for attending to agent technology to cope with the ever-growing complexity of information systems and the increasing difficulty to foresee and plan for all potentially arising situations. As can be seen in [3], many research efforts are dedicated to deploying this emerging technology in the fields of intelligent information retrieval, web assistants, electronic commerce, etc.

However, despite many research efforts to deploy MAS in information-rich environments, this technology seems to have a long way to go before its actual use in large-scale enterprise core applications, such as Enterprise Resource Planning (ERP) applications. The reason is the lack of robustness in the existing MAS. By robustness we mean that both individual agents and agents systems as a whole overcome distur-

T. Wagner and O.F. Rana (Eds.): Infrastructure for Agents, LNAI 1887, pp. 266–278, 2001.

bances, failure, or uncontrolled interactions by reaching well-defined states. In [4], we first presented our means of achieving agent robustness on both levels, namely, *transactions*. In an approach similar to JAFMAS [5], which provides a framework for agent communication, or Aglets [6], which provides an infrastructure for mobile agents, we propose a middleware for the execution of plans generated by agents.

The middleware, illustrated in Fig. 1, receives the agent plan, either complete or incrementally, in the form of a transaction tree. In the tree, the agent actions needed to achieve the predefined goal are specified together with the control flow and control parameters. The middleware is then responsible for the correct and robust execution of these actions. It also automates many procedures that are usually followed in case of failure. Examples of such procedures include automatic retry of failed actions, compensation, and backtracking of parts of the plan. We implement this middleware completely in Java, so that it can execute on all platforms without the need for an extra run-time environment.

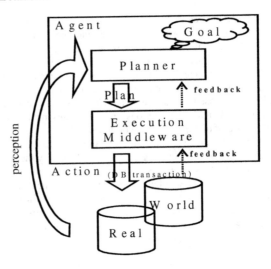

Fig. 1. The execution middleware

A key to the success of this infrastructure in large-scale information systems is its ability to scale. To quantitatively assess the scalability of the proposed middleware, we built a simulator around it. The simulation study also gives a better understanding of the behavior of the transaction trees, and hence the various planning strategies. This is very important in evaluating the overall quality of solutions provided by the MAS. For this reason, we present the simulator as a tool and encourage MAS developers to use it to evaluate their systems before the actual deployment. In this paper, we restrict our analysis to antagonist agents competing on the same database.

The remainder of the paper is organized as follows. Section 2 contains an outline of the agent transaction model. In Section 3, we describe the simulation model and the simulator. We also list the performance indices employed in the evaluation. Section 4 describes the simulation results. Finally, Section 5 summarizes the paper and presents a brief description of our future work.

2 The Agent Transaction Model

Since the vast majority of agent planning techniques is based on hierarchical decomposition (for a good overview, please refer to [7]), we use a model based on open nested transaction trees introduced by Traiger [8] in the early 80s for database management systems. Under this model, a transaction can launch any number of subtransactions, which, in turn, can launch any number of subtransactions, thus forming a transaction tree. In general, a transaction cannot commit unless all its children are terminated. However, if one of the children fails, its parent does not have to abort. It has the choice between:

- ignoring the condition (a non-vital transaction),
- retrying the subtransaction,
- launching another *compensating* subtransaction, or
- aborting.

Subtransactions may commit or abort independently and appear atomic to other subtransactions. A committed subtransaction makes its results available to other subtransactions in other transaction trees as soon as it commits. In case of transaction aborts, its subtransactions must be compensated by executing so-called *compensating transactions* whose role is to mitigate the permanent effects of the original subtransactions.

Fig. 2 is an example of such transaction trees. A *Control Node* is a non-leaf node. It automatically executes within the middleware according to the control parameters supplied to it by the Planner. Typical control parameters include the *number of retries* in case of failure, the *time interval* between retries, and whether the children are to be *undone* or not. For a detailed description of the parameters, please refer to [9]. During normal execution, the children of a control node can execute either in *parallel* or *sequentially*. An *Action Node* is always a leaf node. It submits the agent simple actions to the corresponding database management systems (DBMS) in the form of ACID transactions, i.e., transactions satisfying the *Atomicity*, *Consistency*, *Isolation*, and *Durability* conditions. For a description of these conditions, please refer to [10]. This means that each of these actions returns either success or failure to its parent. For each Action Node, a compensating node is defined. It contains the compensation of the original action.

In order to support agent cooperation in the MAS, their corresponding transaction trees must be coupled in the execution middleware. This concept is completely new to the open-nested transaction models. We introduce the so-called *Synchronization Nodes*. They represent the basic coordination primitives between transaction trees. On the sender side, a node exists and sends a message to the receiver node if a certain condition is met. A typical condition would be a change in the node state such as the commitment of a transaction subtree. On the receiver side, the synchronization node waits for the arrival of the message and commits or aborts according to the message received. Further details concerning agent coupling is beyond the scope of this paper.

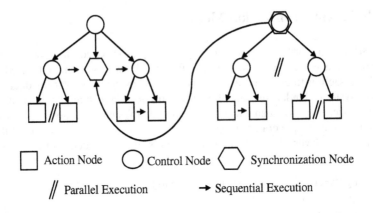

Fig. 2. Two coupled transaction trees

Fig. 3 illustrates a simplified state transition diagram that applies to all node types. At the beginning, the transaction node is in the *Waiting* state until the scheduler starts it. It then moves to the *Executing* state. According to the result of the execution (e.g., success or fail of an action node or the end state of the children of a control node), the node moves either to the *Committing* state or to the *Aborting* state. If aborted, the node waits for a time interval before moving again to the Executing state as long as the number of retries is not yet exhausted. A committed node moves to the *Compensating* state if the *must undo* flag is set in its control parameters and its parent node fails. After compensation, it waits again for execution by the scheduler. Otherwise, the committed node remains in its current state until the root node commits. Then, all the committed nodes in the tree enter the *Terminating* state. However, if the root node fails and exhausts all its retries, all its children enter the *Abandoning* state recursively.

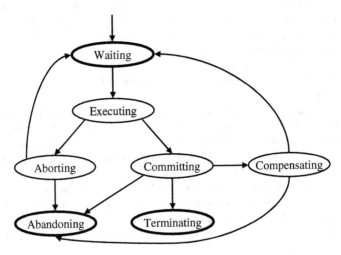

Fig. 3. State transition diagram for a transaction node

3 The Simulation Study

In our simulation study, we analyze the scalability of the middleware under various workload configurations. However, we restrict ourselves to agents acting on the same database, with no cooperation, and having incompatible goals. According to the classification given in [11], this is the case of *antagonist agents* with *collective conflicts over resources*. As illustrated in Fig. 4, we replace the levels above and underneath the middleware with two simulated models. In the following subsection, we describe these models together with the transaction tree model executed by the middleware.

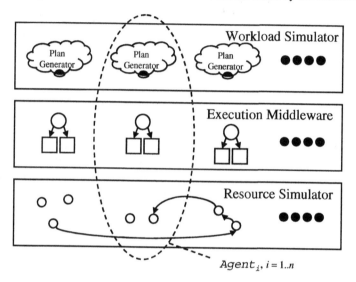

Fig. 4. The simulation environment

3.1 System Parameters

The Workload Model. Each agent is provided with a Plan Generator *(PG)*. This module generates a transaction tree and submits it to the execution middleware. When the middleware finishes execution, the PG generates a new tree and so on. Three parameters specify the tree configuration as illustrated in Fig. 5.

- *Probability of Parallel Execution (P)*: is a Bernoulli trial with probability P that the children of a control node are executed in parallel.
- *Average Number of Children (C)*: is a uniformly distributed random variable between 1 and $2C$; determining the number of children of a control node.
- *Probability of Simple Transactions (S)*: is a Bernoulli trial with probability S that a child is an action node.

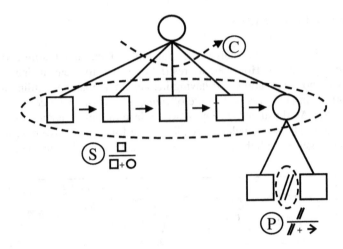

Fig. 5. Parameters for the transaction tree

Since our simulated agents are antagonist, no cooperation takes place. This leads to the absence of any synchronization nodes between the transaction trees. In order to generate a finite tree, $(1-S) \times (C+0.5)$ must be smaller than 1. This restricts our feasible region to that narrow shaded area illustrated in Fig. 6.

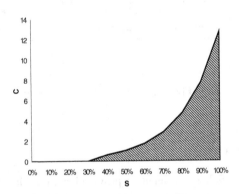

Fig. 6. Feasible region for simulation

The Transaction Tree Model. To get more compact and concrete results, the agents adopt a persevering strategy. This means the following setting of the control parameters. All nodes, both action and control nodes, must be undone in case of failure of the parent node. The number of retries of action nodes is set to 5 in normal mode and to 2 in compensation mode. Compound nodes are also retried twice. In our runs, we fix the time interval between successive retries to 60 seconds for all node types in both operation modes.

The resource model. Execution time of database transactions, normally consisting of read and write operations, is represented by an exponential distribution with mean 15 seconds. To determine whether a transaction is to be *committed* or *aborted*, we construct a *transaction serialization graph*. Each executing transaction is represented by a node in the graph. A directed edge indicates a conflict between two transactions. A conflict occurs if two transactions access the same data object and at least one operation is a write. A transaction is aborted if its introduction results in a cycle in the graph [12]. Edges are added with *two* probabilities: P_1 for nodes belonging to different agents and a lower P_2 for nodes belonging to the same agent. This reflects an assumption about the planning algorithm: the planner tends not to submit conflicting actions simultaneously. P_1 and P_2 are set to 0.03 and 0.01 respectively. Sources for these values as well as mean execution time are taken from standard research in database modeling such as [13], where both the database and transaction sizes are reduced to a small size, while preserving the relationship between them. Fig. 7 illustrates a serialization graph, in which each node is identified by its *agent identifier* ($AgID$) and its *transaction identifier* (TID).

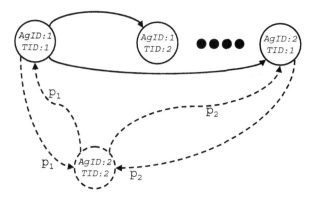

Fig. 7. Inserting a node into the serialization graph

3.2 Performance Indices

It is clear that we cannot provide a unique performance index that combines all possible performance criteria, since the weighting constants are very application-dependent. Therefore, we only identify the most important indices. The first index is the *throughput*, where the number of terminated actions per agent per second is counted. The second index is the *response time* of execution of the whole plan. In this index, we also account for the time wasted in aborted, compensated, and abandoned actions (the different states are explained in Section 2). The *ratio of compensated actions to the terminated ones* is a very important economical measure because of the high cost generally associated with compensation. For example, one gets only a percentage of the full price for a returned theater ticket. A minimization of this ratio is certainly desired. The *ratio of abandoned actions to the terminated ones* accounts for the incidences, in which the execution middleware fails to execute an agent plan and returns control back to the planer. A low value of this metric is a good measure for achieving the design goal of separating planning from the details of execution and the disturbances associated with it. Clearly, the ratio is an index for the ability of the system designer to fine-tune the control parameters of the transaction nodes. The last performance index is the *ratio of aborted actions to the terminated ones*. It accounts for work lost due to conflicting actions. Here also, a lower ratio is desired.

4 Simulation Results

In the simulation study, we explore the workload space, in which all valid values of P, C, and S are used (see Section 3.1). In each experiment, the number of agents is varied between 5 and 100. In the resource simulator, the commit/abort decision plays the major role in the overall performance. Intuitively, it is dependent on the number of concurrently executing transactions and the job mix, i.e., the number of actions each agent is simultaneously having in the model. The results of the experiments form large hypercubes. The good news is that the infrastructure is very *scalable*. It is clear that the performance indices will be negatively affected with the large increase in the number of agents; but there is *no thrashing* in any one of the indices. In the following subsections, we try to isolate each workload parameter and summarize the performance indices in a set of simple figures.

4.1 Effect of Increasing the Degree of Parallel Execution (P)

For the set of curves from Fig. 8[1] to Fig. 12, S and C are fixed to 100% and 3 respectively and the curves are plotted for P varying from 0% to 100%. All performance indices degrade gracefully with the increase in agents; however, the rate depends on P. The throughput and response time of parallel execution of nodes yield better results for under-populated settings. This situation is naturally reversed with the increase in agents (more than 60 agents), in which it is better to submit agent actions sequentially. The compensation ratio, illustrated in Fig. 10, remains in all cases under 10%. However, if compensation results in economically harmful side effects, it is wiser to adopt a conservative strategy and execute agent actions sequentially. This results in almost no compensation. The same applies for the abandon ratio illustrated in Fig. 11. An interesting observation is the abort ratio illustrated in Fig. 12. For an under-populated setting, the abort ratio for more sequential execution is lower than that for a more parallel one. For an over-populated setting, the situation is again reversed. The explanation of this case is simple. The database has a certain capacity for executing transactions without coming into conflicts. For under-populated settings, this capacity is not reached; that is why sequential execution results in a smaller number of concurrent actions and hence a smaller number of aborts. For over-populated settings, the agents with highly parallel execution are either submitting *all* their actions at once or are waiting for retrying *all* their actions. Due to the large wait interval, approx. 4

---

[1] In all figures, the legend starts with the value of S, followed by C, followed by P.

times the execution time, only a fraction of the total number of agents is actually having executing transactions in the resource model, and having a lower overall conflicting rate (remember that $P_1=3P_2$). This results in the better abort ratio for highly populated settings with high degree of parallelism.

4.2 Effect of Increasing the Average Number of Children (C)

For the set of curves from Fig. 13 to Fig. 17, S and P are fixed to 100% and 25% respectively and the curves are plotted for C varying from 3 to 7. Since changing C results in different tree sizes, we normalize the results by dividing them by the average number of action nodes in each tree configuration in order to have a better visual presentation of the graphs. Again, no thrashing is observed in any of the performance indices. Moreover, the values for the normalized (N) response time and compensation ratio, illustrated in Fig. 14 and Fig. 15 respectively, seem to be hardly affected by the change in the tree size. The normalized abandon ratio, illustrated in Fig. 16, is affected by the change in the tree size only for highly populated settings in which a smaller tree yields better results. However, the normalized throughput and normalized abort ratio, illustrated in Fig. 13 and Fig. 17 respectively, are very much affected by the change. The normalized throughput seems approximately to *halve* with the increase of C from 3 to 7 for all populations. The normalized abort ratio also varies by a factor of 2; however in favor of a larger tree. This goes in agreement with the explanation given in Section 4.1.

4.3 Effect of Increasing the Tree Depth (S)

For the set of curves from Fig. 18 to Fig. 22, C and P are fixed to 3 and 25% respectively and the curves are plotted for S varying from 100% to 80%. This leads to a variation of the average depth of action nodes from 2.0 to 4.6. As in Section 4.2, we also normalize the results by dividing them by the average number of action nodes in each tree configuration. Again, no thrashing is observed in these experiments. Similar to Section 4.2, the values for the normalized response time and compensation ratio, illustrated in Fig. 19 and Fig. 20, respectively, are hardly affected by the change in the tree depth. However, the normalized throughput, illustrated in Fig. 18, is greatly affected by the change in S. It is halved if S is reduced to 90% instead of 100%. The decrease is even up to a factor of 3 when reduced to 80%. This is due to the exponential nature of trees. Nevertheless, a deep tree has also some virtues. It allows a better controllability over its subtrees, which reflects the logical partitioning and isolation of planning steps. This can be observed in Fig. 21. The normalized abandon ratio for deep trees is by far better than flat trees. This advantages gains in importance as the number of agents increases. Another virtue is the lower normalized abort ratio illustrated in Fig. 22.

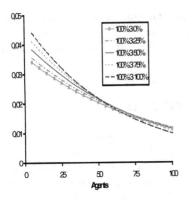

Fig. 8. Throughput for 4.1

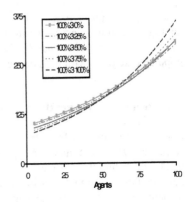

Fig. 9. Response time for 4.1

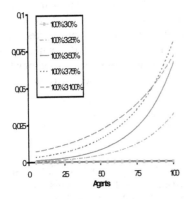

Fig. 10. Compensation ratio for 4.1

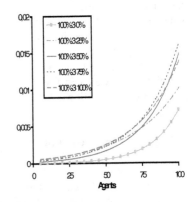

Fig. 11. Abandon Ratio for 4.1

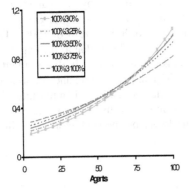

Fig. 12. Abort Ratio for 4.1

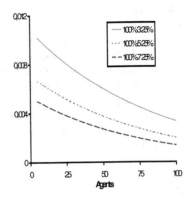

Fig. 13. Throughput (N) for 4.2

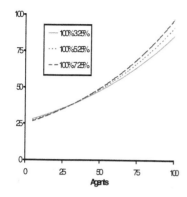

Fig. 14. Response time (N) for 4.2

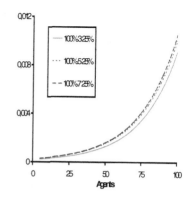

Fig. 15. Compensation ratio (N) for 4.2

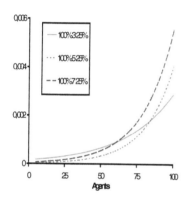

Fig. 16. Abandon ratio (N) for 4.2

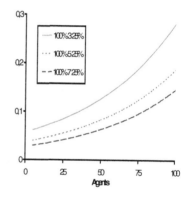

Fig. 17. Abort ratio (N) for 4.2

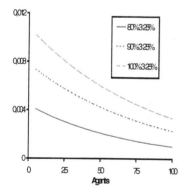

Fig. 18. Throughput (N) for 4.3

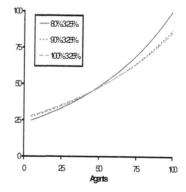

Fig. 19. Response time (N) for 4.3

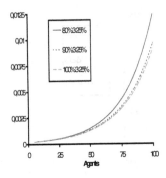

Fig. 20. Compensation ratio (N) for 4.3

Fig. 21. Abandon ratio (N) for 4.3

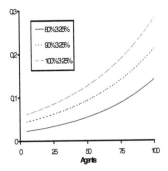

Fig. 22. Abort ratio (N) for 4.3

5   Summary and Future Work

In order to use agent technology in large-scale enterprise core applications, we propose a plan execution middleware, based on an advanced database transaction model, which formally guarantees the robustness of the system on both the level of individual agents as well as the level of the whole system. We built a simulator around this middleware to give a quantitative assessment of the scalability of the middleware.

In this paper, we presented the simulator and the model used in the study. By analyzing the system for a growing number of agents under the various workload configurations, we demonstrate the scalability of our system. The simulation study also reveals a lot about the behavior of the transaction trees and the plans they implement. Here, we restrict ourselves to the case of antagonist agents with self-centered goals. In the future, we want to extend our analysis to consider collaborative agent groups trying to achieve a common goal by developing shared plans that require coordination between the corresponding transaction trees.

References

1. Shen, W., Norrie, D.: Agent-Based Systems for Intelligent Manufacturing: A State-of-the Art Survey. International Journal on Knowledge and Information Systems, Springer-Verlag, (1999).
2. Weiss, G. (ed.): Multi-Agent Systems: A Modern Approach to Distributed Artificial Intelligence. 1st edn. MIT Press, (1999).
3. Klusch, M. (ed.): Intelligent Information Agents: agent-Based Information discovery and Management on the Internet. 1st edn. Springer-Verlag, (1999).
4. Nagi, K., Lockemann, P.: Implementation Model for Agents with Layered Architecture in a Transactional Database Environment. Proc. 1st Workshop on Agent Oriented Information Systems, (June 1999).
5. Chauhan, D., Baker, A.D.: JAFMAS: A Multi-Agent Application Development System. Proc. 2nd International Conference on Autonomous Agents, 100-107, (1998).
6. Lange, D., Oshima, M.: Programming and Deploying Java Mobile Agents with Aglets. 1st edn. Addison-Wesley, (1998).
7. Allen, J., Hendler, J., Tate, A. (eds.): Readings in Planning. 1st edn. Morgan Kaufmann, (1990).
8. Traiger, I.L.: Trends in Systems Aspects of Database Management. Proc. 2nd International Conference on Databases, Wiley & Sons, (1983).
9. Nagi, K.: Transactional Agents: A Robust Approach for Scheduling Orders in a competitive Just-In-Time Manufacturing Environment. Proc. Workshop on MAS in logistics and economical perspectives of agent conceptualization, held within the 23rd German Conference on AI, (September 1999).
10. Gray, J.: The Transaction Concept: Virtues and Limitations. Proc. 7th International Conference on Very Large Data Bases, 144-154, (September 1981).
11. Ferber, J.: Multi-Agent Systems: An Introduction to Distributed Artificial Intelligence. 1st edn. Addison-Wesley, (1999).
12. Bernstein, P., Hadzilacos, V., Goodman, N.: Concurrency Control And Recovery in Database Systems, Addison-Wesley, (1987).
13. Carey, M.J., Franklin, M.J., Livny, M., Shekita, E.J.: Data Caching Tradeoffs in Client-Server DBMS Architectures. Proc. ACM SIGMOD, 357-366, (1991).

Towards a Scalable Architecture for Knowledge Fusion

Alex Gray, Philippe Marti
Department of Computer Science, Cardiff University
Cardiff, UK

Alun Preece
Department of Computing Science, University of Aberdeen
Aberdeen, UK

Abstract

The KRAFT project has defined a generic agent-based architecture to support *knowledge fusion* — the process of locating and extracting knowledge from multiple, heterogeneous on-line sources, and transforming it so that the union of the knowledge can be applied in problem-solving. KRAFT focuses on knowledge in the form of *constraints* expressed against an object data model defined by a shared ontology. KRAFT employs three kinds of agent: *facilitators* locate appropriate on-line sources of knowledge; *wrappers* transform heterogeneous knowledge to a homogeneous constraint interchange format; *mediators* fuse the constraints together with associated data to form a dynamically-composed constraint satisfaction problem, which is then passed to an existing constraint solver engine to compute solutions. The KRAFT architecture has been designed to be scalable to large numbers of agents; this paper describes the features of the architecture designed to support scalability.

1 Introduction

The KRAFT project (Knowledge Reuse And Fusion/Transformation) aims to define a generic architecture for knowledge fusion. Knowledge fusion refers to the process of locating and extracting knowledge from multiple, heterogeneous on-line sources, and transforming it so that the union of the knowledge can be applied in problem-solving. The KRAFT architecture was conceived to support *configuration design applications* involving multiple component vendors with heterogeneous knowledge and data models. This kind of application turns out to be very general, covering not only the obvious manufacturing-type applications (for example, configuration of personal computers or telecommunications network equipment) but also service-type applications such as travel planning (for example, composing package holidays or business trips involving flights, ground travel connections, and hotels) and knowledge management (for example, selecting and combining business rules from multiple heterogeneous knowledge and databases on a corporate intranet).

A key feature of the KRAFT project is that the form of knowledge is restricted to *constraints* expressed against an object data model defined by a shared ontology [8]. This ontology specifies the knowledge available in resources external to the current KRAFT network. The KRAFT architecture supports the following:

- *Knowledge discovery:* locating appropriate on-line sources of knowledge;

- *Knowledge transformation:* transforming heterogeneous knowledge to a homogeneous constraint interchange format;

T. Wagner and O.F. Rana (Eds.): Infrastructure for Agents, LNAI 1887, pp. 279–292, 2001.
© Springer-Verlag Berlin Heidelberg 2001

- *Knowledge fusion:* fusing the constraints with associated data to form a dynamically-composed constraint satisfaction problem (CSP);

- *Problem-solving:* harnessing existing constraint solver engines to compute CSP solutions.

These features — heterogeneous on-line sources, an open, dynamic environment, legacy processing engines — led to the natural choice of an agent architecture as the basic model for the KRAFT specifications [4, 19]. All aspects of the KRAFT architecture are agent-based:

- *facilitator* agents support the description and location of on-line sources through advertising;

- sources are *wrapped* by agent software to transform local knowledge to and from the interchange format;

- *mediator* agents support the querying of sources, and fusion of knowledge from the sources;

- legacy solver engines are provided with agent *wrappers* as front-ends to their services.

An important feature of KRAFT is its *shared ontology* which allows the external resource concepts to be expressed in a common internal representation. This internal KRAFT resource is used by facilitators and wrappers and is managed by a special mediator agent.

KRAFT builds upon work done in the early 1990s on knowledge sharing and reuse, most notably the results of the Knowledge Sharing Effort (KSE) project [12]. Although it did result in a number of practical applications (for example, [6, 10]), the early work on knowledge sharing and reuse has not had the expected impact in the construction of large-scale, open, distributed knowledge systems. One area that was not addressed in the early work was that of *scalability*: few systems used more than 10 agents. However, there is now a rapidly-growing demand for "Internet scale" systems that support the exchange and processing of rich information in areas such as electronic commerce and knowledge management. Any architecture targeting these areas must be designed with scalability in mind. An important aspect of KRAFT is the use of constraints (intensional data) to reduce the quantities of extensional data being transported and so improve scalability.

This paper describes the KRAFT architecture with emphasis on the design features that support scalability. Section 2 presents an overview of the architecture, including the conceptual operations of the main types of agent, and the implementation design. Section 3 examines how scalability has been designed into the architecture as a whole, and the individual agents. Section 4 concludes.

2   The KRAFT Agent Architecture

An overview of the generic KRAFT architecture is shown in Figure 1. KRAFT agents are shown as ovals. There are three kinds of these: wrappers, mediators, and facilitators. All of these are knowledge-processing entities, and are described in sections 2.1, 2.2, and 2.3. External services are shown as boxes. There are three kinds of these: user agents, resources (typically databases or knowledge bases), and solvers. All of these external services are producers and consumers of knowledge: users supply their requirements to the network in the form of constraints via a user agent service, and receive results in the same way. Resources store, and can be queried for, knowledge and data. Solvers accept CSPs and return the results of the solving process. Within a KRAFT network, the constraints and data are expressed using the concepts defined in the shared ontology.

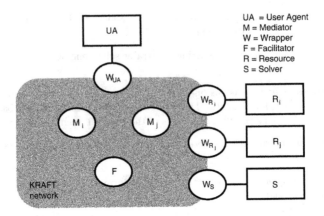

Figure 1: Overview of the generic KRAFT architecture.

KRAFT agents communicate via messages using a nested protocol suite. KRAFT messages are implemented as character strings transported by a suitable carrier protocol. A simple message protocol encapsulates each message with low-level header information, including a timestamp and network information. The body of the message consists of two nested protocols: the outer protocol is the *Constraint Command and Query Language* (CCQL) which is a specialised subset of the Knowledge Query and Manipulation Language (KQML)[11]. Nested within the CCQL message is its content, expressed in the *Constraint Interchange Format* (CIF).

In the current implementation, KRAFT messages are syntactically Prolog term structures. An example message is shown below. The outermost **kraft_msg** structure contains a **context** clause (header information) and a **ccql** clause. The message is from an agent called **storage_inc** to an agent called **pc_configurator**. The **ccql** structure contains, within its content field, a CIF expression (in the implementation, CIF expressions are actually transmitted in a compiled internal format). CIF is described further in Section 2.1.

```
kraft_msg(
    context(1,id(19), pc_configurator, storage_inc,
        time_stamp(date(29,9,1999), time(14,45,34))),
    ccql(tell, [
        sender : storage_inc,
        receiver : pc_configurator,
        reply_with : id(18),
        ontology : shared,
        language : cif,
        content : [
            constrain
                each d in disk_drive
                    such that name(vendor(d)) = "Storage Inc"
                    and type(d) = "Zip"
                at least 1 p in ports(host_pc(d))
                to have type(p) = "USB"
        ])
    )
```

The following sub-sections examine the operations of each of the three kinds of KRAFT agent in more detail.

2.1 Wrapper Agents

Wrappers are agents that act as proxies for external resources — commonly, these will be "knowledge suppliers". Wrappers serve two purposes: they *advertise* the capabilites of the resource to a facilitator, when the resource comes on-line (see Section 2.3), and they *transform* knowledge between the common interchange format used within a KRAFT network, and the internal format used privately by the resource. In both these tasks they utilise the shared ontology.

In a configuration design context, component suppliers make their catalogue databases available on the network. Locally to each supplier, the databases will have different semantics and assumptions. In printed catalogues, these assumptions often appear as asterisked footnotes or "small print". For example, the product catalogue for (fictitious) disk drive vendor, Storage Inc, may have the following "small print" associated with each of its range of Zip disk drives: *this Zip disk drive requires a PC with a USB-type port.* This kind of small print can readily be expressed as constraints in a database catalogue. For example:

```
forall z in zip_drives :
    port_types(connected_pc(z)) must include "USB";
```

This constraint would be stored in Storage Inc's catalogue database, but note that it refers to a property of the PC (**port_types**) to which the drive would be connected in a configured PC system (stored as the **connected_pc** attribute of the Zip disk drive **z**).

The locally-stored constraints will typically be expressed against a local data model (defined by a local ontology) for the product catalogue. In order to fuse together constraints from multiple heterogeneous product catalogues, it is necessary to translate the constraints to a common *constraint interchange format*, expressed in the terms of a *shared ontology* as is commonly done in knowledge-sharing systems[12]. The following constraint shows the above small print Zip disk constraint translated from Storage Inc's local constraint language to the KRAFT Constraint Interchange Format (CIF) language, expressed in the terms of a shared ontology [17] for PC system configuration:

```
constrain
    each d in disk_drive
        such that name(vendor(d)) = "Storage Inc"
        and type(d) = "Zip"
    at least 1 p in ports(host_pc(d))
to have type(p) = "USB";
```

KRAFT CIF is based on the CoLan language used to express semantics in the object database P/FDM[3]. The terminology used in this transformed constraint (for example, the concept **disk_drive**, meaning all disk drive components, the attributes of this concept, **vendor** and **type**) must be defined in the shared ontology for the PC design domain. Some of the transformations needed here were:

- *Addition of contextual information.* In the local Storage Inc database, all constraints implicitly refer to this vendor's products; in the shared ontology, the name of the vendor of the component must be stated explicitly.

- *Mapping classes to attribute values.* In the local Storage Inc database, the type *Zip disk* is represented by the class **zip_drives**; in the shared ontology, "Zip" is the value of the attribute type of elements in the class **disk_drive**.

- *Coping with varying granularities of description.* In the local Storage Inc database, the connected PC is modelled in less detail, with the types of ports being stored in

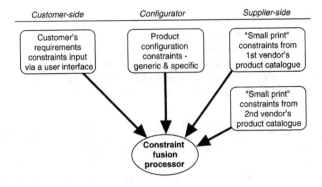

Figure 2: Fusion of constraints from multiple sources.

the attribute `port_types` of the `connected_pc` entity; in the shared ontology, the connected PC of the disk drive (attribute renamed to `host_pc`) is modelled in more detail, with individual ports as entities in their own right, and `type` as an attribute of the `port` entity.

These transformations are implemented within the wrapper agent for each individual vendor, as part of the setting-up needed for the vendor to join the KRAFT network.

2.2 Mediator Agents

Wiederhold definition of a mediator as a component that performs a specific information-processing task, often programmed by an individual domain expert [19]; every mediator "adds value" in some way to knowledge obtained from other agents. In KRAFT, the main tasks performed by mediators are ontology management and knowledge fusion. To perform knowledge fusion, a mediator gathers constraints from other agents (typically wrappers as described in Section 2.1), and processes them to form a coherent CSP at run-time for solving. This is shown in Figure 2. As part of this task, mediators will typically pre-process the constraints in various ways; they will also need to plan and perform selective database queries as explained in [7].

In a typical configuration design application, some constraints will be provided by the customer; others will come from the vendors as discussed above; there will also be constraints coming from the service-provider who will act as the configurator of the product or service provided by the application.

There will typically be several mediators in a KRAFT network: one to perform each distinct value-adding service. For example, in a KRAFT network performing configuration of PC products, there may be a single configurator mediator, or there may be several configurators, perhaps one for each of several different kinds of PC (laptops, generic desktops, special-purpose workstations, etc) or one for each of several distinct subsystems (CPU, peripheral systems, application software bundles, etc).

2.3 Facilitator Agents

Facilitators are the "matchmaker" agents that allow agents to discover one another. As they come online, agents register their identities, network locations, and advertisements of their knowledge-processing capabilities with a known facilitator. When an agent needs to request a service from another agent, it asks a facilitator to recommend an agent that appears to provide that service.

The specification and design for KRAFT's facilitators is informed by the many different definitions of facilitators in the literature [2, 10, 15, 18]. They provide two services within a KRAFT network:

- *Advertisement handling.* When a facilitator receives an advertisement from a wrapper, it is able to process and store this information for further use. An advertisement is a (set of) capabilities that a resource commits to provide. Every resource willing to advertise its capabilities does so first by registering with a facilitator (by sending a CCQL `register` message containing the references and location of the resource), then by sending a CCQL `advertise` message containing the formal description of its capabilities (shown below).

- *Request facilitation.* For a given request, this is the action of finding a (set of) wrapped resources that comply with a satisfiability (or suitability) criterion. In other words, it is the action of finding a resource whose advertised capability matches the requirements derived from the query. This satisfiability criterion depends on the search strategy adopted for the resolution of the query but it is always somewhere in the spectrum bounded by "the most exact match" on one hand and by "the set of all approximate matches" on the other hand. In other words, the satisfiability criterion is a tradeoff between correctness and completeness in the set of solutions.

Following the KQML model [11], CCQL offers two ways for agents to interact with a facilitator:

Recommend-style facilitation: on receiving a query enclosed in a `recommend_one` (or `recommend_all`) message, the facilitator will reply to the agent at the origin of the query, a singleton (or a list) of matching advertisements (including the references to the corresponding resource). The replied advertisement(s) is contained in a `forward` message.

Broker-style facilitation: on receiving a query enclosed in a `broker_one/broker_all` message, the facilitator will send the enclosed query to the most (or all) relevant resource. The answer to the query is then brought back to the facilitator, which in turn forwards the reply to the originator of the query.

A resource capability must be represented intentionally and generically for compactness, but in a way that minimises imprecision. The abstract characteristics of a resource are:

- network information to locate and query the wrapper of the resource;

- the CCQL performatives that the wrapper can handle;

- the intentional content of the resource (or a subset of it);

- an abstract representation of the functionality of the resource.

Advertisements are the basic data structure used to communicate these characteristics. The terms used in the body of advertisements are defined in the shared ontology. The possible components of an advertisement are:

- list of allowed CCQL *performatives*;

- list of available *services*, where each service is defined in the shared ontology;

- list of *domains* that the database can deal with, where each domain is defined in the shared ontology;

- specification of a subset of the CIF language, delimiting the expressiveness of the resource query language within CIF as a whole.

The facilitator encapsulates a database of received advertisements with the above components; the CCQL facilitation operations (forwarding and brokerage) are implemented as queries on this advertisement database.

An example CCQL advertisement message follows (the KRAFT message header is not shown). This advertisement is from the wrapper of a PC software vendor called storage_inc, sent to a facilitator called yellow_pages. The content says that the advertiser can handle CCQL ask_one and ask_all messages, expressed in a subset of CIF corresponding to SQL queries (from the service description, defined in the shared ontology), about ontology concepts storage_device and pc_peripheral.

```
ccql(advertise, [
        sender : storage_inc,
        receiver : yellow_pages,
        reply_with : id(48),
        ontology : advertise_ontology,
        language : cif,
        content : [
            advertisement.performativeList = [ ask_one, ask_all ],
            advertisement.serviceList = [ <database, sql> ],
            advertisement.domainList = [ storage_device, pc_peripheral ] ]
])
```

Each KRAFT network requires at least one facilitator. In a large network, there may be multiple facilitators, either for reasons of specialisation or efficiency.

2.4   Implementation of the KRAFT architecture

Inter-agent communication in KRAFT is implemented by message passing using the Linda tuple-space communication model[5]. A Linda server manages the tuple space; clients connect to the space to write or read tuples (messages). KRAFT uses a Prolog implementation of Linda, where tuples are Prolog term structures: instances of the kraft_msg term structure shown earlier. To send a message, an agent writes it to a Linda server with the name of the recipient; to receive a message, an agent reads any tuples with its own name as the value of the receiver field. An advantage of using this model is that the individual agents do not need to be multithreaded; they choose when to receive any waiting messages synchronously. KRAFT agents can be written in any language provided that they have a Linda client module. Currently, these are available for Prolog and Java agents.

The Linda model is most effective for local-area communication, so to support wide-area KRAFT networks a federated Linda space has been implemented. Each local-area (called a *hub*) has its own Linda server with which local agents interact. The agent namespace has a URL-like *hubname/agentname* syntax. Each Linda server is coupled to a *gateway* agent that relays messages between hubs in a manner similar to an internet router: if a message is posted on the local Linda server with a non-local *hubname* for the recipient, the gateway relays the message to the correct hub gateway agent, which in turn writes it to the hub's local Linda server. This architecture is shown in Figure 3. In the current implementation, the protocol used to carry messages between hubs is TCP via the socket interface; preliminary work has also been done on inter-hub communication using CORBA IIOP [13].

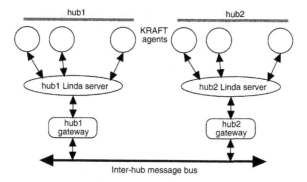

Figure 3: Implementation of the KRAFT architecture.

To support debugging, a *Monitor* user agent has been implemented to trace and display the passage of messages across a KRAFT network, shown in Figure 4. Monitor agents are able to register with the gateway agents in order to display activity at non-local hubs, allowing a user to see interactions across the entire KRAFT network.

3   Designing for Scalability in KRAFT

During the design of the KRAFT architecture, scalability was borne in mind. To this end, six strategies were built-into the architecture:

1. An intelligent strategy for resource querying and constraint solving aims to minimise number of messages, and volume of data transferred, conserving bandwidth.

2. The federated messaging architecture (internet-style) using Linda hubs aims to minimise network traffic, while also being easy to manage and fault-tolerant.

3. Mediators can easily be replicated on their local hub, allowing for concurrent processing and load-balancing.

4. Use of virtual machines for agent implementations (e.g. Java and Prolog) are encouraged, to allow agent mobility in cases where processing needs to be moved local to a resource, or where it is necessary to transfer/replicate an agent on a different hub.

5. Facilitator bottlenecks are avoided by allowing for facilitator replication and specialisation (for example, having a hierarchy of facilitators, similar to DNS), and by using generic advertising to reduce the number of advertisements.

6. The shared ontology supports ontology clusters which in turn allow for evolvability (different worlds) and bottom-up integration of independently-created networks.

Each of these strategies is described in a sub-section below.

3.1   Querying and Solving Strategy

As described in Section 2.2, mediators that perform constraint fusion undertake a combination of operations in constructing a CSP at run-time: gathering and pre-processing a set of constraints from contributing agents, and querying database wrappers in order to populate the domains for the CSP. The two most costly operations here are actually external to the mediator: these are:

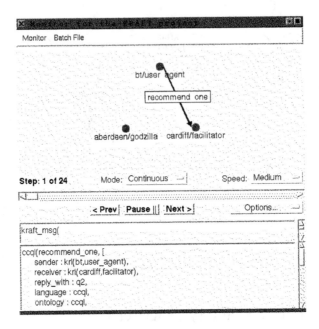

Figure 4: Screenshot of the KRAFT Monitor user agent.

1. the network traffic generated by the constraint and data gathering process; and

2. the constraint solving process carried out by the wrapped solver to which the mediator dispatches the CSP.

The KRAFT architecture is designed to try to minimise both these costs, as follows:

1. In terms of network traffic, constraints are a compact way of transmitting what could otherwise be substantial volumes of data. In a conventional information interchange approach, data instances would be transmitted extensionally, whereas in the constraint approach, each constraint is an intensional definition of a potentially-large amount of data [16].

    Moreover, where it *is* necessary to transfer a number of instances extensionally (for example, to populate a variable domain for a CSP), constraints can be used by the mediator as a *filter* to reduce the number of instances based on what is known about the solution space so far. For example, if it is already known that a PC customer needs at least a 17-inch monitor, there is no point in the monitor vendor shipping instances of 15-inch monitors. The "screen size $>= 17$ inches" constraint would be sent by the mediator to the monitor vendor's wrapper for it to use as part of the internal query on the monitors product catalogue.

2. In terms of constraint solving, the mediator can perform an arbitrary amount of pre-processing on the CSP before sending it to the solver. It can also select what it deems to be the optimal kind of solver for the problem-at-hand. The pre-processing can include simplifying the problem (for example, if redundant constraints are detected) or even aborting the solving process (for example, if a conflict is detected in the CSP that renders it insoluble). Also, the aforementioned process used to build the CSP in terms of gathering instances to populate the variable domains will itself tend to

simplify the CSP by filtering out a significant number of "useless" values (this is similar to the forward-checking technique used in constraint solving [9], but applied in the distributed context).

These normally lead to a reduction in data being transported in the network, and so improve scalability.

3.2   Federated Messaging Architecture

Unlike some agent communication architectures (for example, JATlite[1]) KRAFT does not rely on a centralised message routing mechanism. Routing in KRAFT, like routing in the Internet, is decentralised. The Linda hub architecture shown in Figure 3 allows messages local to a hub to pass unnoticed by other hubs. When the hub is entirely local to a single host, no network traffic at all is generated (messages are passed through the TCP/IP "loopback" interface). The only wide-area network traffic consists of inter-hub messages, which pass between widely-separated gateways. Section 3.4 explains how even this traffic can be minimised.

An important exception here is where monitor agents are configured to monitor activity at more than one hub. In this case, the hub message server is notified to "echo" messages between monitored hubs, and this can lead to substantial network traffic. Therefore, such monitoring is recommended only for testing, and never for use in an operational KRAFT network.

3.3   Mediator Replication

It is conceivable that mediators whose services are much in demand will become bottlenecks. Such bottlenecks are easily detected by the hub servers, which can see that message traffic to and from particular agents is greater than normal, or are not being processed as rapidly as would be desirable. (This is like an office manager observing the "in" and "out" trays of workers in an office: in KRAFT these "trays" are collections of messages on the Linda tuple space managed by the hub server.) Locally, it is relatively easy to clone KRAFT mediators, because these agents do not tend to have persistent storage (if they do, they will typically use a shared private database for this purpose). Therefore, a mediator can be cloned in principle by simply asking the local OS to spawn another instance of the mediator process. The mediator would be passed a unique agent name by the hub server. In this way, mediator services can easily be replicated locally to provide concurrent processing. This technique is equally useful for replicating ontology-management mediators as well as those performing knowledge fusion.

3.4   Agent Mobility

Section 3.3 covers the case where a mediator is replicated locally. It is also possible to replicate a mediator on a different hub. (Or indeed, to relocate the mediator, by replicating it then removing the original.) This is possible when the mediator is implemented in a language that uses a virtual machine environment. KRAFT encourages the use of such languages; currently, the trial systems have been implemented using Prolog and Java. In these cases, the code for the mediator can be encapsulated in an inter-hub message directed to a hub manager. Upon receipt, the hub can spawn an instance of the appropriate virtual machine and pre-load it with the encapsulated agent.

---

[1] http://java.stanford.edu/

This kind of mobility is most advantageous when one wants to move the processing capability closer to the data. Localised communication is always far less costly than wide-area communication, so moving a mediator from a remote hub to the same hub as the data resources can improve performance significantly.

3.5   Facilitator Federations

As the scale of a KRAFT network grows, there is a danger that facilitators will become bottlenecks. A number of strategies are available to avoid this problem.

Normally, each hub will have its own local facilitator, to which requests can be directed without the cost of wide-area traffic. If each of these facilitators is to have knowledge of the entire multi-hub KRAFT network, then they obviously must exchange advertisements among one another. However, recommend requests are typically much more common than advertise requests, so most of their work then will involve local message traffic.

If the network becomes too large to allow each local facilitator to store complete advertisement information, then there are a number of possibilities to reduce the amount of information held by each facilitator. One option is to have *specialist* facilitators, each holding knowledge about a particular area of the shared ontology (for example, in a consumer electronics marketplace, there could be a facilitator that knows about the PC sector, another that knows about the mobile phone sector, and so on). A "meta-facilitator" would be consulted first to locate the appropriate specialist facilitator for a given request. Of course, any of these facilitators could also be replicated if necessary. Another possibility is to partition the facilitation space according to location, where each facilitator would have knowledge about its local hub (or local hubs), and would direct requests that can't be answered locally to a neighbouring facilitator. This approach is essentially similar to the Internet routing scheme.

The use of generic advertisements will reduce the number of advertisements as it eliminates the need to hold specific advertisements. It also reduces the number to be examined when locating appropriate external resources, albeit at the expense of a possibly more complex matching algorithm.

3.6   Ontology Clusters

The schemes outlined in Section 3.5 cover only the cases where the entire KRAFT network uses a single shared ontology, against which all advertisements and requests are expressed. CCQL allows for mutliple ontologies to coexist within the same (using the ontology field in each message) but, more importantly, allows for agents using different ontologies to interoperate by means of *ontology clusters* and inter-ontology mappings. An ontology cluster is a community of KRAFT agents that use the same shared ontology; a cluster that uses shared ontology SO_1 can interoperate with a cluster that uses shared ontology SO_2 if and only if there is an *ontological mapping* from SO_1 to SO_2. Messages with content expressed against SO_1 would be sent to a designated *ontological mediator* that would transform the content to SO_2 before fowarding the message to the intended recipient. This part of the design for the KRAFT architecture is elaborated in [14]. The ontological clusters allow for evolvability (different worlds which must be made to inter-operate) and bottom-up integration of independently-created KRAFT networks.

4   Conclusion

Improving scalability in a distributed environment is concerned with reducing the degradation in performance as the work load increases, where work load can be measured in a number of ways, such as the number of users, activities, resource providers, and sites. Inevitably as the distributed environment grows there is some degradation in performance. In such systems we need to take static and dynamic measures to improve scalability. Dynamic measures reflect the current situation in the distributed system and attempt to respond to fluctuating demand in different parts by ameliorating the factors causing performance degradation. They are measures which respond to feedback from monitors which are evaluating the current performance to identify peaks and/or bottlenecks. Static measures are generally concerned with architectural decisions that have been taken to improve the general scalability of the system and are independent of the dynamic situation. In KRAFT both types of scalability technique have been used. Statically:

- the use of intensional data reduces the quantity of extensional data being transported in the network;

- the use of generic advert representation reduces the number of adverts stored and analysed;

- the use of optimal solvers and filters reduces the amount of extensional data accessed from external sources in CSP;

- the ability to clone at all KRAFT sites the facilitator, mediators and ontology mean that it is possible to design the architecture so that there is no network traffic if a CSP can be solved with local facilities only;

- the Linda hub design means that local messages are processed locally — they also support an easy implementation of monitors which trigger dynamic techniques as the tuples held in a Linda hub show the dynamic state of many of the KRAFT components; and

- the use of ontology clusters and a build-up approach to creating the local shared ontology for a cluster means they reflect their user community needs, which again restricts the number of occasions when there is a need to link to other ontologies in the cluster.

Dynamically: the messages at Linda hubs can be monitored to determine where the bottlenecks are occurring and which agents are involved. As a result of this monitoring, agents can be cloned at the same or another site to reduce network traffic and overall time when an agent is overloaded. Agents can migrate to new sites if the platform configuration at that site and/or the current situation is better suited to their processing needs.

We contend that these static and dynamic features mean that the degradation of performance in a KRAFT environment as workload increases is graceful, and the environment is able to react to fluctuation in usage patterns if this is needed.

Acknowledgements. KRAFT is a collaborative research project between the Universities of Aberdeen, Cardiff and Liverpool, and BT. The project has received funding from the UK Engineering and Physical Sciences Research Council, and BT.

References

[1] J. Andreoli, U. Borghoff, and R. Pareschi, Constraint agents for the information age, *Journal of Universal Computer Science*, 1:762–789, 1995.

[2] Y. Arens, R. Hull, R. King, and M. Siegel, Reference architecture for the intelligent integration of information, Technical report, DARPA — Defense Advanced Research Project Agency, August 1995.

[3] N. Bassiliades and P. M. D. Gray, CoLan: A functional constraint language and its implementation, *Data and Knowledge Engineering*, 14:203–249, 1994.

[4] R. Bayardo et al, InfoSleuth: agent-based semantic integration of information in open and dynamic environments, In *Proc. SIGMOD'97*, 1997.

[5] N. Carriero and D. Gelernter, Linda in Context, *Communications of the ACM*, 32:444–458, 1989.

[6] M. Cutkosky, R. Engelmore, R. Fikes, M. Genesereth, T. Gruber, W. Mark, J. Tenenbaum, and J. Weber, PACT: an experiment in integrating concurrent engineering systems, *IEEE Computer*, 26:8–27, 1993.

[7] P. M. D. Gray, S. M. Embury, K. Y. Hui, and G. Kemp, The evolving role of constraints in the functional data model, *Journal of Intelligent Information Systems*, 1–27, 1999.

[8] P. Gray, A. Preece, N. Fiddian, W. Gray, T. Bench-Capon, M. Shave, N. Azarmi, and M. Wiegand, KRAFT: knowledge fusion from distributed databases and knowledge bases, in *Proc. 8th International Workshop on Database and Expert System Applications (DEXA-97)*, pages 682–691, IEEE Press, 1997.

[9] P. van Hentenryck, *Constraint Satisfaction in Logic Programming*, MIT Press, 1989.

[10] D. R. Kuokka, J. G. McGuire, J. C. Weber, J. M. Tenenbaum, T. R. Gruber, and G. R. Olsen, SHADE: Technology for knowledge-based collaborative engineering, *Journal of Concurrent Engineering: Applications and Research*, 1(2), 1993.

[11] Y. Labrou, *Semantics for an Agent Communication Language*, PhD Thesis, University of Maryland, Baltimore MD, USA, 1996.

[12] R. Neches, R. Fikes, T. Finin, T. Gruber, R. Patil, T. Senator, and W. Swartout, Enabling technology for knowledge sharing, *AI Magazine*, 12:36–56, 1991.

[13] A. Preece, A. Borrowman, and T. Francis, Reusable components for KB and DB integration, in *Proc. ECAI'98 Workshop on Intelligent Information Integration*, pages 157–168, 1998.

[14] M. Shave, Ontological structures for knowledge sharing, *New Review of Information Networking*, 3:125–133, 1997.

[15] N. Singh, M. Genesereth, and M. A. Syed, A distributed and anonymous knowledge sharing approach to software interoperation, *International Journal of Cooperative Information Systems*, 4(4):339–367, 1995.

[16] M. Torrens and B. Faltings, Smart clients: constraint satisfaction as a paradigm for scaleable intelligent information systems, In T Finin and B Grosof (eds) *Artificial Intelligence for Electronic Commerce: Papers from the AAAI-99 Workshop*, AAAI Press, 1999.

[17] P. R. S. Visser, D. M. Jones, T. J. M. Bench-Capon, and M. J. R. Shave, Assessing heterogeneity by classifying ontology mismatches, In *Proc. International Conference on Formal Ontology in Information Systems (FOIS'98)*, IOS Press, pages 148–162, 1998.

[18] G. Wiederhold, Mediators in the architecture of future information systems, *IEEE Computer*, 25:38–49, March 1992.

[19] G. Wiederhold and M. Genesereth, The basis for mediation, In *Proc. 3rd International Conference on Cooperative Information Systems (COOPIS95)*, 1995.

Towards Validation of Specifications by Simulation

Ioan Alfred Letia, Florin Craciun, and Zoltan Köpe

Technical University of Cluj-Napoca,
Department of Computer Science
Baritiu 28, RO-3400 Cluj-Napoca, Romania
{letia,florin,kzoltan}@cs-gw.utcluj.ro

Abstract. The aim is to study the behaviour (in terms of utility) of a large number of autonomous agents under various environmental situations. Our experimental framework is an extension of the Swarm simulator with an array of intelligent agents developed in C++ and Prolog.

1 Specification as Preferences on Obligations

There are many applications for which a wealth of technology is already available towards achieving robust and distributed information systems. But, quoting Victor Lesser [3]: "evaluations have been limited to isolated components, a few example tasks, and small agent groups. Thus, fundamental questions remain to be answered: Is this a sufficient set of technologies with which to produce large and complex multi-agent systems? Can large-scale agent organizations be constructed by appropriately tailoring the dynamic coordination patterns of small groups of agents?"

For self-interested agents, that simply maximize their own utility, it is desirable for reasonable local behaviour to lead to global reasonable behaviour [2]. But if agents are untruthful or deceitful for increasing their utility then harm might arise to the whole society. Various simulation tools have been developed for studying multi-agent coordination [6] and we use Swarm [5] in our framework.

Dynamic goal hierarchies have been used to describe a rational behavior of an agent within a changing environment by defining a preference ordering on the agent's goal set. This idea for a formal theory of practical rationality was later continued with dynamic obligation hierarchies [1] leading to the revision of obligations. Various axioms on preferences have been defined including $Pref(\phi, \psi)(i)$ $\rightarrow \neg Pref(\psi, \phi)(i)$, which says that preferences $Pref(a, \phi, \psi)(i)$ of an agent a for the interval i are asymmetric. $PFObl(a, \phi)(i)$ states that ϕ is among a's *prima facie* obligations for interval i. $Pref(a, PFObl(a, \phi), PFObl(a, \psi))(i)$ says that ϕ is a more important *prima facie obligation* for agent a than ψ. Preferences between *obligations* should satisfy the realism condition:
$Pref(a, PFObl(a, \phi), PFObl(a, \psi))(i) \rightarrow PFObl(a, \phi)(i) \wedge PFObl(a, \psi)(i)$.
A *realisable prima facie obligation* for an agent a for interval i is a *prima facie obligation* of a's for interval i which a can realize on interval i $RPFObl(a, \phi)(i)$ $\leftrightarrow PFObl(a, \phi)(i) \wedge Real(a, \phi)(i)$.

T. Wagner and O.F. Rana (Eds.): Infrastructure for Agents, LNAI 1887, pp. 293–295, 2001.

2 Sample Simulation Scenario

One scenario we have chosen to illustrate how preferences and obligations, as specification, are used to evaluate the behaviour of agents is a grid world with several agents trying to collect objects that pass through it. Objects have utility values in the range 1 to 4 and the agents try to maximize the global utility value of all objects they can collect. A sample of the grid at time $\tau=0$ is depicted in figure 1.

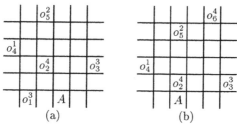

Fig. 1. Sample grid at time (a) $\tau=0$ and (b) $\tau=1$ for an agent A.

All objects move from North to South and the agent A intends to collect the object o_2^4, that is the second object that appeared in the grid from North with utility value 4. Objects with greater utility value are preferred by any agent: $utility(o_i) > utility(o_j) \rightarrow Pref(a,collect(o_i),collect(o_j))$. In this deterministic environment the agent can establish which objects are collect-able and which are not. Example of preferences of agent A in the situation shown in figure 1(a) are:
$Pref(A,PFObl(collect(o_2^4)),PFObl(collect(o_1^3)))(0)$ and
$Pref(A,PFObl(collect(o_2^4)),PFObl(collect(o_3^3)))[0..2]$.

Table 1. Agent preferences, realizable and realized obligations over the interval $[0..2]$.

τ	Preferences on prima facie obligations	Realizable	Real
0	$o_1^3 \prec o_2^4$ $o_3^3 \prec o_2^4$ $o_4^1 \prec o_2^4$ $o_5^2 \prec o_2^4$ $o_4^1 \prec o_1^3$ $o_5^2 \prec o_1^3$ $o_4^1 \prec o_3^3$ $o_5^2 \prec o_3^3$ $o_4^1 \prec o_5^2$	o_2^4 o_3^3 o_4^1 o_5^2	
1	$o_3^3 \prec o_2^4$ $o_4^1 \prec o_2^4$ $o_5^2 \prec o_2^4$ $o_3^3 \prec o_6^4$ $o_4^1 \prec o_6^4$ $o_5^2 \prec o_6^4$ $o_4^1 \prec o_3^3$ $o_5^2 \prec o_3^3$ $o_4^1 \prec o_5^2$	o_2^4 o_4^1 o_5^2 o_6^4	
2	$o_3^3 \prec o_2^4$ $o_4^1 \prec o_2^4$ $o_5^2 \prec o_2^4$ $o_3^3 \prec o_6^4$ $o_4^1 \prec o_6^4$ $o_5^2 \prec o_6^4$ $o_4^1 \prec o_3^3$ $o_5^2 \prec o_3^3$ $o_4^1 \prec o_5^2$	o_2^4 o_5^2 o_6^4	o_2^4

The preferences on obligations, which ones are realizable and which are realized over the interval $[0..2]$ are shown in table 1. But this environment can also be nondeterministic and then agents cannot determine exactly which objects are collect-able and will have to revise this estimation in each time step. In figure 2 the objects are represented by different degrees of grey, based on their utilities. The objects moving down towards the bottom of the grid with different speeds may also disappear. The agents are on the last row of the grid and are represented in black in figure 2.

Fig. 2. Experimental grid with ten agents and utility carrying objects.

3   Discussion

With proper modelling for a given application area the framework can provide statistical information on both achieved behaviour and how much potential exists for improving it. We are currently developing various self-interested agents in our simulation infra-structure. Several specifications ([1, 4] and others) will be evaluated experimentally in terms of utility achieved by agents as a group.

References

1. John Bell and Zhisheng Huang. Dynamic obligation hierarchies. In P. MacNamara and H. Praken, editors, *Proceedings of ΔEON'98*, pages 127–142, 1998.
2. N. R. Jennings, K. Sycara, and M. Wooldridge. A roadmap of agent research. *Autonomous Agents and Multi-Agent Systems*, 1(1):7–38, 1998.
3. Victor R. Lesser. Reflections on the nature of multi-agent coordination framework and its implications for an agent architecture. *Autonomous Agents and Multi-Agent Systems*, 1(1):89–111, 1998.
4. Ioan Alfred Letia. A TLA+ specification for agent communication that enables proofs. In O. Etzioni, J.P. Müller, and J.F. Bradshaw, editors, *Proceedings of the 3rd Annual Conference on Autonomous Agents*, pages 410–411, Seattle, WA, USA, 1999.
5. M. Minar, R. Burkhart, C. Langton, and M. Askenazy. The Swarm simulation system: A toolkit for building multi-agent simulations. Technical report, Santa Fe Institute, 1996. http://www.santafe.edu/projects/swarm/.
6. R. Vincent, B. Horling, T. Wagner, and V. Lesser. Survivability simulator for multi-agent adaptive coordination. In P. Fishwick, D. Hill, and R. Smith, editors, *International Conference on Web-Based Modeling and Simulation*, pages 114–119, San Diego, CA, 1998.

Open Source, Standards and Scaleable Agencies

Stefan Poslad[1], Phil Buckle[2], and Rob Hadingham[2]

[1] Imperial College of Science, Technology and Medicine, Exhibition Road, London, SW7
2BZ, UK.
`s.poslad@ic.ac.uk`
[2] Nortel Networks, London Road, Harlow, Essex, CM17 9NA, UK.
`{pbuckle, rgh}@nortelnetworks.com`

Abstract. Numerous agencies and agent systems have been developed as
vehicles to deliver novel types of e-commerce services to users. However
service agents in one agency are often unable to interoperate or co-operate with
agents from another vendor's agency. Clearly, standardization in this area
would help to create a more ubiquitous market and supporting infrastructure for
agent-based services. We analyze the relevant standards for agents, highlighting
the FIPA (Foundation for Intelligent Physical Agents) agent standards. Standard
specifications ought to be grounded within a practical framework, which
provides a reference implementation for developers and users. We also
highlight the importance of open agent systems and open source
implementations and their role in seeding the market for agent technology.

1 Introduction

Multi-agent (MA) systems are a powerful, relatively new paradigm for accessing and
integrating heterogeneous distributed services. Here, service providers, services users
and intermediaries are represented as autonomous software agents, which interact
using an agent communication language, based on speech acts [1] and use shared
vocabularies called ontologies [2]. The use of the agent communication language
enables agents to interact using semantically rich information.
In a heterogeneous world, concurrent distributed development has lead to many types
of multi-agent systems that are islands of functionality – agents on different types of
platform are unable to interoperate with each other. Agents from different vendors are
likely to use different types of messages and message formats and the meaning and
interpretation of the content is likely to differ. The driving force for interoperability is
partly the customer who strives for simplicity and universality when accessing
multiple services, and partly producers who often need to act in unison to obtain a
critical mass for a sustainable customer-base.
Early adopters, who produce new technology and services, tend to be wary where
there is no commonly agreed standard for interoperability and suspicious of standards
that lacks the support of a large consortium of companies. The standardization process
helps shift the emphasis from the development of the infrastructure to the use of the
infrastructure.

T. Wagner and O.F. Rana (Eds.): Infrastructure for Agents, LNAI 1887, pp. 296–303, 2001.

However, there is inherent high complexity, cost and risk in developing a good practical standard and in developing systems that adhere to the standard. These act as a barrier to users and developers who wish to assess this new technology. Clearly, reference implementations are useful here and there seems two be (at least) two main approaches to develop these. Essentially, reference implementations can be developed under an open license or a closed license. We focus on the latter approach.

The rest of this paper is organized as follows: Section 2 continues with a discussion of issues in standardizing agent systems. In particular, there is a close look at the FIPA agent specifications for multi-agent systems. Section 3 examines the issues in implementing the FIPA agent specifications. Section 4 presents conclusions.

2 Agent Standards

The main driving force for de facto standards from multiple-vendor forums is to seed the market and attain a critical mass of customers, applications and products in the medium and long-term. The seeding of the market is enhanced when the standards are publicly available - they are easier to be taken up by non-members. In standardizing, companies potentially give up a competitive edge in the short-term goal but regain it in the medium to long term by producing products that add value and enhance the standard in a much larger market.

Standards need to be developed at the right time. The development of new products and markets seems to follow a double peak of activity with a dip in between [3]. The optimum time to standardize is towards the end of the first (research) peak or in the dip between the peaks, before the second (development) peak occurs. Standardizing too early before the research is finished can lead to immature, bad standards whereas standardizing too late, once companies have made significant investments, can mean the standards are ignored. We regard MA systems to be somewhere in the dip between the peaks at this stage.

A standard needs to be viable. FIPA seeks to establish or fix a generic core of speech acts in the agent communication language. There are pros and cons to this. Generic patterns do exist at the right level of abstraction and the existence of a generic core can ease interoperability and interaction. A common core may well be a compromise and this may only be realizable after extensive experimentation but this is only natural - robust standards take time to mature. It can also be difficult to define a common denominator, e.g., communication between heterogeneous parties in a wide range of heterogeneous domains, is very diverse. This latter argument has also been applied against the standardization of core facilitator agents such as directory service and management service agents.

Standard specifications rarely consist of complete vertical slices of infrastructure, from provider via some infrastructure, to the user. Often specifications are dependent on other horizontal layers, e.g. they may use an existing software infrastructure. Key issues here are the scope of the specification, how much leverage to make from existing technology and how to link to an existing infrastructure. The scope of MA specifications generally includes the interpretation and handling of ACL (Agent Communication Language) messages, facilitator agents, and the use of, but not the actual specification of an existing software infrastructure such as message transport protocols, and message persistence schema, to underpin agent communication. In

1997, CORBA and OMG's Internet Inter-ORB Protocol (IIOP) showed great promise and FIPA specified it as its mandatory transport protocol.

Finally, standards are not developed in a vacuum. There are often several overlapping standards bodies. If standards are not developed quickly enough for the market in one standards body, they are in danger of being superseded by work in another body. Often standards seek to exploit existing popular standards. There are two important agent standardization efforts that define interoperability between agents on different types of agent platform based on an ACL: KQML (see below) and FIPA. There are also other relevant communication standards initiatives that are not primarily agent-centric, e.g., MPEG-21, W3C XML / RDF and OMG MASIF. These later standards can be regarded as being complimentary to the ACL agent standards - they define the syntax, transport and encoding for message exchange whereas the ACL standards define explicit protocols and semantics for message exchange.

2.1 ACL Agent Standards

The ACL approach is a semantically rich approach. Consider how a new service agent registers itself with a directory facilitator at the ACL level. It issues a register action. This register action is sent within the context of a request speech act. The request speech act is sent within the context of a request conversation or message pattern. This specifies that the request speech act is followed by an agree speech act and then by either an inform, containing the results of the register, or a refuse or a failure message. In addition, the register action is associated with a declarative service description. In contrast, in non-agent approaches, messages are often modeled (or implemented) in terms of an interface that focuses on syntax and data representation rather than on semantics. Such models define a push type of interaction in terms of a message method, parameter types, return data types and the use of object handles to invoke the method.

KQML or Knowledge Query Meta Language was one of the first initiatives to specify how to support the social interaction characteristic of agents using an ACL. KQML was developed at UMBC by Tim Finin et al [4] and has spread throughout the academic community. KQML however isn't a true de facto standard in the sense that there is no consensus on a single specification (or set of specifications) that has been ratified by common agreement. Other differences are that KQML neither defines interaction protocols nor a clear semantics for the use of its speech acts.

FIPA [5] is a non-profit standards organization whose purpose is to promote the development of specifications of generic agent technologies that maximize interoperability within and across agent based applications. Contributors produce their own implementations of the published FIPA specification. FIPA ACL specifications have been released in three phases:

- 1997: FIPA97v1 specifications (7)
- 1998: FIPA97v2, FIPA98v1 specifications (5)
- 2000: new IETF (Internet Engineering task Force) like process, Px000NN specifications (~70)

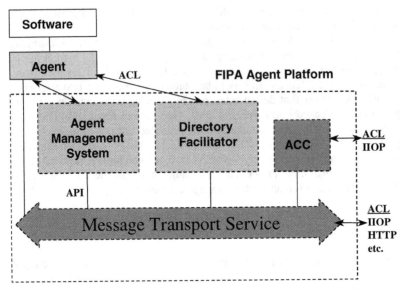

Fig. 1. The FIPA 97 agent reference model

In 1999-2000, the process for producing specifications was revised from yearly cycles to be more IETF-like. Some of these FIPA specifications are revisions of, and hence obsolete the 1997 and 1998 specifications. There are over 70 of these: there are of two types: individual components and profiles that specify how groups of components are inter-linked. So what was termed the FIPA97 agent reference model (figure 1) is now split into several specifications: a management profile, a transport profile and several management and transport component specifications.

This increasing granularity of specifications reflects a move away from supporting single external interfaces towards supporting multiple external interfaces thus easing the maintenance of heterogeneous external interfaces. For example, FIPA in early versions of its specification defined a single so called base-line "transport protocol" - OMG's Internet Inter-ORB Protocol (IIOP). This in essence meant most FIPA agent platforms ran on top of CORBA. There was a growing realization that one transport protocol was not suitable for all domains, for example, an interface has now to been defined to a WAP (Wireless Application Protocol) transport and more may follow.

3 Implementing the FIPA specifications

The FIPA standards in some areas introduce conceptual problems for designers and implementers. For example, the FIPA ACL focuses on an internal agent mental agency of beliefs, desires and intentions and closure is not enforced (agents are not compelled to answer) - these hinder multi-agent co-ordination.

The FIPA specifications are also not intended to be a complete blueprint or specification for building multi-agent system. For example, FIPA standards do not prescribe how to describe existential aspects of how agents in a discrete world, nor do they define error handling although some aspects of error reporting are covered. Some of the practical issues in using the agent standards are discussed in [6]. Useful information for developers is also given in a FIPA output document, the FIPA Developer's Guide [5]. Note that currently, there is no formal or clear mechanism to determine the compliance of a FIPA architecture implementation other than testing the interoperability of heterogeneous FIPA platforms in the field.

3.1 Openness, scalability and Open Source

3.1.1 Openness and scalability

A distributed system is considered open if it is extensible – there is a range of degrees and there exist different models and designs for openness. Openness is linked to re-configurability. If interfaces to the system are explicitly defined, and parts of the system are loosely-coupled then parts can be more easily exchanged and enhanced. Dynamic reconfiguration is a key characteristic of scaleable systems. Minimal openness typically exposes the interface(s) at the highest level of abstraction, for example, the agent platform service API can consist of an agent life-cycle management API, a directory service API and a message transport system API. In an agent platform, communication facilitators coupled with the use of rich message-passing protocols leads to natural support for an open service architecture. Service provider agents and service consumer agents can be dynamically bound and unbound using the facilitator.

Different service domains can require a range of communication support such as more or less negotiation about the protocol characteristics, more or less throughput and more or less security. Openness at lower levels of abstraction in the platform enables these support services to adapt. Depending on the software language and the types of interaction, service links between parts could be statically modified before the session starts or dynamically modified during a session.

Many agent platforms support some boot-strapping process which includes agent synthesis for resident agents. Often an agent shell or agent factory API is defined, the shell contains hooks into the platform to use lower-level services such as a transport service. To synthesis agents, it is not strictly necessary to use the platform API. Providing a standard protocol is used by the platform to exchange messages, the non resident agent can be synthesized externally and can register with the platform using the ACL. Of course, resident and non-resident agents may be managed by the platform differently.

3.1.2 Open source and scalability

An open source implementation can reduce the barrier for the adoption of FIPA standards, enhancing the ability of agent application developers to construct applications using FIPA technology. Minimizing cost is particularly important to encourage take up in education establishments and small medium enterprises. It can also improve software quality through third party development - more eyes, less bugs [7]. Users can directly reduce the time-scale for bug correction by providing their own fixes- this effect can be dramatic within a large user base. Open source is a powerful mechanism for engaging users while the market for FIPA agent technology is developing – it can be regarded as a form of Rapid Application Development in which new user requirements and actual extensions can be incrementally extracted during the development process. FIPA-OS was the first FIPA based platform to be released under an open source license [9] and provides rich and flexible support for agent communication.

3.2 FIPA-OS architecture overview

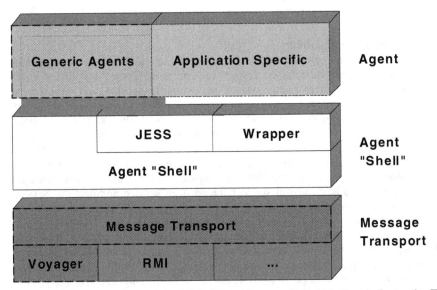

Fig. 2. Schematic diagram of the FIPA-OS architecture. Dotted shading indicates the FIPA defined components

The FIPA reference model (Figure 1) illustrates the core components of the FIPA-OS (Figure 2). In addition to the mandatory components of the FIPA Reference Model, FIPA-OS includes support for:
- agent shells with in-built ACL support and directory service awareness;
- multi-layered support for agent communication;
- message and conversation management;
- dynamic platform configuration to support multiple transports, types of persistence and message encodings.

The FIPA-OS architecture can be envisaged as a non- strict layered model (Figure 2). In a non-strict layered model, entities in non-adjacent layers can access each other directly. The developer is able to extend the architecture not only by appending value-added layers, such as specialist service agents or facilitator agents, on top but in addition, components lower or mid layers can be replaced, modified or deleted. FIPA-OS is described in more detail elsewhere [8].

3.2.1 FIPA-NET

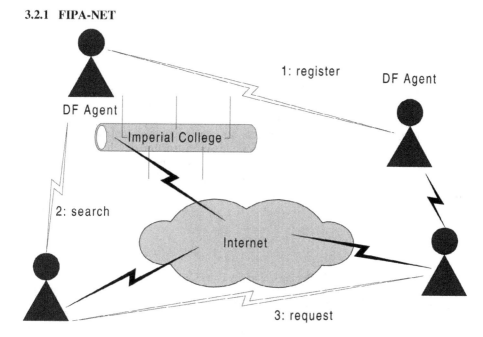

Fig. 3. FIPA-NET: a distributed multi-node FIPA test network that is being used to research into management services such as a Directory facilitator or DF.

In order to research into the management (including scalability, availability and federation) of heterogeneous distributed networks of agent platforms in the field, the CASBAh[1], **C**ommon **A**gent **S**ervice **B**roker **A**rchitecture project [9], is building and testing a network of FIPA platforms in the field called FIPA-NET (Figure 3). FIPA-NET differs from previous FIPA trials [10,11] in that it is not specifically geared to a particular application domain and because it focuses on research into infrastructures. FIPA-NET also differs from the DARPA funded CoABS (Control of Agent Based Systems) Grid whose research includes the integration of very heterogeneous agent platforms and their combined deployment in scenarios such as NEO (Non-combatant Evacuation Operation) [12]. Unlike the CoABS grid, FIPA-NET is more FIPA centric, it not only seeks to use the FIPA ACL but also seeks to test and extend the existing core FIPA middleware services and transport service bindings.

---

[1] The author from Imperial College gratefully acknowledges joint support for the CASBAh project from the UK Engineering and Physical Sciences Research Council (EPSRC) under grant GR/L34440 and from Nortel Networks.

4. Conclusions

Agent technology will realize its full potential, characterized by high levels of multi-agent interactivity occurring across a diverse range of systems and application domains, when it supports a high degree of openness and dynamism. This openness needs to be underpinned using practical standards, and implementations of the standards that can adapt to different computation and communication environments. Building agent services is time consuming and can be expedited by using agent toolkits that enable software developers to create agent based systems whilst removing some of the tedious and often complex infrastructure development. There is now a proliferation of agent-based toolkits that report adherence to agent standards. Release of such toolkits as open source can help seed the generation of a critical mass of agent platforms that can interoperate effectively in the field.

References

1. Searle, J. R. Speech Acts. Cambridge University Press Cambridge, UK (1969).
2. Guarino, N. Formal Ontology, Conceptual Analysis and Knowledge Representation. International Journal Of Human-Computer Studies, Number 5/6 (1995) 625-640.
3. Tanenbaum, A.S. Computer networks. 3rd Edition. Prentice Hall., New jersey (1996) 40-44.
4. Finin, T., Labrou, Y., Mayfield, J. 'KQML as an agent communication language'. In Software agents, Bradshaw JM (ed.), MIT Press (1997) 291-316.
5. FIPA (Foundation for Intelligent Physical Agents) home page. http://www.fipa.org
6. Charlton, P., Cattoni, R., Potrich, A., Mamdani, E. Evaluating the FIPA standards and its role in achieving cooperation in multi-agent systems. "Multi-agent systems, Internet and applications". HICS-33 software technology minitrack, Mawi, Hawaii (2000).
7. Cathedral and Bazaar. http://www.tuxedo.org/~esr/writings/cathedral-bazaar/
8. Poslad, S. J., Buckle S.J., and Hadingham R. The FIPA-OS agent platform: Open Source for Open Standards. Proceedings of PAAM 2000, Manchester U (2000) 355-368.
9. Poslad, S., Pitt J., Mamdani, A., Hadingham, R., Buckle, P. Agent-oriented middleware for integrating customer network services. In Software Agents for Future Communication Systems, Hayzelden, A., Bigham, J., Eds., Springer-Verlag, (1999).
10. Nunez-Suarez, J., O'Sullivan, D., Brouchoud, H., Cros P, Moore, C., Byrne, C. Experiences in the use of FIPA Agent Technologies for the development of a Personal Travel Application. Proceedings of AA2000,Barcelona, (2000) 357-364.
11. Loryman, M., Buckle, P., Major, B. The Cameleon VAB enabled by a FIPA compliant Agent platform. ACTS workshop. Singapore (1999).
12. Giampapa, J., Paolucci, M., Sycara, K. Agent interoperability across multi-agent system boundaries. Proceedings of AA2000,Barcelona, (2000) 179-186.

Infrastructure Issues and Themes for Scalable Multi-agent Systems

Omer F. Rana
University of Wales, Cardiff, UK
o.f.rana@cs.cf.ac.uk

Tom Wagner
University of Maine, USA
wagner@umcs.maine.edu

Michael S. Greenberg
Theophany Holding, USA
mgreenberg@acm.org

Martin K. Purvis
University of Otago, New Zealand
MPurvis@infoscience.otago.ac.nz

Various toolkits have been developed in the research community for constructing multi-agent systems. These toolkits differ in the types of programming languages they support, particular agent services they can be used to implement, and support for visualisation tools to specify agent behaviours. The focus of most tools is on software engineering support for constructing Multi-Agent Systems (MAS) – examples of toolkits discussed in this volume are DECAF, Agora and MADKIT. The approach in these toolkits is to operate at a higher level of abstraction than programming paradigms, enabling the description of particular features which contribute towards "agency". Some research projects have adopted the operating system based approach of specifying an "agent kernel", which provides core low level services for interacting agents. Such core services can include agent interaction, and state management for an executing agent, for instance. Again the emphasis is to shift the focus of creating MAS away from low level aspects such as socket creation and message structure, to defining the relationships between agents, and the role each agent plays within such a relationship. Although such an abstraction is desirable when constructing an agent system for solving a particular problem, it may not be if performance issues, such as response time, are of interest. Performance itself needs a clear definition in the context of MAS, and could be related to (1) wall clock time associated with low level agent infrastructure, contributing towards such application themes as Quality of Service (QoS), and response times to users, or it could be (2) associated with the functionality of the system, such as the efficiency, utility, correctness or capacity to undertake and complete a given role or action. Metrics could be proposed to measure and compare various MAS, and eventually to enable toolkits to support a design process that enables either a particular metric or a collection of metrics to be improved.

The need for a robust, efficient, and scalable infrastructure for MAS is then required, when agents developed using such toolkits are employed in commercial applications. Such an infrastructure should support both (1) the development of new MAS, (2) the deployment of these systems within practical applications. Although tools used by MAS developers will differ from those used by appli-

T. Wagner and O.F. Rana (Eds.): Infrastructure for Agents, LNAI 1887, pp. 304–308, 2001.

cation users, common themes within these two requirements may be used to identify an "infrastructure". We analyse issues in sharing MAS infrastructure, and provide a reference model to facilitate the investigation of scalability. We divide MAS infrastructure into four aspects:

1. *Implementation:* based on implementation technologies, such as Java, CORBA and XML. A common set of implementation technologies have been widely used within the MAS community, and support for standardising services within these technologies may provide a useful foundation for the MAS community. JINI and Voyager are good candidates as core implementation technologies, and existing efforts such as CoABS and FIPA-OS already make use of these.

2. *Co-ordination and Communication:* existing co-ordination policies such as the "Contract Net" are a good example of supporting interaction between collaborating agents. Similarly, work on "Conversation Policies" provides the means to achieve convergence within a society of agents, with a limited number of message exchanges. A co-ordination aspect therefore forms an important part of MAS infrastructure, and is at a higher semantic level than the implementation aspect. One or more domain specific ontologies will also be needed to support MAS co-ordination, and existing work on a common ontology language such as DAML, and the definition of interaction protocols (such as the English auction) in FIPA, are important steps in this direction.

3. A *Multi-Agent behaviour:* aspect is needed to enable the behaviour of each agent that participates in the MAS to be specified. Behaviour may be defined in terms of logic based primitives (such as BDI or temporal logic), or as machine learning algorithms (such as neural networks or genetic algorithms). Each agent may be supported with a scheduler, a planning engine and a knowledge base.

4. An *Organisation:* aspect is provided to support higher level structures that may be "enforced" or may "emerge" between collaborating agents. Such structures may be based upon social systems, biological systems, or fabricated by developers in a particular application domain.

    Some argue that when we have fixed conversation policies, we are installing a mechanism that prevents scalability. There will then be an upper limit, they say, on the number of participants to some of these types of conversations. From this perspective, emergent behaviour is an essential aspect of scalability (i.e. that fixed conversation policies, such as specified by FIPA, stand in the way of emergent behaviour, and thus stand in the way of scalability). Emergent behaviour is therefore intimately associated with scalability, and infrastructural considerations on this issue need to be studied further.

In our definition a MAS involves agents which can undertake one or more roles, and interact with each other to solve a particular problem. All four of these aspects are highly interdependent, and this separation is primarily meant to provide a basis for discussion in the MAS community. For example, BDI control has no temporal component, thus, an agent may reason via BDI that it wants to do tasks A and B, but may not have time for both or it may be unable to coordinate with another agent if it does both because of its temporal constraints, thus, the BDI layer may select some tasks, but need to revise its selection based on feedback from co-ordination and scheduling.

To measure the scalability of the MAS, we must define scalability metrics for each of the aspects defined above. The final objective being the integration of these different scalability metrics to enable (1) comparisons between different MAS, (2) MAS features that contribute towards scalable design.

1   The Role of Standardisation

The standardisation question is often asked by application developers, interested in using a particular toolkit for constructing agent systems. Existing work of FIPA and current efforts towards DAML provide some foundations for building agent tools. However, there is little consensus at present on generic modules that could define agent behaviours, or low level communications mechanisms to support agent interaction.

2   The Search for a "Killer App"

To enable a technology to be more widely adopted, the importance of a 'killer' application is always stressed. The emphasis is generally laid on trying to list benefits that an agent-based approach could offer, above and beyond those offered by existing distributed computing, or logic-based programming approaches. It is generally claimed that such a 'killer' application should be implementable more cleanly, efficiently, and scalably, with an agent based approach, and should demonstrate the effectiveness of agent technology when employed on a large scale. It is also often claimed that the benefits of mobile or intelligent agents are modest when any particular application is viewed in isolation, rather it is a whole set of applications, and their interaction, which could truly demonstrate the effectiveness of a MAS approach to problem solving.

Two domains have so far been investigated as candidates for providing such a 'killer' application, namely electronic commerce and personal/profiling services. The research community has been struggling, it seems, to isolate one application domain that could prove the effectiveness of the MAS approach. Perhaps, a killer application will emerge from a popular internet application that has been ignored by the research community? Tim Finin described "Napster", as an example of an application that would require scable agent technology, in addition to the need for other infrastructure services, such as streaming and security. Similarly, the high performance computing (HPC) community offers applications where scalability is essential, in areas such as the Materials Microcharacterization Collabotory (MMC) work described by Line Pouchard and

David Walker in this volume. There is a clear need to therefore establish better links between existing communities which require high end computational resources (such as TeraFlop machines, and Petabyte data stores), and with an ad hoc community of Internet enthusiasts that has emerged over the last few years. It is likely that the killer application could come from one of these communities, and common activities with these communities should be encouraged. RoboCup Soccer serves a useful purpose in terms of providing an arena for the comparison of relatively small-scale agent applications. In fact it might be appropriate for our community to try and identify other applications (in addition to RoboCup Soccer) at various scales of complexity, which are not "killer apps" but which still may offer useful means and mechanisms for comparing agent technologies. At a minimum, a high quality survey of application domains is needed, especially one which identifies MAS infrastructure needs to support the scaling of such applications.

3   Deployment

Deployment of Multi-Agent Systems (MAS) requires an infrastructure that can scale to the limits of the Internet. The infrastructure should support interoperation between MAS. In order for global adoption it must be engineered for reliability and speed, and support other important considerations, such as security. Many of the issues involved are similar to those in the creation of the Internet, and many of the same engineering techniques apply.

An MAS infrastructure consists of common services and communication paths, that may be employed across a wide range of application domains. Comparable Internet services are FTP, Telnet, DNS, ICMP, etc. MAS services might include service providers such as commerce servers (such as airplane ticketing and stock market interfaces), service brokers (to locate or interact with other service providers), agent name services (for agent access), etc. Communication paths allow interaction between MAS and service providers (which themselves can be MAS) via protocols and ontologies. Interoperability involves MAS coherently interacting with other MAS and service providers for services, communication, and collaborative problem solving, and is the key to a globally scalable and deployable infrastructure. To date, most MAS are developed in isolation as research projects, therefore cooperation between MAS researchers is needed to create MAS that communicate and cooperate. A lot of technology and many standards are available for interoperation (KQML, FIPA-ACL, ANS, many Internet protocols, etc.). Making these research projects interoperate is a concrete step toward an infrastructure. Due to the heterogeneous nature of the computational environment, and the many different applications of MAS, inter-MAS coordination is necessary to create a scalable infrastructure. Again, interoperability is key. When an infrastructure of interoperating MAS exists then MAS proliferation becomes possible to create building blocks for widespread agent deployment.

MAS and their infrastructure must be engineered for industrial use. While many researchers are doing excellent software engineering, most MAS were developed only to prove or explore a line of reasoning, and are not finished products. Good software engineering is a must for dependable infrastructure and MAS. Like interoperability, robustness, dependability, and durability should all be design goals. Projects should use common software engineering techniques, such as formal specifications, source code control systems and extensive quality assurance testing. For MAS to be widely accepted, used and last, they must be dependable. Existing work on software engineering approaches for MAS [3],[4] provide useful first steps in achieving this objective.

To be practical, a scalable MAS infrastructure must be secure. Unfortunately, there is no complete security solution for any computational model [1],[2]. Agents, being more complex than other programming techniques, complicate the problem. Code signing does not assure execution will be correct. There is a huge potential for deception but little or no ability to determine whether one has been deceived. MAS that have sophisticated behaviour (i.e. following multiple non-standard strategies to retrieve documents) may subvert security policies that are inconsistent because they themselves do not scale (i.e. a document is restricted by one access method, but available by another). The potential of MAS delegating authority to other MAS adds more complexity. Any infrastructure must include checks and safeguards to assure as much integrity as possible to limit inevitable problems caused by malicious and accidental MAS execution and interaction. Even so, problems will occur and MAS must be robust enough to handle them.

A scalable MAS infrastructure may be the "killer application" we seek. Many critics of MAS suggest that non-agent techniques work just as well. It is likely that MAS can provide a more reliable service, give better results and handle more complex problems than many non-agent techniques. But, as has been proven time and again, "better" does not necessarily mean widespread adoption. An infrastructure that supports MAS activities and interoperation, and that facilitates the easy inclusion of new MAS, will pave the road to MAS deployment.

References

[1] B. Blakely, "The Emperor's Old Armor," Proceedings of the New Security Paradigms Workshop, 1996.

[2] M. Greenberg, J. Byington, and D. Harper, "Mobile Agents and Security", IEEE Communications, July 1998.

[3] M. Wooldridge and N. Jennings, "Software Engineering with Agents: Pitfalls and Pratfalls". IEEE Internet Computing, May/June 1999.

[4] James Odell, "Agent UML", see web site at: http://www.jamesodell.com/

[5] FIPA: Foundation of Intelligent Physical Agents, See web site at: http://www.fipa.org/

[6] DARPA Agent Markup Language, See web site at: http://www.daml.org/

Index

Bae, D-H. 199
Barber, K. S 41
Barbuceanu, M. 144
Berry, N. M. 188
Botía, J. A. 226
Buckle, P. 296

Clarke, L. A. 64
Cleaver, D. 12
Craciun, F. 293

D'Hondt, T. 166
Decker, K. S. 12
Di Marzo Serugendo, G. 214
Dikaiakos, M. D. 180
Dobson, S. 174

Ferber, J. 48
Flores, R. A. 56

Gasser, L. 1
Garijo, M. 226
Gómez-Skarmeta, A. F. 226
Graham, J. R. 12
Gray, A. 279
Greenberg, M. S. 304
Gutknecht, O. 48

Hadingham, R. 296
Han, I.-J., 199
Hong, J.-E. 199
Horling, B. 102

Jennings, N. R. 246

Kaminka, G. A. 80
Kim, I.-G. 199
Kirkeluten, O. J. 28
Köpe, Z. 293
Kremer, R. C. 56
Krossnes, S. B. 28

Lam, D. N. 41
Lerner, B. 72
Lesser, V. 72, 102, 128
Letia, I. A. 293

Lo, W.-K. 144

Marti, P. 279
Martin, C. E. 41
Matskin, M. 28
McGeary, F. 12
McKay, R. M. 41
McHugh, D. 12
Mersic, M. 12

Nagi, K. 266
Nixon, P. 174
Noda, I. 94
Norrie, D. H. 56
Noy, P. 263

Osterweil, L. 64, 72

Pancerella, C. M. 188
Petrone, G. 177
Poslad, S. 296
Pouchard, L. 192
Preece, A. 279
Purvis, M. K. 304
Pynadath, D. V. 80

Raja, A. 72
Rana, O. F. 304

Sæle, Ø. 28
Samaras, G. 180
Schroeder, M. 263
Stone, P. 94

Tambe, M. 80
Turner, P. J. 246

Van Belle, W. 166
Velasco, J. R. 226
Vincent, R. 102

Wagner, T. 72, 128, 304
Walker, D. W. 192
Walsh, T. 174
Windley, M. V. 12
Woodside, M. 234

Youn, C. 199
Yuan, S.-T. 157

Zhang, X. 72